Inside the World of the Eunuch

Inside the World of the Eunuch

A Social History of the Emperor's Servants in Qing China

Melissa S. Dale

HKU
PRESS
香港大學出版社

Hong Kong University Press
The University of Hong Kong
Pokfulam Road
Hong Kong
www.hkupress.hku.hk

© 2018 Hong Kong University Press

ISBN 978-988-8455-75-1 (*Hardback*)

British Library Cataloguing-in-Publication Data
A catalogue record for this book is available from the British Library.

10 9 8 7 6 5 4 3 2 1

Printed and bound by Paramount Printing Co. Ltd., Hong Kong, China

To Laoda and Child,
You make me proud every day.
Thank you for bringing so much joy into my life.

Contents

List of Illustrations	viii
Acknowledgments	ix
Conventions	xi
Introduction: The Other Side of Eunuch History	1
1. The Palace Eunuch System	14
2. Routes to the Palace	28
3. Unrobing the Emasculated Body	48
4. Entering the Emperor's Realm	66
5. The Parallel World of the Eunuch: Eunuch Society	89
6. Running away from the Palace	107
7. Eunuch Suicide: Punishment, Not Compassion	126
8. Authorized Exits from the System: Sick Leave, Retirement, Discharge, and Death	145
9. Surviving the Fall of the Qing: Chinese Eunuchs Post 1911	170
10. Conclusion	194
Appendix 1: Reign Titles and Dates of the Qing Emperors	201
Appendix 2: Eunuch Suicide Regulations	202
Appendix 3: Eunuch Temples	203
Appendix 4: Eunuch Cemeteries	204
Bibliography	205
Index	215

Illustrations

Figure 3.1 Eunuch in front of Baohua Hall, 1900   49

Figure 4.1 Eunuchs serving   69

Figure 4.2 Group photo of eunuchs   71

Figure 4.3 Zhang Qianhe 張謙和, *Chuxiugong zongguan taijian*
            儲秀宮總管太監   76

Figure 4.4 Empress Dowager Cixi attended by eunuchs, 1903   76

Figure 5.1 Eunuch with dog   96

Figure 8.1 Group of former palace eunuchs at Gang Tie Miao   161

Figure 9.1 Eunuchs scuffling with police, September 1, 1923   183

Figure 9.2 Eunuch of the Imperial Court, Peking   188

Figure 9.3 Eunuchs waiting in front of the palace, ca. 1924   190

Acknowledgments

Over the years, there have been many people who have offered encouragement, guidance, and advice regarding my research on Qing dynasty eunuchs. I am delighted to have the opportunity to formally thank them. This work first began as my doctoral dissertation at Georgetown University, under the guidance of my mentor, Carol Benedict, and committee members, James Millward, Howard Spendelow, and John Witek, SJ. Having worked on this topic on and off for the past seventeen years and throughout the course of several administrative jobs, I am happy to report that I chose a dissertation topic that not only sustained my interest during my doctoral degree program but well beyond. I appreciate the support of the University of San Francisco (USF) College of Arts and Sciences for providing me with a position that allowed me to pursue my interests in administration, teaching, and research. Thank you to my colleagues at the USF Center for Asia Pacific Studies and the Master in Asia Pacific Studies program and my students for indulging me as I shared my passion for eunuchs with them. Words of encouragement over the years from Carol Benedict, James Millward, and Wen-hsin Yeh, even if exchanged briefly at conferences, via email, or while on the job were greatly appreciated. They helped fuel my desire to continue my research, to delve into the life experiences of Qing eunuchs and to share them in print.

Scholars that I have met over the years have been generous with their time and advice. Special thanks to Matthew Sommer for reading several earlier versions of this manuscript and for his willingness to meet and discuss my research; those exchanges proved invaluable. Thanks also to Gail Hershatter and Marta Hanson for their comments on earlier drafts and for encouraging me to develop my line of analysis more, and to Lai Huimin for offering suggestions on my work and sharing materials with me early on. Although I cannot personally thank the anonymous readers who have reviewed my work over the years, I greatly appreciate their comments and suggestions.

Over the course of my research, I have had the pleasure of working with numerous researchers and staff at various institutions. Thank you to the Academia Sinica's Institute of History and Philology for providing me with the affiliation I needed to gain access to the archives as a doctoral candidate and for providing me with a sense of community while working in Taiwan. I am also grateful to the staff and scholars at the First Historical Archives, Beijing, the Palace Museum in Taipei, Stanford University's East Asian Library (especially Kozo Tanaka, Yonghong Yang, and Zhaohui Xue) and Lane Medical Library (Drew Bourn), and the University of California, Berkeley's C. V. Starr East Asian Library (Susan Xue). Thank you also to the editorial team at Hong Kong University Press for the time and energy they put into bringing this manuscript to press.

Finally, I would like to thank my family for being a constant source of support and for their willingness to learn about a topic that has become both a distraction and my passion.

Conventions

As will be seen a Chinese eunuch was more than just an emasculated boy or man, he was a servant of the imperial court. Throughout this study, due to the entrenched nature of the term "eunuch" in the English language, the Chinese term *taijian* 太監 will retain its customary translation.

The hereditary professionals that performed emasculations during the Qing were known as *daozijiang* 刀子匠. While late Qing contemporaries such as George Carter Stent translated this term as "knifers," I have chosen to use the less pejorative term, "knife experts."

I have chosen to use the term "emasculation" rather than "castration," due to its medical accuracy. The medical definition of "emasculation" is the removal of the external male genitalia (scrotum, testes, and penis), whereas "castration" is defined as the removal of the testes. The use of the term is not without its problems, as some might assume that "emasculation" carries the connotation of feminization. Within this work, the "emasculation" is not meant to suggest feminization. Rather, when feminization is meant, that term will be used specifically. When referring to eunuchs during previous dynasties, I have chosen to follow the convention of authors who specialize during those periods and use the term, "castration."

Ages in *sui* 歲 are traditionally calculated using the Chinese lunar calendar, beginning with one year at birth and increasing at the Lunar New Year (not birthdays). Here, *sui* is translated as "years old."

I refer to palaces, buildings, and administrative departments by their romanized Chinese names unless they are well known by their English translation.

Last, throughout this work, I have made every effort to include the Chinese characters for eunuchs' names in order to ensure that they are finally given a voice in the historical record.

Introduction: The Other Side of Eunuch History

Throughout history, eunuchs have been defined by their lack of body parts. Genitally mutilating *one* group to keep *another* pure,[1] rulers have relied on eunuchs as "keepers of the harem," servants who ensured the sexual purity of the palace women, and the legitimacy of the imperial lineage. Societies throughout the world have also castrated or emasculated young boys and men for religious, political, or cultural purposes. While oftentimes labeled erroneously as an exoticism unique to imperial China, eunuchs played roles in the histories of the Roman and Ottoman Empires, served in the Korean imperial court, and continue to exist in contemporary Indian society. In China, the practice of utilizing eunuchs as imperial servants dates back thousands of years to ancient dynasties such as the Shang (1766–1122 BCE)[2] and Qin (221–206 BCE).[3] However, eunuchs are most often associated with dynasties such as the Han (206 BCE–220 CE), Tang (618–907), and Ming (1368–1644), when they served in greater numbers and wielded more political influence.

Emasculating males to become servants for the Chinese emperor was intended to produce a submissive and loyal workforce. Eunuchs were considered to be "ideal servants,"[4] loyal to their masters due to the act's marking of the body and its stigma. In China, emasculation was intended to sever more than body parts. Beyond the physical act of genital mutilation, emasculation carried important social implications for the eunuch. The colloquial term for emasculation, *chu jia* (出家 leaving home) symbolized the act's intention—with the cut of a knife—to destroy former

---

1. This phrase is a slightly modified version of George Carter Stent's comment that eunuchs were symbolic of the lowly position of women in what he termed "eastern despotic countries" as exemplified by "when their husbands or masters conceive it necessary to resort to such horrible mutilations of *one* sex to keep the *other* pure." See George Carter Stent, "Chinese Eunuchs," *Journal of the North China Branch of the Royal Asiatic Society*, New Series, no. 11 (1877): 143.

2. Shih-shan Henry Tsai, *The Eunuchs in the Ming Dynasty* (Albany: State University of New York Press, 1996), 11.

3. Du Wanyan notes that scholars locate the origins of eunuchs in either the Zhou dynasty or the Qin and Han periods. Both Du and Tsai mention the reference to palace eunuchs on oracle bones from the Shang dynasty. See Du Wanyan, *Zhongguo huanguan shi* (Taipei: Wenjin chubanshe, 1996), 9–18 and Tsai, *The Eunuchs in the Ming Dynasty*, 11.

4. Preston Torbert as cited in Evelyn Rawski. See Evelyn S. Rawski, *The Last Emperors: A Social History of Qing Imperial Institutions* (Berkeley: University of California Press, 1998), 163.

familial and social bonds.[5] The stigma of physical disfigurement from emasculation was considered so powerful that it would lead society to ostracize eunuchs
and cause their families to disown them, thereby increasing the dependency of the
eunuch upon his master(s).[6]

Emasculation placed eunuchs in direct opposition to the Confucian philosophy
that served as the source of accepted values and norms for the Chinese government
and society. First, the "reproductive death" resulting from emasculation contributed to the categorization of eunuchs as "other" due to their inability to uphold
the Confucian tenet of filial piety through procreation. Second, the physical act
of marking the body stood as an affront to the belief that one should not harm
one's body as it is given by one's parents. Despite these negative social implications,
many candidates viewed the potential gains associated with service as a palace
eunuch (especially the hope of escaping poverty) as outweighing any conflict with
Confucian philosophy or social norms.

During the Qing dynasty (1644–1911), volunteers rather than prisoners
supplied the imperial court with the majority of candidates for service as palace
eunuchs. Preferring to distance itself from the genital mutilation of young boys and
men, the Qing imperial court relied on licensed professionals to secure and emasculate candidates for service within the Forbidden City. Those unable or unwilling
to pay a professional to perform the procedure often underwent emasculation at
home at the hands of a family member. While an application prerequisite, emasculation alone did not ensure selection as a palace eunuch. As a result, some young
boys and men who had their genitalia excised in the hopes of becoming a palace
eunuch found themselves disfigured and rejected.

Despite eunuchs' intended purpose, histories clearly show that eunuchs were
oftentimes far from the "ideal servants." Histories of eunuchs are full of portrayals
of eunuchs as conniving, corrupt, and selfish individuals who interfered in politics
and amassed personal wealth. Contemporary scholars have been captivated by the
political machinations of powerful eunuchs during the Tang and Ming dynasties,
when eunuchs served in greater numbers and managed to wield power within the
government. As a result, studies on eunuchs during these dynasties have formed the
basis of knowledge for the eunuch population as a whole. This preoccupation with
Tang and Ming eunuchs has led scholars to overlook the histories of eunuchs during
dynasties such as the Qing, when their numbers were reduced and their political
activity was highly restricted, yet their lives were equally as fascinating.

When scholars and authors do include Qing dynasty eunuchs in their studies,
many tend to write about eunuch interference in politics and the corrupt practices
of a small number of notorious eunuchs such as Li Lianying 李蓮英 or An Dehai

---

5. This term is also used to refer to the process of becoming a monk.
6. Preston Torbert, *The Ch'ing Imperial Household Department: A Study of Its Organization and Principal
   Functions, 1662–1796* (Cambridge, MA: Harvard University Press, 1977), 2.

安德海.[7] This narrow focus has perpetuated the stereotypical representation of *all* eunuchs as corrupt, political manipulators.[8] Among the Qing eunuch population, those who held positions of power such as Li or An were few. In reality, only those at the top of the eunuch hierarchy enjoyed such wealth and power. Studies focusing primarily on a small number of notorious eunuchs, rather than the remaining eunuch population, have contributed to the misperception that these eunuchs and their political maneuverings represent Qing eunuchs as a whole.[9] As a result, only one side of eunuch history has been presented. This study aims to contribute to a more nuanced and balanced reconstruction of late imperial eunuch society as a whole and ultimately present the other side of eunuch history.[10]

The Qing dynasty's reliance on eunuchs predates the Manchu invasion of China in 1644. In the early 1600s, as the Manchus established their dynasty and prepared to invade China proper, they began to incorporate eunuchs into their household servant system. This was a departure from traditional Manchu practices of staffing their households with bondservants.[11] Once inside China proper, the Qing expanded their use of eunuchs, finding them to be essential for the functioning of the palace but only if they were utilized in reduced numbers,[12] kept in menial positions, and managed well. While Manchu reliance on eunuchs increased during this period, in comparison with the practices of their Ming dynasty predecessors, this was ultimately a drastic reduction in the size and responsibilities delegated to the palace eunuch population. Only employing some three to five percent of the number of eunuchs previously in the service of the Ming court, the Manchus sent a clear message that the new conquest government would not be relying on eunuchs in the same capacity as their predecessors.

As will be seen, the number of Qing palace eunuchs would fluctuate as supply and demand rose throughout the dynasty, reaching at its peak approximately 3,300

---

7. Two eunuchs who enjoyed great power under the de facto rule of the Empress Dowager Cixi during the late Qing.

8. See Mary Anderson, *Hidden Power: The Palace Eunuchs of Imperial China* (Buffalo: Prometheus Books, 1990); Jonathan Spence, *Emperor of China: Self-Portrait of Kang-Hsi, 1654–1722* (New York: Vintage Books, 1975); and Albert Chan, *Glory and Fall of the Ming Dynasty* (Norman: University of Oklahoma Press, 1982).

9. Currently, the principal information on Qing dynasty eunuchs is found in broad institutional histories of the eunuch system, which span dynasties. These works often capitalize on the exoticism of the eunuch and his supposed knowledge of the secret life of the imperial court within the Forbidden City.

10. Scholars such as Jennifer Jay and Tang Yinian were some of the first to explore the lives of eunuchs. See Jennifer Jay, "Another Side of Chinese Eunuch History: Castration, Marriage, Adoption, and Burial," *Canadian Journal of History* XXVII (Dec. 1993): 459–78. The work of Tang Yinian has been instrumental for the reconstruction of the social history of Qing dynasty eunuchs. This study was inspired in part by several of the topics mentioned in his work (i.e., eunuch runaways and eunuch suicide) and aims to provide further research and analysis on these topics. See Tang Yinian, *Qing gong taijian* (Shenyang: Liaoning daxue chubanshe, 1993).

11. Bondservants were basically slaves who attended to the domestic affairs of the imperial household. See Zheng Tianting, *Qingshi tanwei* (Zhongjing: Duli chubanshe, 1946), 66.

12. During the Ming dynasty (1368–1644) eunuch numbers peaked at 100,000. See Tsai, *The Eunuchs in the Ming Dynasty*, 11. Viewing eunuchs as one of the reasons for the downfall of their predecessors, the Qing capped eunuch numbers at approximately 3,000–3,300.

eunuchs during the reign of the Kangxi emperor (1662–1722).[13] Towards the end of the dynasty, these numbers would steadily decline. In the late Qing, as a series of young emperors came to the throne, eunuchs were not needed in such large numbers, as these emperors were too young to need an empress, imperial consorts, and concubines. During these periods, though, eunuchs continued to be useful, particularly when powerful regents (such as the Empress Dowager Cixi 慈禧太后) relied on individuals outside the civil service, such as eunuchs, to facilitate their hold on power.

During the later years of the dynasty, the palace's once strict control over eunuchs would be repeatedly challenged as eunuchs pushed the boundaries of the limitations put in place to ensure their subservience. Without a strong and engaged emperor on the throne, these regulations would be repeatedly ignored or even relaxed by regents who held the real power at court. Such a scenario created opportunities for eunuchs to reassert themselves and to capitalize on their positions of unofficial power and influence to engage in "intimate politics."[14] While the political maneuverings of a select group of infamous eunuchs are well documented, little is known about the life experiences of the remaining eunuch population.

This study's point of departure is to redirect the scholarly gaze away from a small number of powerful eunuchs and onto the majority of palace eunuchs who never rose to the heights of eunuch power. As a social history of Qing palace eunuchs, this work will explore the life experiences of this group of previously silent inhabitants of the palace. The chapters that follow remind us that as servants of the imperial court, the history of eunuchs is intertwined with that of the palace and the Manchu ruling class. Despite working and living within the seat of imperial power, the majority of Qing palace eunuchs held no real political power, and in the broad scheme of the history of the dynasty, only a small percentage managed to influence politics. What is fascinating about the study of Qing palace eunuchs is not their attempts to gain political power and wealth but rather their interactions with society and those in power.

The importance of this work lies beyond just giving voice to a minority population void of direct political power. Eunuchs, as servants, should not be overlooked in the historical record due to their lack of formal power. As Evelyn Rawski has noted, servants "provide rich insight into the discourse of power."[15] This social history of eunuchs places them at the center of the story and views their interactions

13. As Kutcher notes, the Qianlong emperor, in an attempt to not exceed the number of eunuchs held by his grandfather, the Kangxi emperor, set his eunuch quota at less than 3,300. See Norman A. Kutcher, "Unspoken Collusions: The Empowerment of Yuanming yuan Eunuchs in the Qianlong Period," *Harvard Journal of Asiatic Studies* 70, no. 2 (Dec. 2010): 469. In Rawski's table of the number of eunuchs in palace service from 1750 to 1922, she notes that, in 1750 (during the reign of Qianlong), there were 3,107 eunuchs in service. See Rawski, *The Last Emperors*, Table 1.2, 165.

14. See Mitamura Taisuke, *Chinese Eunuchs: The Structure of Intimate Politics*, trans. Charles A. Pomeroy (Rutland, VT: Charles E. Tuttle, Co., 1970).

15. Rawski, *The Last Emperors*, 160.

with society. As will be seen, the study of Qing dynasty eunuchs contributes to the scholarly discourse on gender, sexuality, class, and labor relations during the late imperial and republican periods. Moreover, due to their assignment to the palace, at the seat of imperial power, and their interaction with the ruling elite, the study of eunuchs also adds depth to legal and institutional histories of the Qing and to our understandings of the principles that underlay Manchu rule and labor relations.

The organization of the work that follows is designed to highlight the key events and aspects of Qing palace eunuch life—tracing the important events in eunuchs' lives from the point of emasculation to employment within the palace, to life as a palace eunuch, to discharge, retirement, and death—focusing on the experiences that eunuchs encountered in their lives inside and outside the palace walls. Moving beyond the 1911 divide, this study also examines the abolition of the eunuch system and the reintegration of eunuchs into society in Republican China.

This study challenges the view of eunuchs as an "exotic" other of only fleeting interest in Chinese studies due to their numerical minority and their indirect involvement in politics. Eunuchs were seen as necessary for the functioning of the imperial court but also as a source of anxiety and constant labor challenges. The following chapters address a number of issues central to late imperial Chinese history: social class, the nature of status groups, and the internal workings of the imperial institution. They also shed new light on more recent historiographical concerns such as the intersections between gender and power, Chinese conceptions of masculinity, the nature of indentured status, medical history, and crime and punishment. In sum, this study recasts and reclaims the past of this previously silent and often miscast group so vital to the imperial court.

A eunuch's raison d'être was to serve the emperor and his court. Spending the majority of their lives behind the palace walls within the imperial seat of power and the inner sanctum of the emperor meant that eunuchs' lives were highly regulated. As will be seen, despite these measures, eunuchs repeatedly tested the boundaries of their role, challenging the restraints put in place to ensure their subservience and curb their attempts to attain political power. An examination of the many regulations that governed eunuchs' lives and the punishments they faced for infractions reveals a tension between the imperial court's need to trust its servants and the distrust and anxiety that permeated their labor relations.[16] This study shows that eunuchs managed to exert a degree of agency in their lives by creating a parallel realm alongside that of the emperor. This realm was most evident after nightfall, when eunuchs were the only men besides the emperor allowed within the inner court, when they congregated while sitting watch or within their shared housing. It is during these late hours of the day and into the night that eunuchs would strengthen their own

---

16. This study aims to build on the foundational work of scholars such as Evelyn S. Rawski who have defined eunuch activities under the rubric of master–servant relations and detailed the "tensions" presented by the contradictory low status of eunuchs and the power enjoyed by some due to their proximity to the emperor and members of his family. See Rawski, *The Last Emperors*.

social bonds and engage in activities that their imperial masters would perceive as most unbefitting a servant of the emperor.

Qing palace regulations regarding eunuch mobility reveal the complexities of unfree status during the Qing dynasty. Eunuchs were servants but not slaves. A eunuch's service was intended to be for life or until he was too ill or too old to serve. During a eunuch's tenure in the palace, the Imperial Household Department restricted his mobility and behavior. Despite these restrictions, eunuchs did receive salaries, time off when they were too ill to work and bereavement leave to mourn the death of a parent.

During the mid- to late Qing, as regulations became more lax, eunuchs were allowed more freedom of mobility. Nevertheless, labor relations between eunuchs and their masters, members of the imperial court and the bondservants that supervised them on behalf of the imperial court, were often strained and tense as eunuchs pushed the boundaries of acceptable behavior and responded to the often oppressive environment in which they worked and lived. Within the palace, minor infractions were often met with corporal punishment. Eunuchs were subject to frequent beatings by their eunuch superiors as a result of their perceived faults and through collective responsibility for those of their associates. Oral histories of late Qing dynasty eunuchs include stories of eunuchs being beaten for miscommunications and minor infractions. Labor relations between master and servant became defined by a management style reliant on corporal punishment and the use of harsh punishments such as exile and manual labor.

The study of eunuchs' lives also sheds light on understandings of gender and ideas of masculinity during the Qing and republican periods. While some studies have labeled eunuchs as a "third sex," this is an example of presentism that does not reflect Qing categorizations of gender and sexuality. As Jennifer Jay's 1993 article revealed, eunuchs identified as male. Moreover, as my analysis will show, while eunuch gender was certainly questioned by others and even seen as a cause of anxiety among the court, gender was not the primary issue in a eunuch's life. Rather, my work reveals that although gender is an interesting theme to explore in eunuch history, the eunuch story is more concerned with eunuch attempts to insert a degree of agency into servile lives governed by a myriad of rules and regulations.

At the most basic level, the aim of this study is threefold: (1) to present new findings, views, and analysis on aspects of the social history of the Qing palace eunuch masses; (2) to fill the historical gap in eunuch histories by focusing on eunuchs during the Qing and continuing the story past the traditional 1911 termination with the fall of the Qing on into the Republican era (1912–1949); and (3) to highlight and build upon the foundational work of scholars in the field, many whose works were formerly available only in Chinese language publications.

Sources

Researching the life experiences of eunuchs is not without its challenges. The servile role that eunuchs played within the palace is reflected in the available archival documents. With the palace focused on recording the political, fiscal, and diplomatic activities of the emperor and his imperial court, eunuchs were only of peripheral importance to those recording the history of the Qing. Eunuchs usually appear in the palace historical record in relation to staffing needs, records of payment, policies governing their administration, and issues of misconduct. As a result, tracing the life experiences of eunuchs is limited by the availability of archival sources. In studying eunuchs during earlier dynasties, scholars had to rely heavily on tomb inscriptions and imperial pronouncements. However, the Qing dynasty archives have preserved a variety of written sources. Despite not being intended for the preservation of eunuch history, Qing archival sources do provide important insight into the challenges eunuchs faced in their lives both within the palace and when trying to reintegrate into society. Rarely do the sources offer opportunities to provide statistical analysis or the ability to track changes over time. Where this is possible, these statistics are more relevant to topics of concern to eunuch institutional history than to social history and are beyond the scope of this study. With the Qing imperial court limiting eunuch literacy to but a chosen few, for whom reading and writing was an occupational necessity, reconstructing eunuch social history becomes even more challenging. In other words, eunuch history recorded by eunuchs is extremely rare. This relative silence in the historical record among eunuchs has led to a discourse on eunuchs often framed by speculation and the perceptions of others, especially the scholar-officials for whom eunuchism symbolized an affront to Confucian values and an avenue of social mobility operating outside the civil service examination system.[17] This fact necessitates careful consideration of official documents, but it does not negate their usefulness.

Archival evidence in the form of edicts, memorials, depositions, and lists, particularly those from the Imperial Household Department, housed in Beijing at the First Historical Archives and in Taipei at the National Palace Museum, detail the selection, training, duties, management, and punishment of palace eunuchs. Moreover, within these documents the voices of eunuchs often resurface in confessions. When combined with oral histories, autobiographies of the last Qing eunuchs, accounts of Western travelers during the late 1800s, and reminiscences of late Qing

---

17. During the Qing, eunuchs were limited in their ability to influence politics; however, some were able to attach themselves to powerful people and benefit from the association with members of the imperial court. Nevertheless, few if any Confucian scholar-officials had positive things to say about eunuchs. Gilbert Chen's study of Ming dynasty eunuchs reveals that this animosity towards eunuchs was already apparent in the previous dynasty. According to Chen, "As a consequence, not a few commoners who were unable to afford the expenses of passing the civil examination or purchasing a degree chose to gain access to privilege by means of eunuchism, a phenomenon harshly decried by some Confucian scholar-officials." See Gilbert Chen, "Castration and Connection: Kinship Organization among Ming Eunuchs," *Ming Studies* 74 (2016), 29, http://dx.doi.org/10.1080/0147037X.2016.1179552.

palace life by palace maidservants and the last Qing emperor, these sources give voice to this previously silent segment of the palace population. As a result, this study does not attempt to provide a comprehensive overview of Qing policies regarding eunuchs but rather insight into the lives of eunuchs during the Qing, how society viewed them, and how they negotiated their identities. While some might see the entire Qing dynasty as too broad a time to adequately cover in one book, in the case of eunuchs one finds that the sporadic nature of archival sources on Qing eunuch social history makes this a necessity. Moreover, limiting this study's focus to the late Qing would preclude the inclusion of interesting cases from the early Qing. As a result, this study has opted to cover the longer time expanse in an effort to build a foundation that others may build on by focusing in future studies on particular time periods.

When the Qing collapsed in 1911, scholars lost an important source of eunuch history. The loss of political power for the Qing also signaled the end of the most abundant source of information on eunuchs and their activities, the palace administration. Due to the illiteracy of most eunuchs, records of the Qing government provide one of the few sources from which scholars can glean information about eunuchs' life experiences. With the birth of the republic, and the Qing court reduced to the maintenance of the palace rather than an empire, the availability of sources on eunuch drops drastically. Hereafter, eunuchs only appear periodically in the historical record, most often in police reports associated with a criminal case. These records, while rare, provide important insight into the fate of eunuchs post 1911. Diaries and autobiographies of the last emperor, Aisin-Gioro Pu Yi 愛新覺羅 溥儀 and his relatives, and the writings of Sir Reginald Johnston, Pu Yi's imperial tutor, also shed light on key events leading to the end of the eunuch system and its aftermath. Newspaper accounts from Chinese- and Western-language newspapers published in China during the mid- to late 1920s also reveal what the expulsion of the eunuchs looked like to those outside the palace as well as society's thoughts on how to deal with the problem of unemployed eunuchs. Last, thanks to the notoriety of the last surviving eunuchs in the mid- to late 1980s, biographies and oral histories provide a means by which eunuchs can finally tell their stories in their own words.[18]

Terminology

In order to understand the life experiences of the Qing palace eunuch, one must become familiar with the terminology used to refer to eunuchs. While in English,

---

18. The majority of eunuchs were illiterate during the Qing dynasty. Oral histories and biographies of some of the last remaining eunuchs have provided eunuchs with a voice in the historical record. See Ma Deqing et al., "Qing gong taijian huiyi," in *Wanqing gongting shenghuo jianwen*, ed. Zhang Wenhui (Beijing: Wenshi ziliao chubanshe, 1982), 173–97; and Jia Yinghua, *Modai taijian miwen: Sun Yaoting zhuan* (Beijing: Zhishi chubanshe, 1993). Late Qing eunuch Xin Xiuming gathered his memories of late Qing palace eunuch life as well as those of his fellow eunuchs in Xin Xiuming et al., *Lao taijian de huiyi* (Beijing: Gugong chubanshe, 2010).

the convention is to translate Chinese terms referring to castrated or emasculated males as "eunuchs," historical records reveal that the Chinese relied on a variety of terms to refer to eunuchs. At his most basic level, a eunuch was defined by his physical body: terms such as *yan* 閹 and *yange* 閹割 described a person who had undergone castration. In Chinese, the following four terms are commonly used to refer to eunuchs: *taijian* 太監, *xiaojian* 小監, *huanjian* 宦監, and *huanguan* 宦官. According to He Guanbiao, the Manchus used *taijian* to refer to their eunuchs.[19] Traditionally, the Chinese term *taijian* has been translated into English as "eunuch." However, this translation obscures the fact that *taijian* refers to more than just an emasculated male; it signifies the title of a eunuch working in the palace or a princely household. As will be seen, this distinction highlights the fact that not all emasculated males obtained employment as eunuchs. Eunuchs without an assignment as an imperial servant were often referred to as *jingshen* 淨身, a term that expressed the purification and release from sexual desire that was believed to follow emasculation. Due to the entrenched nature of the English translation, within this study, *taijian* will retain its traditional translation of "eunuch."

Terminology is also important for understanding the eunuch body. I have chosen to use "emasculation" rather than "castration" to refer to the genital mutilation experienced by eunuchs during the Qing dynasty. According to Drs. Wu Chieh Ping and Gu Fang-Liu, "castration" refers solely to the removal of the testes, whereas "emasculation" indicates removal of both the testes and the penis.[20] In English "emasculation" also implies feminization, but the reader should note that no such inference is made here. At present, for lack of a better medical term that accurately describes the removal of the testes, scrotum, and penis, "emasculation" will be used throughout to refer to the process by which young boys and men became eunuchs. When referencing the procedure during earlier dynasties, I will follow the convention of scholars writing on these periods and use the term "castration."

Before proceeding to a social history of the eunuch, a brief examination of the institutional history of the Qing palace eunuch system is in order. In an effort to provide a basic understanding of the institutional history of the eunuch system, **Chapter 1** traces the beginnings of eunuchs serving in the palace and the rise of eunuch power during the Han, Tang, and Ming dynasties. The remainder of the chapter focuses on the evolution of the eunuch system from its "embryonic" state before the Qing established its rule over China proper to its initial growth during the reign of Shunzhi (r. 1644–1661) to its maturation during the mid-Qing, and finally its gradual decline after the 1850s.

---

19. For information on the derivation and use of the term, *taijian*, see He Guanbiao, "Huanguan tongcheng 'taijian' gao," *Hanxue yanjiu* 8, no. 2 (1990): 201–20.
20. See Wu Chieh Ping and Gu Fang-Liu, "The Prostate in Eunuchs," *EROTC Genitourinary Group Monograph 10—Urological Ontology: Reconstructive Surgery, Organ Conservation and Restoration of Function* (New York: Wiley-Liss, Inc., 1991), 254–55.

Chapter 2 traces the variety of routes that eunuchs took to reach the palace. Despite the different routes taken to the palace, all eunuchs started their journey with the singular act of emasculation. Genital mutilation alone, however, did not ensure the attainment of a position as a palace eunuch. While the government distanced itself from the genital mutilation and sale of young boys and adult men into servitude, the government licensed emasculation professionals and was directly involved in regulating the supply and demand that fueled the eunuch system and determined the fate of these new emasculates. Coercion by family members and the sale of boys does not explain the emasculation of all eunuchs. Many destitute Chinese men, viewing emasculation and employment as a palace eunuch as the remedy to their own and by extension their families' financial problems, volunteered for service. Nevertheless, the irreversible act of emasculation, a prerequisite for even being presented as a candidate for service within the palace, did not ensure employment as an imperial court eunuch. Even if they managed to enter the palace walls, not all eunuch candidates received an invitation to stay. A myriad of palace eunuch prerequisites concerning ethnicity, age, and form of emasculation allowed the Qing to control the selection process.

Chapter 3 aims to unrobe the emasculated body by examining how this form of genital mutilation affected eunuchs both physically and psychologically and by exploring multiple perspectives on how the Chinese eunuch body has been read by others. In addition, eunuchs' self-perceptions of their bodies will be revealed through oral histories and inferred through eunuch practices. As will be seen, despite common knowledge regarding what made one a eunuch, very little appears in the historical record about what this looked like. Emasculation physically marked the eunuch body and caused society to read it as different from that of non-emasculated Chinese males. How the body was read, though, depended upon who was reading it (Han Chinese, the Manchu imperial court, Westerners, or eunuchs themselves). While genital mutilation was intended to subjugate and neuter Chinese men, in reality emasculation rendered eunuchs "sexually and politically charged."[21] Representing a nexus of gender and political power, eunuchs provide unique insight into late imperial views towards masculinity and political power during the Qing.

In **Chapter 4**, one finds that, even though emasculation was a job prerequisite, it did not ensure that a eunuch would be hired as a palace eunuch. Emasculates would undergo training prior to applying for service in the palace. Designed to be the ideal servants for the emperor and his court, eunuch subservience and proper conduct were expected. While eunuchs were not slaves, they were imperial servants living in an environment defined by strict rules of deportment and protocol. Once inside the palace, new recruits quickly discovered that they were no longer a numerical minority but among the majority in a setting in which they were surrounded by their fellow eunuchs. However, in terms of status, the majority of eunuchs occupied

---

21. Charlotte Furth, "Androgynous Males and Deficient Females," *Late Imperial China* 9, no. 2 (Dec. 1988): 15.

positions at the bottom of the social hierarchy within the palace. Physical disfigurement now dictated every aspect of the eunuch's life from entry into the eunuch system, to placement in the eunuch hierarchy, to apprenticeship, to employment opportunities.

In **Chapter 5**, palace eunuchs, seeking agency in their restricted lives, tested the boundaries of subservience to the emperor and the imperial eunuch system. Behind the palace walls, eunuchs operated within two parallel realms, one revolving around the emperor and his imperial court and another in which they challenged the restrictions placed on them by the imperial eunuch system. This chapter focuses on the world of the eunuch, where eunuchs recreated the social bonds that emasculation was intended to deny them. An examination of legal cases and directives on eunuch conduct provides insight into this second, more hidden, realm, one in which opium dens and gambling flourished, eunuchs became drunk and got into fights with one another, and forbidden bonds of intimacy defeated one of the main purposes of emasculation.

By exploring cases of runaway eunuchs, **Chapter 6** aims to contribute to the understanding of unfree status during the Qing dynasty and more broadly to the reconstruction of the social history of eunuchs. The abundance of cases in the historical record of palace eunuchs running away, often repeatedly, reflects poorly on the imperial court's treatment of its eunuchs and effectiveness at times in controlling its eunuch population. Confessions from captured eunuchs reveal that, for many, serving as a palace eunuch proved too restrictive and too oppressive to endure. The repeated flight of eunuchs suggests that, for some, the possibility of punishment was preferable to continued service and waiting for an authorized exit from the system due to old age or sickness. Cases of runaway eunuchs reveal: (1) the tensions that characterized labor relations between the imperial household and its eunuch workforce and (2) that eunuch status does not fit neatly into the binary of free or unfree, it is something more complicated that lies on the continuum in between.

Over the course of their often lifelong tenure in the service of the imperial court, palace eunuchs enjoyed few opportunities to escape their oppressive and highly restricted work environment. **Chapter 7** reveals that, for some palace eunuchs, living and working in the Forbidden City could quickly become stifling. Eunuchs who hoped to terminate their employment with the palace had few options. The Imperial Household Department authorized only three types of exit: discharge because of old age or illness, disciplinary problems, and death. Eunuchs desiring to leave the system of their own volition faced two options: flight or suicide. Since running away involved the possibility of capture followed by beatings, wearing the cangue, and forced labor, suicide provided eunuchs with one of the few ways in which they could determine when they would permanently exit the system.

Chapter 8 examines how the Qing viewed its responsibility towards palace eunuchs when they were either too sick or too old to serve. The Qing envisioned that their responsibility for the livelihood of a palace eunuch would end as soon as he was no longer able to perform his duties. Upon discharge from the system, the government restored the eunuch's commoner status, classifying him as a *weimin taijian* (為民太監 commoner eunuch). Having taken this action, the government attempted to sever all ties and relinquish all responsibility for its former servants. Qing regulations stipulated that retired eunuchs were to return to their native places and support themselves. However, eunuch reintegration into society ran into obstacles upon implementation.

While for many in Chinese society the fall of the Qing and the rise of the republic signaled a new beginning and an interest in all things modern, the end of empire placed eunuchs in a precarious position. **Chapter 9** reveals that, with their raison d'être no longer viable, eunuchs struggled to survive. This chapter chronicles the last days of the Qing palace eunuch system after the fall of the Qing and the rise of the republic in 1911 in addition to eunuch survival strategies in the years that followed. For some palace eunuchs, life would continue as usual in the years that followed as they continued to serve the "little court." By 1924, though, the realities of the republic and the calls for modernity would become readily apparent. Pu Yi, the former Xuantong emperor (r. 1909–1912), would abruptly expel the remaining eunuchs from the palace and force them onto the street with their belongings. Now considered remnants of the imperial past, eunuchs faced the challenge of surviving outside the palace walls in a society that no longer needed their services. While some would capitalize on their former knowledge of the imperial court in order to earn money, others found that they would need to reinvent themselves and find alternate career paths in order to survive.

In sum, this study of palace eunuchs in late imperial China recasts and reclaims the past of this previously silent numerical majority within the imperial court. Redirecting the focus away from a few notorious individual eunuchs to the eunuch population as a whole, one finds a lifestyle that differed greatly from that of the stereotypical eunuch in terms of status, power, and wealth. As noted by Shih-shan Henry Tsai in his 1996 study of Ming dynasty eunuchs, the time has come for "a more in-depth study of eunuchs in general"[22] to provide a counterbalance to the stereotypical representation of the corrupt eunuch. Now, over twenty years later, the historical lens must be widened beyond the traditionally narrow focus on a small number of corrupt individual eunuchs to encompass the entire palace eunuch population. As a social history of Qing dynasty and Republican era eunuchs, this work examines a complicated social group whose emasculation and employment located them at the center of the empire, closer to the emperor than any other men, yet also subjected them to servile status and marginalization by society. While certainly oppressed, eunuchs were not mere victims, but actively endeavored to have a degree of agency in their lives by either recreating the social bonds that emasculation and eunuch employment denied them or through flight from the palace and at

22. Tsai, *The Eunuchs in the Ming Dynasty*, 9.

times even suicide. Ultimately, with the cut of the knife, emasculation irrevocably altered the eunuch's entire being and rendered him into something other than male in the eyes of the Qing imperial house and Chinese society.

1

The Palace Eunuch System

China's practice of castrating young boys and men can be traced back to the beginnings of its imperial system. Some scholars, citing references to castration on oracle bones, note the presence of eunuchs in China over 3,000 years ago, during the Shang dynasty (1766–1222 BCE). Despite this early reference to castration,[1] it was not until the Western Zhou dynasty (1046–771 BCE) that one finds evidence of eunuchs being used within the palace as attendants for imperial women. By the Qin (221–206 BCE) and Han (206 BCE–220 CE) dynasties, the increasing number of eunuchs in the service of the court had necessitated the creation of an institutionalized palace eunuch system.

The Eunuch System Prior to the Qing Dynasty

The history of the Chinese eunuch system is intertwined with the expansion of imperial political power[2] and the role of the emperor as the son of heaven. As the political unification of China gave rise to dynasties, so did the emperor's need to exhibit his power symbolically through a lifestyle of lavishness and extravagance. While the building of palaces and a capital city manifested imperial power through architecture, the emperor also projected symbolic power by surrounding himself with a surplus of women and a palace full of servants. Beyond symbolic reasons, the imperial court relied on eunuchs for practical reasons. As palace servants, eunuchs were viewed as essential for the maintenance of the imperial harem and the smooth operation of the imperial household.[3]

---

1. Du Wanyan, *Zhongguo huanguan shi* (Taipei: Wenjin chubanshe, 1996), 9. Kutcher notes that, although the Shang castrated prisoners of war, it was not until the Zhou dynasty that eunuchs were employed by the government. See Norman A. Kutcher, "Unspoken Collusions: The Empowerment of Yuanming yuan Eunuchs in the Qianlong Period," *Harvard Journal of Asiatic Studies* 70, no. 2 (Dec. 2010): 453.
2. Du, *Zhongguo huanguan shi*, 3.
3. As Evelyn S. Rawski has noted, the emperor needed servants for practical and symbolic reasons. See Evelyn S. Rawski, *The Last Emperors: A Social History of Qing Imperial Institutions* (Berkeley: University of California Press, 1998), 160.

In the early dynastic period, imperial courts relied on eunuchs who had under-gone castration as a form of punishment (*gongxing* 宫刑)[4] to staff their palaces.[5] One of the five mutilating punishments (*wuxing* 五刑) mentioned in the *Shujing* 書經,[6] castration was listed alongside other corporal punishments such as tattoo-ing, cutting off the nose, cutting off the feet, and execution.[7] Beyond bodily harm, castration punished the individual and his family through the ending of his branch of the patrilineal line. Within the legal system, castration served as an alternative to the death penalty, especially for minors. Many of these eunuchs had not committed any crime but found themselves castrated as a result of the practice of collective responsibility. For instance, in cases of attempted revolt, the guilty party was sen-tenced to execution. In addition, all male members of the felon's family over the age of fourteen would receive death sentences. Those below the age of fourteen would be castrated and sent to serve as palace eunuchs.[8] In 547, the Western Wei dynasty abolished castration as a form of punishment. In 581, the Sui dynasty revised their list of corporal punishments and removed castration from among the choices.[9] While this ruling made clear that the castration of ethnically Han Chinese boys and men was not allowed, the need for eunuchs as servants continued unabated. In later dynasties, castration as a form of punishment would appear again. For example, during the early Ming dynasty, the Hongwu emperor 洪武 (r. 1368–1398) allowed for a variety of corporal punishments, including castration, only later in his reign to prohibit them.

When the penal system was no longer a reliable source of supply, human traf-ficking in young non-Han Chinese boys filled the void. During the Sui dynasty and even later during the Ming (1368–1644), the courts turned to human trafficking in non-Han Chinese boys and men obtained through raiding expeditions, slave markets, and tribute.[10]

Despite official prohibitions against castration and the social stigmatization attached to it, Han Chinese still voluntarily underwent castration to become palace eunuchs. Viewing castration as an avenue for upward mobility, many men and boys willingly chose to become eunuchs, thus enabling dynasties with large eunuch systems such as the Ming to meet their demand.

Over time, as the Chinese dynastic system became more reliant on hereditary succession, emperors came to view eunuchs as uniquely qualified to serve within the court. Physically incapable of both procreation and sexual function, a eunuch's

---

4. *Xing* 刑 is a general term for punishments involving mutilation.
5. J. K. Rideout, "The Rise of the Eunuchs during the T'ang Dynasty, Part One (618–705), *Asia Major* 1.1 (1949): 54.
6. *The Book of Documents* or *Classic of History*. One of the Five Classics of ancient Chinese literature.
7. Mitamura Taisuke, *Chinese Eunuchs: The Structure of Intimate Politics*, trans. Charles A. Pomeroy (Rutland, VT: Charles E. Tuttle Company, 1970), 55.
8. Rideout, "The Rise of the Eunuchs during the T'ang Dynasty," 54.
9. Rideout, "The Rise of the Eunuchs during the T'ang Dynasty," 54 and Zhengyuan Fu, *Autocratic Tradition and Chinese Politics* (New York: Cambridge University Press, 1993), 112.
10. Rideout, "The Rise of the Eunuchs during the T'ang Dynasty," 54.

value for the court became based upon his inability to perform sexually. Within the palace, this physical inability gave eunuchs access to women that was denied to non-emasculated males. Within the *Zhou li* (The Rituals of Zhou), the dynasty's "blueprint of the ideal government," the government's intended role for eunuchs was clearly laid out: eunuchs were to ensure both the purity of the imperial lineage and the chastity of the palace women. A sixteenth-century commentary on the *Zhou li* further explains the government's need for eunuchs. "'Women were in the inner quarters of the palace and could not go out. Men [other than the emperor] were in the outer palace and could not go in. Eunuchs could function in both places.'"[11] Beyond their physical impairment, emasculation rendered eunuchs social outcasts and in theory ensured their reliance on their master. An act that both marked the body physically and stigmatized the person socially, emasculation was designed to create a loyal and subservient servant, unfettered by family ties or responsibilities and wholly dependent upon his master for his livelihood. As will be seen, the eunuch system was built upon assumptions that did not meet realities.

This combination of factors, both physical and social, explains the court's preference for eunuchs to perform duties it would not assign to non-emasculated men. One might ask, though, why some of these duties, especially the care of palace women, needed to be assigned to an emasculated male? What value did emasculated servants provide that maidservants could not? First and foremost, maidservants were not social outcasts who had permanently left their families to serve the imperial court. As such, their loyalties and subservience were not absolute. Second, eunuchs were seen as capable of performing tasks that women physically or socially could not. As Du Wanyan, states, a eunuch had a man's strength, without his sexual ability.[12] Beyond physical strength, eunuchs continued to possess much of the social power associated with men in China's Confucian patriarchal society. While Du describes castration as "turning [a man] into 'half woman,'"[13] as will be seen in Chapter 3, the procedure did not alter the eunuch's gender identity. Eunuchs continued to self-identify as men. Last, as "agents of the imperial will,"[14] eunuchs had access to people and places that others did not. As the commentary from the *Zhou li* points out, eunuchs were able to cross the inner–outer court divide. This access also carried political value for the imperial court; eunuchs facilitated the administration of the palace and acted on behalf of the emperor as a counterbalance to the civil service bureaucracy. Overall, eunuchs' physical and social impairments uniquely qualified them for roles and access denied to others, both men and women.

While deemed essential for the symbolic, political, and administrative needs of the imperial court, eunuchs were also a constant source of anxiety and tension. Throughout history, emperors were well aware of the potential political power of

---

11. Wang Yingdian, *Zhou li zhuan* as cited in Kutcher, "Unspoken Collusions," 453.
12. Du, *Zhongguo huanguan shi*, 3.
13. Du, *Zhongguo huanguan shi*, 3.
14. Rawski, *The Last Emperors*, 160.

individual eunuchs and the group as a whole if left unchecked. As early as the Qin dynasty, eunuchs had already become notorious for their involvement in politics. Throughout Chinese history, if eunuchs were involved in politics, scholars reasoned that their interference had weakened the dynasty and ultimately contributed to its downfall.[15] Despite these potential drawbacks, all governments that ruled China throughout three millennia employed eunuchs. Eunuchs are best known, though, for their activities during the Han, Tang, and Ming dynasties, when their numbers increased and these courts struggled to maintain a balance between the need for eunuchs and eunuchs' rising power.

An examination of the institutional history of eunuchs throughout China's imperial system reveals a common theme: the link between the rise of eunuch political power and individuals with indirect holds on power. The ability of eunuchs to influence politics can be directly attributed to the rise of "intimate politics." Facilitating the power of those without direct access to power, such as women of the court and their families, eunuchs benefited when their masters/benefactors gained political power and influence at court. During the Han, six dowager empresses promoted eunuchs to positions that allowed them to cross the divide from servile status to influencing politics.[16] By the Later Han (25–220 CE), eunuch factions carried enough influence to assist the emperor in overthrowing a rival faction and in another instance, to help bring an emperor to the throne.[17]

When a small number of eunuchs exerted political influence through intimate politics, it created tensions between eunuchs and their masters that resonated throughout the eunuch system. Dynastic histories are replete with instances of eunuchs pushing and oftentimes breaking the boundaries of the servile roles they were intended to play within the court and the attempts of the court to rein eunuchs in. Histories of the eunuchs during the Tang dynasty (618–907) note such tensions between eunuchs and their masters. The Tang imperial court continued to rely on eunuchs in their traditional role as "guardians and servants of the Imperial Harem,"[18] but over time some eunuchs managed to influence politics. Eunuchs were viewed as an "undesirable necessity" for the care of the imperial women. Official historians note that the imperial court managed to keep eunuchs in their "proper place" until the abdication of the Empress Wu 武后 in 705.[19] Hereafter, eunuchs were appointed to positions of command in the palace guard and army that enabled them to "participate in the decision-making process."[20] According to Shih-Shan Henry Tsai, eunuchs became "virtual king makers" during the Tang, inserting themselves into the selection of some seven of the last eight Tang emperors and wielding such power

---

15. Taisuke, *Chinese Eunuchs*, 18. See also Kutcher, "Unspoken Collusions," 454.
16. Shih-Shan Henry Tsai, *The Eunuchs in the Ming Dynasty* (Albany: State University of New York Press, 1996), 12.
17. Kutcher, "Unspoken Collusions," 454.
18. Rideout, "The Rise of the Eunuchs during the T'ang Dynasty," 53.
19. Rideout, "The Rise of the Eunuchs during the T'ang Dynasty," 53.
20. Tsai, *The Eunuchs in the Ming*, 12.

that officials in the capital and provinces were forced to "ingratiate themselves" to eunuchs.[21] As with the Han dynasty, scholars have assigned blame to eunuchs for contributing to the fall of the Tang. Eunuchs would "pay a heavy price" for their involvement in politics. In 903, the warlord Zhu Quanzhong executed hundreds of eunuchs and ordered all eunuchs involved in military affairs to commit suicide.[22] Well aware of the potential hazards of allowing eunuchs too much political power, succeeding dynasties such as the Song and the Yuan would continue to rely on eunuchs but in a much-diminished capacity.

The eunuch system would reach its "zenith" during the Ming dynasty, a period in which eunuch numbers and power swelled.[23] Rather than attributing the rise of eunuch power solely to the decline in quality of emperors, especially those characterized as young, weak, and/or totally disinterested in government, Robert Crawford argues that the basis for eunuch power lay in their role as a check on the bureaucracy and as a tool to "bolster imperial authority."[24] Despite eunuchs' role as a "rival power group" that could be used to balance the power of scholar-officials, early rulers such as the Ming founder, Emperor Hongwu, distrusted eunuchs and advised that they should not be allowed to "intervene in governmental affairs." Those who disobeyed were to be beheaded.[25] Despite this admonition, one finds eunuch numbers and power expanding during the Ming, even during Hongwu's rule, from one hundred at the beginning of the Ming to more than 400 by the end of his reign. After his death, his successors would ignore his warnings about keeping eunuchs out of politics. During periods in which the court faced internal rebellions and foreign invasions, eunuchs repeatedly found opportunities to step in and fill power vacuums.

In the early years of Ming rule, the court established the Directorate of Palace Eunuchs (*Neishijian* 內史監) to handle the administration of eunuchs serving within the inner court. After 1400, the government's increasing reliance on eunuchs necessitated a reorganization of the eunuch institutional structure into twenty-four offices (*ershisi yamen* 二十四衙門)—all designed to manage aspects of the palace administration ranging from staff supervision, to imperial provisions and food, to gunpowder, to the imperial insignia and tent, to the imperial stables.[26] Within the directorates, eunuch hierarchy became stratified with eunuchs being assigned ranks and titles. As Crawford notes, "At this point, they [eunuchs] had ceased to be entirely personal tools used at imperial discretion and became instead an institutionalized bureaucracy with its own inner development and history."[27]

---

21. Tsai, *The Eunuchs in the Ming*, 12.
22. Tsai, *The Eunuchs in the Ming*, 12.
23. Robert B. Crawford, "Eunuch Power in the Ming Dynasty," *T'oung Pao*, Second Series, vol. 49, livr. 3 (1961): 115.
24. Crawford, "Eunuch Power in the Ming Dynasty," 116–17.
25. In 1384, the Hongwu emperor had an iron sign hung over the palace gate that stated this. See Crawford, "Eunuch Power in the Ming Dynasty," 119.
26. For a complete list, see Crawford, "Eunuch Power in the Ming Dynasty," 122.
27. Crawford, "Eunuch Power in the Ming Dynasty," 122.

According to Tsai, during the Ming, eunuchs became a "fully developed third branch of Ming administration that participated in all the most essential matters of the dynasty."[28] Beyond the above-mentioned responsibilities, the government assigned eunuchs to play roles outside the capital city, ranging from guarding and managing imperial tombs to working in supply depots and granaries, to even serving as military commanders.[29] Eunuchs holding military assignments defended the northern borders against the Mongols, led an all-eunuch military battalion, and even commanded China's maritime fleet to the coasts of eastern Africa during the famous maritime missions known for their eunuch commander, Zheng He.

During the Ming, eunuchs were no longer merely servants of the emperor and his family. By the sixteenth century, ranking eunuchs had become "powerful bosses" with their own servants and attendants.[30] In addition to political power, Ming eunuchs wielded considerable economic power as they controlled the wealth of the empire via the Palace Treasury.[31] As might be expected, as the number of offices controlled by eunuchs were increasing so was the number of eunuchs needed to staff them. This number would rise from 10,000 in the fifteenth century to 70,000 in the palace (some 100,000 in total) by the end of the dynasty in 1644.[32] Viewing emasculation as a means to achieve wealth and power, many eunuchs volunteered for service, creating a ready supply of emasculates for the government.

The Qing Eunuch System

During the early 1600s, Jurchen tribes rising in the northeast would coalesce into a group known as the Manchus and eventually challenge the Ming dynasty's control over China. By 1636, the Manchus had established their own dynasty known as the Qing 清 and soon after began to rely on eunuchs as palace servants. Early Qing rulers such as Taizu (Nurhaci) (r. 1616–1626) and Taizong (Hongtaiji) (r. 1627–1643) utilized eunuchs in their service but not in numbers large enough to warrant the creation of an institutionalized eunuch system.[33] At this time, eunuchs also existed in the palaces of the *han* and Jurchen *beile* princes.[34] Here, eunuchs performed the role for which they are well known in history, that of ensuring the "purity of the ruling family's bloodline" by preventing illicit relations between

28. Tsai, *The Eunuchs in the Ming*, 221.
29. For a discussion of eunuch assignments during the Ming, see Tsai, *The Eunuchs in the Ming* and Crawford, "Eunuch Power in the Ming Dynasty."
30. Tsai, *The Eunuchs in the Ming*, 33.
31. Huang Tsung-hsi as cited in Crawford, "Eunuch Power in the Ming Dynasty," 140.
32. Crawford, "Eunuch Power in the Ming Dynasty," 123–24.
33. *Qingshi* (Taipei: Guofang yanjiuyuan, 1961), 卷 119, 1428.
34. Yu Huaqing, *Zhongguo huanguan zhidushi* (Shanghai: Renmin chubanshe, 1993), 447. Charles Hucker defines *beile* as a "title of imperial nobility (*chueh*), originally a descriptive term for a tribal chief but awarded by the founder of the imperial line, Nurhachi [Nuerhachi], to his own brothers, sons, and nephews." See Charles A. Hucker, *A Dictionary of Official Titles in Imperial China* (Stanford: Stanford University Press, 1985), 371.

bondservants (*baoyi* 包衣), enslaved captives from battle, and the palace women.[35] According to Yu Huaqing, these eunuchs were the forcibly emasculated sons and younger brothers of bondservants.[36] During this period, eunuchs, such as those in the service of Nurhaci's eleventh son, Babuhai[37] (1596–1743), were male slaves and low servants.[38] While the origins and use of these eunuchs differed radically from the majority of those employed by the Qing once inside China proper after 1644, as will be seen, their status did not.

The Manchus' limited use of eunuchs during the early Qing relates directly to their bondservant system. Prior to the creation of the banners[39] (1601), the Manchus employed bondservants in private households to provide menial labor and agricultural work.[40] From 1615 to 1620, the bondservants belonging to the emperor and the Manchu princes were organized into companies similar to the Banner system.[41] Bondservants in private hands eventually became known as household slaves, while those of the imperial household retained the designation of bondservant.[42] From this point on, bondservants were a hereditary servile people registered in the banners, who attended to the domestic affairs of the imperial court, serving as messengers and runners, and attendants of the imperial household.[43] These tasks encompassed those normally attended to by eunuchs in the Han Chinese imperial courts such as the Ming. According to Zheng Tianting, "the bondservant system in reality was the same as the eunuch system."[44] Zheng overlooks one important difference: the Manchus did not require bondservants to undergo emasculation. According to the *Qingshi* 清史, prior to taking over control of China proper, the Qing "relied on the old Ming system for the private apartments of the emperor."[45] The Manchu eunuch system, still in its "embryonic form" prior to the Shunzhi reign (1644–1661), utilized eunuchs according to their physical inabilities, specifically their inability to have sexual relations or engage in illicit relations with the women of the palace.

As the Ming dynasty neared collapse, palace eunuchs actively pursued employment with those they perceived as the potential victors in the battle for China. One Ming eunuch who was in charge of Beijing's garrison even facilitated the rebel Li

35. Yu Huaqing, *Zhongguo huanguan zhidushi*, 447.
36. Yu Huaqing, *Zhongguo huanguan zhidushi*, 447.
37. The eleventh of Nurhaci's sixteen sons. See Fang Chao-ying, "Nurhaci," in *Eminent Chinese of the Ch'ing Period (1644–1912)*, ed. Arthur W. Hummel (Washington, DC: Government Printing Office, 1943; reprint, New York: Paragon Book Gallery, Ltd, 1967), 598.
38. Zheng Tianting, *Qingshi tanwei* (Zhongjing: Duli chubanshe, 1946), 66.
39. "The banners were large civil-military units created from 1601 on to replace the small hunting groups of Nurgaci's [Nurhaci's] early campaigns. Banners were made up of companies, each composed (at least in theory) of three hundred warrior households." See Rawski, *The Last Emperors*, 61.
40. Jonathan Spence, *Ts'ao Yin and the K'ang-hsi Emperor* (New Haven: Yale University Press, 1988), 7.
41. Spence, *Ts'ao Yin and the K'ang-hsi Emperor*, 8.
42. Spence, *Ts'ao Yin and the K'ang-hsi Emperor*, 8.
43. See Zheng Tianting, *Qingshi tanwei*, 64 and Rawski, *The Last Emperors*, 167.
44. Zheng Tianting, *Qingshi tanwei*, 65.
45. *Qingshi*, 卷 119, 1428.

Zicheng's entry into Beijing by opening the gate to the city.[46] Once inside, Li found a crowd of Ming eunuchs waiting to welcome him at the imperial residences.[47] Ming eunuchs also greeted the Manchu regent, Dorgon,[48] as he entered the Shanhai Pass with the Qing imperial carriage.[49] Well aware of the Ming dynasty's problems with eunuchs and the perception that they had contributed to the weakened state of the dynasty, the Manchus were wary of these eunuchs. Nevertheless, they absorbed many former Ming eunuchs into their system.[50]

Once the Manchus established their dynasty inside China proper in 1644, their reliance on eunuchs increased both in scale and in scope. As the Manchu's rule over China expanded, so did their administrative and symbolic need for palace eunuchs. Ming eunuchs' intimate knowledge of the many facets involved in ruling the Chinese empire and the administration of the palace had the potential to facilitate China's new rulers in their transition to power. For a conquest dynasty such as the Qing, eunuchs would have been important sources of institutional knowledge and a means to balance the power of the Han Chinese bureaucracy. Eunuchs also fulfilled the Manchus' immediate administrative needs of staffing the newly acquired Forbidden City and serving the women of the court. Symbolically, eunuchs also contributed to the emperor's desire to "awe and impress subjects" with symbols of "conspicuous consumption."[51]

As a conquest dynasty, the Manchus came to rule with their own traditions concerning the imperial harem and how to administer their palace. The Manchu imperial practice of possessing fewer empresses and concubines than their Han Chinese predecessors initially resulted in the Manchus needing fewer eunuchs to attend to their women. In addition, they relied on their own system of governance to manage their household, the Imperial Household Department (*Neiwufu* 內務府).[52] This system would place bondservants in positions overseeing palace eunuchs. These factors, combined with an anxiety about the potential of a resurgence of eunuch power, resulted in a drastic reduction in the number of palace eunuchs. The Manchus would make it their policy to keep eunuch numbers low and to relegate eunuchs to menial positions. During the course of the Qing, the Manchus would employ at most 3,300 eunuchs, some three to five percent of the former 70,000 to 100,000 eunuchs.[53] While comparatively small, the Qing's reten-

46. Zheng Tianting, *Qingshi tanwei*, 65.
47. Zheng Tianting, *Qingshi tanwei*, 65.
48. Shunzhi's regent from 1644 to 1650.
49. Zheng Tianting, *Qingshi tanwei*, 65.
50. *Guochao gongshi* as cited in Preston Torbert, *The Ch'ing Imperial Household Department: A Study of Its Organization and Principal Functions, 1662–1796* (Cambridge, MA: Harvard University Press, 1977), 48–49.
51. Rawski, *The Last Emperors*, 181.
52. According to Rawski, the *Neiwufu* (Imperial Household Department) was created in during the 1620s. See Rawski, *The Last Emperors*, 179.
53. Shih-shan Henry Tsai notes that, at the end of the Ming dynasty, there were 100,000 castrated males in the population. See Tsai, *The Eunuchs in the Ming*, 26. According to Ding Yanshi, the overall trend during the Qing suggests a decline in the number of eunuchs from 2,866 during the reign of Qianlong, to 2,638 during the reign of Jiaqing, to 1,989 during the reign of Guangxu, and finally 800–900 during the reign of the last

tion of many former Ming eunuchs represented an enlargement of both the scale and the scope of eunuch employment within the Qing palace.

Initially, the Qing limited eunuchs to their traditional role of keepers of the imperial women. Suspicions concerning the involvement of eunuchs in the downfall of the Ming led the regent, Dorgon, to restrict the influence of eunuchs within the court. Dorgon continued the Manchu tradition of delegating eunuch management to the Imperial Household Department (*Neiwufu*), which was created prior to the establishment of Qing rule within China proper.[54] Faced with an overabundance of Ming eunuchs, the Qing dynasty attempted to restrict the role and employment requirements for eunuch service within the palace. In the years immediately following the establishment of rule inside the pass, the Qing dynasty issued edicts which "prohibited the eunuchs from handling the income from the imperial estates (1644), from participating in court audiences (1645), . . . from going to the capital to seek employment (1646) [and abolished] . . . eunuch posts, such as those connected with revenue and construction works."[55] While these measures succeeded in reducing the eunuch workforce, they did not result in a total reduction of eunuch influence within the court.

In the years immediately following the death of Dorgon in 1650 and Shunzhi's assumption of personal rule, the young emperor utilized the palace eunuchs to "strengthen his own imperial position against the power of the Manchu princes."[56] Shunzhi first increased his reliance on eunuchs by allowing their presence in the Throne Hall, "the seat and source of imperial power."[57] Later, in 1653, Shunzhi strengthened eunuch power even further by abolishing the Imperial Household Department and establishing the Thirteen Yamen (十三衙門 Thirteen Eunuch Bureaus). This ruling released eunuchs from their subordinate position under a management system controlled by bondservants and replaced it with a system of joint rule by both eunuchs and bondservants. Despite this elevation of eunuch power within the Qing court, palace eunuchs faced regulations that restricted their mobility and influence in governmental affairs.[58]

---

emperor, Xuantong. See Ding Yanshi, *Wanqing gongting yishi* (Taipei: Shijie wenwu chubanshe, 1984), 186. Evelyn Rawski notes a 1751 edict fixing the number of palace eunuchs at 3,300. See Rawski, *The Last Emperors*, 164. Norman Kutcher's table plotting the annual census of eunuchs for years with records from 1747 to 1806 notes that Qianlong did not exceed the 3,300 quota set by his grandfather, Kangxi. See Kutcher, "Unspoken Collusions," Fig. 1.

54. Although there is no clear date for the establishment of the Imperial Household Department, Chang Te-ch'ang (Zhang Dechang) prefers the date of 1628 as quoted in the genealogy of a *baoyi* official. See Chang Te-ch'ang, "The Economic Role of the Imperial Household in the Ch'ing Dynasty," *The Journal of Asian Studies* 31, no. 2 (Feb. 1972): 245.

55. Torbert, *The Ch'ing Imperial Household*, 22.

56. Lawrence Kessler, *K'ang-hsi and the Consolidation of Ch'ing Rule, 1661–1684* (Chicago: University of Chicago Press, 1976), 26.

57. Chang Te-ch'ang, "The Economic Role of the Imperial Household in the Ch'ing Dynasty," 248.

58. Torbert, *The Ch'ing Imperial Household*, 23.

The Shunzhi emperor's death from smallpox on February 6, 1661[59] signaled the reassertion of power by the Manchu princes to the detriment of Qing palace eunuchs. With the heir apparent only seven years old at the time of his father's death, the regency of four Manchu elders (Soni, Suksaha, Ebilun, and Oboi) quickly moved to restrict further eunuch influence within the court. The regents utilized Shunzhi's will,[60] in which he expressed his regret over having created the Thirteen Yamen, as a pretext for abolishing them and reinstating the Imperial Household Department. As a result, the regents returned eunuchs to their former subordinate position under the management of bondservants.

During the reign of the Kangxi emperor (1662–1722), the Manchus restored the Imperial Household Department to power. In 1677, the Kangxi emperor further consolidated control over the palace eunuchs with the establishment of the *Jingshifang* (敬事房 Office of Eunuch Affairs) as a unit within the Imperial Household Department.[61] This office handled the screening, transfer and appointment, and reward and punishment of imperial palace eunuchs.[62] In addition to managing eunuch affairs, the *Jingshifang* was responsible for such duties as the recording of the births and deaths of the imperial family.[63]

Considering eunuchs as basically yin 陰 in nature,[64] Kangxi kept a watchful eye over their movements and activities. Throughout his sixty-one-year reign, one finds numerous regulations prohibiting eunuchs from "gambling, excessive drinking, fighting," speaking with outsiders about palace matters, and so forth.[65] Despite Kangxi's general distrust of eunuchs, the informal and friendly style of his letters to the eunuch Gu Wenxiang reveals the emperor's ability to view individual eunuchs in a positive light.[66] Nevertheless, Kangxi endeavored to keep his personal relations with eunuchs from interfering with governmental affairs, as revealed in his comment: "In my court I never let them [eunuchs] get involved with government— even the few eunuchs-of-the-presence with whom I might chatter or exchange family jokes were never allowed to discuss politics."[67] It is also during the reign of Kangxi that the emperor enacted sumptuary laws to govern the employment of eunuchs. From 1701, aside from the palace, only nobles and officials of the first two ranks were allowed to have eunuchs employed within their households.[68]

59. Kessler, 25.
60. This will is now considered by many scholars to be a forgery.
61. Wang Shuqing, "Jingshifang," *Gugong bowuyuan yuankan*, no. 2 (1979): 64.
62. Yu Huaqing, *Zhongguo huanguan zhidushi*, 451. Hereafter, "imperial palace eunuchs" will refer to eunuchs employed by the emperor within his palaces, as opposed to those employed in the personal residences of princes, marquis, and grand ministers.
63. Wang Shuqing, "Jingshifang," 64.
64. Jonathan Spence, *Emperor of China: Self-Portrait of K'ang-hsi* (New York: Vintage Books, 1988), 45. Yin is the principle in Chinese philosophy that is characterized as feminine, passive, negative and weak.
65. Yu Huaqing, *Zhongguo huanguan zhidushi*, 454.
66. For examples of these letters, see Spence, *Emperor of China*, 156–66.
67. Spence, *Emperor of China*, 45.
68. Rawski, *The Last Emperors*, 181.

The Yongzheng emperor (1723–1735) also distrusted eunuchs, perhaps due to the involvement of certain eunuchs in the power struggle that broke out over succession following his father's death. Eunuchs loyal to Yongzheng's rivals for the imperial throne such as Zhou Jinchao (loyal to Yinreng) and Wei Zhu (the eunuch in charge of the Inner Chancery of Memorials who was an important player in the Yinsi faction) may have contributed to Yongzheng's desire to restrict the influence and power of palace eunuchs.[69] Throughout his reign, Yongzheng attempted to reform eunuch behavior as well as curb their influence within the court. Yongzheng's numerous edicts attempting to rectify eunuch conduct such as drinking and gambling, being lazy messengers, complaining, cursing at people on the street, being arrogant, and speaking in a loud voice[70] suggest that he was frustrated that eunuchs were not acting according to their designated servile role. Torbert argues that, within these edicts that scolded eunuchs for bad conduct, the emperor repeatedly reminded eunuchs of their "moral indebtedness to him."[71] Contrary to the popular characterization of Yongzheng as a despotic ruler who rose to power by killing his brothers, Torbert casts him as a "skillful administrator" who utilized favors and rewards, such as establishing a loan fund to help eunuchs meet unexpected expenses and providing shelter and stipends for elderly eunuchs, to win the allegiance of the eunuch workforce.[72]

The Yongzheng emperor also endeavored to prevent eunuch families from abusing their sons' positions within the court. In an edict from 1726, he declared that eunuch relatives would "not be able to take advantage of the power of inner palace eunuchs to perform improper and illegal acts."[73] Yongzheng also prohibited the fraternization of eunuchs directly serving him with those employed throughout the rest of the palace. In 1730, he ordered that "eunuchs [directly] serving the emperor should also not drink, play chess [or] dominoes (*gupai*) [or] gossip with other eunuchs."[74] Clearly, the Yongzheng emperor desired to keep the intimate affairs of his household as well as the governmental affairs of the empire beyond the reach of the majority of the outer court eunuch population.

In contrast to his father's management style, the Qianlong emperor (r. 1736–1795) managed eunuchs by directly attacking their routes to power and influence within the palace. As will be seen, Qianlong promoted a policy of eunuch illiteracy, seeing no need for eunuchs to recognize more than a few characters. Qianlong also endeavored to curb eunuch influence in governmental affairs. In an edict from 1745, Qianlong declared that eunuchs "'should not engage in conversations with outer court officials,' '[nor] should [they] exchange friendly visits with princes,

69. For information on the succession struggle, see Silas H. L. Wu, *Passage to Power: K'ang-hsi and His Heir Apparent, 1661–1722* (Cambridge, MA: Harvard University Press, 1979), 156–76.
70. See *Guochao gongshi*, ed. Yu Minzhong (Taipei: Taiwan xuesheng shuju, 1965), 史三, 訓諭.
71. Torbert, *The Ch'ing Imperial Household*, 50.
72. Torbert, *The Ch'ing Imperial Household*, 51.
73. Edict cited in Yu Huaqing, *Zhongguo huanguan zhidushi*, 454.
74. Edict cited in Yu Huaqing, *Zhongguo huanguan zhidushi*, 454.

marquis, and men in high places.'"[75] Scholars such as Zheng Tianting and others have characterized Qianlong as a "stern manager of eunuchs" who became more lax in the later years of his reign.[76] More recent scholarship by Norman Kutcher finds that the Qianlong emperor was not as strict in his management of eunuchs as earlier studies have attempted to show.[77] Kutcher argues that, in response to shortages in the supply of eunuchs, particularly young eunuchs, the emperor quietly granted them more privileges, especially those serving him at his primary residence, the *Yuanmingyuan*.[78]

In the years that followed, the Jiaqing emperor (r. 1796–1820) would not only continue on with the well-known theme of attempting to prevent the resurgence of eunuch power but also the leaking of palace secrets and sensitive information. Eunuch involvement with officials and nobility outside the palace continued to plague the emperor during his reign period. In an effort to prevent the leaking of palace information, Jiaqing prohibited eunuchs previously employed by banner-men from returning to the private households of their former employers.[79] The rise in the number of eunuchs fleeing the palace in favor of employment in princely households during this period, and Jiaqing's moves to prevent princes from exceeding their eunuch quotas, suggests that the emperor's strict control over his eunuch workforce was creating tense labor relations within the palace. Jiaqing's suspicions of eunuchs would prove well founded in 1813, when, during the Eight Trigrams Uprising, eunuch members of the rebel group facilitated the entry of rebels into the palace.[80] That same year, Jiaqing became suspicious of requests for eunuch leave from the palace and prohibited eunuchs from going outside the palace alone, requiring that they travel in groups of two or three.[81] Undoubtedly, the possible disastrous results of eunuch involvement with people and groups outside the palace prompted Jiaqing and later his successor, the Daoguang emperor (r. 1821–1850), to further restrict eunuch mobility and eunuch relationships with those outside of the Forbidden City. Throughout his reign, Daoguang continued to work towards severing eunuch connections with those outside the imperial court. In light of the relatively recent attempt to invade the palace during his predecessor's reign, in 1827, Daoguang also took measures to prevent eunuchs from possessing weapons within the court.[82]

---

75. Edict cited in Yu Huaqing, *Zhongguo huanguan zhidushi*, 455.
76. See Kutcher, "Unspoken Collusions," 450.
77. Kutcher, "Unspoken Collusions," 451.
78. Kutcher, "Unspoken Collusions," 451.
79. Kutcher, "Unspoken Collusions," 455.
80. For information on eunuch involvement in the Eight Trigrams Uprising, see Clara Wing-chung Lau, "Jiaqing jingji 'guiyou zhi bian' zhong taijian suo banyan de jiaose" 嘉慶京畿「癸酉之變」中太監所扮演的角色, *Dongfang wenhua* 東方文化 2 (1984): 87–106 and Susan Naquin, *Millenarian Rebellion in China: The Eight Trigrams Uprising of 1813* (New Haven: Yale University Press, 1976), 148, 175–83.
81. *Qinding Da Qing huidian shili* 欽定大清會典事例 [Imperially commissioned collected regulations of the Qing dynasty] , 卷 1217 as cited in Yu Huaqing, 456.
82. *Qinding Da Qing huidian shili*, 卷 1217 as cited in Yu Huaqing, 456.

From the initial inception of the Qing eunuch system through the reign of Daoguang in 1850, Qing emperors continuously enacted policies aimed at preventing a reassertion of eunuch influence and power within the imperial court and throughout the empire. Countless edicts decreased eunuch numbers, prevented them from handling imperial funds, restricted them from interfering in politics, and lessened their opportunities for involvement with individuals or groups outside the palace by confining them within the palace walls, except when on official business.

After 1850, Qing emperors gradually became laxer in their previously vigilant stand against the reassertion of eunuch influence within the court. As noted by Wang Shuqing, a series of young, weak emperors manipulated by members of the imperial court such as China's last female regent, the Empress Dowager Cixi, contributed to the increased power and political activity enjoyed by late Qing eunuchs.[83] Operating outside the traditional power structure, Cixi relied on "intimate politics" through eunuchs to ensure her hold over politics. In 1869, Cixi's favoritism of eunuchs became readily apparent to those outside her inner circle. That year, Cixi sent one of her favorite eunuchs, An Dehai 安德海 (1844–1869), to supervise the Imperial Textile Factory at Nanjing, a post formerly occupied by bondservants. Traveling down the Grand Canal in style, flying imperial insignia with female musicians on board, and demanding bribes from local officials, An attracted the attention of local officials, who assumed that his claim to be on an imperial mission was fraudulent. In response, An and six of his associate eunuchs were executed; others were sent to Heilongjiang to serve as slaves.[84] In another case of favoritism, Cixi promoted Li Lianying 李蓮英 to rise above the rank of fourth grade, allowing him to obtain the rank of second grade.[85] Cixi's favoritism of An and Li was a source of rumors and criticism; Chinese and foreign writers even alleged that neither had been emasculated but were in fact fully functional males with whom the empress dowager engaged in illicit relations.[86]

Desiring to keep her eunuch favorites happy, Cixi lapsed into practices common during periods of eunuch power (the Han, Tang, and Ming dynasties) such as allowing eunuchs to have sons employed as officials.[87] This practice blatantly disregarded one of the benefits of employing eunuchs, namely the lack of offspring that might form factions and interfere in the government. During the reign of Tongzhi (1862–1874), eunuchs who facilitated the political influence of Cixi, such as An and Li, and those in the upper echelons of the eunuch hierarchy, enjoyed extravagant lifestyles and positions previously unheard of in the Qing. These eunuchs ate lavish

---

83. Wan Yi, Wang Shuqing, and Liu Lu, *Qingdai gongtingshi* (Shenyang: Liaoning renmin chubanshe, 1990), 499.

84. Rawski, *The Last Emperors*, 189–90.

85. Wan Yi et al., *Qingdai gongtingshi*, 498.

86. See Keith McMahon, "The Polyandrous Empress: Imperial Women and Their Male Favorites," in *Wanton Women in Late Imperial Chinese Literature*, ed. Mark Stevenson and Wu Cuncun (Leiden: Brill, 2017), 29 and 47.

87. Wan Yi et al., *Qingdai gongtingshi*, 498. As will be seen, some men became eunuchs after having children; other eunuchs, incapable of fathering their own children, chose to adopt.

meals, wore expensive clothing, and even had their own eunuchs who waited on them.[88] Overall, eunuchs during the latter period of the Qing dynasty worked in an environment that provided them with opportunities for advancement and power actively denied to earlier generations of Qing palace eunuchs. As this work will show, when eunuchs were in short supply or their assistance was needed to facilitate access to politics, previously strict regulations became relaxed. As a result, by the late Qing, eunuchs were routinely allowed greater freedom of mobility to interact with their families, network with other eunuchs, and live a life beyond the confines of the palace walls.

By the reign of Xuantong (1909–1912), with the Qing's former hold over power clearly waning, eunuchs became bolder in their attempts to subvert the traditional master–servant power structure. While on the surface eunuchs continued the façade of eunuch subservience, planning for their survival after the potential fall of the dynasty became paramount. During the chaotic final years of the dynasty, some eunuchs fled the palace in greater numbers while those who stayed behind looked for ways to fund their future life outside the palace eunuch system. As will be seen, eunuchs were routinely accused of stealing palace treasures during this period. As Chapter 9 will show, while the dynasty would fall in 1911, the eunuch system would not. With the Articles of Favorable Treatment allowing Pu Yi, the former Xuantong emperor, to remain in residence within the Forbidden City and provided with a stipend to maintain some form of his former imperial lifestyle, the eunuch system, albeit in an abbreviated form, persisted. The palace eunuch system would continue for another eleven years until July 1923, when, in a sudden move, Pu Yi would assemble all the eunuchs and inform them that their services were no longer needed. Pu Yi's pronouncement summarily brought to an end the Qing's reliance on eunuchs and abolished the three-millennia-old imperial eunuch system.

---

88. Wan Yi et al., *Qingdai gongtingshi*, 499.

2
Routes to the Palace

Unlike many of their counterparts in earlier dynasties who received sentences of emasculation as a result of their unfree status, the majority of Qing palace eunuch candidates voluntarily subjected themselves to genital mutilation as a prerequisite for appointment.[1] The Qing required that all applicants to the palace eunuch system have undergone the procedure of having their external male genitalia (scrotum, testes, and penis) excised in total prior to applying for service. Given that emasculation was not forced upon Qing eunuchs, why would young boys and men in a Confucian society that revered filial piety and the continuance of the family line allow themselves to become emasculated and labeled as "unfilial" or as "social outcasts"?

As one traces the routes taken by eunuch candidates to reach the palace, one finds paths peopled with the "socially inferior"[2] of Qing society, families and individuals who viewed emasculation as their ticket to social advancement, wealth, and power. For others, it was merely a way to ensure survival and a source of livelihood for the family. As will be seen, although eunuchs took a variety of routes to reach the palace, they all started their journey with the singular act of emasculation. Genital mutilation alone, though, did not ensure the attainment of a position as a palace eunuch. While the government distanced itself from the genital mutilation and sale of young boys and adult men into servitude, it was directly involved in regulating the supply and demand that fueled the eunuch system and determined the fate of these new emasculates.

During the Qing, emasculation was "voluntary" in the sense that the majority of young boys and men did not undergo genital mutilation as a form of punishment imposed by the government. As will be seen, "voluntary" did not necessarily equate to individual choice in the matter. Privatization of the process, in which the government authorized professionals known as *daozijiang* (刀子匠 knife experts) to supply

---

1. For information on the foreign and domestic sources of eunuchs during the Ming dynasty, see Shih-shan Henry Tsai, *The Eunuchs in the Ming Dynasty* (Albany: State University of New York Press, 1996), 17–21.
2. Albert Mann, "The Influence of Eunuchs in the Politics and Economy of the Ch'ing Court 1861–1907" (MA thesis, University of Washington, 1957), 19. Mann includes "mean people" (*jianmin* 賤民) among the sources of Qing eunuchs. I have yet to find any evidence within the historical record to support this claim.

the court with eunuchs, distanced the court from direct involvement in the physical transformation of Chinese males into eunuchs. Licensure enabled the government to contract out the recruitment, screening, and emasculation of prospective eunuch applicants yet retain control over the actual hiring process and limit the number of eunuchs entering the system. Privatization also allowed the government to disassociate itself from the human trafficking and physical mutilation of young boys and men. Despite this, the court's preference for eunuchs emasculated prior to the onset of puberty created the demand necessary to sustain the sale of young boys. En route to the palace, kidnappers, *daozijiang*, and even family members facilitated the trade in emasculates. As will be seen, the status of these children, some of whom were volunteered by their parents and some of whom were sold into bondage to a *daozijiang* only later to be hired as palace servants, reveals the complexities of ideas of unfree status during the Qing.

Coercion by family members and the sale of boys does not explain the emasculation of all eunuchs. Many destitute Chinese men, viewing emasculation and employment as a palace eunuch as the remedy to their own and by extension their families' financial problems, volunteered for service. Nevertheless, the irreversible act of emasculation, a prerequisite for even being presented as a candidate for service within the palace, did not ensure appointment as an imperial court eunuch. Even if eunuchs managed to enter the palace walls, not all candidates received an invitation to stay.

With the government removed from direct involvement in the emasculation process, *daozijiang*, kidnappers, and family members often determined the fate of boys and men. Within a patriarchal and hierarchically organized society such as the Qing, the wishes of elders and the good of the family took precedence over individual concerns, especially those of minors. In the case of emasculation, this resulted in the complete negation of a boy's rights over his own body.

To families oppressed by poverty, learning that someone from their area had become wealthy as a eunuch made emasculation appear more attractive[3] and as a possible remedy to their financial situation. *Daozijiang* preyed upon the desperation of the poor and sold them a glorified picture of the eunuch lifestyle.[4] This picture proved too enticing to resist for many families oppressed by poverty. Determining their son's and by extension the family's fate, parents rather than the soon-to-be-emasculate offered the final consent just prior to the excision of the child's sexual organs. When asked *houhui bu houhui* (後悔不後悔 Will you regret it?),[5] the parent's or sponsor's negative response would serve as the only permission necessary for the *daozijiang* to proceed. These parents allowed the excision of their son's genitalia in

---

3. Ma Deqing et al., "Qing gong taijian huiyi lu," in *Wanqing gongting shenghuo jianwen*, ed. Zhang Wenhui (Beijing: Wenshi ziliao chubanshe, 1982), 173–74.

4. Ma Deqing et al., "Qing gong taijian huiyi lu," 176.

5. George Carter Stent, "Chinese Eunuchs," *Journal of the North China Branch of the Royal Asiatic Society*, New Series, no. 11 (1877): 171.

exchange for the hope their son might obtain employment as a palace eunuch and provide the family with a source of livelihood.

Again and again throughout the historical record, poverty appears as the primary motivating factor behind emasculation. Poverty, when coupled with visions of the power and an assumed life of leisure inside the Forbidden City, proved attractive to applicants faced with the alternatives of hunger, begging, or even crime. When asked whether he had been emasculated by choice, one late Qing eunuch replied:

> Why not? It seemed a little thing to give up one pleasure for so many. My parents were poor, yet by suffering that small change I could be sure of an easy life in sur-roundings of beauty and magnificence; I could aspire to intimate companionship with lovely women unmarred by their fear or distrust of me. I could even hope for power and wealth of my own. With good fortune and diligence, I might grow more rich and powerful than some of the greatest officials, in the empire.[6]

Other applicants fell prey to rumors of the leisurely life enjoyed by eunuchs. George Carter Stent describes the motivations of another late Qing eunuch applicant:

> A few years ago a newly-married young man expressed a strong desire to become a eunuch, as he said he should then have nothing to do but eat, drink, and sleep. His relatives endeavored to dissuade him from so insane an idea, and refused to become surety for him; whereupon he attempted to perform the operation on himself, but did it so clumsily that no one would employ him. He, therefore, had mutilated himself for life without gratifying his desire of living the easy life of a eunuch.[7]

The court screened applicants to ensure that poverty had been the primary motivation for their emasculation. When the candidate had not entered the system via a *daozijiang*, the grand ministers of the Imperial Household Department were ordered to investigate the eunuch's background.[8] Clearly, the palace endeavored to select candidates who had become emasculated out of financial desperation. Those who had ulterior motivations such as desire for power and political influence could become problematic in a system that aimed to suppress eunuch "interference" in politics. At times, the government did encourage families to send one of their sons to become a eunuch. In the very early years of the Qing, during the third year of Shunzhi (1646), the statutes noted that, if a commoner family had more than four or five sons, then one should be sent to apply to become an emasculate.[9] It is interest-ing to note that the Qing was actively encouraging the emasculation of young men

---

6. John Blofeld, *City of Lingering Splendour: A Frank Account of Old Peking's Exotic Pleasures* (London: Hutchinson, 1961; reprint, Boston: Shambhala, 1989), 58–59.

7. Stent, "Chinese Eunuchs," 169.

8. *Qinding Da Qing huidian shili* 欽定大清會典事例 (*QDDQHDSL*) [Imperially commissioned collected regula-tions of the Qing dynasty], ed. Li Hongzhang et al. (Shanghai: Shangwu yinshuguan, 1909), 卷1216，內務府，太監事例，選驗太監，嘉慶19年.

9. *QDDQHDSL*, 卷1216，內務府，太監事例，順治3年.

at time when there was a surplus of unemployed Ming eunuchs seeking employment. One can surmise that the Qing, considering the loyalty of these former Ming eunuchs to be suspect, would have preferred to create a new applicant pool.

In sum, financial desperation combined with illusions of the power and wealth of those working in proximity to the imperial court supplied the Imperial Household Department with applicants for its eunuch system. These were the "socially inferior" among Qing society: families and individuals willing to sacrifice genitalia and procreation for an alternate route to social advancement, wealth, and power. These were young boys/families and even adult males who shared a willingness to subject their children or themselves to physical mutilation in exchange for the hope of a steady source of income and the possibility of a life of leisure and/or political power in the service of the imperial court.

Daozijiang

Young men and boys interested in becoming eunuchs could register their names with a *daozijiang*.[10] Due to the secrecy involved in maintaining the hereditary nature of the profession and the apparent lack of information in the Qing palace archives concerning *daozijiang*, one must rely on the recollections of late Qing palace eunuchs and Western physicians and scholars living and working in China at the time for information on these individuals and their practice. Granted monopolies by the government until they were revoked in 1900,[11] *daozijiang* were enlisted in one of the three banners of the Imperial Household Department and carried the rank of the seventh grade.[12] One confession from a runaway eunuch during the fifty-eighth year of Qianlong (1793) reveals that some *daozijiang* families had been in the profession for generations. This eunuch described himself as having been emasculated by a fourth-generation *daozijiang*.[13] The entire livelihood of these men depended on their success in the recruitment, emasculation, and future employment of young boys and men as eunuchs.[14]

Late Qing contemporaries recalled that, during the Guangxu period (ca. 1895), two well-known *daozijiang*, Bi Wu (畢五 Bi "the Fifth") and Xiaodao Liu (小刀劉 "Pocket Knife" Liu), performed emasculations in Beijing. Bi operated an

---

10. *Daozijiang* are also referred to as a *yahang* (牙行 guild).

11. In 1900, the government revoked the licensure of the *daozijiang* and assigned the Imperial Household Department's Judicial Department to perform emasculations. Du Wanyan does not cite any reason for the change. See Du Wanyan, *Zhongguo huanguan shi* (Taipei: Wenjin chubanshe, 1996), 23. See also Ma Deqing et al., "Qing gong taijian huiyi" in Zhang Wenhui, ed., *Wanqing gongting shenghuo jianwen*, 177.

12. Du Wanyan, *Zhongguo huanguan shi*, 22 and Dan Shi, *Mémoires d'un Eunuque dans la Cité Interdite*, trans. Nadine Perront (Marseille: Editions Philippe Picquier, 1991; reprint, 1995), 105.

13. *Guoli Gugong Bowuyuan* [National Palace Museum], Taipei 國立故宮博物院, *Gongzhong dang zouzhe* 宮中檔 奏摺 [Secret Palace Memorials], *Jiaqing chao* 咸豐朝 [Jiaqing reign period], 404007353, 故宮 093158.

14. George Carter Stent's 1877 account notes that these men were "recognized" by the government but not paid by it. See Stent, "Chinese Eunuchs," 170.

establishment on Nanchang Street while Liu had one outside Di'an Gate.[15] The memoirs of Yu Chunhe, a eunuch during this same period, also include *daozijiang* "Fine Blade" Liu, who performed emasculations on Fangzhuang Street next to Di'an Gate.[16] Recollections of late Qing palace eunuchs note that four times a year (spring, summer, winter, and fall), Bi and Liu would each supply the palace with at least forty emasculates.[17] As a result, these two *daozijiang* ensured a supply of 160 new eunuch recruits each year.

Those who chose to begin the application process with a *daozijiang* benefited from the *daozijiang's* experience in performing the procedure as well as his ability to facilitate the applicant's entry into the palace. Aware of the traits the palace found desirable in their eunuch staff, *daozijiang* routinely screened their applicants for qualities such as "appearance, conversation, intelligence and cleverness, and strength."[18] According to the late Qing eunuch Yu Chunhe, this pre-emasculation examination could leave the applicant feeling humiliated. In Yu's case, *daozijiang* Bi looked Yu over from head to toe and then used his hands to examine between Yu's thighs.[19] If, as in the case of Yu, the applicant passed the *daozijiang's* test, the applicant would proceed to the next step in the process, the emasculation.

Sought out as prey by kidnappers or viewed as a commodity by their families, young boys also found themselves delivered to the *daozijiang's* "shed" (*changzi* 廠子)[20] as a result of human trafficking. In one record from the fifty-eighth year of Qianlong (1793), it was reported that a young Manchu boy, nine-year-old Li Zhu, had been drugged and forced to become emasculated. It was recommended that Li be handed over to the Imperial Household Department and assigned to serve in the inner court.[21] In another case from the sixteenth year of Daoguang (1836), one learns that eunuchs themselves were also involved in the trafficking of young boys to become emasculates. In this case, two discharged eunuchs were arrested for luring over ten young boys from the road, forcing them to become emasculated by a local *daozijiang*, and selling them as emasculates. At the time of the arrest, seven of the boys had already been emasculated and sold, while four others had been rescued before the procedure had been performed.[22]

Parents also trafficked their own children; those in need of quick and ready cash could sell their sons directly to a *daozijiang*. As Nadine Perront points out, parents would sell their seven and eight year old sons for a sum of money that would

15. Jin Yi and Shen Yiling, *Gongnü tan wanglu* (Beijing: Forbidden City Press, 1992), 103. Note that Ma Deqing et al. locate the *daozijiang's* shed inside the gate. See Ma Deqing et al., "Qing gong taijian huiyi lu," 176-77.
16. Dan Shi, *Mémoires d'un Eunuque*, 12.
17. Wan Yi, Wang Shuqing, and Liu Lu, *Qingdai gongtingshi* (Shenyang: Liaoning renmin chubanshe, 1990), 497. See also Ma Deqing et al., "Qing gong taijian huiyi lu," 176.
18. Ma Deqing et al., "Qing gong taijian huiyi lu," 176.
19. Dan Shi, *Mémoires d'un Eunuque*, 106.
20. Stent, "Chinese Eunuchs," 170.
21. *Guoli Gugong Bowuyuan, Junjichu* 軍機處 057869，乾隆 58年7月26日.
22. *Guoli Gugong Bowuyuan*, 軍機處069938，道光16年2月8日.

only feed the family for a few months.[23] However, emasculation and employment of the boy as a eunuch did ensure that at least the boy would not starve. Unlike the sale of girls, in which the families often retained financial ties to the child,[24] the sales of boys to a *daozijiang* were final. In return for a sum of money, parents rescinded their parental rights over the child to the *daozijiang*. Whereas young girls kidnapped and sold to brothels might hope to eventually be bought back by their families, the physical mutilation of emasculation prevented these boys from ever returning to their previous lives. The purchase and emasculation of young boys became a lucrative scheme for *daozijiang* who required their "adopted sons"[25] to turn over their entire salaries from their employment as eunuchs to them.[26] As a result, eunuchs from these *daozijiang* "families" found themselves held in bondage by two masters, their imperial employers and their *daozijiang* "fathers."

Once sold, some young men attempted to buy back their freedom. However, the high price put on their freedom could have appeared insurmountable to those already in desperate financial straits and forced some young men to acquiesce to emasculation. At the age of seventeen, Yu Chunhe found himself sold to a *daoziji-ang*. Yu had been lured to the *daozijiang's* shed by a man from his village known as "Uncle Qian," who had promised to help him find employment. The monetary value placed on Yu's freedom (the one hundred *taels* to cover what the *daozijiang* had paid for him) combined with the threat of Bi accusing him of fraud in a system in which Bi claimed to have connections, led Yu to acquiesce to emasculation. After refusing to eat, drink, or even speak for two days and two nights, Yu lost the will to fight and informed Bi that he could perform the emasculation whenever he desired.[27]

Qing law prohibited young boys and men from being emasculated against their will or from being deceived into undergoing emasculation.[28] However, because society placed the needs of the family above the individual, such laws did little to protect young boys from their own family members. Also, as Yu Chunhe's case reveals, *daozijiang* circumvented the law and utilized pressure and coercion to produce emasculates. Prior to performing the emasculation, *daozijiang* required all potential candidates to sign a waiver stating that the procedure was voluntary. Despite the omission of any direct mention of death,[29] the document seems to have acted as a release that freed the *daozijiang* from fault in case "problems" were to arise in the future. Those who chose to break this binding contract faced lawsuits and fees.

---

23. Dan Shi, *Mémoires d'un Eunuque*, 12.

24. Gail Hershatter, *Dangerous Pleasures: Prostitution and Modernity in Twentieth-Century Shanghai* (Berkeley: University of California Press, 1997), 182.

25. It remains unclear whether these adoptions were made legal or for how long these new eunuchs had to hand over their salaries to their *daozijiang*.

26. Ma Deqing et al., "Qing gong taijian huiyi lu," 177.

27. Dan Shi, *Mémoires d'un Eunuque*, 110–12.

28. *Da Qing lüli anyu* 大清律例按語 [Code of the Great Qing with Remarks and Comments], 冊33卷65, 刑律雜犯, 31.

29. Jin and Shen, *Gongnü tan wanglu*, 105.

Daozijiang such as Bi also asked for final verbal consent before proceeding with the excision of the genitalia. However, as Yu Chunhe recalled, *Daozijiang* Bi was not interested in his response. After his emasculation, Yu asked Bi, "before starting the procedure, you had told me you were going to give me some medicine. Instead, you forced an egg into my mouth and asked me if I would have any regrets." Bi responded that he had inserted the egg into Yu's mouth to keep his airway open and to help him breathe during the procedure. As for the question, "Will you regret it?" *Daozijiang* Bi remarked that this was merely a way to get Yu to open his mouth so that he could insert the egg.[30] However, technically, no one could challenge Bi on the point that he had not asked for Yu's consent to perform the procedure.

Regardless of the route taken to reach him, the *daozijiang* required payment in order to perform the emasculation. Playing the role of the eunuch's master, the *daozijiang* required that his "pupils" present him with offerings such as a pig or a chicken or a bottle of *baijiu* 白酒.[31] The actual cost of the procedure was determined on a sliding scale depending upon the financial situation of the applicant's family.[32] Those unable to pay the *daozijiang* the required fees could arrange to pay off their debt after they entered the palace. In addition to these offerings and fees, applicants had to prepare supplies for use during their recovery period. These included: (1) thirty *jin* (斤) of millet (the equivalent of a month's worth of rations), (2) several big corn cobs for use in heating the *kang* (炕 raised heated bed), (3) several stalks of sesame (to be burnt into an ash for placement under the body for purification purposes), and (4) fifty sheets of window paper to keep the wind out.[33] Once all of the above requirements had been met, the *daozijiang* would proceed with the emasculation of the applicant.

Emasculation as Punishment

While less common, the government did sentence young men to emasculation as a form of punishment. Norman A. Kutcher notes that, during the Qing period, the Qianlong emperor increased the supply of *Yuanmingyuan* eunuchs by calling for sons of rebels who had killed more than three or four members in a family to be emasculated.[34] In another case from the fifty-fourth year of Qianlong (1789), a Grand Council report from the governor of Zhejiang listed thirty-seven young boys (sons of bandits from Taiwan who were under the age of fifteen) who were to be sent in two waves to the capital to be emasculated, where they would serve the

---

30. Dan Shi, *Mémoires d'un Eunuque*, 118–19.
31. Jin and Shen, *Gongnü tan wanglu*, 105. *Baijiu* is a spirit usually distilled from sorghum or maize.
32. Jin and Shen, *Gongnü tan wanglu*, 105.
33. Jin and Shen, *Gongnü tan wanglu*, 105–6.
34. See Norman A. Kutcher, "Unspoken Collusions: The Empowerment of Yuanming yuan Eunuchs in the Qianlong Period," *Harvard Journal of Asiatic Studies* 70, no. 2 (Dec. 2010): 473.

Imperial Household Department as eunuchs assigned to sweeping the palace.[35] The list notes the name and age of each boy, many of whom were under the age of nine, some as young as four years old. While the palace favored eunuch recruits who were emasculated prior to the onset of puberty, after the age of nine, this list reveals that, in cases of punishment, the age limit could be lowered. For our discussion, it is important to note that archival documents recording instances of emasculation by punishment during the Qing appear to be motivated by the palace's need for eunuchs rather than the desire to teach rebels or murderers a lesson by subjecting their sons to emasculation as a form of collective punishment.

Palace Applicants

While the Qing distanced itself from the emasculation of eunuch applicants, the government remained directly involved in the recruitment process. Aside from entering the eunuch system via a *daozijiang*, applicants could register their names and offer their services (*touchong* 投充) to the Qing court.[36] Within the counties of Daxing 大興 and Wanping 宛平 in Shuntian Prefecture 順天府, applicants could register their names with two individuals authorized by the government to compile lists of eunuch hopefuls.[37] Candidates could also register with the Board of Rites at the county level or from within the capital.[38] For example, during the Yongzheng reign (1723–1735), one candidate first registered in Wuqing 武清 County was forwarded to Wanping County and then on to the Board of Rites.[39]

In 1776, the Qianlong emperor rerouted the application process.[40] Suspicious that the recent shortage of eunuch applicants was due to extortion by Board of Rites employees, the Qianlong emperor revoked the board's responsibility for eunuch registration and ordered applicants to register their names with the Imperial Household Department. The emperor's suspicions were not totally unfounded. During the reign of Kangxi, extortion had also frustrated the efforts of eunuch candidates to enter the system. For example, Li Tianfu 李天福, an emasculate arrested for trying to sell himself into slavery, revealed the problems eunuchs encountered when dealing with Board of Rites employees. When asked why he had not entered the palace system, Li replied, "It's not easy for us to enter the palace [system]. When you register at the Board of Rites, applicants are only allowed to enter after giving the runner several *taels*. We are strongly encouraged to give this money. We decided to become eunuchs because our families are poor. Since I was unable to enter [service]

35. *Guoli Gugong Bowuyuan*, 臺匪緣坐犯屬年在十五歲以下應行解京闍割起數名單, 軍機處檔奏摺件, 039376 and 039377.

36. *QDDQHDSL*, 卷1216, 內務府, 太監事例, 選驗太監, 順治18年.

37. *Da Qing huidian* as cited in Tang Yinian, *Qing gong taijian* (Shenyang: Liaoning daxue chuanshe, 1993), 36.

38. Albert Mann locates eunuch registration at the prefectural level. See Mann, "The Influence of Eunuchs," 44.

39. *Gongzhong dang Qianlong chao zouzhe (GZDQLCZZ)* 宮中檔乾隆朝奏摺 [Secret palace memorials of the Qianlong period], no. 28, 乾隆32年8–12月 (Taipei: National Palace Museum, 1984), 310.

40. *QDDQHDSL*, 卷1216, 內務府, 太監事例, 選驗太監, 乾隆41年.

in the palace, I decided to sell myself."[41] Despite the Qianlong emperor's attempt to rid the application system of extortion, problems persisted. In 1785, nine years after removing the Board of Rites from the application process, the Qianlong emperor once again complained that extortion within the selection process was causing a shortage of applicants.[42]

Transfers

During the Qing, eunuchs also arrived at the palace as transfers from the princely households. As described by Albert Mann, the service of a prince or princess could become a "kind of probationary apprenticeship for the more advantageous post at court."[43] Entry into the eunuch system via princely households proved relatively easy for candidates since they were not subject to the same employment requirements as palace applicants, such as restrictions on age, native place, and ethnicity, and were hired directly by the individual princes. The ease of obtaining a position in a princely household combined with knowledge of the practice of transferring eunuchs to the palace allowed many eunuchs to circumvent the strict employment criteria of the palace and ultimately created an alternate route into palace service.

Eunuchs were most likely to be transferred to the palace during periods in which the palace faced a shortage of applicants. Sumptuary laws put in place by the Jiaqing emperor (r. 1796–1820) both limited the number of eunuchs allowed to princes and created a ready supply of trained eunuchs for the court.[44] In 1809, faced with a deficit of some 300 eunuchs, the Jiaqing emperor turned to the princely households to fill the openings. Princes who possessed eunuchs in excess of the legal quotas were required to select three or four to send to the palace.[45]

Young emasculates serving in princely households had an even greater chance of being transferred. Shortages of candidates who could fulfill the palace's employment criteria, specifically the age requirement, forced the court to look elsewhere for eunuchs to meet its demands. For example, in 1808, the Jiaqing emperor had expressed concern over the age of eunuch recruits. Faced with a shortage of young applicants and fearful of older eunuch recruits potentially causing problems if allowed to serve within the palace, the emperor looked to the princely households for a remedy. The emperor decreed that recruits older than twenty years of age be given to imperial princes (*qinwang* 親王) and commandery princes (*junwang* 郡王) in exchange for eunuchs in their service who were under twenty years old.[46] By

---

41. First Historical Archives, Beijing, *Kangxi chao manwen zhupi zouzhe quanyi* (Beijing: Zhongguo shehui kexue chubanshe, 1996), entry 4041, 1620.
42. *QDDQHDSL*, 卷1216，內務府，太監事例，選驗太監，乾隆50年.
43. Mann, "The Influence of Eunuchs," 48.
44. *Qinding zongrenfu zeli*, no. 1, 卷6, 20.
45. First Historical Archives, Beijing, *Neiwufu* 內務府 [Imperial Household Department]，*Kuaijisi* 會計司 [Office of Accounts]，嘉慶14年11月.
46. *QDDQHDSL*, 卷1216，太監事例，嘉慶13年.

the late Qing, Stent notes, "Every fifth year each prince is required to furnish, for the use of the palace, eight young eunuchs. These must have been previously well trained, and before they enter on their duties in the palace, must be inspected and guaranteed to be pure eunuchs—i.e., properly emasculated, clean in person, and free from all disease."[47] In exchange, princes were paid 250 *taels* per eunuch.[48]

Emasculation

The single most important job requirement of all eunuch candidates was fulfilled through the act of emasculation. Young boys and men who underwent emasculation by a *daozijiang* would begin their transformation at one of the "sheds" (*changzi* 廠子) located near the palace. What happened inside the walls of the shed, how *daozijiang* removed the external male genitalia (scrotum, testes, and penis) and turned boys and men into eunuchs, was a closely guarded secret due to the hereditary nature of the profession. As a result, descriptions of the procedure during the Qing, either in English or in Chinese, appear to be derived from the accounts of two Westerners living and working in China during the late 1800s, that of Dr. Georges Morache (1869), a physician in the French army and member of the French legation in Beijing, and George Carter Stent (1877), an independent scholar of Chinese culture and language, British legation guard, and later member of the Chinese Maritime Customs.[49] Relying on knowledge of the procedure obtained from "informants," Morache and Stent each recount the steps involved in the emasculation process. Without further detail on these informants, one can only assume that they are eunuchs or family members who might have been present during the procedure. Despite the challenges these sources cause for scholars today in determining their veracity, they have become the only extant sources (besides oral histories of late Qing eunuchs) on the emasculation procedure.

According to Morache, the procedure would commence with the "patient" being plunged into a very cold bath to numb the senses. Then the genitalia would be wrapped in a silk-like packet and excised with one pass of the knife. To stem the bleeding, a handful of styptic power would be immediately applied to the wound. Stent's account, published in the *Journal of the Royal Asiatic Society*, with its additional detail, has become the most often-cited source on the emasculation procedure.[50] According to Stent, potential eunuchs could undergo emasculation

---

47. Stent, "Chinese Eunuchs," 167.
48. Stent, "Chinese Eunuchs," 167.
49. Georges Morache, «Les misère en *Pékin*», in *Pékin et ses habitants: Étude d'hygiène* (Paris: J.-B. Baillière, 1869). For a discussion of Western medical accounts on emasculation and Chinese eunuchs, see Melissa S. Dale, "Understanding Emasculation: Western Medical Perspectives on Chinese Eunuchs," *Social History of Medicine* 23, no. 1 (April 2010): 38–55.
50. Stent's description of the process, despite lacking in specifics on the "informant" who supplied this information, is the most-often cited source in English and Chinese language publications on the emasculation procedure, due to its level of detail.

by a *daozijiang* and receive recovery care for six *taels*.[51] The procedure was performed with the "candidate or victim" situated in a reclining position on a *kang*. The candidate's waist supported by one individual, two others would then hold his legs apart during the procedure, which would proceed as follows:

> The operating "knifer" [*daozijiang*] then stands in front of the man—with his knife in his hand—and enquires if he will ever repent. If the man at the last moment demurs in the slightest, the "knifer" will not perform the operation, but if he still expresses his willingness, with one sweep of the knife he is made a eunuch.
>
> The operation is performed in this manner: white ligatures or bandages are bound tightly round the lower part of the belly and the upper part of the thighs, to prevent too much hemorrhage. The parts about to be operated on are then bathed three times with hot pepper-water, the intended eunuch being in the reclining position as previously described. When the parts have been sufficiently bathed, the *whole*—both the testes and penis—are cut off as closely as possible with a small curved knife, something in the shape of a sickle. The emasculation being effected, a pewter needle or spigot is carefully thrust into the main orifice at the root of the penis; the wound is then covered with paper saturated in cold water and is carefully bound up. After the wound is dressed the patient is made to walk about the room supported by two of the "knifers," for two or three hours, when he is allowed to lie down.[52]

Later descriptions of the emasculation process, by Western physicians such as Drs. J.-J. Matignon and W. Korsakow, published in medical journals during the late 1890s, provide more medical detail to our understanding of emasculation. These accounts note alternate forms of anesthetic, including preoperative procedures utilized to reduce blood flow and pain, the use of either "sturdy scissors" or three knives varying in shape and size (from a sickle shape, to a small hatchet, to a long cleaver), and the different materials used for plugs placed in the urethra (wood, lead, pewter, and tin).[53]

For three days following the surgery, the candidate was prohibited from drinking anything since he was unable to urinate during this period. The surgery would be deemed a success if, when the spigot was removed (three days after the surgery), the emasculate could urinate. Since post-operative recuperation necessitated not wearing clothing below the waist,[54] emasculation during the months of late spring and early summer offered advantages. Favorable temperatures as well as low mosquito and fly populations[55] made recuperation more comfortable and helped prevent infection. The new eunuch would be considered totally healed in about one hundred days.

51. Stent, "Chinese Eunuchs," 170–71.
52. Stent, "Chinese Eunuchs," 170–71.
53. See Dale, "Understanding Emasculation," 40–46.
54. Jin and Shen, *Gongnü tan wanglu*, 106.
55. Tang Yinian, *Qing gong taijian*, 38.

The emasculate's severed genitalia, known as *bao* (寶 treasure) were preserved in a "pint measure" and kept high on a shelf. Since the possession of *bao* was required for eunuch promotions and needed to be placed in the coffin at the time of burial, *bao* were highly prized. Moreover, if the emasculate or his family failed to ask for these after the procedure, the *daozijiang* could make a considerable profit by selling or renting *bao* to eunuchs for use in burials or promotions. Stent cites that eunuchs in the late Qing would often pay as much as fifty *taels* to purchase a set of *bao*.[56]

According to Stent, death resulting from the actual surgery (often caused by the inability to urinate) was quite rare and occurred in "about two out of a hundred cases."[57] However, postoperative complications were not uncommon. Imprecision by the *daozijiang* led some eunuchs to suffer from urinary incontinence, making it necessary for them to wear a large handkerchief wrapped around their loins.[58] According to Dr. J.-J. Matignon who treated several eunuchs during the late Qing, those eunuchs whose surgeries resulted in complications often sought the help of foreign doctors.[59] Western medicine, and its use of catheters which aided in the flow of urine, undoubtedly saved the lives of many eunuchs.[60] As will be seen, the failure of the *daozijiang* to excise the genitalia in total could also impede the candidate's ability to obtain and retain a position as a palace eunuch.

Self-Emasculation

Eunuch candidates who were unwilling or unable to pay to have the procedure performed by a *daozijiang* could opt for the riskier and more painful method of self-emasculation (*zigong* 自宮).[61] Ma Deqing 馬德清, a eunuch during the reign of Guangxu, recalls the day his father emasculated him without anesthetic or taking any measures to control the bleeding. "The year I turned nine, perhaps it was the thirty-first year of Guangxu (1905), my father called me in, held me down in the shop, and emasculated me with his own hands . . . Please remember at this time, there weren't any anesthetics, injections, or things to stop the bleeding . . . To forcibly hold down a child who is kicking and screaming and cut off his reproductive organs

---

56. Stent, "Chinese Eunuchs," 172.
57. Stent, "Chinese Eunuchs," 171.
58. Jin and Shen, *Gongnü tan wanglu*, 147.
59. For examples, see Dale, "Understanding Emasculation."
60. See J.-J. Matignon, *Superstition, Crime et Misère en Chine : Souvenirs de Biologie Sociale* (1899 ; reprint, Paris: Masson and Cie, 1900), 185–86, 189.
61. Although *zigong* may be translated as "voluntary castration" (see Jennifer Jay, "Another Side of Chinese Eunuch History: Castration, Marriage, Adoption, and Burial," *Canadian Journal of History* XSVII (Dec. 1993): 464), I prefer to follow Shih-shan Henry Tsai's translation of the first character 自 *zi* as "self" rather than "voluntary" (see Tsai, *The Eunuchs in the Ming Dynasty*, 22). Ma's recollection and the fact that many young boys found themselves denied a choice in the matter reveals that the soon to be emasculate was not always willing. Translating *zigong* as "self-emasculation" avoids this implication while highlighting the fact that these emasculations were not carried out by *daozijiang*. Two late Qing eunuchs recalled that, during the late Qing, only a small percentage of eunuchs became emasculated in this manner. For information on the frequency of this practice, see Ma Deqing et al., "Qing gong taijian huiyi lu," 176.

. . . That child is in so much pain!"[62] After being emasculated by his father, a tube was inserted into Ma's urethra and he was allowed to recuperate for the standard one hundred days, during which time dressings of white wax (*baila* 白蠟), sesame oil, and powder from the Chinese prickly ash were applied.[63]

The government's policy towards self-emasculation fluctuated with the supply and demand of eunuch applicants. Officially, the government followed the Ming precedent of prohibiting the practice. During the Ming dynasty, "inconsistency" and "leniency" in enforcing bans against self-emasculation by emperors such as Chenghua (r. 1464–1487) had contributed to a supply of eunuchs far in excess of the demand.[64] During the 1470s, unemployed self-emasculates became a "political headache and social nuisance," storming the Board of Rites and demanding employment on more than one occasion.[65] By the end of the Ming, self-emasculates only exacerbated Ming eunuch supply and demand problems. In 1623, 20,000 eunuch candidates competed to fill 3,000 openings.[66]

During the early Qing, prohibitions against self-emasculation allowed the government to limit the number of emasculated males in the population.[67] Early Qing emperors such as Shunzhi ordered that self-emasculates and those involved in the act be sentenced to decapitation and their families exiled to a distant place for military service.[68] Preston Torbert describes how the number of living Ming eunuchs diminished over time, such that prohibitions against self-emasculation revealed a more humanitarian side of the Manchu rulers. Torbert suggests that the Manchus aimed in part with these bans to protect boys from being forcibly or deceitfully castrated [emasculated].[69] However, leniency in enforcing the ban, particularly during the reign of Qianlong, reveals that Qing emperors often excused self-emasculations that had been motivated by poverty. Moreover, as Norman Kutcher has shown, the Qianlong emperor preferred to have the *Yuanmingyuan* staffed with young eunuchs.[70] Rather than turning away self-emasculates, the Qianlong emperor allowed them to be hired for service in Rehe.[71] Contrary to the good intentions of the government, such acts of mercy by Qing emperors had the adverse effect of encouraging future acts of genital mutilation performed by fathers on sons or by men upon themselves.

62. Ma Deqing et al., "Qing gong taijian huiyi lu," 174.
63. Ma Deqing et al., "Qing gong taijian huiyi lu," 174.
64. Tsai, *The Eunuchs in the Ming Dynasty*, 22.
65. Tsai, *The Eunuchs in the Ming Dynasty*, 22.
66. Mitamura Taisuke, *Chinese Eunuchs: The Structure of Intimate Politics*, trans. Charles A. Pomeroy (Rutland, VT: Charles E. Tuttle Co., 1970), 71.
67. Tang Yinian, *Qing gong taijian*, 37.
68. *QDDQHDSL*, 卷1216，內務府，太監事例，禁令.
69. Preston Torbert, *The Ch'ing Imperial Household Department: A Study of Its Organization and Principal Functions, 1662–1796* (Cambridge, MA: Harvard University Press, 1977), 40.
70. Kutcher, "Unspoken Collusions."
71. *Zongguan neiwufu xianxing zeli* as cited in Wan Yi et al., *Qingdai gongting shi*, 496–97.

Entry into the Palace

Having their genitalia removed did not ensure that the emasculate would obtain employment as an imperial court eunuch. Applicants first had to pass a pre-employment physical and fulfill a variety of age, character, and ethnicity requirements. These requirements appear to have applied to all applicants, regardless of their point of entry. Even recruits who had been sent to the palace by an authorized *daozijiang* had to undergo further examination by the staff of the Imperial Household Department. While the screening and the recommendation from these agents of the government undoubtedly improved the applicant's chances of acceptance, the final decision on whether or not these now physically altered boys and men would obtain a position rested with the Imperial Household Department.

The palace selection process began with a physical examination of the applicant, intended to verify that the candidate was an emasculate. Previous studies such as that by Albert Mann have stated that emasculation occurred after an applicant had been hired. According to Mann, in a practice dating to 1661, applicants would undergo emasculation after satisfying all the pre-employment requirements and then recover in the eunuch quarters within the palace.[72] Mann may be referring to Xu Ke's description of the eunuch selection process. Xu Ke notes that, after being emasculated by the palace, eunuchs recuperated (avoided the wind for one hundred days) in the private apartments of the palace.[73] However, palace archival records reveal that emasculation was a prerequisite for even commencing the selection process.

Evidence from as early as the eighteenth year of the Shunzhi reign (1661) supports the argument that applicants were required to have undergone emasculation prior to being selected to serve. In that year, the emperor ordered the *Kuaijisi* (會計司 Office of Accounts) and the *Zhangyisi* (掌儀司 Department of Ceremonial) to each send an official to supervise an elderly eunuch in verifying that applicants who had been sent to or who had registered with the Board of Rites had already been emasculated.[74] Here, the reference to eunuchs as "eunuchs who had been sent to or had offered their services to the Board of Rites" as opposed to "new eunuch hires" (*xinjing taijian*) suggests that emasculation came before being hired, in the chronology of the application process.

Such physical examinations (pre-employment physicals) proved more accurate than did the presentation of one's *bao*.[75] Since, as discussed above, an emasculate's *bao* were often retained by the *daozijiang* and could be rented, borrowed, bought, and sold for use during promotion or burial, physical examinations provided the

---

72. Mann, "The Influence of Eunuchs," 44.
73. Xu Ke, *Qingbai leichao* 清稗類鈔 [Unofficial sources on the Qing arranged by categories] (1917; reprint, Taipei: Taiwan Shangwu yinshuguan, 1966), vol. 4, 1.
74. *QDDQHDSL*, 卷1216, 內務府，太監事例，選驗太監，順治18年.
75. Jennifer Jay suggests that, during certain periods of Chinese history, emasculates retained their *bao* as proof of their emasculation. See Jay, "Another Side of Chinese Eunuch History, 464.

Qing palace with a more accurate idea of the veracity of the claim of emasculation. Applicants who failed to pass the pre-employment physical were rejected on the grounds that their bodies were "impure"[76] (*shenzi bu jing* 身子不淨), terminology that suggests that the male genitalia had not been totally excised, and sent back to their native place. During the reign of Yongzheng, the palace rejected the emasculate Zhao Ben 照本 for this reason. Zhao was sent back to his native place of Wuqing County 武清, Shuntian Prefecture 順天府, only to be rejected again during the reign of Qianlong, when he attempted to obtain employment as a eunuch at the home of a marquis (*wugong yefu* 五公爺府).[77]

Biological (natural) eunuchs would have also failed this examination and been refused entry into royal service.[78] Charlotte Furth argues that the prohibition against biological eunuchs stemmed from both the belief that those with sexual anomalies were "inauspicious omens" and the Manchu attempt to rid the court of the sexual decadence associated with the fall of the Ming. The sexual dysfunction of biological eunuchs may have proven difficult for the court to verify. Assumed physical dysfunction did not always equate to physical incapability. Emasculation (the excision of the male genitalia in total) allowed the court some degree of certainty that the eunuchs were not only sexually dysfunctional but also physically incapable of engaging in sexual relations and in procreating.

Age

The imperial court further limited the eligibility of eunuchs by restricting the age at which eunuchs could enter the palace. Age requirements fluctuated throughout the dynasty, depending upon eunuch supply and demand. For example, during the reign of Yongzheng alone, the emperor first capped the age limit at seventeen, then at twenty-six, and then removed the criteria of age altogether. Specifically, in 1724, the Yongzheng emperor restricted eunuch age upon entry into imperial service to those seventeen and under.[79] However, in an imperial decree from that same year, the emperor ordered that applicants twenty-six and younger be admitted.[80] Decrees issued in 1733 and 1735 reveal that age temporarily ceased to be a selection criterion and applicants were to be admitted regardless of their age.

Despite the fluidity of age requirements, the overall trend suggests a preference for males emasculated before the age of twenty.[81] Eunuchs emasculated prior to the onset of puberty were especially prized; they were considered easier to manage as well as pure in sexual desire. As described by Torbert, the Qianlong emperor's

---

76. *GZDQLCZZ*, 乾隆32年10月初6日，310.
77. *GZDQLCZZ*, 乾隆32年10月初6日，310.
78. Charlotte Furth, "Androgynous Males and Deficient Females," *Late Imperial China* 9, no. 2 (Dec. 1988): 24.
79. *Guochao gongshi*, ed. Yu Minzhong (Taipei: Taiwan xuesheng shuju, 1965), 47.
80. *QDDZHDSL*, 卷1216，內務府，太監事例，選驗太監，雍正2年.
81. Yu Huaqing, *Zhongguo huanguan zhidushi* (Shanghai: Renmin chubanshe, 1993), 481.

decision to require written bonds from local government officials, in addition to the usual proof of guarantor for applicants over the age of fifteen, reveals a suspicion of older eunuchs.[82] The court's preference of young emasculates is also apparent in the Jiaqing emperor's complaints in 1808 about many of the new eunuchs being twenty or thirty and being from other provinces.[83] He declared that those under twenty could be employed by the palace but that those who were too old or from other provinces were to be sent to princes and traded with eunuchs serving in princely establishments who were twenty and younger.

Rules governing the age at which eunuch applicants had undergone emasculation became even stricter after the 1813 Eight Trigrams Uprising, during which eunuchs facilitated the entry of Eight Trigrams rebels into the palace. In the year following the incident (1814), the Jiaqing emperor decreed that only applicants sixteen and under who had never been married or fathered children would be allowed to join the palace workforce. The emperor further attempted to alleviate his fear of eunuchs emasculated at a later age by trading older palace applicants with eunuchs under the age of fifteen who were already employed by imperial princes.[84] Palace applicants who did not meet the palace's criteria would be sent to the princely households.[85]

The emperor's suspicions of eunuchs emasculated as adults were not unfounded. Post-pubertal emasculates were among those eunuchs involved in the 1813 Eight Trigrams Uprising. For example, one such eunuch rebel, Mu Qi 穆七, had been married and fathered two sons before undergoing emasculation.[86] However, the age at the time of emasculation was not an absolute indicator of the eunuch's reliability. Among the confessions of Eight Trigrams eunuch rebels in which the age at the time of emasculation is listed, one finds that some of the eunuchs who participated in the incident, such as Yu Jiqing 于吉慶, had undergone emasculation as children (in Yu's case, age ten).[87]

Ethnicity

There has been considerable confusion amongst Western historians concerning the ethnicity of eunuchs. Many Western accounts from the nineteenth century assumed that all eunuchs were Manchu. The late Qing contemporary Reginald Johnston criticized these accounts and attempted to clarify the matter by arguing that all eunuchs were Chinese.[88] Johnston was correct in his assertion that "dynastic house-law

---

82. Torbert, *The Ch'ing Imperial Household Department*, 40.
83. *QDDQHDSL*, 卷1216，內務府，太監事例，選驗太監，嘉慶13年.
84. *QDDQHDSL*, 卷1216，內務府，太監事例，選驗太監，嘉慶13年.
85. *QDDQHDSL*, 卷1216，內務府，太監事例，選驗太監，嘉慶13年.
86. *Guoli Gugong Bowuyuan*, Taipei, *Gongci dang* 供詞檔，99.
87. *Guoli Gugong Bowuyuan*, Taipei, *Gongci dang* 供詞檔，63.
88. Reginald Johnston, *Twilight in the Forbidden City* (London: Victor Gollancz Ltd., 1934; reprint, Wilmington, DE: Scholarly Resources, 1973), 221–22. Frank Dorn also writes that "All the eunuchs were Chinese." See

strictly forbade the employment of Manchu eunuchs."[89] However, the effectiveness of this ban depended upon an emperors' willingness to enforce it. In reality, while the majority of eunuchs were Han Chinese, some were from other ethnic groups.

In 1724, perhaps in a move to protect the integrity of Manchus and bannermen, it was decreed that eunuchs from banner families were ineligible for service as eunuchs.[90] Since banners were primarily a political rather than an ethnic division,[91] it is difficult to ascertain from this decree if it was directed specifically at preventing Manchus from becoming eunuchs or more broadly from prohibiting the hiring of eunuchs from banner families. Those found responsible for hiring a bannerman as a eunuch, including the *shouling taijian* (首領太監 supervisory eunuch) who performed the inspection and the eunuch's guarantor, would be punished.[92] Nine years later, in 1733, the emperor reversed this ban and allowed bannermen to become eunuchs. Those discovered already serving in the palace were allowed to remain. Although no reason is given for this reversal of policy, the simultaneous relaxation of age restrictions so that age ceased temporarily to be a factor suggests a shortage of eunuch candidates.

Eunuch transfers into palace service from princely households provide some insight into why early Qing emperors prohibited bannermen from becoming eunuchs. Some Qing emperors were very suspicious of the loyalties of these eunuchs to their former employers and feared that they might divulge palace secrets. Potential security leaks and political conflicts would have proven even greater if the eunuch was a bannerman. The Yongzheng emperor's need for eunuchs may have outweighed previous reservations against hiring eunuchs with banner origins.

Native Place

The palace also screened applicants according to their native place. As stated above, in 1808, the Jiaqing emperor complained about the number of new eunuch recruits who were from "other provinces" and ordered that these emasculates be sent to serve in the princely households rather than in the palace.[93] During the Qing, a disproportionate number of eunuchs were from the northern provinces surrounding the capital. Most eunuchs originated in the capital area and its environs, for example from the cities of Beijing and Tianjin, the provinces of Zhili and Shandong, and Shuntian Prefecture.[94] In *Qingbai leichao*, the late Qing contemporary Xu

---

Frank Dorn, *The Forbidden City: The Biography of a Palace* (New York: Charles Scribner's Sons, 1970), 215.

89. Johnston, *Twilight in the Forbidden City*, 222.

90. *QDDQHDSL*, 卷1216，內務府，太監事例，選驗太監，雍正2年.

91. The division was essentially between conquerors and the conquered. The "conquest elite" included Manchu, Mongol, and Han Chinese. See Evelyn S. Rawski, *The Last Emperors: A Social History of Qing Imperial Institutions* (Berkeley: University of California Press, 1998), 59.

92. *QDDQHDSL*, 卷1216，內務府，太監事例，選驗太監，雍正2年.

93. *QDDQHDSL* 卷1216，內務府，太監事例，選驗太監，嘉慶13年.

94. Yu Huaqing, *Zhongguo huanguan zhidushi*, 479. For a list of the specific provinces in Zhili and counties in Shuntian from which eunuchs originated, see Tang Yinian, *Qing gong taijian*, 36.

Ke notes the prevalence of eunuchs from Hejian Prefecture.[95] Headstones from Enjizhuang 恩濟莊 Cemetery , a eunuch cemetery established by Qianlong in 1738, also provide clues about the origins of Qing eunuchs.[96] Of the 300 headstones still extant in 1958, Liu Jingyi and Lu Qi list information on eighty-five. Of these, thirty provide information on the deceased's native place. From these thirty, one finds that twelve came from Shuntian Prefecture, six from Hejian Prefecture, and the remainder from Tianjin and various other locations. George Carter Stent's findings from the late Qing support Hejian Prefecture as a common source of Qing and even Ming eunuchs.[97] Pu Jia and Pu Jie narrow the field even further, tracing the origins of Qing eunuchs to specific counties within Hebei Province. They also add that a small number of eunuchs were of Mongolian origin.[98] This predominance of eunuchs from northern China suggests a Qing preference for eunuchs proficient in the Mandarin language as well as eunuchs not associated with areas in southern China known for Ming loyalist activities in the early years of the Qing.

Background Checks

Aside from these eligibility restrictions, Qing eunuch recruitment involved background checks and personality profiles. As evidenced by an edict from 1751, in which the Qianlong emperor noted that the bad habits of new eunuch recruits were unacceptable and warned that they might lead to transgressions, eunuch demeanor played an important role in ensuring an obedient workforce.[99] However, it was not until 1814 that Qing emperors ordered that, after verifying that applicants to the Board of Rites had undergone emasculation, investigators should determine the temperament and examine the background of the eunuch applicants.[100] As a result, selection favored applicants who appeared docile and subservient.[101] Investigations also aimed to determine if the applicant had a criminal record. The government often required written bonds from the local government in the applicant's native place as a further measure to guarantee the integrity of eunuchs.

Eunuch candidates who the palace found to be both physically pure and in fulfillment of the above job requirements would then enter into imperial service. With emasculation and its accompanying physical transformation now complete, the eunuch entered the palace and a lifestyle far removed from the one he had left outside the palace walls.

---

95. Xu Ke, *Qingbai leichao*, vol. 4, 1.
96. See Liu Jingyi and Lu Qi, "Qingdai taijian Enjizhuang yindi," *Gugong bowuyuan yuankan* 3 (1979): 51–58.
97. Stent, "Chinese Eunuchs," 168.
98. Pu Jia and Pu Jie, *Wanqing diwang shenghuo jianwen*, vol. 1 (Taipei: Juzhen shuwu chubanshe, 1984), 217.
99. Edict cited in *Guochao gongshi* (A history of the palace during the Qing period), vol. 1, ed. Yu Mingzhong (Taipei: Taiwan xuesheng shuju, 1965), 100.
100. *QDDQHDSL*, 卷1216，內務府，太監事例，選驗太監，嘉慶19年.
101. Yu Huaqing, *Zhongguo huanguan zhidushi*, 481.

Palace Rejects

The often strict eunuch employment criteria combined with the requirement that applicants become emasculated prior to "interviewing" with the palace suggests that a population of emasculates not employed by the palace existed during the Qing. As mentioned, many of these "palace rejects" may have found employment in princely households. With sumptuary laws limiting the number of eunuchs princely households could legally employ, some simply may have never obtained the positions they had been emasculated for.

Glimpses into the lives of these desperate men who underwent emasculation in hopes of obtaining employment as eunuchs only to be rejected suggest that they had difficulty reintegrating into society. During the late Ming, when the supply of emasculates far outnumbered demand, unemployed emasculates earned a living in bathhouses serving their employed brethren.[102] In the little information we have from the Qing, one finds that these rejected emasculates banded together and even turned to lifestyles removed from the mainstream of society, such as monasticism. In 1767, Zhao Ben, the above-mentioned emasculate who had been rejected for being labeled "impure," had become a monk.[103]

Conclusion

During the Qing dynasty, young boys and men underwent emasculation in order to apply for service as a palace eunuch. The great majority of these men were not criminals, prisoners of war, or tributes who, as a result of their unfree status, had been sentenced to the punishment of emasculation. These were the poor of Qing society, young boys and adult males who volunteered to become emasculated. Yet, an examination of the emasculation experiences of Qing eunuchs and the routes taken to reach the palace suggests that we need to rethink the "voluntary" nature of the eunuch supply system.

The Manchus' preference for prepubescent emasculates created an environment in which children found themselves volunteered for service by their elders. Among the "socially inferior" of Qing society and those living in poverty, the needs of the individual, or in this case the child, succumbed to the needs of the family. Denied the right to decide the fate of their own bodies, children listened as their parents or guardians consented to the emasculation procedure by a *daozijiang* or watched in horror as their parents physically restrained them and excised their genitals at home without the aid of anesthetic. Desperation among the lower rungs of Qing society

---

102. Tsai, *The Eunuchs in the Ming Dynasty*, 48.
103. Zhao was a sixty-five-year-old itinerant monk arrested for getting into a fight with a shopkeeper. Zhao revealed in his confession that, finding himself in abject poverty after the death of his wife during childbirth, he had become emasculated. Labeled "impure" during his physical examination, Zhao was rejected as a eunuch candidate. See GZDQLCZZ, 乾隆32年10月初6日，310.

and the demand created by the palace for young emasculates created an atmosphere conducive to the sale of young boys, a market often obscured by the better-known sale of young girls into prostitution. *Daozijiang*, as brokers, traded with kidnappers and even parents in the sale of this human commodity.

The fate of these young boys sold to *daozijiang* further reveals the complexities of unfree status in Qing China. Their purchase entitled the *daozijiang* to assume the role of both father and master. *Daozijiang* also benefited financially from these transactions for years, as their emasculated "sons" were required to send money to them. In addition, their employment by the palace as eunuchs resulted in years of servitude in an environment in which the needs and desires of the imperial court took precedence. Ultimately, these young boys found themselves held in bondage by two masters, their *daozijiang* and the Qing court.

Physical disfigurement alone did not ensure that the emasculate would obtain employment as a palace eunuch. The government's distancing itself from the emasculation process allowed the Qing to disassociate itself from the human trafficking and genital mutilation of boys and men despite the fact that these practices were fueled by the imperial court's demand for eunuch recruits. The imperial court's preference for young emasculates, perceived as thoroughly pure and easier to train and manage, further contributed to the demand for young boys in particular.

Eunuch procurement for the palace would ebb and flow according to supply and demand. In order to meet the palace's needs, the northern provinces (Zhili and Shandong) surrounding the capital as well as cities such as Tianjin and the capital itself became centers of recruitment for eunuch candidates. Qing regulations concerning age, character, and ethnicity would fluctuate according to the palace's needs. Prohibitions against bannermen becoming eunuchs reveal that, while the Qing relied on eunuchs to staff the palace, it was a practice that the imperial court only deemed fit for Han Chinese.

Early Qing regulations that screened applicants for age, character, and ethnicity requirements initially limited the number of eunuchs in the population as planned. However, as the years progressed and the excessive numbers of Ming eunuchs diminished, such strict employment criteria contributed to shortages in the palace's supply of eunuchs. Early efforts to ban self-emasculation and protect boys from being emasculated through deceit or force later became relaxed as the Qing excused self-emasculations motivated by poverty. The demand for eunuchs to fill the many vacancies, as many as 300 at times, necessitated both an easing of hiring restrictions and using alternate sources for eunuchs, namely the princely households. For those emasculates unable to obtain a position with the palace, few employment options remained available in a society that labeled eunuchs as social pariah. As will be seen, for those emasculates selected by the palace, their entry into the palace would forever alter both their lifestyle and their being.

3

Unrobing the Emasculated Body

Curiosity about the emasculated[1] body has attracted the attention of scholars, travel writers, and society throughout the ages. Chinese eunuchs, however, shared little about the life altering experience of emasculation and its effects on the body. This relative silence has led to a discourse on emasculation and the eunuch body framed by speculation and the perceptions of others. While many understood in general terms what a eunuch was—a man without his genitalia—few outside the eunuch community had any idea about what this really entailed. As a result, mystery surrounded the eunuch body.

Whereas other forms of disfigurement in China, such as the bound foot, were a source of curiosity and fascination among Chinese and Westerners alike, the eunuch body did not receive the same amount of attention or exposure. Accessibility played a key role in understanding the eunuch body. During the Qing dynasty, eunuchs lived the majority of their lives within the Forbidden City. As a result, very few Chinese and/or Westerners came into contact with or even saw a eunuch. Compounding this lack of accessibility was the fact that the eunuch body was covered by his robe and unseen by but a select few.[2] Eunuchs closely guarded their privacy, especially their defining features (or lack thereof), in an attempt to retain some sense of modesty and decorum and perhaps more importantly to protect themselves from social ridicule. As a result, academic discourse on the eunuch body was virtually nonexistent until the late 1800s, when Western physicians working in Beijing began treating eunuchs for urological problems.

This chapter aims to unrobe the emasculated body by examining how this form of genital mutilation affected eunuchs both physically and psychologically and by exploring multiple perspectives on how the Chinese eunuch body has been read by others and by eunuchs themselves.[3] As will be seen, despite common knowledge regarding what made one a eunuch, very little appears in the historical record about

---

1. As stated in the introduction to this work, I have chosen to use the term "emasculation" rather than "castration," due to its medical accuracy.
2. Western physicians practicing medicine in Beijing in the late 1800s were among the select few non-eunuchs to examine the eunuch body and record their observations. See Melissa S. Dale, "Understanding Emasculation: Western Medical Perspectives on Chinese Eunuchs," *Social History of Medicine* 23, no. 1 (April 2010): 38–55.
3. The majority of eunuchs were illiterate during the Qing dynasty.

Figure 3.1
Eunuch in front of Baohua Hall, 1900

what this actually looked like. Emasculation physically marked the eunuch body and caused society to read it as different. How the body was read, though, depended upon who was reading it (Han Chinese, the Manchu imperial court, eunuchs themselves, or Westerners). While genital mutilation was intended to subjugate and neuter Chinese men, in reality emasculation rendered eunuchs "sexually and politically charged."[4] Representing a nexus of gender and political power, eunuchs provide unique insight into late imperial views towards masculinity and political power during the Qing. Operating outside the boundaries of the masculine role defined by Confucianism, eunuchs were feminized and viewed as potential political and sexual threats.

Post Emasculation: Physical and Psychological Changes

Central to any study of the eunuch body is an understanding of the physical effects of the act of emasculation. Whether performed by a *daozijiang* (刀子匠 knife expert), a parent, or oneself, the ultimate result was the same—the rendering of the male body into a eunuch through the excision of the external male genitalia (scrotum, testes, and penis). The physical changes to the male body did not end with the amputation of the genitalia. Emasculation caused the eunuch's body to

---

4.   Charlotte Furth, "Androgynous Males and Deficient Females," *Late Imperial China* 9, no. 2 (Dec. 1988): 15.

continue to undergo physical changes as a result of the removal of the testes, the main source of testosterone production in the male. Eunuchs experienced hormonal changes and exhibited symptoms similar to those found in cases of spontaneous primary hypogonadism,[5] in which the body experiences a drastic and sudden drop in testosterone levels.

The age of the eunuch at the time of emasculation, before or after puberty, determined the extent to which these hormonal changes resulted in physical changes. Eunuchs emasculated prior to the onset of puberty presented the most physical changes. The drastic reduction of testosterone, which aids in the closure of bone growth plates, would have presented in eunuchs by tending to make them grow more slowly and to be above average in height.[6] Dr. Ferdinand Wagenseil's 1933 study of the morphological changes associated with emasculation in Chinese eunuchs found that, on average, eunuchs were taller than Chinese men. The tallest eunuch in his study of thirty-one eunuchs had been emasculated before puberty. In comparison with non-emasculated men, eunuchs exhibited shorter torsos and longer legs and noticeably broader pelvises. While a eunuch's arms and legs were longer than normal, Wagenseil found that their legs were noticeably longer. Eunuchs were also more likely to have bowed or crossed legs.[7] Wagenseil also observed that twenty of the thirty-one eunuchs in his study had kyphosis of the spine.[8] The delay in the closure of bone plates would also have increased the likelihood of eunuchs having elongated fingers and larger hands than normal.[9]

In addition, lacking the opposing activity of testosterone on estrogen, eunuchs experienced an increase of fatty tissue and exhibited fat distribution patterns more typical of females than males, such as wide hips and gynecomastia (breast enlargement).[10] According to Dr. G. Morache, eunuchs who had been emasculated at a young age also tended to be obese.[11] Wagenseil also noted that the eyebrows, beard, and body hair of eunuchs were reduced. He also found that eunuchs had

---

5. J. S. Jenkins, "The Voice of the Castrato," *The Lancet* 351 (June 20, 1998): 1878. For a description of the symptoms of hypogonadism, see http://www.mayoclinic.org/diseases-conditions/male-hypogonadism/basics/symptoms/con-20014235. Accessed August 2, 2016.
6. Raymond T. Morrissy, ed., *Lovell and Winter's Pediatric Orthopedics*, 3rd ed., vol. 1 (Philadelphia: J. B. Lippincott Co., 1990), 249.
7. F. Wagenseil, "Beiträge zur Kenntnis der Kastrationsfolgen und des Eunochoidismus beim Mann," *Zeitschrift für Morphologie und Anthropologie*, Band XXXII, Heft 3. d. 26, H. 2 (1933): 463–64. Thank you to Jan Vaeth for help translating these sections from German to English.
8. Wagenseil as cited in Jean D. Wilson and Claus Roehrborn, "Long-Term Consequences of Castration in Men: Lessons from the Skoptzy and the Eunuchs of the Chinese and Ottoman Courts," *The Journal of Clinical Endocrinology & Metabolism* 84, no. 12 (1999): 4332.
9. Morrissy, ed., *Lovell and Winter's Pediatric Orthopedics*, 249. When comparing eunuch and non-eunuch hands and fingers, Wagenseil did not find any real difference. Studies of eunuchs in other cultures, such as the 1896 study of eunuchs in Constantinople, found that eunuchs had elongated fingers and hands. See Drs. Hikmet (Hamdi) and Felix Regnault as cited in George Junne, *Black Eunuchs of the Ottoman Empire: Networks of Power in the Court of the Sultan* (London: I.B. Tauris, 2016).
10. Wagenseil, "Beiträge zur Kenntnis der Kastrationsfolgen," 464.
11. G. Morache, *Pékin et ses habitants : Étude d'hygiène* (Paris: J.-B. Baillière, 1869), 135.

more wrinkles on the face than did non-emasculated men.[12] As palace recruitment records reveal a preference for young emasculates, especially those who were emasculated as boys, or at least prior to age fifteen or at most age twenty,[13] the majority of eunuchs would have exhibited these physical characteristics.

Emasculation would also affect the young male's voice by preventing it from deepening naturally during puberty. According to Morache, eunuchs who were emasculated as youths had a "special timber" to their voices.[14] In eighteenth-century Europe, this physical characteristic gave rise to the practice of castrating young boys to perform opera. As will be seen, the Chinese also valued the eunuch voice and assigned them to the palace theaters to entertain the imperial court. While Europe's castrati only experienced "partial excision" of their male genitalia (castration as opposed to emasculation), like Qing eunuchs, the removal of the testes resulted in the "deliberate induction of hypogonadism."[15] Castrati and Chinese prepubertal emasculates shared the physical attributes of unusual tallness, smooth skin, a lack of facial hair, wide hips, and gynecomastia.[16]

Emasculation as an adult produced quite different and far fewer physical manifestations than those exhibited in prepubescent emasculates. Western physicians working in Beijing in the mid- to late nineteenth century such as Morache claimed that those emasculated as adults were difficult to distinguish from unemasculated males.[17] Kutcher cites the case of one eunuch who had been emasculated at thirty-six *sui* who commented, "Because I was castrated in middle age, my face could grow a beard and people couldn't tell that I was a eunuch."[18] Unable to produce testosterone after the body had taken on the characteristics of adult males, these eunuchs would typically only experience a lightening of the beard and an increase in fatty tissue, such as breast enlargement (gynecomastia). During the late Qing, when eunuch recruits were not meeting palace demands, the palace was forced to loosen its age restrictions, which resulted in the acceptance of more eunuchs who had been emasculated after the onset of puberty. As a result, during the late Qing, some eunuchs would have revealed fewer of these defining physical characteristics.

With emasculation marking the body beyond the hidden genital region, one can assume that the majority of Qing palace eunuchs did not look like typical Chinese men. In addition to these physical markers, an emasculate could be recognized by

12. Wagenseil, "Beiträge zur Kenntnis der Kastrationsfolgen," 463–64.
13. *Qinding Da Qing huidian shili* 欽定大清會典事例 (QDDQHDSL) [Imperially commissioned collected regulations of the Qing dynasty], ed. Li Hongzhang et al. (Shanghai: Shangwu yinshuguan, 1909), 卷 1216，內務府，太監事例，選驗太監，嘉慶13年.
14. Morache, *Pékin et ses habitants*, 135.
15. Jenkins, "The Voice of the Castrato," 1877.
16. Jenkins, "The Voice of the Castrato," 1878 and Meyer M. Melicrow and Stanford Pulrang, "Castrati Choir and Opera Singers," *Urology* 3, no. 5 (May 1974): 665.
17. Morache, *Pékin et ses habitants*, 135.
18. NWFZA 05-0489-061 JQ 6.6.14 as cited in Norman A. Kutcher, "Unspoken Collusions: The Empowerment of Yuanming yuan Eunuchs in the Qianlong Period," *Harvard Journal of Asiatic Studies* 70, no. 2 (Dec. 2010): 474, note 67.

his distinctive gait. When a eunuch walked he would "lean slightly forward, take short steps, keep the legs close, [while] at the same time turning the toes outward."[19] Overall, eunuchs were described as having an "indescribable *je-ne-sais quoi* [something that cannot be described] which those who have not been emasculated do not have."[20] Many Chinese, especially those who had never encountered a eunuch before, might not have immediately read the body as a eunuch. Physical indicators, though, would have alerted people to the fact that this individual was different.

The hormonal imbalance caused by emasculation also caused psychological changes in eunuchs. Lacking the opposing activity of testosterone on estrogen, which in turn led to the presence of higher levels of estrogen in eunuchs than in the average male, emasculates were reported to have suffered from hot flashes and mood swings.[21] Other accounts describe eunuchs as being "hysterical" and "easily moved to violent anger" but also "easily appeased, readily amused, depressed, timid, honest, and charitable."[22] These apparent contradictions may be explained in part by the fact that eunuchs, like non-emasculates, were individuals who exhibited a wide range of personalities and psychological states.

Eunuchs emasculated against their will, especially those who had their genitals forcibly removed by their own fathers, no doubt harbored great resentment and deep psychological wounds. For example, more than fifty years after his emasculation by his father, the late Qing eunuch Ma Deqing 馬德清 found the experience extremely painful to talk about. Ma claims that the day his father cut off his sexual organs was the day that he disassociated himself from his family.[23] The French physician J-J. Matignon found that feelings of hatred toward their fathers were common among his eunuch patients.[24] Finally, sexual frustration may have also presented itself in eunuchs since, as will be seen, complete removal of the external male genitalia does not appear to have totally eradicated the eunuch's sexual desire.

Reading the Eunuch Body: Sexuality and Gender

Emasculation and the resulting eunuch body complicated the efforts of others to determine how to read the eunuch body. In order to understand the categories into which eunuchs were placed in terms of sexuality and gender, one must first have an understanding of the meanings of these categories during the Qing. According to Charlotte Furth, in a society dominated by Confucian social morals, sexual

---

19. George Carter Stent, "Chinese Eunuchs," *Journal of the North China Branch of the Royal Asiatic Society*, New Series, no. 11 (1877): 178.

20. Stent, "Chinese Eunuchs," 178.

21. Sir C. A. Gordon, *An Epitome of the Reports of the Medical Officers to the Chinese Imperial Maritime Customs Service from 1871 to 1882* (London: Baillière, Tindall and Cox, 1884), 225.

22. Gordon, *An Epitome of the Reports*, 225.

23. Ma Deqing et al., "Qing gong taijian huiyi lu," in *Wanqing gongting shenghuo jianwen*, ed. Zhang Wenhui (Beijing: Wenshi ziliao chubanshe, 1982), 175.

24. J.-J. Matignon, *Superstition, Crime et Misère en Chine: Souvenirs de Biologie Sociale* (1899 ; reprint, Paris: Masson and Cie, 1900), 196.

normalcy was defined by reproductive capabilities. With society viewing "sexual action or initiative . . . a male attribute,"[25] hermaphrodites and eunuchs were viewed as sexually female. Furth's point that Chinese society did not allow for an intermediate status between the sexes,[26] is particularly important to reflect on when one considers eunuch gender. If one continues this line of reasoning, then, eunuchs should not be labeled as a "third sex" as some scholars have chosen to do.[27] As will be discussed, labeling a eunuch as such is a form of presentism that does not align with eunuch self-perceptions of their gender identity. According to Furth's analysis, sexual inability or the incapacity to uphold the tenets of filial piety through procreation, would have resulted in eunuchs being categorized as female. With Confucian teachings espousing that one should not intentionally harm the body given by one's parents, as well as the importance of reproduction and continuance of the family line, emasculation and the "reproductive death"[28] it "implied" placed the eunuch in direct opposition to Confucian morality and subject to social stigmatization.

In addition, Chinese biological thinking, based on yin-yang 陰陽 cosmological views,[29] considered male and female to be best understood as two poles on a continuum. The yin pole is commonly associated with females, but yin should not be translated as "female" or conversely yang translated as "male."[30] In the yin-yang dichotomy, yin both compliments and is the opposite of yang. Utilized as a way of describing phenomena and complementary opposites, yin is associated with the qualities of dark and cold while yang describes the qualities of light and hot. Confucian ideology also used the yin-yang dichotomy to describe hierarchical relationships. In these relationships, yin commonly described the inferior position of a female to a male. As will be seen, the classification of eunuch gender as more yin than yang by Confucian society carried important implications for eunuch social and political roles.

By design, eunuchs were intended to be submissive and devoid of family ties that might interfere with their loyalty to the imperial court. Within the palace, the yin-yang duality also defined power relations, differentiating the inhabitants of the inner and outer courts based upon their access to power. The inner court was gendered yin (female) and inhabited by women and groups that gained power in part through intimate contact with the emperor; as a result, these inhabitants (including eunuchs) were described as conniving and corrupt. The outer court was

25. Furth, "Androgynous Males and Deficient Females," 6. Although Furth's argument relies on Ming historical and literary sources, it remains relevant for this discussion of the Qing as an example of Han Chinese social views towards sexuality and gender.
26. Furth, "Androgynous Males and Deficient Females," 19.
27. Wang Yude, *Shenmi de di san xing: Zhongguo huangguan daxiezhen* (Wuchang: Huazhong ligong daxue chubanshe, 1994).
28. Furth, "Androgynous Males and Deficient Females," 15.
29. Furth, "Androgynous Males and Deficient Females," 3.
30. See Susan Brownell and Jeffrey N. Wasserstrom, "Introduction: Theorizing Femininities and Masculinities," in *Chinese Femininities and Chinese Masculinities: A Reader*, ed. Susan Brownell and Jeffrey N. Wasserstrom (Berkeley: University of California Press, 2002), 1–31.

gendered yang (male) and associated with those who rose to power through the civil service exam. Thus, the feminization of eunuch gender involved more than the eunuch's low standing on the sexual hierarchy due to his inability to procreate or penetrate. Eunuch political maneuvers that for the most part took place outside the routine channels of the bureaucracy, through inner palace coalitions or factions, aroused the suspicion of scholar-officials, who expressed their resentment to such by stigmatizing and feminizing eunuchs. The ability of eunuchs with the cut of the knife to bypass the years of study and expense associated with the traditional route to power, via the civil service exam, led some scholar-officials to distrust eunuchs and regard the motives of Chinese men who became emasculates as self-serving. Characterizations of eunuchs as more yin than yang facilitated scholar-officials' attempts to negate a potential rival political power within the government.

Conceptions of Chinese masculinity as expressions of *wen* (文 literary) and *wu* (武 martial) further contribute to understanding perceptions of eunuch gender during the Qing dynasty. While masculinity could be either *wen* or *wu*, the ideal was a combination of both.[31] During the Qing, such dichotomies would have been particularly pronounced, as native Han Chinese relied on literary knowledge to obtain access to political power in the face of Manchu domination of the military sphere. Literary knowledge geared toward success in the civil service exams served as one way in which Han Chinese men expressed their masculinity. As noted by Louie and Edwards, "Participation or success in the imperial examinations was a respected component of the masculine image."[32] Thus, the potential for eunuchs to access power via emasculation (and not the civil-service exam) threatened the political power of Han Chinese scholar-officials and by extension one of the main sources from which they derived their masculinity.

Eunuch involvement in activities associated with the other main component of masculinity, military prowess, may have also elicited an unfavorable response from the scholar-official class. Following the Ming precedent of creating a eunuch-exclusive military battalion within the palace, the Yongzheng emperor called for the selection of 200 outer court eunuchs to be trained in military arts such as archery and firearms. Once trained, these eunuchs would be divided into two companies of Imperial Guards (*suwei* 宿衛) to protect the emperor.[33] Specifying the selection of older eunuchs who were strong and healthy, the emperor revealed his perception that at least some eunuchs possessed martial (*wu*) abilities. During the Ming, such eunuch battalions had run into stiff opposition from one of the grand secretaries and the Minister of War on the grounds that such units were "egregious," "threatening to

---

31. Kam Louie and Louise Edwards, "Chinese Masculinity: Theorizing Wen and Wu, *East Asian History* 8 (1994): 144.

32. Louie and Edwards, "Chinese Masculinity," 146.

33. *Guochao gongshi* 國朝宮史 [A history of the palace during the Qing period], ed. Yu Minzhong 于敏中, 史3, 訓諭 3, 雍正2年5月24日, 48. The Yongzheng emperor may have viewed a guard comprised of eunuchs as more loyal than guards who may have supported the imperial princes who had opposed his rise to power.

the security of the palace," and "contrary to military norms."[34] While the reaction to the Yongzheng emperor's edict is not noted, later restrictions on eunuch possession of weapons within the palace (particularly after the 1813 Eight Trigrams Uprising in which eunuch members of the Eight Trigrams facilitated the entry of rebels into the palace)[35] suggest that the scholar-officials would have opposed eunuch involvement in martial activities. By prohibiting eunuchs from obtaining an education or participating in military activities, two key components of the masculine identity in Qing China, scholar-officials feminized eunuch gender and thus limited eunuch political power.

The physical inability of eunuchs to penetrate during intercourse also contributed to Confucian society's categorization of eunuch gender as yin. Here, Matthew Sommer's argument concerning why male-male intercourse was regarded as threatening during the Qing also provides insight into how eunuch sexual inability or the disfigured body would have affected readings of eunuch gender. According to Sommer, male-male intercourse was not criminalized during the Qing as a result of homophobia. Rather, during the Qing, intercourse between males was seen as threatening because it had the potential to upset the "gender hierarchy" by subverting the male's typical sexual role from the penetrant to the penetrated.[36] Sommer argues, "In late imperial China, common sense held that to be penetrated would profoundly compromise a male's masculinity; for this reason, powerful stigma attached to a penetrated male."[37] While it remains unclear if eunuchs continued to remain sexually active post emasculation, one can infer that the inability to assume the male's sexual role (as the penetrant) would have further contributed to the feminization of eunuch gender. For eunuchs, biological function (or in this case dysfunction) contributed to their inability to assume the social role of penetrator and thus resulted in the reading of the eunuch body as feminine.

With Confucian society viewing eunuchs' social role as "servile, feminized inhabitants of the inner quarters," one might assume that eunuchs were unquestionably gendered female; however, as Furth points out, eunuch political power during the Ming dynasty resulted in gender "ambiguities."[38] Yet, by the Qing dynasty, with the Manchus drastically reducing eunuch numbers and their potential to interfere in politics, one can assume that Confucian society tended to locate eunuch gender closer to the yin pole and that their potential "political charge" was greatly reduced.

In sharp contrast to Confucian society's labeling of eunuch gender as feminine, eunuchs themselves continued to self-identify as gendered male. According

---

34. Shih-shan Henry Tsai, *The Eunuchs in the Ming Dynasty* (Albany: State University of New York Press, 1996), 66–67.

35. See Susan Naquin, *Millenarian Rebellion in China: The Eight Trigrams Uprising of 1813* (New Haven: Yale University Press, 1976), 96.

36. Matthew Sommer, *Sex, Law, and Society in Late Imperial China* (Stanford: Stanford University Press, 2000), 117.

37. Sommer, *Sex, Law, and Society in Late Imperial China*, 118.

38. See Furth, "Androgynous Males and Deficient Females," 15.

to Jennifer Jay, "The writings by eunuchs give no indication of even a slight change in gender identity after castration. Even their sexuality, or rumours of it, remained male-oriented."[39] While the act of emasculation rendered eunuchs physically disfigured and physically incapable of reproduction and penetration during sexual intercourse, it did not alter the eunuch's self-identification as male. Eunuchs were not homosexuals or those with sexual anomalies such as hermaphrodites or transsexuals looking for sexual reassignment through emasculation.[40] As Jay has noted, eunuchs "remained unquestionably male in gender identity and role . . . They . . . married, adopted children, ran the households as male heads of the family when off duty or when retired from the palaces . . . Even their sexuality, or rumours of it, remained male-oriented."[41]

Building upon this foundational research, further examination reveals that while gender identity was a non-issue for eunuchs (they were simply boys and men who had undergone emasculation), how others have read and labeled the eunuch body led to multiple interpretations of sexuality and gender during the Qing. Whereas Han Chinese society labeled eunuchs as feminine, the Manchu imperial court questioned this classification and considered whether emasculation really altered eunuch gender. Working with eunuchs daily, the Manchu court may have discovered what eunuchs believed themselves: that despite Confucian society's reading of the eunuch body as female, emasculation did not reassign a eunuch's gender; it remained unaltered as male. Given that a palace eunuch's raison d'être was based upon his inability to perform sexually and the assumption that emasculation extinguished all sexual desire, this revelation would have proven disconcerting for the court. As will be seen, uncertainty about the actual effects of emasculation on the eunuch body and gender identity created a sense of unease and anxiety among eunuchs' Manchu masters.

Imperial Anxiety about the Eunuch Body

Suspicions concerning the validity of Confucian classifications of eunuch gender as more feminine than masculine, or more yin than yang, compounded the imperial court's initial suspicions of eunuch loyalty. Initially, the Manchus appear to have accepted Chinese perceptions of eunuch gender as more yin. In 1689, the Kangxi emperor described eunuchs as "yin 陰 with a disposition that was not like ordinary men. When older they are already feeble and their speech and movements are like babies. Outwardly, they appear respectful and virtuous. Inwardly, they are really unfathomable."[42] It is clear that the Kangxi emperor both identified eunuchs

---

39. Jennifer W. Jay, "Another Side of Chinese Eunuch History: Castration, Marriage, Adoption, and Burial," *Canadian Journal of History* XXVIII (Dec. 1993): 465.
40. Jay, "Another Side of Chinese Eunuch History," 463.
41. Jay, "Another Side of Chinese Eunuch History," 465.
42. *Guochao gongshi*, 史 2，訓諭 2，康熙28年4月，30.

with the yin principle and feared that eunuchs were not the "ideal servants" they were intended to be. To the Kangxi emperor, eunuch motives and loyalty were questionable.

Preceding dynasties had utilized emasculation as a way to purify men to work in the inner court. As described by Stent, eunuchs were assigned to attend to the women of the imperial court. "All eunuchs are considered pure (*chên* [*zhen*] 真 or *ch'ing* [*qing*] 清,) but boys who are made eunuchs when under ten years of age are termed 'thoroughly pure' (*t'ung-chên* [*tongzhen*] 通真). These are specially prized, and are employed by the ladies of the palace with as much freedom as if they were girls; performing such offices as ought only be done by women—some of them of a nature it would be impossible to describe here." Stent notes that "these boy-eunuchs are supposed to be free from the least licentiousness—even in thought;—in fact, they are considered to be devoid of all feelings of that kind whatsoever."[43] Initially, the Manchus accepted Chinese beliefs and practices regarding eunuchs and the effectiveness of emasculation in achieving its intended goals. Eventually, though, this acceptance of eunuchs as purified, feminized servants of the palace gave way to uncertainty about the effects of emasculation on eunuch gender. The imperial court's utilization of eunuchs within the palace, especially in the late 1800s, suggests that the imperial court tended to question the effect of emasculation on a eunuch's gender. Daily interaction with eunuchs suggested to the imperial court that gender classification encompassed more than the ability to penetrate during intercourse and the ability to procreate. Despite beliefs that emasculation purified the body, and by extension gave eunuchs access to serve women in ways no non-emasculated male would ever be allowed, one finds that, within the palace, uncertainty surrounded its true effects of upon the body.

This suspicion was reflected in biannual physical examinations to ensure that the eunuchs were still "clean." Twice a year, once in the spring and once in the fall, the Imperial Household Department examined eunuchs.[44] Throughout the dynasties, rumors had circulated that some young boys and men had avoided having their genitalia removed before obtaining employment as eunuchs. During the Qing, such rumors surrounded the relationship of the Empress Dowager Cixi and one of her eunuch favorites, An Dehai. The presence of these pseudo-eunuchs, or as Furth calls them "eunuchs in name only,"[45] within the palace created the potential for sexual scandals and power rivalries to arise within the imperial sanctum. The ability of non-emasculated males to obtain employment as palace eunuchs would have been a direct assault on the basic reasons for the maintenance of the eunuch system, namely the protection of the rulers' two prized possessions: "dynastic power" and their "women."[46] One might even argue that eunuchs should be added to Matthew

---

43. Stent, "Chinese Eunuchs," 177.
44. Jin Yi and Shen Yiling, *Gongnü tan wanglu* (Beijing: Forbidden City Press, 1992), 41.
45. Furth, "Androgynous Males and Deficient Females," 15.
46. Li Kan, "Tan Qingdai de taijian," *Gujin wenshi yuekan* (March 1942): 29.

Sommer's list of males who elicited fear among Chinese society, males who stepped outside normative male roles such as monks and cross-dressers. Most people were unable to view the eunuch body and determine its dysfunction, so fear may have led people to think that some eunuchs were really sexual predators in disguise or, if truly emasculated, then feminized, political sycophants operating within the palace walls.

Suspicions of bribery facilitating the entry of non-emasculated males into the eunuch system,[47] as well as fears of "regeneration"[48] of excised genitalia, necessitated these post-employment physical examinations. Stent attributes the institution of post-employment physical exams to an incident between Liu Zhongtang[49] and a chief eunuch during the Qianlong era. In response to being treated disrespectfully by this eunuch, Liu memorialized the emperor, calling for a re-examination of the purity of the entire eunuch staff. Liu claimed that, during the Ming, the regeneration of eunuchs' "mutilated organs" had led to "licentiousness and disorder in the palace between the eunuchs and ladies."[50] In an attempt to prevent such a reoccurrence, the emperor heeded Liu's advice and ordered the examinations and re-emasculation if necessary. According to Stent, while deaths among first time emasculates were rare, those who underwent emasculation a second time, or had their genitals "swept clean" (*saojing* 掃淨), were often "swept dead" (*saosi* 掃死).[51]

Cases in which the penis was not excised in entirety at the time of emasculation may have contributed to anxiety over what is now considered a medical impossibility, namely the regeneration of excised genitalia. Such a discovery had the potential to threaten the purity of the imperial lineage if the testes remained functional and the chastity of the palace women if some sexual function remained. Some eunuchs worked in intimate contact with women of the inner court daily, so eunuchs with sexual capabilities had the potential to form not only sexual relations with palace women but political relationships as well, embodying the very essence of *jian* (姦 sexual and political betrayal). This suggests that the implementation of the biannual exams stemmed from anxiety about the potential sexual threat posed by both pseudo-eunuchs infiltrating the palace and actual emasculates who might regenerate their sexual organs after emasculation. In order to protect both the chastity of the women of the court and the purity of the imperial lineage, it may have been simply viewed as safer to err on the side of caution and repeatedly examine the palace eunuch population. As a result, some eunuchs underwent emasculation two or three times to ensure no genitalia remained extant and that the wound was completely flat.[52]

---

47. Jin and Shen, *Gongnü tan wangle*, 41.
48. Jay, "Another Side of Chinese Eunuch History," 466.
49. Stent refers to Liu as "president"; however, he does not indicate what Zhong was the president of. See Stent, "Chinese Eunuchs," 162–63.
50. Stent, "Chinese Eunuchs," 162.
51. Stent, "Chinese Eunuchs," 162–63.
52. Jin and Shen, *Gongnü tan wanglu*, 41.

The uncertainty about emasculation's effectiveness in extinguishing the male libido also led to prohibitions to prevent amorous relationships from developing between eunuchs and female members of the palace staff. The Imperial Household Department's prohibitions against such relationships are one example of efforts to err on the side of caution in case suspicions about the persistence of the eunuch libido were well founded. During the Qing, the imperial court employed young Manchu women to serve as ladies-in-waiting to the women of the Qing court. Selected at the age of thirteen or fourteen, they would serve until the time they returned home to marry.[53] Working alongside eunuchs daily, it was only natural for relationships to form between members of the two groups. The severity of palace regulations aimed at preventing relationships between eunuchs and maidservants, relationships known as *duishi* 對食, reveals that this was considered a serious matter. Maidservants who addressed eunuchs in familial terms, who referred to eunuchs as *boshu* (伯叔 uncle) or *xiongdi* (兄弟 brother), faced punishment and expulsion and her family faced exile to Xinjiang.[54]

Despite these prohibitions, during the late Qing, marriages between the eunuchs and maidservants were not uncommon.[55] Mark Elliott's suggestion that there was "a chronic shortage of marriageable females in the banners"[56] would also suggest that at the core of Manchu prohibitions against eunuch–maidservant relationships (*duishi*) were fears about the efficacy of emasculation in eradicating sexual desire and neutering eunuchs. *Duishi* relationships threatened to deprive the banner community of eligible marriageable women and thus the ability to sustain the purity of the Manchu race inside China proper. By the end of the Qing, such concerns about Manchu fertility appears to have dissipated or become overshadowed by intimate politics. By the late Qing, the Empress Dowager Cixi arranged marriages between palace eunuchs and Manchu maidservants, perhaps in an attempt to keep happy those who facilitated her access to power. One such match resulted in the marriage of an eighteen *sui* Manchu maidservant who had served the Empress Dowager from the age of thirteen to a eunuch surnamed Liu, who was the informally adopted son (*gan erzi* 乾兒子) of the empress's favorite, Li Lianying 李蓮英.[57]

In many ways, the sexual and political threat posed by eunuchs is very similar to the anxiety generated by monks during the Qing dynasty. Monks, like eunuchs, operated outside the social roles established by the Confucian ethical system.[58]

---

53. Jin and Shen, *Gongnü tan wanglu*, 5.
54. *Qinding gongzhong xianxing zeli* 欽定宮中現行則例 (QDGZXXZL) [Imperially authorized laws and regulations of conduct within the palace] (Reprint, Taipei: Wenhai chubanshe, 1979), 卷3，宮規，404.
55. QDGZXXZL, 卷3，宮規，404.
56. Mark C. Elliott, *The Manchu Way: The Eight Banners and Ethnic Identity in Late Imperial China* (Stanford: Stanford University Press, 2001), 255.
57. Jin and Shen, *Gongnü tan wanglu*, 2.
58. For a discussion of how Chinese society viewed monks with suspicion, see Sommer, *Sex, Law, and Society in Late Imperial China*, 100.

Like monks, eunuchs were supposed to be celibate, never marry,[59] and live away from their families. It is interesting to note that the colloquial term for "eunuch" is *chu jia* (出家 quitting home), the same term that is used for an individual who left home to become a Buddhist monk or nun. Living outside the confines of the Confucian family order, monks, like eunuchs, were often perceived as threatening. Both groups were supposed to remain celibate; however, suspicion surrounded the sexual activities of monks and eunuchs. Eunuchs posed both a sexual and a political threat, mainly to the imperial court due to their physical proximity to the emperor, whereas monks were seen as more of a sexual threat to society. It is interesting to note that these two groups often overlapped, as some eunuchs lived out their retirement in Buddhist temples and monasteries (see Chapter 8).[60]

The duties performed by eunuchs within the inner quarters further suggest an uncertainty about the effectiveness of emasculation in eradicating the male libido. During the Qing, the imperial court employed female servants rather than eunuchs to attend to the most intimate care of the women of the court. The assignment of female attendants to duties such as assisting their masters with bathing and dressing, and sitting watch while the women of the court slept[61] further suggests that the imperial court was unsure if eunuchs continued to have sexual urges and to identify their gender as male post emasculation.

It is interesting to note that the "thoroughly pure" became sullied by age. According to Stent, eunuchs emasculated prior to the onset of puberty (the "thoroughly pure") would be replaced by new prepubertal emasculates and assigned to duties outside "the private apartments of the ladies."[62] Changing perceptions of eunuch purity over their life course suggests an ambiguity in the government's ideas about eunuch sexuality and gender. Moreover, the fact that older eunuchs were removed from the inner quarters suggests an underlying suspicion of the effectiveness of emasculation in eradicating sexual desire.

Rumors of the ability of the libido to survive emasculation likely held some degree of truth. Initially, the Chinese believed that the complete excision of the male genitalia would leave the eunuch totally devoid of sexual function and rid him of sexual desire. If performed so that the genitalia were cut off entirely, emasculation caused sexual deficiency and often total impotence, but it did not remove sexual desire in all eunuchs. In Europe, some castrati were also known to have maintained

---

59. As discussed in previous chapters, emasculation was intended to produce a group of servile people unhindered by family ties. The stigma of emasculation was thought to be so strong that it would lead to the severing of family ties and prevent eunuchs from marrying. As my research shows, many eunuchs maintained relations with their families post emasculation and employment by the palace. In addition, by the end of the Qing dynasty, members of the imperial court were actively promoting eunuch marriage.

60. After retiring from service as palace eunuchs, some lived out their lives in eunuch retirement associations housed in Buddhist temples and monasteries. Some powerful eunuchs even became Buddhist abbots in later years. See Ma Deqing et al., "Qing gong taijian huiyi lu," 196. For a discussion of Qing eunuch retirement associations, see Chapter 8.

61. Xin Xiuming, *Lao taijian de huiyi* (Beijing: Beijing Yanshan chubanshe, 1992), 67.

62. Stent, "Chinese Eunuchs," 177.

their libido post castration.[63] However, for the castrati, the removal of only part of their genitalia (castration as opposed to emasculation) left them with the organs necessary to function sexually even if with some deficiencies.

The presence of the libido post emasculation suggests both the desire and, in some cases, the ability of eunuchs to act on their sexual urges. Here, Frank Dorn's negative portrayal of eunuchs as "sexless and frustrated"[64] has some merit. Although his depiction of eunuchs as "sexless" doesn't appear to align with eunuch self-perceptions, sexually "frustrated" seems more of an appropriate description of the sexual lives of the majority of eunuchs. Zhang Delang, a late Qing eunuch with three wives, is even reported to have frequented a prostitute in the Japanese concession of Tianjin.[65] On one occasion, Yu Chunhe, a eunuch in his service, describes an intimate scene between Zhang and the prostitute. Yu even describes how he became aroused while witnessing a sexual encounter between Zhang and the prostitute. In his memoirs, Yu comments that, while he watched Zhang and the prostitute, his own body was "burning with fever and desire" (J'étais brûlant de fièvre et de désir).[66]

Dissatisfaction with their sexual dysfunction may have led some eunuchs to seek treatment. Jay suggests that eunuchs emasculated post puberty may have been able to "to reduce the effects of castration" and experience "'dry-run orgasm with diminished sensation'" with the help of hormone therapy.[67] Eunuchs may have also relied on dildos[68] as sexual aids to facilitate their sexual relations.

Aside from anxiety about the effects of emasculation on the body, Manchu–eunuch labor relations suggest that the imperial court viewed eunuchs as gendered male. Palace employment of eunuchs as palace guards and regulations against eunuchs wielding knives in the palace suggest that, despite their impotence, they were considered able to perform roles that female maidservants could not. Moreover, Qing reports attempting to deal with instances of eunuch-upon-eunuch violence and eunuchs getting into altercations and stabbing one another with knives (see Chapter 5) did not align with Confucian portrayals of eunuchs as effeminate. Interacting with eunuchs daily within the palace, the Manchu imperial court suspected that eunuchs were simply men without genitalia.

Western Attempts to Read the Chinese Eunuch Body

To the Western observer and reader, there was no confusion about how to read the eunuch body. It was simply and undeniably gendered female. Historical, literary,

---

63. Jenkins, "The Voice of the Castrato," 1879.
64. Frank Dorn, *The Forbidden City: The Biography of a Palace* (New York: Charles Scribner's Sons, 1970), 215.
65. Dan Shi, *Mémoires d'un Eunuque dans la Cité Interdite*, trans. Nadine Perront (Marseille: Editions Philippe Picquier, 1995), 225.
66. Dan Shi, *Mémoires d'un Eunuque dans la Cité Interdite*, 225.
67. Jay, "Another Side of Chinese Eunuch History," 466.
68. Bronze dildos were discovered in Han dynasty tombs. Asian Art Museum of San Francisco, "Tomb Treasures" Exhibit. http://www.asianart.org/regular/tomb-pleasures, accessed August 13, 2017.

and medical records are filled with the word "feminine" in descriptions of eunuchs. To the Western observer, the removal of the male genitalia signaled the removal of the eunuch's manhood. Given that much of the discourse about the eunuch body stems from the interaction between Western physicians and eunuchs in China during the late 1800s, these perceptions have undoubtedly influenced how scholars have viewed eunuch gender.

With the arrival of more and more Westerners to China in the mid- to late 1800s, in the years following the Opium Wars, the eunuch body became an object of fascination and study. The Chinese eunuch body became both an example of backward China and a source of medical insight for Western proponents of eugenics.[69] Prior to this time, during the period of early missionary activity, foreign trade, and political delegations, the eunuch body did not attract the attention of Western writers or artists. While eunuchs frequent the pages of Western traveler accounts of their encounters with China, they are mentioned only as the gatekeepers of the Chinese emperor. Early on, Westerners realized that eunuchs were often the first line of communication between them and the Qing court. These references typically mentioned the eunuch's attire, his demeanor, but not the appearance of the body. What a eunuch actually looked like was left to the reader's imagination. The eunuch body remained absent in Western traveler accounts until the late 1800s, when physicians began to become interested in eunuchs and emasculation.

Western travelers and missionaries to Chinese repeatedly mention their interaction with eunuchs as they attempted to reach the imperial court both physically and culturally. To members of foreign delegations, eunuchs were seen as a channel through which they might access the emperor to deliver goods or messages from their governments. Eunuchs were also viewed by missionaries as objects of proselytization, whose access to the inner sanctum of the palace might serve as a method of reaching the female inhabitants of the palace as well as the emperor himself.

Missionaries' and travelers' encounters with eunuchs during the 1700s and 1800s reveal little about the eunuch body. Important sources of information about the palace, such as the account of the Catholic priest Matteo Ripa (1682–1746), who spent thirteen years in the palace, mention contact with eunuchs but offer no descriptions of the eunuch body. This disinterest in the eunuch body continues in the 1800s, with writers such as Sir Isaac Taylor Headland and his wife, Lady Headland (Marion Sinclair), who had frequent and intimate contact with the Empress Dowager Cixi during the more than twenty years she served as a physician to many women of the court. Perhaps overshadowed by writers' fascination with the Empress Dowager and her hold on power, eunuchs are only described as wearing long robes and as a potential means to sharing the gospel with the members of the imperial court.[70]

---

69. See Dale, "Understanding Emasculation."
70. Isaac Taylor Headland, *Court Life in China: The Capital, Its Officials and People* (New York: Fleming H. Revell Company, 1909), 97.

The Chinese eunuch body was finally unrobed in the 1860s, when Westerners physicians in China began documenting their treatment and interaction with eunuchs at Western dispensaries and hospitals in the capital. Curiosity about the eunuch body and how Western medical techniques such as catheterization alleviated and even saved the lives of eunuchs suffering from urological problems became the focus of numerous articles published in medical journals. At the same time, eunuchs and their bodies became a subject of great interest among American physicians and politicians considering castration as a possible "remedy" for resolving issues of sexual and psychological deviancy.[71]

For some of these medical professionals and self-proclaimed scholars of China, the study of eunuchs also provided the context to express their views on the backwardness or exoticism of China. The eunuch body became a symbol of China's backward practices, allowing writers an opportunity to offer social commentary about Chinese culture and its practices, especially related practices such as polygamy. As Stent noted, "polygamy; were it not for that eunuchs would be as rare as unicorns."[72] It is this social commentary that sets the tone for Stent's overwhelmingly negative descriptions of the eunuch body.

Stent writes, "eunuchs, taken as a whole, may be considered repulsive looking, but young eunuchs are often very handsome and feminine in appearance; indeed, one can almost imagine some of them to be young women dressed in men's clothing."[73] Stent complicates eunuch gender classification by presenting it as more female in the case of young eunuchs, only later to state that they are more androgynous in their later years. Stent writes, "as they grow older there is something painfully comical in their appearance; on seeing them one cannot help fancying they bear a resemblance to old women, who forgetting their age and sex, are masquerading in male attire."

Stent's account reveals that Westerners also read the eunuch body as something other than male. He writes, "eunuchs may be known by the voice, the want of hair on the face, cringing manner, hangdog, bloated appearance (in some)."[74] Stent later adds, "in fact there is something grotesque—if I may be allowed the expression—in their voices, not by any means pleasant to listen to"[75] and notes that the eunuch's "face is bare as a billiard ball."[76] Stent, like other Westerners writing during this time, viewed the eunuch body through the lens of Orientalist stereotypes about Chinese culture, society, and its government.

Characterizations of eunuchs as ugly and feminized continued well past the end of the Qing. In addition to visual manifestations of emasculation, aural ones contributed to how Westerners read the eunuch body as female. One need only to

71. See Dale, "Understanding Emasculation."
72. Stent, "Chinese Eunuchs," 183.
73. Stent, "Chinese Eunuchs," 178.
74. Stent, "Chinese Eunuchs," 178.
75. Stent, "Chinese Eunuchs," 179.
76. Stent, "Chinese Eunuchs," 179.

read about the chance encounter of an American living in Beijing in the 1930s with a former palace eunuch to grasp how the voice could influence how one read the eunuch body. Approached from behind by the eunuch while walking through Beihai Park, Blofeld's initial reaction was that the "soft, feminine voice" that addressed him belonged to a woman. Once Blofeld turned, the eunuch's face was barely visible due to the night. Had it been daylight, he might have mistaken the eunuch for a woman but as it was night he knew that it was highly unlikely "in Peking to encounter a woman walking alone in a solitary place at night."[77] Had the eunuch not introduced himself as such, Blofeld suggests that he would have read the body as feminine.

In each of the above-mentioned examples, Western male writers feminized the eunuch body. It is interesting to note that Katherine Carl, one of the few Western females who spent time in the palace and interacted with eunuchs, did not. Carl spent several months as an inhabitant of the palace while she painted the Empress Dowager Cixi's portrait for the 1904 St. Louis World's Fair. In describing Cixi's chief eunuch, Li Lianying, Carl writes:

> In person he is tall and thin. His head is, in type, like Savonarola's. He has a Roman nose, a massive lean jaw, a protruding lower lip, and very shrewd eyes, full of intelligence, that shine out of sunken orbits. His face is much wrinkled and his skin like old parchment. Though only sixty years old, he looks seventy-five, and is the oldest eunuch in the Palace. He has been there since the age of ten.[78]

Even in the case of the eunuch's wrinkled face, Carl does not compare Li to an old woman.

Conclusion

Emasculation proved to be a life-altering event for the eunuch candidate, one that physically and socially marked the body. Curiosity about how emasculation affected and changed the eunuch body has captivated writers for the last 150 years. Despite this curiosity, few had actually seen the unrobed eunuch body, as eunuchs rarely shared the extent of the damage caused by genital mutilation. This chapter has attempted to unrobe the eunuch body to reveal how the complete removal of the external male genitalia not only resulted in sexual dysfunction but also led to different interpretations of eunuch gender.

Emasculation was intended to create a subjugated and neutered male, yet in reality it sparked a charge—a political charge fueled by the eunuch's proximity to the seat of imperial power and a sexual charge fueled by uncertainties regarding how to read the eunuch body. These uncertainties led to speculation by different segments of society regarding how to label eunuch gender. Operating outside the boundaries

---

77. John Blofeld, *City of Lingering Spendour: A Frank Account of Old Peking's Exotic Pleasures* (London, 1961; Reprint, Boston: Shambhala, 1989), 58.
78. Katherine A. Carl, *With the Empress Dowager of China* (1906; reprint, New York: KPI, Limited, 1986), 125.

of the masculine role defined by Confucian norms—the ability to penetrate during sexual intercourse and to procreate—eunuchs were feminized and labeled yin. For eunuchs, emasculation removed their genitalia but not their identity as male.

For the Manchu imperial court, their daily interaction with eunuchs suggested that Confucian labels were inaccurate. The possibility of genitals regenerating and the failure of emasculation to extinguish all sexual desire only augmented the Manchu court's distrust of eunuchs. Vigilance against not only perceived political but sexual betrayal fueled the court's obsession with efforts to maintain purity in an attempt to protect the chastity of the women of the palace as well as the sanctity of the imperial lineage. Repeated checks to ensure the prevention of pseudo-eunuchs resulted in the repeated genital mutilation of those found to be "impure." The palace's employment patterns for eunuchs further suggests an uncertainty regarding the practice of assigning eunuchs as if they were feminized servants. The use of eunuchs as guards and in roles designed to protect the emperor and his family reveals the tendency of the Manchu imperial court over time to view eunuchs as more yang than yin.

Westerners also studied eunuchs, who were viewed as a curiosity, in an effort to determine the effects of emasculation on the body. While the medical discourse on eunuchs has furthered the discipline in providing first-hand accounts of eunuch medical history, Western accounts have contributed to misperceptions about eunuch gender. By applying Orientalist stereotypes to China, rather than viewing eunuchs through the lens of Chinese society, the Manchu imperial court, and most important of all, eunuchs themselves, nineteenth-century Western scholars made assumptions about eunuch gender that have now been proven false. As such, eunuchs were not objects of study in their own right but rather symbols of Chinese backwardness in Orientalists' discourses on imperial China. In sum, this chapter reveals that discussions of eunuch gender require more nuanced understandings of how emasculation altered the physical body but left the eunuch's gender identity unchanged.

4

Entering the Emperor's Realm

As one passed through the gates of the Forbidden City and entered the palace, it was as if one had entered another world. While "all under heaven" was the emperor's realm, it was never felt so much as here within the seat of imperial power and the residence of the emperor. Here, surrounded by buildings and statues "symbolizing the longevity of the emperor and his everlasting power,"[1] eunuchs would begin the work for which they had been created—to wait upon their imperial masters as servants. The act of emasculation had physically altered these young boys and men, turning them into something other than men in the eyes of Chinese society and the Qing court. Outside the palace walls, among society, eunuchs were in the minority and shunned as social outcasts.

Once inside the palace, emasculates found themselves in a unique environment. No longer the numerical minority, eunuchs quickly became absorbed into the palace eunuch community and hierarchy. Spending most of their hours working within the palace, new recruits joined the ranks of a large palace servile staff (bondservants, maidservants, wet nurses, etc.) whose life and work pivoted around the service of the emperor and the imperial court. Among the palace servant community, just as among society, the majority of eunuchs occupied positions at the bottom rung of the social hierarchy. Physical disfigurement and servile status now defined the eunuch's life and identity.

Assuming a New Identity

Emasculation had physically altered these young boys and men. The next step, entry into the palace eunuch system, would complete their metamorphosis. In the early stages of the transformation of emasculates into palace eunuchs, their status as servants of the imperial court became readily apparent. Even prior to their entry into the palace, new recruits found their identities eclipsed by the wants and needs of their imperial masters. Once the physical transformation was complete, eunuch recruits would be given new names that symbolically represented the end of their former

---

1. *Gugong* 故宫 [The Palace Museum] (Beijing: The Forbidden City Publishing House of the Palace Museum, 1990), 11.

lives as they joined a group of eunuch candidates for palace service. A review of palace archival records of eunuch applicants reveals that groups of applicants shared the same first characters in their given names. For example, in an undated list of forty applicants, in every case, the eunuch's first name began with the character *lian* (連 to connect; together with).[2] In another list of twenty-three eunuch applicants examined by the *Kuaijisi* (會計司 Office of Accounts) and the *Zhangyisi* (掌儀司 Department of Ceremonial), each one had the character *jin* (進 to enter) as the first character of his given name.[3] An examination of the characters selected for these new names suggests that names were chosen to express ideas such as loyalty or the attainment of happiness.[4] If the names were selected by the *daozijiang*, these symbolic meanings would have been an excellent marketing tool to improve the likelihood of the eunuch candidate being selected as a palace eunuch.

The commonality of characters in eunuch names suggests that eunuch recruits took new names at the time of their emasculation, perhaps reminiscent of the practice in China of men taking on new names to mark their transformation into Buddhist monks. The Chinese practice of using the term 出家 *chu jia* to symbolize the cutting of family ties for both monks and eunuchs suggests that these two groups might also have shared the practice of taking a new name to represent the transformation. For eunuchs, the taking of new names may have signified both their physical transformation and perhaps even provided information about their point of entry into the system, such as the *daozijiang* who had performed the emasculation and presented these candidates as a group to the palace, just as Chinese families often named their children with the same first character, adding a second character to differentiate between siblings of the same sex. These first characters also indicated peer groups within the palace eunuch population.

Basic Training

The Imperial Household Department continued to mold emasculates into eunuchs (*taijian* 太監) during a period of basic training prior to the recruits' actual entry into the palace. With the majority of eunuchs coming from poor families, a period of education in the etiquette and deportment required of imperial servants was an absolute necessity. In the initial stages of instruction conducted at the *Shenxingsi* (慎刑司 Judicial Department, Imperial Household Department), which lasted several

---

2. First Historical Archives, Beijing, *Gongzhong* 宮中 [Palace], *zajian* 雜件 [Miscellaneous documents] 1272，*Renshilei taijian* 人事類太監 [Eunuchs].

3. First Historical Archives, Beijing, 宮中，雜件1200，人事類太監媽媽女子, 正4月28日. No year is listed on this document.

4. Characters such as *xin* (信 trustworthy), *zhong* (忠 loyal), *fu* (福 fortune), and *xi* (喜 happiness) are among the most common eunuch names. See Norman A. Kutcher, "Unspoken Collusions: The Empowerment of Yuanming yuan Eunuchs in the Qianlong Period," *Harvard Journal of Asiatic Studies* 70, no. 2 (Dec. 2010): 478.

days or by some accounts up to two weeks,[5] new recruits studied the rules and regulations of the palace, court etiquette, and the basics of eunuch service.[6] According to L. C. Arlington and William Lewisohn, palace eunuchs "were instructed in their duties and correct deportment" at the *Dagaodian* or *Dagaoxuandian* (大高殿 or 大高玄殿 Hall of High Heaven), which was located at the southwest corner of Coal Hill.

Preston Torbert suggests another mechanism for eunuch training, the sending of eunuch recruits to the *Yuanmingyuan*. Torbert cites a 1754 edict which he claims suggests that new eunuchs were sent to serve as "grounds keepers" in the *Yuanmingyuan*, from which those who performed well on the job were promoted to work in the imperial palace. However, a closer inspection of this edict reveals that this "promotion" of *Yuanmingyuan* eunuchs was not the norm. The edict specifically refers to instances in which there were few middle-aged recruits and numerous young recruits entering the palace. To remedy the situation, the Qianlong emperor ordered that good eunuchs from the *Yuanmingyuan* be selected to supplement the lack of older (mature) eunuchs and that new recruits be sent as their substitutes. While admittedly some young eunuchs did work in the *Yuanmingyuan* prior to being transferred to the palace to serve, based on this edict one should not infer that all young eunuchs received their training there. As Kutcher notes, the Qianlong emperor preferred to have the *Yuanmingyuan*, his primary residence, staffed with young eunuchs.[7]

Instructors utilized lessons and group and individual exercises followed by critiques of the recruit's performance by his classmates to familiarize these new eunuchs with the ways of the palace.[8] Oral histories of late Qing palace eunuchs provide us with rare glimpses into the training eunuchs received. First, new recruits had to master the complexities of forms of address within the palace. For example, the emperor was to be addressed as *Wansuiye* (萬歲爺 Lord of 10,000 Years) , the empress dowager as *Lao Foye* (老佛爺 The Old Buddha), and the imperial concubines as *zhuzi* (主子 master). Since eunuchs did not like to be called *taijian*, superiors were to be addressed as *shifu* (師父 teacher) and those in the same generation were to be called by their surnames followed by *ye* (爺 term of respect).[9] New recruits also learned which words the palace considered taboo. For example, characters that possessed the same sounds as characters in the emperor's name were not allowed to

5. Dan Shi, *Mémoires d'un Eunuque dans la Cité Interdite*, trans. Nadine Perront (Marseille: Editions Philippe Picquier, 1991 ; reprint, 1995), 124.

6. See L. C. Arlington and William Lewisohn, *In Search of Old Peking* (Peking, 1935; reprint, New York: Paragon Book Reprint Corp, 1967), 132; Preston Torbert, *The Ch'ing Imperial Household Department: A Study of Its Organization and Principal Functions, 1662–1796* (Cambridge, MA: Harvard University Press, 1977), 43; and *Guochao gongshi*, ed. Yu Minzhong, vol. 1 (Taipei: National Palace Museum, 1984), 102.

7. Kutcher, "Unspoken Collusions," 458.

8. Dan Shi, *Mémoires d'un Eunuque dans la Cité Interdite*, 129.

9. Xin Xiuming, *Taijian tan wanglu* (Beijing: Gugong chubanshe, 2015), 224.

be spoken. Eunuchs possessing the same characters or similar-sounding characters in their own names found themselves forced to change their names.[10]

Aside from forms of address, recruits were instructed in how to receive orders from their employers. A eunuch's listening skills were particularly important since, within the palace, a superior's instructions were to be understood the first time.[11] Asking a superior to repeat or explain an instruction was not allowed. As will be seen, this often led to misunderstandings and a eunuch being punished for not delivering the correct item to his master.

Basic training also required that eunuchs master the numerous forms of salutations and prostrations required for service within the palace. In the memoir of the late Qing eunuch Yu Chunhe, Yu commented that, in retrospect, a eunuch's life was spent on his knees.[12] When to kneel, whether to kneel with one leg or two, and when to add a *ketou*[13] 磕头 all required instruction.[14]

Figure 4.1
Eunuchs serving

10. Xin Xiuming, *Taijian tan wanglu* (2015), 224.
11. Dan Shi, *Mémoires d'un Eunuque dans la Cité Interdite*, 127.
12. Dan Shi, *Mémoires d'un Eunuque dans la Cité Interdite*, 125.
13. The ceremonial act of prostrating and knocking the head on the ground.
14. Ma Deqing et al., "Qing gong taijian huiyi lu," ed. Zhang Wenhui (Beijing: Wenshi ziliao chubanshe, 1982), 181.

Ordinary acts of daily life became so complicated once performed inside the palace walls[15] that basic training even included lessons in these areas. New recruits studied, among other things, how to carry items (not too high or too low but at the level of one's eyebrows), how to serve tea or food, how to assist one's master in smoking a water pipe or lighting a cigarette, and how to dress one's master. In a mere fourteen days, recruits could only receive instruction in the bare minimum of the palace rules and regulations for proper service.[16] The remainder of eunuch training would be left to apprenticeship and experience once the eunuch had been selected for imperial service.

Labeled by Assignment

Prior to entering the palace, new recruits received designations that would become as basic to their identities as their name, age, and native place.[17] Those eunuchs not already associated with a banner (i.e., new recruits who were not transfers from a princely household) would each be assigned to a banner such as the "White Bordered Banner" or the "Red Bordered Banner" and placed under the supervision of an individual bannerman or a bannerman family. Banner designations would serve as a form of identification for the eunuch and provide the palace with a further layer of supervision of the eunuch staff.[18]

Once the recruits had completed their basic training, they would be escorted into the palace. On the chosen day, in the early morning, the recruits, dressed in the attire of an apprentice eunuch (a robe [*paozi* 袍子], a pair of black boots, and a belt),[19] would be led en masse into the palace by a *zongguan taijian* (總管太監 assistant chief eunuch) to receive their assignments and begin their duties. Records from the late Qing indicate that, once they had arrived at the *Yangxindian* (養心殿 Hall of Mental Cultivation), they would kneel in audience with the principals of the palace such as the empress dowager, the emperor, and the other ladies of the court. Slips of wood on which were written the recruit's name, age, and native place provided individuals of the court with information to aid in their selection.[20] Should additional information be desired, the name of the recruit would be called and the eunuch asked to respond to questions. In the late Qing, the Empress Dowager Cixi would select first, favoring recruits who were young, intelligent, and literate. The emperor would then make his selections, followed by the empress, and the imperial

---

15. Dan Shi, *Mémoires d'un Eunuque dans la Cité Interdite*, 126.
16. Dan Shi, *Mémoires d'un Eunuque dans la Cité Interdite*, 130.
17. Within palace archival records, references to a particular eunuch are routinely followed by the eunuch's name, age, native place, and banner assignment.
18. See Ma Deqing et al., "Qing gong taijian huiyi lu," 178.
19. See Ma Deqing et al., "Qing gong taijian huiyi lu," 178 and Dan Shi, *Mémoires d'un Eunuque dans la Cité Interdite*, 131.
20. See Ma Deqing et al., "Qing gong taijian huiyi lu," 178–79.

concubines.[21] After the women's quarters had made their selections, the remaining recruits would be dispersed for service among the forty-eight departments (*chu* 處) within the system.[22]

Their assignments now designated, eunuchs took on an essential piece of their new persona. These assignments would function as labels that, along with their name, native place, and age at the time of emasculation, would become the defining characteristics of a eunuch, required in all official correspondence. Having become emasculated and received his assignment to work within the palace, the emasculate's rebirth was now complete.

Figure 4.2
Group photo of eunuchs

21. Xin Xiuming, *Lao taijian de huiyi* (Beijing: Beijing yanshan, 1987), 16.
22. Xin Xiuming, *Lao taijian de huiyi* (1987), 16.

Master–Apprentice System

Once a palace eunuch was assigned his duties, his training continued with a period of apprenticeship under a eunuch superior. The master, usually an older eunuch with the rank of *zongguan taijian* (總管太監 assistant chief eunuch) or *shouling taijian* (首領太監 supervisory eunuch)[23] would act as the recruit's instructor as he learned how to perform his assignments within the palace. New recruits did not receive systematic training;[24] instead, they learned by following their superiors around in the performance of their duties. Recalling their training, three eunuchs from the late Qing noted, "[we] had to rely on [our] own devices, the master never gave explicit demands, and very rarely instructed [us], wanting us to teach ourselves."[25]

While the role of eunuchs as servants of the imperial court is understood, less well known is that, during the apprentice period, eunuchs worked as servants for other eunuchs. During this period, eunuchs trained by serving their eunuch superiors. Eunuchs would wait on their superiors—drawing water for their bath, helping them dress—and only retiring for the evening after their master's wants and needs had been satisfied.[26] One recruit recalls, "I would prepare his tea, I would go to find his breakfast at the kitchens and return to wake him up. I would help him get dressed, I would serve him his meal, then while he was attending to his work, I would tidy up . . . In the evening when he was tired, I would massage his legs."[27] During this period of the eunuch's training, a recruit's primary responsibility was serving his master/teacher well.[28] In addition, recruits were responsible for completing their duties for the imperial court. For example, when not occupied with the service of his master, the eunuch Yu Chunhe would clean the floors and replace the candles in the sanctuaries and devotional rooms within the palace.[29] Yu notes that he always completed his tasks "with diligence and application, concern and discretion"[30] and that his master was always happy with his work, but not all master–apprentice relations were as amicable. The threat of collective punishment for infractions committed by their disciples ensured that masters closely supervised their subordinates. If a master noticed an error, his apprentice would receive a harsh reprimand, a slap on the face for repeated minor offenses, or a beating for errors deemed more serious.[31] Apprentices who learned quickly and performed their duties well earned the favor of their masters and increased their chances of promotion.[32]

---

23. Zhao Rongsheng and Wei Ziqing, "Jinggong he bai shifu" [Entering the palace and honoring your master] in *Wanqing gongting yishi*, ed. Ding Yanshi (Taipei: Shijie wenwu chubanshe, 1984), 207.
24. Pu Jia and Pu Jie, *Wanqing diwang shenghuo jianwen*, vol. 1 (Taipei: Juzhenwu chubanshe, 1984), 234.
25. Pu Jia and Pu Jie, *Wanqing diwang shenghuo jianwen*, vol. 1, 234.
26. Wan Yi, Wang Shuqing, and Liu Lu, *Qingdai gongtingshi* (Shenyang: Liaoning renmin chubanshe, 1990), 501.
27. Dan Shi, Mémoires d'un Eunuque dans la Cité Interdite, 134.
28. Ma Deqing et al., "Qing gong taijian huiyi lu," 179.
29. Dan Shi, *Mémoires d'un Eunuque dans la Cité Interdite*, 135.
30. Dan Shi, *Mémoires d'un Eunuque dans la Cité Interdite*, 134.
31. Pu Jia and Pu Jie, *Wanqing diwang shenghuo jianwen*, 234.
32. Ma Deqing et al., "Qing gong taijian huiyi lu," 179.

Educated Eunuchs

Basic instruction in eunuch etiquette and duties served the needs of those eunuchs performing menial labor and attendant duties. However, eunuchs assigned to bureaus such as the *Zoushichu* (奏事處 Chancery of Memorials) had to attain literacy through a period of education in reading and writing. During the early Qing, the palace followed the Ming dynasty precedent in educating eunuchs. During the Ming, upon entering the eunuch system, some 200–300 eunuchs would be selected to receive an education at the *Neishutang* 內書堂.[33] Eunuch education began around the age of ten.[34] Each student would be supplied with a copy of the "Thousand Character Essay"[35] and the *Four Books*.[36] Over time, both the quantity and quality of the formal education that eunuchs received decreased, due to the attempts of Qing emperors such as Kangxi and Qianlong to prevent eunuch intervention in the government. The Kangxi emperor's often-quoted remarks about eunuchs reflect Qing efforts to keep them in menial positions. Spence summarizes Kangxi's views as follows:

> For eunuchs are basically Yin in nature. They are quite different from ordinary people; when weak with age they babble like babies. In my court I never let them get involved with government—even the few eunuchs-of-the-presence with whom I might chatter or exchange family jokes were never allowed to discuss politics . . . Whereas in the later Ming Dynasty, besides being so extravagant and reckless, they obtained the power to write endorsements on the emperors' memorials, for the emperors were unable to read the one- or two-thousand-character memorials that flowed in; and the eunuchs in turn passed the memorials on to their *subordinates* to handle.[37]

As a result, emperors such as Kangxi endeavored to keep eunuch education at a minimum and only accessible to those for whom it was an occupational necessity. Policies such as those of Kangxi, denying all but a few an education, helped maintain a eunuch's subservience and his inability to interfere in politics.

During the Qing, young eunuchs selected to receive an education studied under a Han Chinese instructor sent from the *Wanshandian* (萬善殿 Hall of Ten Thousand Virtues).[38] In the early years of the Qing dynasty, Asitan (d. 1683 or 1684), a Manchu official (bondservant of the Imperial Household) and translator who possessed the *jinshi* 進士 degree,[39] served concurrently as a secretary in one

---

33. Xu Ke, *Qingbai leichao* (1917; reprint, Taipei: Shangwu yinshuguan, 1966), 6.
34. Xu Ke, *Qingbai leichao*, 6.
35. According to Giles, "a composition in one thousand different characters, arranged so as to yield sense." See Herbert A. Giles, *A Chinese English Dictionary* (Shanghai, 1912; reprint, Taipei: Ch'eng Wen Publishing Company, 1972), 211.
36. *The Great Learning, the Doctrine of the Mean*, the *Analects*, and the *Mencius*.
37. Jonathan D. Spence, *Emperor of China: Self-portrait of K'ang-hsi* (New York: Vintage Books, 1988), 45–46.
38. Xu Ke, *Qingbai leichao*, 6.
39. A third degree graduate under the imperial examination system. Often translated as "doctorate."

of the Thirteen Yamen and as a tutor in the palace school for young eunuchs.[40] Asitan, a native speaker of Manchu, instructed the young eunuchs in the Manchu language until he lost his position in 1661, after the Thirteen Yamen were abolished and replaced by the Imperial Household Department.

The fate of eunuch education remains unclear from this date until Kangxi established the eunuch school known as the *Zhangfang Guanxue* (長房官學 The Eunuch School located in the Apartments of the Eldest Son) in 1696.[41] From this point until 1796, a period of one hundred years, more than ten young eunuchs at a time received an education at the eunuch school.[42] As during the reign of Shunzhi, one Han Chinese was sent to instruct the young eunuchs. The Qianlong emperor would later comment that eunuchs had always been educated by a Han Chinese instructor who lived with his eunuch students in a dormitory and instructed them in how to recognize simple characters.[43] Eunuchs studying the *Qingshu* (清書 Manchu language books) were instructed in Manchu in the *Zhangfang* while those studying the *Hanshu* (漢書 Chinese language books) were taught how to read and write Chinese characters in a nearby location. In both instances, the young eunuchs received instruction from copyists sent from the Imperial Household Department rather than from Han Chinese sent from the *Wanshandian*.[44]

Qianlong's downgrading of the quality of instructors of eunuch education from Han Chinese associated with the *Wanshandian* to Imperial Household Department copyists reflects the emperor's belief that providing eunuchs with an education would only lead to eunuch abuses and interference in the government as in the Ming. "He asserted that 'literacy only made it easier for eunuchs, such as those in the Directorate of Ceremonial in Ming times, to satisfy their own greed and ambitions. What harm is there in eunuch illiteracy?' he asked rhetorically. 'All they need to be able to do is recognize a few characters and that's all.'"[45] Eunuchs from the late Qing attest to the small numbers of literate eunuchs at court. The rural origins of the majority of eunuchs ensured that less than twenty percent entered the palace able to recognize characters.[46] Denied access to an education once they were employed by the court, the majority of eunuchs remained illiterate.

While mid- and late Qing emperors regarded an educated eunuch as an invitation to eunuch meddling in the government, women of the court appear to have favored and even promoted the education of eunuchs in their service. For example, the Empress Dowager Cixi selected literate eunuchs as her attendants. With the education of Manchu women discouraged until the early 1900s, literate eunuchs

---

40. Walter Fuchs, "Asitan," in *Eminent Chinese of the Ch'ing Period (1644–1912)*, ed. Arthur W. Hummel (Government Printing Office, Washington, DC, 1943; reprint, Taipei: SMC Publishing Inc., 1991), 14.

41. Date cited in Torbert, *The Ch'ing Imperial Household Department*, 29.

42. *Guochao gongshi*, ed. Yu Minzhong, vol. 5, 卷 73，官制 2，2209.

43. *Guochao gongshi*, ed. Yu Minzhong, vol. 5, 卷 73，官制 2，2209.

44. *Guochao gongshi*, ed. Yu Minzhong, vol. 5, 卷 73，官制 2，2209.

45. Torbert, *The Ch'ing Imperial Household Department*, 49.

46. Xin Xiuming, *Lao taijian de huiyi* (1987), 16.

provided a valuable service for the women of the court.[47] According to one Manchu palace maidservant, in this respect, the position of maidservants was lower than that of the eunuchs, since some eunuchs were given the opportunity to learn how to read.[48] Educated eunuchs enabled women of the palace to read books as well as write letters to friends.[49] The Empress Dowager Cixi arranged to have two eunuchs read to her and tell her stories.[50] Cixi even ordered young eunuchs to study foreign languages, suggesting that she relied on eunuchs as translators.[51]

The Stratification of Eunuch Society

As new members of the palace eunuch society, eunuch recruits entered the social hierarchy at the bottom rung. During the Qing, eunuch titles and ranks were "highly stratified."[52] At the very top of the eunuch pyramid of power sat the chief eunuch (*Gongdian jiandu lingshi taijian* 宮殿監督領事太監 or *Qianqinggong zongguan* 乾清宮總管 or *dazongguan* 大總管), who answered to the Imperial Household Department and the emperor concerning matters of eunuch conduct.[53] Directly under the chief eunuch were the *zongguan taijian* (總管太監 assistant chief eunuchs) who assisted their superior in the management of the palace eunuchs.[54] *Shouling taijian* (首領太監 supervisory eunuchs), who bore the responsibility for eunuchs within their departments, were supported in their duties by *fushouling taijian* (副首領太監 assistants to *shouling taijian*) chosen from the populace of *taijian* (太監 unranked eunuchs). During the early and mid-Qing, eunuch rank could not surpass grade four; however, by the late Qing, some eunuchs were eunuchs of the third or second grade.[55] However, the majority of eunuchs, who served as palace attendants, did not even possess rank.

Eunuch attire reflected the highly stratified nature of palace eunuch society. Photographs of late Qing eunuchs in attendance of the Empress Dowager Cixi present eunuch attire in its finery. Clothed in elaborately embroidered gowns and wearing hats, the eunuchs in these photographs present only one aspect of eunuch dress. As mentioned, new recruits wore simple blue robes (*paozi* 袍子) and a green unlined upper garment (*guazi* 褂子). These items had been recycled and dyed for repeated use.[56] Regulations stipulated that only eunuchs possessing rank could wear

47. Isaac Taylor Headland, *Court Life in China: The Capital, Its Officials and People* (New York: Fleming H. Revell Company, 1909), 231.
48. Jin Yi and Shen Yiling, *Gongnü tan wanglu* (Beijing: Forbidden City Press, 1992), 17.
49. Headland, *Court Life in China*, 231.
50. Xin Xiuming, *Lao taijian de huiyi* (1992), 37.
51. Xin Xiuming, *Lao taijian de huiyi* (1992), 188.
52. Evelyn S. Rawski, *The Last Emperors: A Social History of Qing Imperial Institutions* (Berkeley: University of California Press, 1998), 165.
53. Torbert, *The Ch'ing Imperial Household Department*, 42.
54. Torbert, *The Ch'ing Imperial Household Department*, 42.
55. Yu Huaqing, *Zhongguo huanguan zhidushi* (Shanghai: Renmin chubanshe, 1993), 466.
56. Xin Xiuming, *Lao taijian de huiyi* (1992), 64.

Figure 4.3
Zhang Qianhe 張謙和,
Chuxiugong zongguan taijian
儲秀宮總管太監

Figure 4.4
Empress Dowager Cixi attended by eunuchs, 1903. Photograph by Yu Xunling, ocw.mit.edu, public domain, https://commons.wikimedia. org/w/index.php?curid=21925529

hats. The color of the hat, ranging from red to different shades of blue, to white or gold, revealed the eunuch to be of the second through eighth grades respectively.[57] The type of bird embroidered on a eunuch's robe also indicated his official rank and title.[58] Even wearing particular items of clothing, such as the wearing of the *magua* (馬褂 a short riding jacket), was a right reserved for those in the upper echelons of the eunuch hierarchy, specifically *zongguan* and *shouling taijian*.[59]

Eunuch attire also varied according to the season and the occasion. Eunuchs wore gray and blue in the spring, dark green and camel in the summer, blue and gray in autumn, crimson and violet on birthdays, and green and purple on death anniversaries.[60] Western observers, apparently unaware of the above variations, when describing late Qing eunuchs would note: they "invariably dress in sombre coloured garments (bought by themselves), such as an ash-coloured long coat (p'ao-tzu [*paozi*] 袍子), and over this a dark-blue shorter coat (kua-tzu [*guazi*] 褂子), trowsers of some dark material, and always the official hat and boots when on duty or out walking;—the boots are more square at the toes than those generally worn by officials."[61] According to J.-J. Matignon, eunuchs could be easily spotted due to their "somber costume and their square-tipped shoes which were almost always boots made out of silk or wool."[62] Eunuchs in service during the late Qing note that all eunuchs wore green shoes, while in reality the style of shoe depended on the eunuch's rank. The complexity of eunuch attire according to rank reflects just one form of stratification within eunuch society.

Aside from rank, the proximity of the eunuch's duties to the emperor determined eunuch status.[63] At the most fundamental level, there were two types of Qing palace eunuchs, inner court eunuchs (*neigong taijian* 內宮太監) and outer court eunuchs (*waiwei taijian* 外圍太監).[64] Inner court eunuchs directly served the emperor, his empresses and concubines, and imperial sons and princesses.[65] Outer court eunuchs only indirectly served the imperial court and were under the management of the various *yamen* of the *Jingshifang*, the Imperial Household Department, or the *Libu* (禮部 Board of Rites), the *Gongbu* (工部 Board of Works), etc.[66] Albert Mann has characterized the difference in "the prestige value" of the two groups as "roughly equivalent to those of house and field work in American slavery."[67]

---

57. Pu Jia and Pu Jie, *Wanqing diwang shenghuo jianwen*, vol. 1, 205.

58. Pu Jia and Pu Jie, *Wanqing diwang shenghuo jianwen*, vol. 1, 205.

59. Li Guang, "Qingji de taijian" in *Wanqing gongting shenghuo jianwen*, ed. Zhang Wenhui (1982), 160.

60. Pu Jia and Pu Jie, *Wanqing diwang shenghuo jianwen*, vol. 1, 205.

61. George Carter Stent, "Chinese Eunuchs," *Journal of the North China Branch of the Royal Asiatic Society*, New Series, no. 11 (1877): 178.

62. J.-J. Matignon, *Superstition, Crime et Misère en Chine: Souvenirs de Biologie Sociale* (Paris: Masson et Cie, 1899), 193.

63. Rawski, *The Last Emperors*, 166.

64. Tang Yinian, *Qing gong taijian* (Shenyang: Liaoning daxue chubanshe, 1993), 24.

65. Tang Yinian, *Qing gong taijian*, 24.

66. Tang Yinian, *Qing gong taijian*, 24.

67. Albert Mann, "The Influence of Eunuchs in the Politics and Economy of the Ch'ing Court 1861–1907" (MA thesis, University of Washington, 1957), 53.

The Qing divided inner court eunuchs into five groups based mostly on whom they served: the emperor, the empress and concubines, the empress dowager, the imperial sons and princess, and the general service system.[68] According to Tang Yinian, during the Qing, these five groups consisted of approximately 400–500 eunuchs, in other words twenty to twenty-five percent of the Qing palace eunuch workforce. In direct contact with the imperial family, inner court eunuchs enjoyed a higher status and considerably more power than outer court eunuchs.

The majority of Qing palace eunuchs fell under the outer court eunuch designation due to the menial nature of their duties. Outer court eunuchs were managed by the *Jingshifang* as well as their individual departments. Outer court eunuchs could also be divided into five groups: those who worked in the imperial gardens, parks, altars, and temples; the *zongguan* within the Imperial Household Department; those in the imperial tombs and the Imperial Household Department; those who entertained the imperial family as actors and musicians; and those serving in miscellaneous capacities.[69] While outer court eunuchs received lower pay and fewer privileges than their counterparts within the inner court, they did possess one advantage. Living outside the palace, these eunuchs were not subject to many of the strict rules and etiquette requirements imposed upon eunuchs of the inner court.

Duties

One of the most fundamental reasons behind the Chinese practice of emasculation, to ensure the purity of the imperial line, has led many to assume that eunuchs served no other purpose than to serve the imperial concubines and to facilitate the emperor's sexual encounters with the members of his harem. Captivated by this image of eunuchs as "keepers of the harem," many historians have reconstructed an extremely limited view of the role of eunuchs within the palace. By focusing solely on eunuchs in these roles, scholars have left readers with the impression that eunuchs served the court merely as attendants for the women of the court. Unofficial histories of the palace perpetuate this stereotype by feeding the imaginations of their readers with descriptions of the nightly process of choosing the emperor's sexual partner, the delivery of the chosen empress or concubines (naked and wrapped in a blanket), and the recording of the time of the sexual encounter. However, as Harold Kahn correctly points out, more reliable official histories which do not include such accounts, respect the privacy of the emperor's sex life and reveal only the eunuch's mundane duties such as waiting attendance, standing guard, and keeping the palace clean.[70]

Many inner court and outer court eunuchs found themselves relegated to performing menial labor such as opening and closing the palace gates, standing guard,

---

68. Tang Yinian, *Qing gong taijian*, 24.
69. Tang Yinian, *Qing gong taijian*, 188.
70. Harold L. Kahn, *Monarchy in the Emperor's Eyes* (Cambridge, MA: Harvard University Press, 1971), 52–54.

sweeping, cleaning, or serving. However, eunuchs performed a myriad of duties within the palace. The memoirs of Pu Yi, the last Qing emperor, give one an idea of the wide variety of roles eunuchs filled within the palace. Eunuch duties included:

> transmitting imperial edicts, leading officials to audiences, and receiving memorials; handling official documents of the various offices of the Household Department, receiving money and grain sent by treasuries outside the palace, and keeping a fire watch; looking after the books of the library, the antiques, calligraphy, paintings, clothing, fowling-pieces, bows and arrows: keeping the ancient bronzes, the *objects de virtue*, the yellow girdles granted to meritorious officials, and fresh and dried fruit; fetching the Imperial Physicians to attend in the various palaces, obtaining the materials used in the palace by outside builders; burning incense before the records and precepts of the emperor's ancestors, their portraits, and the gods; checking the comings and goings of the officials of the various departments, keeping the registers of the attendance of the Hanlin academicians and of the watches of the officers of the guard; storing the imperial seals; recording the actions of the sovereign; flogging offending eunuchs and serving women; feeding the various living creatures in the palace; sweeping the palace buildings and keeping the gardens tidy; checking the accuracy of the chiming clocks; cutting the emperor's hair; preparing medicine; singing opera; reciting classics and burning incense as Taoist monks in the City Temple; becoming lamas in the Yung Ho Kung [*Yonghegong*] as substitutes for the emperor; and many other duties.[71]

Clearly, eunuchs served the court as more than keepers of the harem. Although eunuchs certainly provided this service for the court, they also performed the numerous daily tasks necessary to keep the palace running smoothly. An examination of several of the duties cited in Pu Yi's list, particularly those requiring specialized training, presents a more balanced portrayal of the services that eunuchs provided the court.

Eunuch Clergy

Eunuchs trained in the various religions of the court—Buddhism, Daoism, and Tibetan Buddhism—played a vital role in the dissemination and practice of religion inside the palace walls. From their appointments to the numerous Buddhist, Daoist, and Tibetan Buddhist temples located within the Great Within (*da nei* 大內),[72] eunuch religious clergy especially attended to the spiritual needs of the women of the palace. Eunuch priests gave these women, who were prohibited from engaging in any unsupervised contact with non-emasculated males, access to religion. However, the dismissal of all eunuchs serving as Buddhist monks and Daoist priests during the Daoguang reign period (1821–1850) resulted in palace women having

---

71. Aisin-Gioro Pu Yi, *From Emperor to Citizen: The Autobiography of Aisin-Gioro Pu Yi*, trans. W. J. F. Jenner (Beijing, 1964; reprint, New York: Oxford University Press, 1987), 62–63.
72. Xin Xiuming, *Lao taijian de huiyi* (1992), 93.

access only to lama eunuchs connected to the *Zhongzhengdian* (中正殿 the center for Tibetan Buddhist ritual in the Forbidden City).[73] Late Qing contemporaries such as Stent note that eighteen lama eunuchs, representing *Luohan* (Arhats) or "the attendants of Kuan-yin [*Guanyin*], 觀音, the goddess of mercy", served the women of the palace.[74] Palace regulations record the number of lama eunuchs as even higher, listing twenty-five specific positions for eunuch lama service within the palace. Within the *Zhongzhengdian*, three eunuchs served as *shouling lama*, and twelve as *lama taijian*. Two eunuchs were also studying the Tibetan Buddhist faith. For an hour sometime between 5 a.m. and 7 a.m., these eunuchs could be found in the courtyards of each palace, chanting scriptures and expiating the sins of the dead (*chaodu* 超度).[75] In addition to "attending to" the religious needs of the palace women, lama eunuchs were responsible for chanting sutras and substituting for the emperor at the *Yonghegong* (雍和宫 Palace of Eternal Harmony or The Yonghe Temple).[76] In the early morning on the first and fifteenth of each month, lama eunuchs would lead eunuchs from each of the large Tibetan Buddhist temples into the palace to chant and expiate sins (*chaodu*).[77] Eight eunuchs (one *shouling lama* and seven *lama taijian*) were also assigned to perform spiritual functions at the imperial tombs.[78]

Travel accounts such as those of Stent and Matignon present service as a eunuch lama as a highly sought-after position since, as such, eunuchs would receive double pay (as both eunuch and priest).[79] However, salaries of *lama taijian* listed in the *Palace Regulations* do not support this claim. In fact, one finds the pay of the highest-ranking lama eunuchs, three *taels* per month, to be comparable to that of other eunuchs within the palace possessing the same rank. Moreover, the remaining lama eunuchs received salaries at the same level (two *taels*) as the majority of palace eunuchs.[80]

Christian missionaries soon discovered the benefits of eunuch catechists in the dissemination of religion among the palace women and sought to convert eunuchs to their faith. While it remains unclear how many eunuchs practiced Christianity during the Qing, one periodically finds references to Christian eunuchs in Western sources. For example, in the writings of the Jesuit Antoine Thomas (1644–1709), Thomas notes the tolerance of the Kangxi emperor towards one particular Christian eunuch who was appointed as the prefect of the garden of the empress even after refusing to offer sacrifices to the Manchu and Chinese gods in the presence of the

---

73. Xin Xiuming, *Lao taijian de huiyi* (1992), 194.

74. Stent, "Chinese Eunuchs," 173.

75. Xin Xiuming, *Lao taijian de huiyi* (1992), 194.

76. Aisin-Gioro Pu Yi, *From Emperor to Citizen*, 173.

77. Xin Xiuming, *Lao taijian de huiyi* (1992), 194–95.

78. *Qinding gongzhong xianxing zeli* 欽定宮中現行則例 (QDGZXXZL) [Imperially authorized laws and regulations of conduct within the palace] (Reprint, Taipei: Wenhai chubanshe, 1979), 卷4，728–29.

79. Matignon, *Superstition, Crime et Misère en Chine*, 190.

80. QDGZXXZL, 卷4，705.

emperor.[81] At present, the extent of influence that Christian eunuchs had upon the religious beliefs of the imperial court remains unclear.

The involvement of eunuchs in religious roles within the court is fascinating, since their physical disfigurement prevented them from fully participating in religious offerings. According to Stent, eunuchs were allowed to enter temples to burn incense and to fast but were prohibited from mounting the platform to confess and be absolved by a priest. Stent adds, "In this, however, they are not worse off than many others, for no cripple or deformed person, no one short of an eye, finger, or any portion of the body, nor any woman in her courses, etc., can ascend the dais."[82] Despite this form of religious discrimination, eunuchs managed to serve as religious leaders and attend to the spiritual needs of the inhabitants of the palace. More detailed accounts of the role of eunuchs in performing spiritual functions must be found before one can fully understand this apparent contradiction.

Actors

Qing eunuchs also served as actors and singers, performing Chinese opera for audiences within the imperial court, especially the women of the palace. Undoubtedly, eunuch actors emasculated prior to the onset of puberty and the resulting deepening of the male voice would have been highly valued in the female roles. As with the castrati in Europe, removal of the testes prolonged the ability of the eunuch to sing in ranges much higher than that of non-emasculated adult men. According to Stent, the Qing employed some 300 eunuch actors specifically for providing theatrical performances for the palace women. However, eunuch actors performed for much wider audiences, including the emperor, princes and grand ministers, and even foreign visitors to the palace such as the American artist Katherine Carl.[83] The recollections of the late Qing eunuch actor Geng Jinxi 耿進喜 support the contention that eunuch actors performed for more than female audiences.[84] Geng, who entered the palace in 1894, at the age of fifteen *sui*, was sent to study military plays and the *xiaosheng* 小生 role[85] at the *Shengpingshu* (升平署 Court Theatrical Bureau, colloquially referred to as the *Nanfu* 南府) after he caught the attention of the empress dowager. Geng notes that he also performed for the emperor. However, he never performed for audiences in which both the emperor and the empress dowager

81. John Witek, SJ. "Reporting to Rome: Some Major Events in the Christian Community in Peking, 1686–1687," in *Echanges Culturels et Réligieux entre la Chine et l'Occident*, ed. Edward J. Malatesta, SJ, Yves Raguin, SJ, and Adrianus C. Dudink (Taipei: Ricci Institute, 1995), 307–8.

82. Stent, "Chinese Eunuchs," 178.

83. Xin Xiuming, *Lao taijian de huiyi* (1992), 100. See Katherine Augusta Carl, *With the Empress Dowager of China* (1906; reprint New York: KPI Limited, 1986), 58–63.

84. Geng recalled his time spent within the palace at a national conference of those in the traditional opera profession convened by the Department of Culture in 1950. See Zhu Jiyan, "Taijian tan wanglu: Ningshougong taijian Geng Jinxi tan," *Zijincheng* 1 (1980): 42.

85. A role in Chinese opera.

were present. According to Liana Chen, the Empress Dowager Cixi employed 180 eunuchs in her own theater troupe that often performed alongside civilian actors at her many theatrical performances.[86]

Designated as outer court eunuchs, these eunuchs lived in and fell under the jurisdiction of the *Shengpingshu*, located outside the palace but still within the confines of the Imperial City.[87] Here, eunuchs specializing in the arts studied music and acting.[88] Positions as eunuch actors could often bring added benefits. Actors who attracted the attention of the emperor or an empress were often rewarded with gifts or favored treatment.[89] The lifestyle of eunuchs attached to the *Shengpingshu* appears to have been quite different from that of eunuchs living within the palace. Due to their training in the arts, *Shengpingshu* eunuchs had extended ties to their eunuch masters (teachers). Each of the different roles customary to Chinese drama had a master, a disciple, an elder master, and a grandson disciple (*tusun* 徒孫).[90] Such connections, when combined with the specialized training these eunuchs received, made leaving the *Shengpingshu*, to serve in another capacity within the palace, a difficult if not impossible task.[91]

Eunuch Physicians

Eunuchs also served in positions requiring a degree of knowledge in medicine. Records from the Imperial Pharmacy indicate that eunuch doctors treated the female inhabitants of the palace. One memorial from the Kangxi period sent in by officials from the Imperial Household Department reports the birth of a princess by an imperial concubine. According to the eunuch physician (*taijian daifu* 太監大夫) in attendance, both the imperial concubine and the princess were doing well.[92] Eunuch physicians, due to their emasculation would have been given access to women denied to male physicians, namely the ability to easily enter the women's quarters within the palace and to treat their female patients. As eunuchs were routinely assigned to assist their female masters in performing intimate tasks such as dressing, one can assume then that it would not have been unusual for a eunuch physician to be allowed to touch a female patient, either to take her pulse or to assist with the delivery of a royal child.

The ability to treat the women of the palace also exposed eunuch doctors to being charged with medical malpractice when their treatments had unintended

---

86. Liana Chen, "The Empress Dowager as Dramaturg: Reinventing Late-Qing Court Theatre," *Nan Nü: Men, Women and Gender in Early and Imperial China* 14, no. 1 (2012): 23–24, 39–40.
87. Xin Xiuming, *Lao taijian de huiyi* (1992), 99.
88. Xin Xiuming, *Lao taijian de huiyi* (1992), 99.
89. Stent, "Chinese Eunuchs," 174.
90. Xin Xiuming, *Lao taijian de huiyi* (1992), 181.
91. Xin Xiuming, *Lao taijian de huiyi* (1992), 181.
92. First Historical Archives, Beijing, *Kangxi chao manwen zhupi zouzhe quanyi* (Beijing: Zhongguo shehui kexue chubanshe, 1996), 1538, entry 3711.

consequences. In a malpractice case from 1713, Wang Jinchao 王金超, a eunuch physician, was charged with contributing to a female patient's death.[93] According to the memorial, Wang, who is characterized as someone who "did not understand medical books or the properties of medicines," attempted to treat a young woman suffering from gastrointestinal problems over the course of three days. After taking the medicine prescribed by Wang, the patient could no longer eat. At this point, Wang gave the patient another medication. Shortly thereafter, on the third day of treatment, the patient died. Aside from his lack of knowledge in medicine, Wang was criticized for his failure to alert those in charge or his supervisor of the severity of the woman's illness so that they could have called in a physician from the outside, presumably a non-eunuch physician. What is interesting is that, according to Wang, he was notified about the patient five days earlier than the official account stated and started treatment that day but was told the following day when he went to examine the young patient that she was doing better and that there was no need to see her. Four days later, a eunuch from the Imperial Pharmacy was sent to get Wang, but upon his arrival he was once again informed that the young patient was doing better. That day, however, the patient developed a fever and a dry mouth. At this point, Wang was given access to the patient. In the end, Wang was sentenced to wear the cangue for three months, to receive one hundred lashes, and exiled to herd animals in Wula[94] 烏拉. The other eunuchs involved in calling Wang to come to treat the patient were also punished for their failure to contact a qualified physician when the young woman was so clearly seriously ill. These two eunuchs were sentenced to wear the cangue for two months, receive one hundred lashes, and sent to be supervised by their eunuch superior. Eunuchs serving in the Imperial Pharmacy during this episode were also punished for their involvement but received lesser sentences.

Eunuch doctors also appear to have treated commoners outside the palace walls. In a case of malpractice from 1814, *Yuanmingyuan fushouling taijian* 副首領太監 Miao Jinyu 苗進玉 was arrested and charged with the death of commoner Xu Zhu 徐柱 outside the Fuyuan Gate 福園門.[95] In the brief record, the location in which Miao treated Xu is noted as well as the cause of death, namely Miao's incorrect needling technique (*wu zhen* 誤針). The document also makes clear that eunuch doctors, like other eunuchs who received specialized training, should know their place and be supervised by their respective departments so that such occurrences could be prevented in the future.

Miao's case also provides insight into where eunuch doctors received their training. Eunuchs are noted as receiving medical training at the Imperial Pharmacy. Records indicate that, at a given time, two eunuch sub-department heads and twenty eunuch subordinates were assigned to this department. Their responsibilities

---

93. First Historical Archives, Beijing, *Kangxi chao manwen zhupi zouzhe quanyi*, 878, entry 2193.
94. Present day Jilin Province. Wula was located just north of the city of Jilin 吉林 on the 1820 map of Tan Qixiang. "Wula" is a Chinese transliteration of Manchu *ula* (a large river).
95. *QDGZXXZL*, 嘉慶19年潤2月初7日，139–40.

included summoning doctors to feel pulses, preparing medicine, sitting watch, etc.[96] Serving in such positions, these eunuchs would have become familiar with the use of medications to treat different diseases and the art of feeling pulses. While criticized for their lack of medical understanding or punished for their misdiagnosis and failed treatments of their imperial patients in the two above-mentioned cases, these eunuch medical practitioners must have provided a beneficial service for the Qing imperial court and its inhabitants; otherwise, eunuchs would have been prohibited from working in that capacity.

The case of Wang Jinchao reveals that eunuch doctors were considered subordinate in their roles to other doctors. When questioned, two eunuchs working in the Imperial Pharmacy recounted that, when Wang was preparing the medication, they had specifically asked him if he had consulted with a doctor from the outside (*waimian daifu* 外面大夫) about the prescription to which he replied "yes." In his interrogation, Wang confirmed that he had consulted a doctor before administering the prescription. At present, it remains unclear if eunuch doctors treated other eunuchs. In the few records found to date that mention eunuch doctors, one can clearly see that, despite the assignment of eunuchs to roles in health care, a eunuch doctor's medical skills, and right to even treat patients without supervision are clearly called into question.

Living Quarters

Within the palace, eunuchs congregated in living quarters known as *tatan* 他坦, situated throughout the Forbidden City and its environs. The locations of the various *tatan* were determined by the eunuch's department and the nature of his duties. Eunuchs of the inner court, those who directly served the emperor or those connected to the various palaces within the Forbidden City, lived in close proximity to their employers. Eunuchs of the Presence (those in the service of the emperor) lived in quarters situated in the narrow passageways between the walls that ran east to west within the palace.[97] These locations, adjacent to the sewage drainage system for the palace,[98] reflect the subservience of all eunuchs to the emperor, regardless of rank or position. Within each of the palaces, the *tatans* were located at the sides of the main building, allowing the eunuch to "be readily summoned when wanted."[99] He Rong'er, a late Qing Manchu maidservant, recalled that the more aged eunuchs of the palace tended to live together in an alley (*hutong*) running north to south on the east side of Beihai.[100]

---

96. Tang Yinian, *Qing gong taijian*, 194.
97. Du Wanyan, *Zhongguo huanguan shi* (Taipei: Wenjin chubanshe, 1996), 51.
98. Hashikawa Tokio, "Kangan Oboegaki," *Bungei Shunju* (Dec. 1959): 254.
99. Stent, "Chinese Eunuchs," 177.
100. Jin and Shen, *Gongnü tan wanglu*, 19.

Outer court eunuchs, who made up approximately seventy-five percent of the eunuch workforce, were not allowed to live within the Forbidden City. Instead, the Qing housed the majority of their eunuch staff in the various *yamen* found within the environs of the Forbidden City.[101] According to Tang Yinian, upon entering the system, these eunuchs would be given an allowance for rent ranging from 500 to 800 *wen* 文, determinant on position and rank.[102] Rooms appear to have been shared by eunuchs. Sun Yaoting 孫耀庭, the last surviving Qing eunuch, roomed with a *zongguan taijian* from the acting troupe (*xiban*) and later a *xiao taijian* in the service of the imperial concubine Duan Kang.[103] Eunuchs who had been discharged due to sickness, retirement, or crimes did not receive housing.

Eunuchs also received monthly compensation for their services in the form of money and rice.[104] The amount of pay and rice a eunuch received corresponded to his rank within the eunuch hierarchy. During the Qing, the average eunuch's monthly salary could range from two to eight *taels* 兩 per month and from one to eight *hu*[105] 斛 of rice. As seen below, the minority of eunuchs in the upper echelons of the eunuch hierarchy received comparatively much higher salaries.

> During the reigns of Guangxu and Xuantong, *dazongguan* [received] one hundred *taels* of food money . . . , forty *pin* 品 of vegetables, and two *tang* 湯 per month, *shouling taijian* [received] fifty *taels* of food money, thirty *pin* of vegetables, and two *tang* per month; *xiao taijian* [received] ten *taels* of food money, four *pin* of vegetables, and one *tang*; each department's *shouling taijian* [received] ten *taels* of food money, three *pin* of vegetables, and one *tang*.[106]

The amount of allowance each eunuch received depended upon the location of his duties rather than rank; some locations did not pay an allowance to those in the upper echelons of the eunuch hierarchy.[107] Eunuch salaries were intended to supply the eunuch with enough funds to cover the costs of food and clothing. In addition, Qing eunuchs routinely supplemented their salaries with gifts or money given on special occasions. These included imperial births and marriages, birthdays, and festivals. On such occasions, eunuchs might receive goods such as leather, jewelry, jade, brocade, or silk.[108]

While the salaries of eunuchs in the upper echelons of the eunuch hierarchy such as those holding the posts of *zongguan* or *shouling* allowed for luxuries such as private kitchens, most eunuchs lived more modest lifestyles.[109] During the late Qing,

101. Tang Yinian, *Qing gong taijian*, 60.
102. Tang Yinian, *Qing gong taijian*, 60.
103. Lan Jie, "Zai shi taijian Sun Yaoting tingyou gongji," *Zijincheng* 4 (1993): 42.
104. Tang Yinian, *Qing gong taijian*, 60.
105. A unit of dry measure.
106. Pu Jia and Pu Jie, *Wanqing diwang shenghuo jianwen*, 210.
107. Yu Huaqing, *Zhongguo huanguan zhidushi*, 483.
108. *Wanqing gongting yishi*, ed. Ding Yanshi 191.
109. Pu Jia and Pu Jie, *Wanqing diwang shenghuo jianwen*, 210.

eunuchs would often pool their resources and save time and money by "form[ing] messes" in which each would supply a certain amount of meat, vegetables, etc.[110] For example, during the late Qing, eunuchs serving in the Empress Dowager Cixi's palace all ate together in one building.[111]

Eunuchs could find all the necessities of daily life within the confines of the Forbidden City. According to the late Qing eunuch Xin Xiuming, inner court eunuchs could visit the tailor, have their heads shaved, their clothes starched, or even have a bite to eat at one of the *tatan* that lined the Western River just outside of the *Neiyoumen* (內右門 Inner Right Gate).[112] According to Geng Jinxi 耿進喜, a eunuch actor during the late Qing, eunuchs could also eat at the *Siheyi* 四合義 and *Daheyi* 大合義 restaurants, both located in a building next to the wall of the Eastern Shenwu Gate. Geng noted that these restaurants catered exclusively to eunuchs employed by the Imperial Household Department.[113] Xin Xiuming adds that Siheyi Restaurant was a small restaurant run by a Mr. Wang located within the Forbidden City along the Western River. Here, eunuchs could order a *jiangrou juanbing* (醬肉卷餅 soy sauce beef roll) or a bowl of bean porridge and not spend a lot of money. According to Xin, this restaurant's clientele was not exclusively eunuchs; workers also dined there, finding it more convenient than going outside the palace to eat.[114]

Conclusion

Despite the enormity of the impact of emasculation upon a recruit's physical being, the act was merely the first step in his transformation into a palace eunuch. Entrance into palace service completed the metamorphosis of the emasculate into eunuch. As a palace eunuch, the emasculate found that his physical disfigurement now defined every aspect of his life, from his identity, to his status, to his assignments.

As the recruit entered the Forbidden City and service as a palace eunuch, he lost his old identity both in name and in history. He now became identified through social markers such as a new shared surname, his point of entry into the eunuch system (via a certain *daozijiang* or grouping of eunuch recruits), or native place. Even the eunuch's assignment within the palace came to define him. From that moment on, in official correspondence throughout the eunuch's life to his tombstone in death, his name, native place, age at the time of emasculation, and palace designation would become the essential elements of his identity.

The emasculate's new status as a servant of the imperial court became readily apparent as soon as he entered the palace eunuch system. New eunuch recruits, despite joining the ranks of the palace's servile staff, soon found themselves at the

---

110. Stent, "Chinese Eunuchs," 177.
111. Zhu Jiyan, "Taijian tan wanglu: Ningshougong taijian Geng Jinxi tan," *Zijincheng* 2 (1980): 40.
112. Xin Xiuming, *Lao taijian de huiyi* (1992), 7.
113. Zhu Jiyan, "Taijian tan wangle," *Zijincheng* 2 (1980): 40.
114. Xin Xiuming, *Lao taijian de huiyi* (1992), 130.

bottom of the social hierarchy within the palace. As residents of the palace, eunuchs found their freedoms of mobility, leave, association, and fraternization with Chinese society eclipsed by the wants and needs of the emperor and his court. Trained under the master–apprentice system, eunuchs quickly discovered that the emperor was not their only master. During the apprentice period, the eunuch masses waited on their eunuch superiors as servants, an act that reveals the complicated status of eunuchs within the palace. While emasculation was designed to keep them submissive, palace practices enabled some eunuchs to rise above their intended status at times and to enjoy service designed for the emperor (albeit the eunuch supervisor could easily claim that this was all for the good of emperor and ensuring that the eunuch received the training necessary to wait on his imperial masters).

Emasculation, the most important criterion for palace eunuchs, defined the nature of eunuch employment. Fascination with the role of eunuchs in facilitating the sexual encounters between the emperor and members of his harem has resulted in the stereotypical representation of eunuchs as solely "keepers of the harem." In reality, Qing eunuch duties were multifaceted. Qing eunuchs performed a myriad of duties designed to keep the palace and the government operating smoothly. While many eunuchs found themselves delegated to perform menial duties within the palace such as sweeping and cleaning, eunuchs also served in positions requiring specialized training such as medicine, acting, and religion. Eunuchs whose roles pushed the boundaries of their servile position, such as those practicing medicine, found themselves judged by a different set of standards than those of their non-emasculated counterparts, especially when something went wrong.

The Qing palace eunuch workforce encompassed a wide variety of eunuch ranks and duties; hierarchies of rank and prestige stratified the eunuch workforce. *Zongguan* and *shouling taijian* were few in number, and attaining such positions was often an unrealistic goal for the majority of eunuchs. Most eunuchs spent their careers relegated to the position of the unranked. Efforts to prevent eunuch intervention in the government during the early and mid-Qing ensured that few eunuchs ever rose above the fourth grade. The physical location of the eunuch's appointment, as well as whom he served, also determined the eunuch's prestige within the palace and among society. Within the eunuch hierarchy, only inner court eunuchs enjoyed direct contact with the emperor and the imperial family. Making up twenty to twenty-five percent of the eunuch workforce, inner court eunuchs enjoyed privileges and prestige rarely afforded the remaining seventy-five percent of eunuchs. However, outer court eunuchs, by benefit of their appointment outside of the inner sanctum of the emperor, often enjoyed advantages in increased mobility and freedoms rarely afforded to their inner court counterparts.

Emasculation also determined the amount of education eunuchs would receive. With emperors such as Qianlong desiring to confine eunuchs to roles similar to maidservants (albeit emasculated ones), eunuch education became viewed as an invitation to eunuch corruption and interference in the government. As a result, only a select few among the eunuch population attained literacy. However, the specialized nature of some eunuch duties, particularly those in the Chancery of Memorials, ensured that a small percentage of eunuchs continued to receive instruction in reading and writing. Moreover, the reliance of the Manchu women of the court on literate eunuchs to teach them the Classics and to facilitate their correspondence with friends and communication with foreign visitors ensured the perpetuation of some degree of eunuch education within the palace.

Emasculation and employment within the palace both physically and socially altered the eunuch. As described by Albert Mann, eunuchs became "creatures of Court life."[115] Inside the palace walls, eunuchs lived their lives to satisfy the wants and needs of their masters. As a result, the wants and needs of the eunuch population routinely were ignored, regulated, and often prohibited.

As will be seen, a small number of eunuchs, uninhibited by restrictions on the eunuch lifestyle intended to suppress eunuch political activity and power, manipulated eunuch society to meet their individual desires for power and wealth. Within the decorum and etiquette of the palace, these eunuchs created a parallel world, a world that catered to eunuchs' and palace inhabitants' desires to escape from the drudgery of palace life.

---

115. Albert Mann, "The Influence of Eunuchs in the Politics," 24.

5

The Parallel World of the Eunuch

Eunuch Society

Restrictions placed on eunuch responsibilities and demands of subservience to the imperial court successfully prevented Qing eunuchs from obtaining overt and recognized political power like their Ming predecessors had. However, systematic suppression of eunuchs did not eradicate their ability to recreate the social and familial bonds denied them or to find opportunities to pursue financial gain and power. Accounts of Qing palace life reveal that alongside the decorum and restrictions of palace life existed a parallel world, a world in which eunuchs recreated the bonds denied them and where some even engaged in activities considered unseemly for a servant of the emperor.

The palace eunuch system was based on the premise that eunuchs were designed to be the ideal servants for the emperor and his imperial court. The Qing perpetuated the belief that emasculation would transform eunuchs into submissive and loyal beings due to social ostracism and their lack of family ties. In reality, ensuring that eunuchs fulfilled their intended role proved to be a constant challenge for the Qing. While subservience was demanded and enforced when not readily given, eunuchs continuously challenged the role in which the system placed them. An examination of eunuch activities within the palace reveals an inherent tension that defined labor relations between eunuchs and their masters. According to Evelyn Rawski, James Scott's analysis of domination and resistance exemplifies this relationship, or the "silent struggle," between the emperor and the palace eunuch population. Rawski writes:

> As long as the dominant group successfully projects the appearance of overwhelming coercive force, implicit rejections of the public discourse tend to remain underground. In the imperial discourse, eunuchs and bondservants should be hardworking and efficient, utterly loyal and devoted to the emperor. Yet the criminal cases display lazy, thieving, gossiping betrayers of the imperial trust, whose existence contradicts the central tenet of the Qing social order, namely that the emperor's persona commands complete obedience.[1]

---

1. Evelyn S. Rawski, *The Last Emperors: A Social History of Qing Imperial Institutions* (Berkeley: University of California Press, 1998), 161.

While not all eunuchs fit the stereotypical profile of "lazy, thieving, gossiping betrayers of the imperial trust," the actions of the majority reveal that the ideal for eunuchs was not always the reality.

Within the palace walls and the environs of the palace, eunuchs endeavored to balance the submissiveness required of them by the imperial court with a degree of agency in their lives by sustaining their ties with the outside world, creating their own society, and engaging in activities that disrupted the harmony of the palace. Despite emasculation's intended cessation of a eunuch's ties with society and his family, eunuchs openly continued their interaction with the world outside the palace, especially with their families. They also actively created new bonds by forming native place associations with their fellow eunuchs and relationships with other palace servants. They also engaged in prohibited forms of entertainment such as drinking, gambling, and drugs—behavior that not only disrupted the harmony of the imperial residence but also directly contradicted the absolute power of the emperor.

Contact with Families

While emasculation was intended to sever the eunuch's ties with his family and thereby ensure his loyalty to the emperor, in reality many eunuchs still retained some measure of contact with their natal families. Despite the fact that some eunuchs hated their fathers for "volunteering" them for emasculation, familial bonds often remained intact, as eunuchs regularly sent money home, spent leave with their families, and attended their parents' funerals. He Rong'er 何榮兒, a late Qing Manchu maidservant, reveals that the inhabitants of the palace were allowed to visit with their families once a month. On a set day at the beginning of each month (*chu'er* 初二), people living within the palace could visit with their families at secluded location to the west of the Shenwu Gate (*Shenwumen* 神武門). Here, palace inhabitants could have conversations with their family members as well as give gifts of clothing or remit to them part or all of their monthly salaries.[2] Limiting family visits to one location, the palace enabled itself to both control and monitor contact between the palace staff and their families. Contact between some palace inhabitants and their family members could be even less frequent than once a month. In fact, some Manchu maidservants did not see their families for two or three years.[3] Transportation difficulties and costs of travel from the servant's family home to the palace contributed to the prolonged intervals between such visits.

While service in the palace may have lessened the frequency of contact with their families, these ties remained intact. Archival records reveal that filial responsibilities survived the transformation of sons into eunuchs. Eunuchs could not

---

2. Jin Yi and Shen Yiling, *Gongnü tan wanglu* (Beijing: Forbidden City Press, 1992), 19–20.
3. Jin and Shen, *Gongnü tan wanglu*, 19–20.

continue the family line, but they could in their own ways continue to respect their parents. When a eunuch's father or mother died, he could request leave to attend the funeral. Eunuchs in the upper echelons of the hierarchy would receive sixteen days off to attend a parent's funeral; other eunuchs would receive twelve days.[4] Eunuchs also spent time with family while on leave from the palace. Some eunuchs, as will be seen, even relied on their families to shelter then after they ran away from the palace.

During the reign of Qianlong (1736–1795), Norman A. Kutcher notes that the emperor allowed eunuchs to live and interact with others outside the palace walls. As a result, the *Yuanmingyuan* became much more porous during this time period.[5] Some eunuchs assigned to the *Yuanmingyuan* even spent time with their families every day. Kutcher cites the 1771 case of Liu Jinxin 劉進喜, who had drowned at age eleven. Details of the case revealed that Liu's father had routinely picked his son up every night from the palace.[6] When describing the official policy towards eunuchs at the time, Kutcher notes that that Qianlong's need to staff the *Yuanmingyuan* with young eunuchs created an atmosphere in which "the misdoings of eunuchs ought to be ignored."[7] In addition to needing to sustain the number of eunuchs (as Kutcher notes), the Qing may have considered these young eunuchs to be less of a threat due to their youth. Moreover, the lax enforcement of rules regarding contact with families, a separation that was one of the key tenets of the eunuch system, may have been due to the *Yuanmingyuan* being more of a garden-like atmosphere than the real seat of imperial power. Records from the Forbidden City noting the need to request leave to exit the palace for such everyday tasks as visiting the barber suggest that rules were enforced more strictly there.[8] The high incidence of eunuchs running away repeatedly from the Forbidden City also supports the argument that eunuch mobility may have been more restricted there as well.

As Susan Naquin has noted in her study of the Eight Trigrams Uprising of 1813, during which eunuch Trigram members facilitated the entry of the rebels into the palace, "eunuchs did not live in isolation inside the Forbidden City." Confessions of eunuchs involved in the uprising reveal that they continued to have contact with

---

4. Yu Huaqing, *Zhongguo huanguan zhidushi* (Shanghai: Renmin chubanshe, 1993), 490.
5. Norman A. Kutcher, "Unspoken Collusions: The Empowerment of Yuanming yuan Eunuchs in the Qianlong Period," *Harvard Journal of Asiatic Studies* 70, no. 2 (Dec. 2010): 475.
6. First Historical Archives, Beijing, *Neiwufu zou'an* 05-0283-04 as cited in Kutcher, "Unspoken Collusions," 475, note 71.
7. Kutcher, "Unspoken Collusions," 475.
8. In two separate undated documents from the First Historical Archives, Beijing, archived under the miscellaneous files, one notes eunuchs who had not returned after going out to have their heads shaved. First, in the thirteenth year of Tongzhi (1873), eunuch Su Wenzhi 蘇文志, had requested leave to have his head shaved and not returned. See First Historical Archives, Beijing, 宮中，雜件1017，人事類太監. Also, in the fourth year of the Daoguang reign (January 31, 1824–February 17, 1825), eunuch Wang Zhide 王志得 had requested leave to have his head shaved. See First Historical Archives, Beijing, 宮中，雜件 1019，人事類太監. As will be seen, this was one errand that gave eunuchs the means to run away from the palace eunuch system.

their families.[9] Naquin even cites the example of the father of the eunuch rebel Liu Te-ts'ai (Liu Decai) facilitating meetings between the eunuch and his rebel master via messages he left for his son at the western gate of the Forbidden City.[10] However, financial incentives motivated eunuchs to join the rebels, so contact between these eunuchs and their family members may have been more frequent than normal. Evidence suggests that the Jiaqing emperor increasingly limited eunuch contact with those outside the palace after the suppression of the Eight Trigrams.[11] In one case from the twenty-second year of his reign (approximately five years after the uprising), inner court eunuch Wang Fu 王幅 was interrogated regarding his sending of five letters.[12] Wang's letter-writing campaign began when his younger brother (*xiongdi* 兄弟) traveled to the capital to deliver a letter from their mother informing him of the violent death of his elder brother (*xiongbao* 兄胞), who had been killed by two commoners who had beaten and stabbed him. Readers of Wang's letters can immediately sense his stress about his inability to be at home dealing with the situation. Wang expresses to the man he had write the letters for him that he was unable to get leave from the palace and, since his mother was elderly, he didn't know how she was doing and he could not be at peace [until he knew]. Wang's case reveals that, despite difficulties in transportation and communication (most eunuchs were illiterate), they managed to maintain contact and have strong bonds with their families.

Eunuch Leave

In addition to bereavement leave, eunuchs were allowed to request leave from the palace for special occasions, such as a family wedding. To attend a male relative's wedding, a eunuch would receive three days of leave.[13] In addition to time restraints placed on eunuch leave, the Imperial Household Department restricted how eunuchs spent their time away from the palace. Officials from the *Zongwufu* (總務府 Office of General Affairs) were sent to check up on eunuchs to ensure that they did not travel freely, attend the theater, fraternize with other eunuchs, gamble, or fail to return to the palace at the end of their leave.[14] As will be seen, eunuchs could also request sick leave in order to recuperate from illness.

9.   Susan Naquin, *Millenarian Rebellion in China: The Eight Trigrams Uprising of 1813* (New Haven: Yale University Press, 1976), 96.
10. Naquin, *Millenarian Rebellion in China*, 148.
11. *Qinding Da Qing huidian shili* 欽定大清會典事例 (QDDQHDSL) [Imperially commissioned collected regulations of the Qing dynasty], 卷 1217 as cited in Yu Huaqing, *Zhongguo huanguan zhidushi*, 456.
12. *Guoli gugong bowuyuan*, Taipei, 軍機處 052713，嘉慶22年8月21日.
13. Yu Huaqing, *Zhongguo huanguan zhidushi*, 490.
14. Yu Huaqing, *Zhongguo huanguan zhidushi*, 490.

Family Life

Living out the majority of their lives behind the palace walls and allowed only limited time off from their duties, some eunuchs actively took measures to create their own families. The act of emasculation rendered eunuchs sexually deficient and physically incapable of reproduction. However, the removal of the body parts necessary for reproduction did not erase the eunuch's desire for a family.

Eunuch marriage was not a rarity, particularly among eunuchs who had undergone emasculation after puberty. As Jennifer Jay has shown, some eunuchs married and had children prior to emasculation.[15] Eunuchs even married after emasculation and while serving in the palace. Despite prohibitions against amorous relationships between eunuchs and palace maidservants, marriages between the two were not uncommon.[16] Eunuchs also married women who already had children, an often ideal situation for the infertile eunuch. Eunuchs also created their own families by adopting children. As described by Jay, eunuchs such as Li Lianying 李連英 (1848–1911), adopted biological nephews and nieces, a practice customary among Ming and Qing eunuchs.[17]

Despite early and mid-Qing attempts to hire only eunuchs who had never been married or fathered children,[18] shortages in the supply of candidates resulted in the relaxation of earlier restrictions. During the late Qing, the palace was both aware of and conciliatory towards eunuchs who had families. Geng Jinxi, a Ningshou palace eunuch, recalls an occasion when the Empress Dowager Cixi learned that a thirty-year-old eunuch in her service was married and had children. Upon hearing this, she then commented jokingly, "Oh, I see. You have a wife and a son, and still wanted to serve as a eunuch. Not bad."[19] During the late Qing, the Empress Dowager Cixi even arranged marriages between palace eunuchs and Manchu maidservants. One such match resulted in the marriage of an eighteen *sui* Manchu maidservant who had served the Empress Dowager Cixi from the age of thirteen, to a eunuch surnamed Liu, who was the informally adopted son (*gan erzi* 乾兒子) of the Empress's favorite, Li Lianying.[20] Earlier palace restrictions on eunuch mobility also appear to have been relaxed during the late Qing, enabling eunuchs with wives and families living outside the palace to "go out and spend a few days with them occasionally."[21]

15. Jennifer Jay, "Another Side of Chinese Eunuch History: Castration, Marriage, Adoption, and Burial," *Canadian Journal of History* XVIII (Dec. 1993): 467.
16. *Qinding gongzhong xianxing zeli* 欽定宮中現行則例 (QDGZXXZL) [Imperially authorized laws and regulations of conduct within the palace] (Reprint, Taipei: Wenhai chubanshe, 1979) 卷3，宮規，404.
17. Jay, "Another Side of Chinese Eunuch History," 475.
18. *Qinding Da Qing huidian shili* (QDDQHDSL), ed. Li Hongzhang et al. (Shanghai: Shangwu yinshuguan, 1909), 卷1216，內務府，太監事例，選驗太監，嘉慶13年.
19. Zhu Jiyan, "Taijian tan wanglu: Ningshougong taijian Geng Jinxi tan," *Zijincheng* 2 (1980): 41.
20. Jin and Shen, *Gongnü tan wanglu*, 2.
21. George Carter Stent, "Chinese Eunuchs," *Journal of the North China Branch of the Royal Asiatic Society*, New Series, no. 11 (1877): 169.

Through marriage and adoption, eunuchs may have attempted to fulfill the social responsibilities of men; however, negative social perceptions hindered eunuchs' efforts to achieve acceptance. The inability of eunuchs to reproduce, as well as the social stigma connected to emasculation, would have complicated their attempts to find a bride. However, money could often overcome such seemingly insurmountable obstacles. According to one eunuch's widow (the same palace maidservant given in marriage to eunuch Liu), once eunuchs obtained wealth either through their position or the theft of an expensive item, they would want to buy a wife, build a house, and "establish some semblance of family."[22] Such eunuchs were labeled "fake old cocks [roosters]" (*jia laogong* 假老公),[23] a term perhaps even more derogatory than *laogong* (老公 old rooster), since it implied more than simply the eunuch's inability to reproduce but also society's unwillingness to accept his family as "real."

This prejudice continued even after the fall of the Qing dynasty. A note in the local gossip section of the *Dagongbao* in 1923 echoes this sentiment. The headline reads, "Must Escape. Why would a eunuch want a wife?" The source reveals that "Li so-and-so," a eunuch living on the rice market street outside the Xuanwu Gate, had reported to the police that his wife had "escaped." The paper promised to look into the matter further, since it appeared that the eunuch was not telling the whole story. From the gossip columnist's choice of words, specifically "escaped" rather than "ran away," and the headline "Why would a eunuch need a wife?", it is clear that society viewed eunuch marriage as not only a farce but a form of bondage.[24] Stent echoes this sentiment in his reference to the marriage of the infamous Qing eunuch An Dehai 安德海. Stent writes, "He also had a wife—an unnecessary appendage to a eunuch—but one which he conceived his riches and power entitled him to indulge in."[25]

As discussed by Jay, writings by eunuchs do not suggest any change in eunuch gender post emasculation.[26] However, studies of the Chinese homosexual tradition, such as that by Bret Hinsch, present eunuchs as "the sexual favorites of emperors from the Han to the Qing."[27] Manchu-professed hostility towards Chinese homosexual customs resulted in the criminalization of homosexuality and its shrouding in secrecy. Despite Hinsch's heavy reliance on literary sources due to the dearth of archival evidence on homosexuality during the Qing, the suggestion that even a small percentage of eunuchs engaged in homosexual activities in not unrealistic. However, at present it remains unclear whether these homosexual liaisons existed

22. Jin and Shen, *Gongnü tan wanglu*, 99.
23. Jin and Shen, *Gongnü tan wanglu*, 99.
24. *Dagongbao*, April 1, 1923, 2.
25. Stent, "Chinese Eunuchs," 164.
26. Jay, "Another Side of Chinese Eunuch History," 465.
27. Bret Hinsch, *Passions of the Cut Sleeve: The Male Homosexual Tradition in China* (Berkeley: University of California Press, 1990), 63.

due to an emperor satiating his sexual desires with his servant or whether homosexuality was prevalent or even existed amongst the eunuch population.

Manchu motives for criminalizing homosexuality indirectly support the speculation that homosexuality existed among the palace eunuch population. According to M. J. Meijer, the Qing criminalized homosexuality because it threatened to prevent men from fulfilling their duties to their ancestors and from carrying on the family name.[28] Since emasculation "implied" "reproductive death," the possibility of being labeled "unfilial" for committing a homosexual act may not have inhibited some eunuchs from such liaisons. During the Ming dynasty, Chinese society had condoned homosexuality as long as it was a temporary act or a "male dissipation" that some males experienced before marriage and the fulfillment of familial responsibilities. Eunuchs inclined to become homosexuals would have had no such reasons to discontinue their same-sex activities. The restricted lifestyle of eunuchs may have also created an environment favorable to homosexuality. Palace eunuchs match Furth's criteria for men who might engage in homosexual relations. They were "unmarried and impoverished bachelors," and because palace women were legally and physically sexually off limits, they lived in an "all male environment."[29] In the end, due to the secrecy surrounding homosexual activity during the Qing, the final word on the existence or prevalence of homosexual activity among palace eunuchs may never be more than speculation.

Eunuch "Esprit de Corps"

With limited contact with family members and marriage a remote possibility for many eunuchs during the early and mid-Qing, eunuchs turned to their fellow emasculates to provide them with pseudo-familial bonds. Shared experiences such as genital mutilation and its accompanying physical and social changes combined with the demands of imperial service created strong bonds among the eunuch brethren. Moreover, the master–apprentice system facilitated the formation of eunuch society. Throughout his period of service within the palace, a master would train numerous apprentices[30] and in the process create his own social network. Katherine Carl, the American artist in residence at the palace while she painted the Empress Dowager Cixi's portrait in 1903, attests to the strong bonds among eunuchs. Carl writes that she noticed a "feeling of '*esprit de corps*' among them [the eunuchs]—a spirit of mutual helpfulness."[31] During the late Qing, native place associations, such as that formed by eunuchs from Shandong, assisted young emasculates in entering

28. M. J. Meijer, "Homosexual Offences in Ch'ing China," *T'oung Pao* LXXI (71) (1985): 129.
29. Charlotte Furth, "Androgynous Males and Deficient Females," *Late Imperial China* 9, no. 2 (Dec. 1988): 13.
30. Ma Deqing et al., "Qing gong taijian huiyi lu," in *Wanqing gongting shenghuo jianwen*, ed. Zhang Wenhui (Beijing: Wenshi ziliao chubanshe, 1982), 179.
31. Katherine Augusta Carl, *With the Empress Dowager of China* (1906; reprint, New York: KPI Limited, 1986), 126–27.

the palace eunuch system.[32] Native place ties may have filled a void in the lives of eunuchs as they lived out their lives inside the palace walls separated from their families. This "mutual helpfulness" could often be limited to apprentices trained under the same master, since masters often promoted their individual interests as they endeavored to advance their disciples beyond those of other eunuch masters.[33] Undoubtedly, the Qing's utilization of the apprentice–master system as a teaching tool had the unintended effect of creating and cementing eunuch bonds and may have even contributed to the formation of eunuch cliques.

Pseudo-familial bonds with fellow eunuchs and servant coworkers often compensated for their segregation from society. Shared experiences such as emasculation and similar work environments cemented bonds among the eunuchs and the other servile employees of the palace. Native place associations and master–apprentice bonds further created ties among the eunuch populace and often assisted young emasculates in entering the palace system and in obtaining promotions. As mentioned, eunuchs often formed familial type bonds with Manchu maidservants (*duishi* 對食) assigned to the same palace. Aware that such relationships could lead to conflicting loyalties as well as romantic liaisons, Qing emperors criminalized such encounters.

Figure 5.1
Eunuch with dog

32. Jia Yinghua, *Modai taijian miwen: Sun Yaoting zhuan* (Beijing: Zhishi chubanshe, 1993), 464.
33. Carl, *With the Empress Dowager of China*, 127.

Within the palace, eunuchs actively created a society that attempted to alleviate the oppressive atmosphere that characterized the eunuchs' work and home
environment. Accounts of late Qing palace life reflect the stolen moments in which
eunuchs chatted with their coworkers or shared an inexpensive meal with their
fellow eunuchs at one of the palace restaurants catering to eunuch clientele. Some
eunuchs found companionship and an escape from the loneliness and drudgery
associated with palace life by raising dogs. During the late Qing, American artist
Katherine Carl found hundreds of dogs living within the palace. Twelve eunuchs
served the Imperial Kennel, caring for the dogs of the imperial court.[34] Those dogs
owned by the Empress Dowager Cixi slept on silk cushions with eunuchs in attendance to bathe and take them for their daily exercise outdoors. Eunuchs also raised
dogs of their own within the palace.[35] Even in this aspect of a eunuch's life, status
played a role. Within the palace, the owner's class lines appear to have dictated the
color and breed of the dog. Reflective of their status, eunuchs' and maidservants'
dogs were usually inferior breeds.[36] According to the late Qing eunuch Xin Xiuming
eunuchs were particularly fond of raising the palace dogs known as *longgou* 龍夠.[37]

Forbidden Entertainment

In addition to forming familial and social bonds, eunuchs subverted their required
submissiveness by engaging in prohibited forms of entertainment and leisure activities. This parallel world of the eunuch served as a counterbalance to days of performing menial servant work within the palace. This realm, existing alongside that
of the emperor, was most evident after nightfall, when eunuchs were the only males
besides the emperor allowed within the inner court and most outer court eunuchs
enjoyed a break from their duties. It is during these late hours of the day and into
the night that eunuchs would recreate the social bonds denied them and engage
in activities that their masters would perceive as most unbefitting of an emperor's
servant. Records of eunuch infractions and legal cases related to these recreational
activities provide a glimpse into the other side of eunuch life and reveal the tension
between the imperial court's need to trust their servants and the distrust that permeated their relations.

Gambling

Having few forms of recreation available to them, eunuchs liked to spend their leisure
time gambling. One late eunuch is quoted as saying "if we 'do not like gambling we

---

34. Tang Yinian, *Qing gong taijian* (Shenyang: Liaoning daxue chubanshe, 1993), 197.
35. Carl, *With the Empress Dowager of China*, 54.
36. Mao Xianmin, "Wanqing gongting 'yanggou re," *Zijincheng* 4 (1994): 46.
37. Xin Xiuming, *Lao taijian de huiyi* (Beijing: Beijing yanshan chubanshe, 1992), 134.

have no pleasure.'"[38] Eunuchs would place bets on quail or cricket fights or other games of chance (*paigu*).[39] In 1689, the Kangxi emperor noted that some eunuchs looked like beggars as a result of squandering their monthly salaries on gambling.[40] Records reveal that gambling was very common among eunuchs in the ninth year of the Qianlong emperor's reign (1744).[41]

Despite the popularity of gambling, Qing rulers viewed it and other eunuch recreational activities as a dereliction of eunuch duties and a source of problems among its eunuch population. Gambling was often accompanied by drinking, which in turn could lead to instances of violence. Associating gambling with increases in theft (often due to gambling debts) and violence, Qing emperors repeatedly responded to instances of eunuch gambling with harsh punishments. In the mid-1700s, *Guochao gongshi* notes that eunuchs caught gambling within the palace would be punished by sixty blows of the *ban* (板 flattened bamboo).[42] In actuality, punishments could be harsher than those listed in the regulations. In one case from 1704, four eunuchs were caught gambling while sitting watch some time after dusk. As punishment, each eunuch was sent out of the palace into the capital city to wear the cangue for two months and then received one hundred lashes. The severity of the punishment depended upon the amount of money gambled, here only "200–300 *qian* 錢" each, and the number of eunuchs involved.[43]

According to the Palace Regulations published in the mid-1800s, eunuchs caught gambling received punishments ranging from wearing the cangue, to corporal punishment and temporary banishment, to the death penalty.[44] First-time offenders were to be sentenced to wear the cangue for three months, receive forty blows from the *ban*, followed by exile to the Eastern and Western Tombs to serve. For second-time offenders, the sentence increased in severity to death by strangulation. During the first year of the Xianfeng reign period (1851), noting that there were no eunuchs currently serving at the imperial tombs, the punishment was changed to three months wearing the cangue, forty blows from the *ban*, and exile to Dasheng Wula[45] to serve as a slave to an official for three years, after which time the eunuch was to be sent back in to serve in the outer court.[46]

The statutes also became more specific, differentiating between those who ran gambling halls and those who were patrons. The location of the gambling, within the inner court or in the outer court, was irrelevant in these cases; instead the statutes

38. Stent, "Chinese Eunuchs," 180.
39. QDGZXXZL 卷4，處分，795.
40. *Guochao gongshi* 國朝宮史, ed. Yu Minzhong, 訓諭2，29，康熙28年3月25日.
41. *Guochao gongshi* 國朝宮史，史四，訓諭4, 91，乾隆9年2月22日 (March 24, 1744).
42. *Guochao gongshi*, vol. 2，官制，775.
43. First Historical Archives, Beijing, *Kangxi chao manwen zhupi zouzhe quanyi* (Beijing: Zhongguo shehui kexue chubanshe, 1996), 958, entry 2449.
44. QDGZXXZL, 卷4，處分，793–98.
45. In Present-day Jilin Province. Wula was located just north of the city of Jilin 吉林 on the 1820 map of Tan Qixiang. "Wula" is a Chinese transliteration of Manchu *ula* (a large river).
46. QDGZXXZL, 卷4，處分，793–94.

focused on the number of eunuchs involved in the gambling and whether or not the eunuch received a percentage of the profits. Eunuchs who set up opportunities/dens for gambling for a small number of people and made money off the arrangement were sentenced to wear the cangue for two months, receive forty blows from the *ban*, and exiled to Heilongjiang to serve as a military slave. Those who repeated their mistakes would be sentenced to execution. Those promoting gambling involving a larger number of eunuchs were sentenced to strangulation regardless of whether or not it was their first offence. Clearly, the Qing were interested in removing instigators of eunuch gambling from the palace and its environs.

Collective punishment was also used as a strategy to prevent eunuchs from gambling. Eunuch supervisors whose subordinates were caught gambling found their monthly salaries fined for periods ranging from two months to two years, the harsher punishments being saved for supervisors who were aware of a problem but failed to report it. The Qing also relied on eunuchs to police each other. Eunuchs serving alongside eunuchs caught gambling could also face punishment if they had knowledge of such activities but did not report them. Eunuchs who were suspicious but did not report anything to their superiors, regardless of whether they knew the details or not, would be sentenced to wear the cangue for two months and receive forty blows from the *ban*, after which time they would be sent back to their original position to continue serving.

It is important to note that eunuchs in this instance were not singled out by the Qing for gambling. Statutes reveal that gambling among the military and commoners was also met with harsh punishments. Gamblers were sentenced to wear the cangue for two months and receive one hundred blows from the *zhang* (杖 heavy bamboo used for beating criminals).[47] The sentences for wearing the cangue were exactly the same; the only difference was the number of blows and the type of instrument used to inflict them. Eunuchs received fewer blows from the lighter bamboo rod.[48]

Since much of eunuch gambling occurring during the evening hours while all other men except the emperor and the imperial doctor were required to be beyond the walls of the inner court, and while many eunuchs sat watch, Qing emperors were forced to rely on eunuchs to police themselves in this matter. During periods when the palace demands for eunuchs exceeded the supply, sending gambling offenders to the imperial tombs to serve or exile may have been more of a threat than a reality. Such harsh punishments for gambling sent a clear message that such acts of disobedience would not be tolerated; however, in practice the Qing may have found it difficult to implement such punishments without resulting in too large of a drain on its palace eunuch supply. In practice, sentences appear to have been more lenient at times, as shown in the statute from the Xianfeng period, in which exile to

---

47. *Qinding da qing lüli* 欽定大清律例，卷34，刑律，雜犯，同治9年 (1870).
48. The document uses the character 版, which has the same sound but a different meaning (blocks for printing; register). This appears to be an error in writing the character in the original.

Heilongjiang was reduced to three years of exile to Dasheng Wula, after which time the eunuch was sent back to the palace to resume service.

Suspicions about eunuch gambling also led the palace to conduct searches to ensure that eunuchs were not involved in any prohibited activities or that they were not in possession of any weapons. In the third year of the Xuantong reign (1911), various departments in the inner and outer palace reported that their search for knives, spears, gunpowder, weapons, and people seeking money through gambling had been completed.[49] The persistence of eunuch gambling as an imperial "headache" throughout the dynasty attests to the ability of eunuchs to manipulate their environment, albeit to a small extent.

Drinking

Drinking alcohol also provided eunuchs with a form of prohibited entertainment. Eunuchs caught drinking alcohol contributed to increased tensions between eunuchs and their superiors and eunuchs and their imperial masters. Palace Regulations forbid eunuchs from drinking alcohol within the palace during the day and punished offending eunuchs with sixty blows from the *ban* and fined their *shouling* eunuch six months' pay.[50] Eunuchs drinking at night could also be a problem. In one case from 1722, two eunuchs came to their superior late at night to report that eunuch Jin Tinglin 金廷林 was drunk and being noisy.[51] Their superior responded, "He is very close to the emperor's living quarters; why is he being noisy?" They were sent away due to the lateness of the hour and told to come back in the morning. As it got later, the situation with Jin deteriorated further; he wouldn't quiet down and eventually brandished a knife. When questioned about the incident, Jin claimed that he was noisy because he had cut his left hand when he had hit it against a rock. Other eyewitness accounts, though, added that Jin had cursed at his superiors and even brandished a sword. Jin's bad behavior only earned him a sentence of wearing the cangue for two months and one hundred lashes (from the whip, *bian*). In this detailed case, involving several eyewitness accounts, it is repeatedly noted that Jin had cursed at his superior and had a weapon inside the palace.

The Qing often linked drinking and gambling within the statutes.[52] While seen as an escape for many eunuchs, such practices could lead to devastating consequences. In a case from the eighth year of the Daoguang reign (1828),[53] the Board

---

49. First Historical Archives, Beijing, Gongzhong 宮中 [Palace], zajian 雜件 [Miscellaneous documents], Renshilei taijian 人事類太監 [Eunuchs]，奏單，宣統3年4月初1日.

50. *Guochao gongshi*, vol. 2, 官制, 775.

51. First Historical Archives, Beijing, *Kangxi chao manwen zhupi zouzhe quanyi* 康熙潮滿文朱批奏摺全譯 [A complete translation of Manchu vermilion endorsements and palace memorials from the Kangxi court] (Beijing: Zhongguo shehui kexue chubanshe, 1996), 1512, entry 3936.

52. *Guochao gongshi*, 國朝宮史, 訓諭2，29，康熙28年3月25日.

53. First Historical Archives, Beijing, Zongguan Neiwufu 總管內務府 [Imperial Household Department], Daoguang 道光, zalu dang 雜錄檔 [Miscellaneous Archives], 05-0651-004，道光8年9月初7日.

of Punishment investigated the apparent suicide of *Yuanmingyuan* palace eunuch Sheng Liang 生梁. Their findings determined that Sheng had killed himself by hanging. Interviews with his fellow eunuchs noted that Sheng had gambled with them on several occasions, during which he lost repeatedly (eight or nine strings of cash each time). The investigation concluded that Sheng, who often gambled and drank heavily, had killed himself after his debts became overwhelming. Since Sheng committed suicide inside the palace compound, his family was subject to exile in the empire's borderlands to serve as military slaves. As Sheng had no family, this was not necessary. Eunuchs who had gambled with Sheng, though, were sentenced to wear the cangue for two months and to receive forty lashes.

Drinking and gambling also became linked with cases of eunuchs running away. As will be seen, eunuchs running away from the palace proved to be a chronic problem throughout the dynasty. Qing interrogations of captured runaways often inquired if they had run away due to gambling debt. Drinking and getting drunk outside the palace could also motivate eunuchs to run away. In the seventh year of the Jiaqing reign period (1802), Zhao Shijie 趙士傑, a fourth-generation eunuch, was arrested for running away after getting drunk in a wine shop outside the palace. Realizing that he would not have time to return to the palace before sunset, he rented a room for the night and ultimately ended up running away.[54]

Eunuchs Quarreling and Fighting

Contrary to stereotypical representations of eunuchs as docile and submissive, the historical record reveals that eunuch-upon-eunuch violence was not uncommon within the palace. While not every case stemmed from drinking or gambling, legal cases reveal that the Kangxi's emperor's concerns about such activities leading to violence were not unwarranted. Drinking and gambling were often linked to cases of eunuchs caught quarreling and fighting. Eunuchs caught arguing with and fighting one another within the palace were subject to sixty blows from the *ban*. It is interesting to note that this was the same punishment applied to eunuchs caught drunk within the palace during the day.[55] The case of Department of Ceremonial eunuch Du Ming 杜明 (1739) suggests that earlier representations of eunuchs as meek and feminine did not match the realities of eunuch behavior. Here, Du is charged with stabbing eunuch Liu Erqi 劉爾奇.[56] According to Du's confession, he was a palace theater eunuch suffering from a preexisting illness who had asked a fellow eunuch to help him go pick up some things. Du's supervisor didn't approve of this. Du claimed that another eunuch, named Liu, who was with his supervisor at the time, hit him for no reason. Du cursed at his supervisor and as a result was

54. *Guoli Gugong Bowuyuan* [National Palace Museum], Taipei, *Gongzhong dang zouzhe* 宮中檔奏摺 [Secret Palace Memorials], *Jiaqing chao* 嘉慶朝 [Jiaqing reign period] 404007353, 故宮093158, 嘉慶7年2月9日.
55. *QDGZXXZL*, 777.
56. First Historical Archives, Beijing, 5全宗，29卷，30 號，乾隆4年4月28日.

forced to show his subservience by dropping to the ground to *ketou* 磕頭. In addition, Du was fined two to three days of pay. Du also states that his illness flared up again and he was throwing up blood continuously. When he ran into Liu outside the palace, Liu had made a comment that infuriated him so much that he stabbed Liu in the leg three times. Liu's confession presents quite a different account of the events that transpired between the two. According to Liu, he had simply run into Du when he had gone out to buy vegetables. Du had been hiding and ran up behind him and attacked him. Du stabbed Liu in both legs. According to Liu "the pain was unbearable." The fight that ensued between the two was so big that it brought people out of their homes. When Du's supervisor arrived, Du dropped the knife and was arrested. Du was punished according to the precedent set during the Kangxi reign: eunuchs wielding a knife were sentenced to cut grass at Weng Mountain[57] 甕山. Undoubtedly, the punishment would have been more severe if the crime and the ensuing fight had broken out inside the palace instead of outside the palace walls.

In one undated case involving a fifty-year-old eunuch named Liu Kuaizui 劉快嘴 we learn that Liu had been sent to cut grass at Weng Mountain as a punishment for stabbing a man with a small knife.[58] In another undated roster for Weng Mountain, a forty-one-year-old eunuch surnamed Jin 靳 was listed as having gotten drunk in the palace in the middle of the night and brandishing a knife while cursing at his supervisor. Jin had already completed the first two stages of his punishment—wearing the cangue for three months and receiving one hundred lashes from a whip—and was now being sent to cut grass.[59]

As Kutcher has noted, eunuchs could resort to violence in order to protect their perceived territory (section of the palace). He reveals how an altercation between two groups of eunuchs stemming from a fight over access to crabs in a culvert in the *Yuanmingyuan* would eventually lead to one eunuch being murdered by another. As Kutcher notes, the dialogue recounted in the confession, with each group questioning the right of the other to be there, is "filled with territorial sentiment."[60]

These cases remind us that eunuchs were not the docile, submissive servants they have traditionally been portrayed to be. Eunuchs became angry, they cursed at each other, and oftentimes held grudges that they would act upon with violence. Drinking and gambling among eunuchs only compounded these problems. Eunuchs fighting and stabbing each other with knives stands in stark contrast to

---

57. Weng Mountain (so named because of its similarities in appearance to a tall earthen jar) in Ziyang County, in nearby Shanxi province, further supports this conclusion. For the location of Weng Mountain, see Zhang Qiyun, ed., *Zhongwen da cidian*, vol. 22 (Taipei: Zhongguo wenhua yanjiusuo, 1967), 9420.

58. Academia Sinica 中央研究院近史所，近史所，Taipei, 內務府堂人事類，A字號，MC2911，上駟院，Box. No. 95，鍘草太監花名.

59. Academia Sinica 中央研究院近史所，近史所，Taipei, 內務府堂人事類，A字號，MC2911，上駟院，Box No. 95，鍘草太監花名. This is most likely the same Jin Tinglin who was arrested in 1722 although the account of his arrest does not mention him being sent to cut grass but the rest of the facts are the same. The characters for his name are also different in the first account but the sounds are the same in both.

60. First Historical Archives, *Neiwu zou'an* 208 (QL 48.8.19) as cited in Kutcher, "Unspoken Collusions, 488.

traditional understandings of eunuch behavior and their depiction as the emperor's submissive servants.

Opium Smoking

Eunuchs also engaged in opium use both within and outside the palace as a form of escape and to alleviate pain. Palace records reveal that eunuchs were opium users as well as sellers. Despite the severity of palace regulations designed to prevent eunuch opium use, eunuchs appear to have continued to smoke opium in their rooms and in eunuch-run opium dens within the palace. While late Qing recollections of eunuch opium use tend to downplay its occurrence, with one eunuch citing it was "rare," the need for Qing emperors to repeatedly add harsher punishments to deal with eunuch opium smokers suggests that it was more frequent than these recollections suggest.

The Qing responded to eunuchs caught smoking opium with severe punishments. Eunuchs caught smoking opium within the inner court, regardless of whether they were first-time offenders or addicts, faced strangulation. This death sentence sent a clear message to eunuchs that this form of entertainment was considered an affront to the emperor, as the act was committed within the walls of the emperor's personal residence. In addition, due to the Qing's preference for enacting collective punishment, the eunuch's family and fellow eunuchs would also suffer for his crime. The eunuch's family would be exiled to the borders of the empire, to Xinjiang, to serve as slaves for the military. The eunuchs' superior, regardless if he knew of the eunuch's activity or not, was also exiled, not to Xinjiang but to Heilongjiang, to serve as a slave for the military. Even the eunuch's roommate received punishment and was exiled. These harsh punishments for the eunuch offender and the implementation of collective punishment for his associates and family members suggest that eunuch opium smoking within the palace was enough of a problem for the authorities to place specific statutes on the books.[61]

The statute makes clear that eunuchs were also involved in selling opium. Authorities were urged to verify if eunuchs were suspected of dealing opium, and once verified, to sentence the seller to the same punishment as the user. Eunuchs caught smoking in outer court *tatan* and public places would be sentenced to wear the cangue for six months, after which time they were to be sent to the border. Eunuchs caught smoking opium while on leave or at a private residence or another locale could face sentences as severe as wearing the cangue in perpetuity without the possibility of clemency.[62]

During the tenth year of the Guangxu reign (1885), eunuch Wang Xilian 王喜連 was arrested after getting into an argument with unemployed bannerman (*sula* 蘇拉) Guo Taoqi 郭掏氣, who had visited Wang in his room to use his drug

---

61. *QDGZXXZL*, 卷4，處分，820.
62. *QDGZXXZL*, 卷4，處分，822–23.

paraphernalia. The two had gotten into an argument after Wang obstructed Guo from doing so despite his expressed need to smoke opium to treat his abdominal pain.[63] Wang's possession of drug paraphernalia for smoking opium is not addressed directly in the document, but mention is made that he is over seventy years old, which may account for him receiving a pardon in this case.

Such strict punishments did not deter late Qing eunuchs from using and selling opium within the Forbidden City itself. The extent to which the eunuch populace participated in opium smoking and gambling remains uncertain. In 1877, some thirty years after the end of the first Opium War (1839–1842), Stent writes:

> Most of the eunuchs smoke opium, and to enable them to indulge in this habit without quitting the palace, seven or eight opium dens are opened in its precincts; this is not only a convenience for them, but for officials who may have business in the palace, but are compelled to wait about the outer courtyards. These opium dens are called "smoking establishments["]; (煙館); the fact of their being in the palace is notorious, but no doubt it is considered policy to shut the eyes—officially—to their existence.[64]

Sun Yaoting, who entered the palace as a eunuch at the age of fifteen,[65] became the accountant (bookie) for an opium dealer (another eunuch) inside the palace. According to Sun, during the late Qing, four to five opium dens operated inside the palace walls; one of these was located within the inner court.[66] On his first visit to this opium den, Sun witnessed ten eunuchs reclining on *kang* (炕 raised heated bed) smoking opium in a smoke-filled room.[67]

The late Qing contemporary Pu Jia also noted that there were a lot of eunuchs who smoked opium inside the palace.[68] In contrast, recollections of three late Qing palace eunuchs interviewed in the 1960s present opium smoking as a rare occurrence within the palace.[69] Moreover, these eunuchs portray eunuch involvement with opium as nothing more than a servant helping his master with the water pipe.[70] Katherine Carl writes that the Empress Dowager Cixi detested the drug and imposed harsh punishments on eunuchs found to "indulge" in it.[71] According to Carl,

> They were not only deprived of so many months' pay and loss of their buttons, but were sometimes banished from the Palace for a certain length of time, and even severe corporal punishment would be ordered. These stringent measures did not prevent some of them, however, from indulging surreptitiously in the narcotic, but

---

63. First Historical Archives, 敬事房2462，宮中雜件 (舊整) 2462，光緒10年5月初4日.
64. Stent, "Chinese Eunuchs," 180.
65. 16 *sui.*
66. Jia, *Modai taijian miwen*, 78.
67. Jia, *Modai taijian miwen*, 78–79.
68. Pu Jia, "Qinggong huiyi," in *Wanqing gongting shenghuo jianwen*, ed. Zhang Wenhui (Beijing: Wenshi ziliao chubanshe, 1982), 24.
69. Ma Deqing et al., "Qing gong taijian huiyi lu," 182.
70. Ma Deqing et al., "Qing gong taijian huiyi lu," 182.
71. Carl, *With the Empress Dowager of China*, 127.

they took the most extreme precautions to prevent its being found out. Her Majesty has unusually acute olfactories, especially for opium. This, it seems, can be detected by its odor, which hangs around the clothes, and like the odor of the rose, one 'can break the vase, it lingers there still.' But it seems that the eunuchs have special linen clothes, which they put on for smoking, and these are given to be washed, immediately the fascinating pipe is finished. Unless one is an habitual smoker, the drug has very little outward effect and except by the odor, it cannot be detected.[72]

Punishments appear to have been more lenient for cases in which eunuch were caught smoking opium in the outer court or in their own quarters as opposed to the inner court. Eunuchs caught smoking opium in the outer court would be sentenced to wear the cangue for six months, followed by exile to the borders of the empire rather being sentenced to death by strangulation.[73] Even retired eunuchs caught smoking opium could face punishments as severe as the death sentence.

The subsistence levels of eunuch salaries suggest that many eunuchs would not have been able to financially afford opiates. However, as with gambling, opium smoking among eunuchs may have motivated them to steal in order to support their drug habits. While the extent of eunuch drug use remains unclear, it is known that opium smoking among the Qing nobility was not uncommon. In fact, Rawski attributes the rise in opium sales in China during the nineteenth century to opium addiction among this group.[74] Such a market for opium use, especially within a group possessing such considerable access to the palace, could have provided lucrative business opportunities for eunuchs involved in the palace drug trade in opium.

Conclusion

In response to the often oppressive environment in which they lived and worked, eunuchs sought to create their own society. As a result, eunuchs existed within two parallel realms: one in which they served the emperor and operated in an environment dictated by rules that served as visible manifestations of the emperor's absolute rule, and the other in which eunuchs governed themselves and attempted to create a sense of agency in a very restrictive environment. In this parallel world, eunuchs actively recreated the bonds that emasculation and servile life were intended to deny them.

Desiring to build connections and a sense of community with others, eunuchs compensated for their segregation from society by forming pseudo-familial bonds with fellow eunuchs and palace servants. Shared experiences such as emasculation and similar work environments cemented bonds among the eunuchs and the other servile employees of the palace. Native place associations and master–apprentice

---

72. Carl, *With the Empress Dowager of China*, 127.
73. QDGZXXZL, 卷4，處分，822.
74. Rawski, *The Last Emperors*, 90.

bonds further created ties among the eunuch populace and often assisted young emasculates in entering the palace system and in obtaining promotions.

Some eunuchs attempted to circumvent the physical and social limitations of emasculation and palace service through marriage and the adoption of children. Eunuchs shared the desires of their unemasculated counterparts for marriage, children, and family life. While many eunuchs succeeded in finding a bride and adopting children, social acceptance of these families often eluded these eunuchs.

Accounts of late Qing palace life reflect the stolen moments in which eunuchs chatted with their coworkers or shared an inexpensive meal with their fellow eunuchs at one of the palace restaurants catering to eunuch clientele. Other eunuchs found happiness in such simple pleasures as raising dogs. Palace disciplinary records also reveal that eunuchs engaged in activities that the court deemed unbefitting of an imperial servant: drinking, gambling, smoking opium, and even relationships with women.

A small number of eunuchs, uninhibited by restrictions on the eunuch lifestyle intended to suppress eunuch political activity and power, manipulated eunuch society to meet their individual desires for power and wealth. Within the decorum and etiquette of the palace, these eunuchs created a palace underworld that at times catered to eunuchs' and palace inhabitants' desires to escape the drudgery of palace life through gambling and illicit drug use.

As described by Albert Mann, eunuchs became "creatures of Court life."[75] The eunuch lifestyle revolved around the service of the emperor and his court. Inside the palace walls, eunuchs lived their lives to satisfy the wants and needs of their masters. As a result, the wants and needs of the eunuch population were routinely ignored, regulated, and often prohibited. Qing rulers viewed eunuch recreational activities as both a dereliction of eunuch duties and a social problem if eunuchs gambled away their savings. The Imperial Court was concerned that eunuch gambling debt could lead eunuchs to steal items, get into fights, and resort to violence. Qing regulations and statutes repeatedly use the phrase *taijian bu shou guiju* (太監不守規矩 eunuchs aren't observing with the rules), a phrase that makes clear that that eunuchs were perceived to be acting in ways that did not fit their station in life or show adequate respect to the imperial will, especially within the emperor's residence and seat of imperial power. Despite the imperial court's best efforts, eunuchs actively worked to rebuild the bonds emasculation was intended to deny them.

---

75. Albert Mann, "The Influence of Eunuchs in the Politics and Economy of the Ch'ing Court 1861–1907" (MA thesis, University of Washington, 1957), 24.

6

Running away from the Palace*

During the Qing dynasty, young boys and men voluntarily underwent emasculation to become eunuchs. Envisioning a life of power and wealth working in proximity to the emperor, or at the very least a job providing room and board, the benefits of emasculation appeared to outweigh the costs of genital mutilation. Once inside the palace though, new recruits faced the realities of the eunuch system: restrictions on their mobility, harsh working conditions, and punishments. Moreover, if a eunuch was unhappy with his work environment, he rarely had the option of quitting or leaving the system, as terms of service were for life. During the Qing, eunuchs were not released from service unless they were deemed too ill or too old to serve. For many eunuchs, running away from the palace provided a much quicker, albeit more dangerous, exit from the palace eunuch system.

This chapter explores official records of palace eunuch flight, capture, and confessions[1] and finds that the punishments imposed on runaway eunuchs reveal that restricted mobility and harsh punishments often became too oppressive for the palace eunuch workforce to endure. Faced with impending beatings for often

---

* Many thanks to the *Journal of the Royal Asiatic Society* for permission to reprint this chapter, which first appeared as "Running Away from the Palace: Chinese Eunuchs during the Qing Dynasty," *Journal of the Royal Asiatic Society* 27, issue 1 (Jan. 2017): 143–64. The article has been slightly modified to blend with the rest of the book.

1. Cases of eunuchs running away cited in this chapter are based largely upon archival documents found in Beijing in the First Historical Archives and in Taipei at the National Palace Museum Library. Here, one can find an abundance of documents in the *Gongzhong dang* (宮中檔 *Secret Palace Memorials*) and the archives of the *Junjichu* (軍機處 Grand Council), which record cases of palace eunuchs running away during the Qing. While numerous, records of runaway eunuchs do not lend themselves to a statistical analysis of eunuch runaways (the number of eunuchs running away during particular reign periods or from different departments). The archives appear to have preserved interesting cases rather than lists of runaway eunuchs and those captured. Few documents detail the number of runaway eunuchs at a given time, so it remains unclear if the extant documents in the archives are complete or are only those that have survived in the historical record. This lack of statistics also makes it difficult to ascertain the number of eunuchs who did not attempt to run away. Not all eunuchs wanted to leave the system. For eunuchs in the upper echelons of the eunuch hierarchy, life as a palace eunuch presented opportunities to amass power and wealth. However, this was life for a select few. As will be seen, for unranked eunuchs, those who made up the majority of eunuch runaways, life would have been quite different and much more challenging. Despite the lack of statistics on runaway eunuchs, these archival records are vital for understanding eunuch social history and labor relations within the Forbidden City. In particular, confessions of runaway eunuchs provide scholars with one of the few instances in which we can hear eunuch voices and obtain first-hand information about their life experiences.

minor infractions, for eunuchs, flight from the system represented an act of agency in a life filled with rules and regulations set by others. However, as will be seen, the difficulties that eunuchs faced trying to survive outside the system ensured that escape from the palace and attempting to sever ties with the eunuch system without authorization would prove exceedingly difficult.

The abundance of cases of runaway eunuchs in the historical record reflects poorly on the Qing dynasty's treatment of its eunuchs and effectiveness at times in controlling its eunuch population. By exploring such cases, this chapter aims to contribute to the understanding of unfree status during the Qing and more broadly to the reconstruction of the social history of eunuchs. As the majority of palace eunuchs were illiterate, these reports give voice to eunuchs and reveal: (1) the tensions that characterized labor relations between the imperial household and its eunuch workforce and (2) that eunuch status does not fit neatly into the binary of free or unfree status but rather is something more complicated that lies on the continuum in between.

The palace eunuch system was based on the premise that eunuchs were created to serve the emperor and his imperial court. As Chapter 5 has shown, labor relations between eunuchs and their masters reveal tensions, as eunuchs challenged the rules and pushed and even crossed the boundaries of what the imperial court deemed acceptable behavior for a eunuch. While from the emperor's point of view some eunuchs undoubtedly did "betray the imperial trust,"[2] cases of runaway eunuchs reveal there is more to the story; here one finds clues to eunuchs' motivations behind their actions. As palace eunuchs spent the majority of their lives behind the walls of the Forbidden City, many endeavored to balance their expected submissiveness with a degree of agency in their own lives. Flight from the system was just one of the ways eunuchs did just that.[3] Running away, for many eunuchs, was a direct response to their treatment by their employers. The following analysis is designed to take the reader through the course of a eunuch's flight from the palace, commencing with possible escape routes and ending with his capture and punishment.

Running Away: Eunuch Escape Routes

Little information appears in the historical record concerning eunuch escape routes. Due to the highly restrictive nature of entry and exit from the Forbidden City, eunuchs intending to flee from the palace had to look for opportunities to facilitate their escape. Running errands such as going to buy vegetables[4] or wontons

---

2. As stated in Chapter 5, Evelyn Rawski notes that Qing criminal cases involving eunuchs "display lazy, thieving, gossiping betrayers of the imperial trust." See Evelyn S. Rawski, *The Last Emperors: A Social History of Qing Imperial Institutions* (Berkeley: University of California Press, 1998) 161.

3. For other ways, such as the creation of a eunuch society within the palace, see Chapter 3.

4. First Historical Archives, Beijing, 宮中，雜件，人事類太監1018，逃走太監，自鳴鐘首領李三喜.

often provided eunuchs with the pretext they needed to get beyond the watchful eye of their superiors and outside the palace walls.

Going to have their head shaved by one of the barbers who set up shop outside the palace walls also created opportunities for eunuch flight.[5] The frequency with which eunuchs shaved their heads before running away is intriguing. Eunuchs, like other men in Qing society, wore their hair in a queue drawn from the hair at the top of the head (a style that requires the front and sides of the head to be regularly shaven). Xin Xiuming 信修明, a eunuch during the late Qing, notes in his recollections that eunuchs of the inner court could visit the barber as well as have something to eat at one of the shops (*tatan* 他坦) that lined the western river located outside the Inner Right Gate (*Neiyoumen* 內右門).[6] One can speculate that these *tatan*, located outside the walls of inner court, might have provided eunuchs with an excuse for leaving the heavily guarded residence of the emperor and his family and placed them one step closer to their attempted unauthorized exit from the palace.[7]

Eunuchs also ran away while on leave from the palace. During the reign of Jiaqing (1796–1820), the failure of eunuchs to report for duty after having been on leave became such a problem that the emperor stipulated that they were to have an escort to and from the location they would be staying at during their leave.[8] However, these measures did not prevent eunuchs from escaping in the interim. This problem persisted into the Xianfeng reign period (1851–1861); in 1856, Li Dongji 李冬吉, a twenty-two-year-old (*sui* 歲)[9] Yuanping native serving as a eunuch in the *Yuanmingyuan* requested leave and ran away for the second time.[10] During the same year it was reported that Zhang Ming 張明, a forty-six-year-old eunuch in the service of the *Yulinglongguan* (玉玲瓏館 Skillfully Worked Jade House) in the *Yuanmingyuan*, had still not returned from leave. This was also his second time running away.[11]

The palace considered eunuch flight as a dereliction of duty and immediately launched searches for missing eunuchs. Descriptions of the runaway's face and body (*mianmao shenzhong* 面貌身中 or *mianmao tie* 面貌帖) provide glimpses into how the Qing endeavored to capture escaped eunuchs. It is interesting to note that, aside from mentioning the color of a eunuch's facial skin and whether or not it was pockmarked, the remainder of the description detailed only the clothing or uniform the eunuch would have been wearing at the time of his escape. For example, Li

---

5. First Historical Archives, Beijing, 宮中，雜件，人事類太監1019，逃走太監，自鳴鐘首領張得成 and First Historical Archives, Beijing, 宮中，雜件，人事類太監1018，逃走太監承乾宮首領張得福8月初2.

6. Xin Xiuming, *Lao taijian de huiyi* (Beijing : Beijing yan shan chu ban she, 1992), 7. *Tatan* in this case refers to both eunuch living quarters and places where eunuchs could get something to eat. *Tatan* were also located within the Forbidden City and *Yuanmingyuan* as well.

7. A visit to the barber outside the palace would have facilitated a eunuch's attempt to disguise himself as a monk.

8. Du Wanyan, *Zhongguo huanguan shi* (Taipei: Wenjin chubanshe, 1996), 125.

9. Ages in *sui* 歲 are traditionally calculated using the Chinese lunar calendar, beginning with one at birth and increasing at the Lunar New Year (not birthdays). Here, *sui* is translated as translated as "years old."

10. First Historical Archives, Beijing, 總管內務府，雜錄檔136，咸豐6年正月–6月.

11. First Historical Archives, 總管內務府，雜錄檔136，咸豐6年正月–6月.

Yi 李義, a eunuch from the *Jingrengong* (景仁宮 Palace of Benevolent Prospect), was described as having: "a yellow face, and wearing a spring hat, a blue cotton robe, a green cloth unlined outer coat, and green cloth boots."[12] In another case, escaped eunuch Wang Xiangrui's 王祥瑞 description lists the following information: "wearing a spring hat, a blue robe and green outer coat, spring cloth boots, and white skin without pock marks."[13] The lack of distinguishing physical characteristics besides skin color or blemishes suggests that the eunuch may have been seen in social rather than physical terms in this instance. This is noteworthy, since a eunuch's social role and identity stemmed from the physical feature he lacked, his genitalia. However, here a eunuch's clothing rather than physical features differentiated him from the rest of the population. In the case of escaped eunuch Zhang Feng 張鳳, the authorities were told to circulate his age, appearance, clothing, disguise, and coloring (*nian mao yizhuang yanse* 年貌衣裝顏色) to help aid in his capture.[14] In 1763, Zhao De 趙德, a eunuch assigned to the *Yuanmingyuan*, was so bold as to escape by horse. The thirty-five-year-old Yuanping native's escape caused an announcement to be circulated noting his clothing and his mode of transportation, riding a black horse.[15] In each of these cases, wanted posters focused on a eunuch's clothing more than his physical attributes.

When contrasted with descriptions of non-emasculated fugitives, this becomes even more apparent. For example, the Qing Code of 1740 required authorities to provide a detailed record of a fugitive's age, appearance, place of origin, the presence of facial hair and/or a mole, etc.[16] According to Susan Naquin, during the Qing, lists of wanted criminals contained "the name (including aliases), age, residence, physical description, and crime of men wanted by the government. Pictures might even be drawn to aid in the identification."[17] For example, the fugitive Liu Shih-ming (aka Lo Shu-t'ou), who had escaped from exile, was described as, "39 *sui*, of medium build, of light complexion, without pockmarks, with slight whiskers and a tattoo on his face (branding him as an exiled criminal)."[18]

More likely, the absence of detailed physical markers on eunuch runaway notices may be attributed to the fact that eunuch physical characteristics were a given in Qing society. While young eunuchs could and often did pass as non-emasculated males, adult eunuchs would have exhibited physical characteristics that marked them as such. Adult eunuchs who had been emasculated prior to the onset of puberty would have had extremely low levels of testosterone and would

12. First Historical Archives, Beijing, 宮中，雜件，人事類太監1017, 10月15日.

13. First Historical Archives, Beijing. 宮中，雜件，人事類太監1018, n.d. Case from 咸豐3年2月27日.

14. *Guoli Gugong Bowuyuan*, Taipei, 宮中檔奏摺, 乾隆朝403020746, Box 2743，乾隆30年6月3日.

15. *Guoli Gugong Bowuyuan*, Taipei, *Junjichu dang zhejian* 軍機處檔摺件009751，故宮009822，乾隆24年1月29日.

16. "Da Qing Lüli 大清律例 (1740)," Legalizing Space in China, http://lsc.chineselegalculture.org/eC/DQLL_1740/5.6.13.387.3.

17. Susan Naquin, "True Confessions: Criminal Interrogations as Sources for Ch'ing History," *National Palace Museum Bulletin* XI, no. 1 (March–April 1976): 12.

18. Susan Naquin, "True Confessions," 12.

therefore have lacked secondary sexual characteristics. These eunuchs would have exhibited a lack of facial hair, high voices, longer hands and fingers, and increased height (see Chapter 3). If a eunuch was still a child at the time of running away, many of these markers would not have appeared yet, and the young eunuch might have been able to successfully pass as a non-emasculated boy. However, in the case of older eunuchs, the above-mentioned physical changes may have made eunuchs appear more noticeable in a crowd. Such physical markers may have contributed to the arrest of the eunuch Bao Desheng 鮑的生. In 1842, while attempting to flee exile in Dasheng Wula 大牲烏拉,[19] Bao aroused the suspicions of the Shanhai Pass border guards. What gave Bao away? According to the arresting guards, he simply "looked like a eunuch" (*xing si taijian* 形似太監).[20] In the end, official descriptions of eunuch runaways based on their attire may have proven useless since, as we will see later, eunuchs often sold their clothes once they were outside the palace, in order to obtain money for food.

One disguise that did prove successful for some runaway eunuchs was to pretend they were monks by shaving their heads and donning religious attire. Since eunuchs often retreated to monasteries after retirement,[21] the presence of eunuchs at temples or among society would not have aroused the suspicions of the authorities. For example, Zhu Xiang 朱祥, a eunuch in the Imperial Library, tried to hide so that he would not have to endure a beating. Unable to find a hiding place, Zhu cut off his queue, took the alias of Li Fang 李芳, and joined the staff of the *Wanshandian* (萬善殿 Hall of Ten Thousand Virtues) as a monk.[22]

Surviving outside the System

While records indicate that many eunuchs succeeded in the initial act of running away, surviving outside of the palace walls and/or the eunuch system proved more difficult. As stated, the eunuch system was based upon the premise that emasculation rendered Han Chinese males into ideal servants who were totally reliant on their imperial masters. Since emasculation marked the body, it was believed that it would make eunuchs into social outcasts and thus increase a eunuch's reliance on his master. In fact, eunuchs would have found it very difficult to survive outside the eunuch system. The high instances of repeat offenders in cases of eunuch flight, especially when eunuchs had run away up to five or six times, suggests that providing for themselves while on the run, evading capture, and ultimately surviving outside the system proved challenging.[23]

19. Present-day Jilin Province. Wula was located just north of the city of Jilin 吉林 on the 1820 map of Tan Qixiang. "Wula" is a Chinese transliteration of Manchu *ula* (a large river).

20. Guoli Gugong Bowuyuan, 宮中檔奏摺, 道光朝005580, packet #33, crate #2719, 道光22年4月11日.

21. Ma Deqing et al., "Qing gong taijian huiyi lu," in *Wanqing gongting shenghuo jianwen*, ed. Zhang Wenhui (Beijing: Wenshi ziliao chubanshe, 1982), 196.

22. Du Wanyan, *Zhongguo huangguan shi*, 124.

23. I have yet to find any palace records that indicate the number of eunuchs assigned to the Forbidden City who

Once he was outside the palace walls, the eunuch's immediate concerns were obtaining travel money and food and avoiding arrest. In their confessions, captured eunuchs repeatedly mention selling their clothes in order to have money to buy food. In 1819, five-time runaway Sun Yong'an 孫勇安 ran out of money and, fearing arrest, turned himself in. In the following deposition, Sun recounts the events leading up to his fifth escape attempt and his surrender to the authorities:

> I am a forty-four *sui* native of Wuqing District. Formerly, when I ran away for the fourth time, I was sent to Heilongjiang to be a slave. During the ninth month of the eighteenth year of Jiaqing (Sept. 24–Oct. 23, 1813), having completed my six-year term of exile, I was freed and sent back in to the Department of Ceremonial. Later, I was transferred to the *Shuhuochu* (熟火處 Cooking Fire Department) to serve. This year, my *shouling taijian* [supervisory eunuch] Xu Jinxi sent me to accompany the hunt (*suiwei*). I did not have the money to buy a saddle or the [necessary] clothing and I could not borrow [the money] because I am usually not on friendly terms with my co-workers, and since [my] starting date was drawing near and [I] still had not yet borrowed [the money], I came up with the idea to run away. This year on fifteenth day of the second month (March 18), I ran away to a neighborhood outside of the *Xuanwumen* (Gate of Proclaimed Military Strength) where I found a small inn to stay and hide out in. Every day I moved and was without a fixed location. When I met people who questioned me, I lied and said that I was a eunuch on leave from an outer palace (*waifu*) who was unable to enter the city because it was late. Since it appeared that I had already used up the money [I obtained] from selling the clothes off my back to buy food and fearing that the punishment would be harsher if I was captured, I turned myself in to the Department.[24]

Clearly, Sun had no set destination in mind other than leaving the palace when he escaped. Never staying in one location more than one day, Sun focused on avoiding capture and feeding himself while on the run. Attempting to evade the authorities, Sun did not find other forms of employment but rather relied on money he obtained from selling the clothes off his back to support himself.

Eunuchs who chose to disguise themselves as monks appear to have had greater success in sustaining themselves for longer periods of time. Pretending to be itinerant monks, eunuchs would have met both the needs of eluding the authorities and obtaining food (through begging for alms). Other eunuchs such as the fifteen-year-old runaways Zhao Rong 趙榮 and Zhao Yu 趙玉 prolonged their freedom by hiring themselves out as laborers—cutting bramble, bundling sorghum, chopping

---

succeeded in running away and surviving outside the system; undoubtedly there were some who succeeded. According to Kutcher, during an eight-year period, the *Fanyichu* arrested seventy-five runaway eunuchs and were in "hot pursuit" of twenty-two others. See Kutcher, "Unspoken Collusions: The Empowerment of Yuanming yuan Eunuchs in the Qianlong Period," *Harvard Journal of Asiatic Studies* 70, no. 2 (Dec. 2010): 476. The *Fanyichu* 番役處 was a division of the *Shenxingsi* 慎刑司 responsible for the capture of escaped eunuchs. As this chapter is based primarily upon arrest records of captured runaway eunuchs, it is unclear how many might have evaded capture. If surviving outside the system was easy, one surmises that the number of repeat offenders would have been lower.

24. First Historical Archives, Beijing, 內務府，張儀司3779，嘉慶24年3月18日.

firewood, and cutting grass.[25] Due to their young age, these eunuchs may not have exhibited the distinctive physical characteristics of eunuchs yet and found it easier to blend in with society and to obtain work outside the system.

Some eunuchs tried to evade the authorities and lengthen their stay outside the palace by hiding out in relatives' homes. For example, one eunuch stayed with his adopted son's daughter.[26] In another case a eunuch, who had been exiled for stealing from his employer, a prince, ran back to the capital and hid out at his uncle's house until poverty forced him to apply once again to become a palace eunuch.[27] However, a runaway's relatives were often reluctant to harbor the fugitive, especially one who worked for the imperial court. As will be seen, families of runaway eunuchs, whether they were involved in helping the eunuch evade capture or not, faced collective punishment. Some may have never known that their eunuch relative was a fugitive, as some runaways merely told them that they were out on leave.

Other eunuchs extended their time outside the palace walls by working in the princely establishments of princes, dukes, and grand ministers. Well aware of this practice, the Qing attempted to prevent runaway eunuchs from looking at princely establishments as safe havens. The *Qinding zongrenfu zeli* (Imperially authorized laws and regulations of the court of the imperial clan) announced that, in 1802, Hu Jinyu 胡進玉 ran away for the second time, took an alias, and applied to work for a prince. After his arrest, Hu was exiled to Heilongjiang to serve as a military slave.[28] Later, the Qing stipulated that, when receiving eunuch applicants, princes, dukes, and grand ministers must look into the eunuch's circumstances and contact the Imperial Household Department to ensure that the applicant was not a runaway.[29]

The practice of eunuchs running away from service at the palace only to then apply to serve as a eunuch at a princely establishment may have been attributed to the inability of eunuch runaways to sustain themselves outside the system. The salary of a eunuch in the service of an imperial prince (*qinwang* 親王), commandery prince (*junwang* 君王), *beile* or *beile* prince (*beizi* 貝子) was very low compared to that of a palace eunuch.[30] Since princely establishments varied in size and wealth, the salaries of eunuchs employed by princes would also have varied.[31] Moreover, one can assume that the prestige associated with serving in a princely household was certainly less than that of a eunuch assigned to the imperial court.

25. *Gongzhong dang Jiaqingchao zouzhe* 宮中檔嘉慶朝奏摺 (*GZDJQCZZ*), no. 20, pt. 2, vol. 30 (Taipei: National Palace Museum, 1993–1995), 431.

26. First Historical Archives, Beijing, *Kangxi chao manwen zhupi zouzhe quanyi* (Beijing: Zhongguo shehui kexue chubanshe, 1996), 1118, entry 2822.

27. *Qingdai neige daku sanjian manwen dang'an xuanbian* 清代內閣大庫散件滿文檔案選編 [Selections from the archives of the Grant Secretariat of the Qing dynasty] (Tianjin: Tianjin guji chubanshe, 1991)，doc. 11, 26–27. This case clearly shows how difficult it was for eunuchs to survive outside the system.

28. First Historical Archives, Beijing 中國第一歷史檔案館, *Qinding zongrenfu zeli* 欽定宗人府則例 [Imperially commissioned regulations of the Imperial Clan Court], 例（八），職制王公毋許濫收太監，卷28，15.

29. First Historical Archives, Beijing, 內服務，會計司 8560，嘉慶9年6月16日.

30. Li Guang, "Qing ji de taijian," in *Wanqing gongting shenghuo jianwen*, ed. Zhang Wenhui, 161.

31. Li Guang, "Qing ji de taijian,"161.

Sources from the late Qing reveal that life was not necessarily better for eunuchs serving in princely households. Pu Jie's[32] recollection of an incident involving a eunuch employed by his family during the late Qing reveals that beating the servants was also a part of the daily routine in princely households. On one occasion, Pu Jie's mother ordered a eunuch to bring her some sugar (*táng* 糖). Thinking that she said "soup" (*tāng* 湯), a word that sounds similar but differs in tone and meaning, he brought her a bowl of soup. That night, the eunuch received several tens of blows from the large flattened bamboo (*daban* 大板) for his mistake.[33] "[Thus] beaten, he could not sit down on a stool for several days, [and] at night when it was time to sleep, [he] had to lie down on his side or face down on the bed.[34] Like palace eunuchs, these eunuchs lived in oppressive surroundings and operated under the same type of master–apprentice system in which collective responsibility ensured the perpetuation of beatings and the suppression of the eunuch population.[35]

Service in a princely establishment did offer the eunuch some advantages. Restrictions on the eunuch's mobility would have certainly been relaxed, giving eunuchs more freedom. Moreover, serving outside the palace, eunuchs would have had more contact with society. It remains unclear how much palace eunuchs would have known about the lives of their counterparts serving in the princely establishments. The cases presented here reveal that, for some eunuch runaways, princely households provided a source of food and money and a place to hide from authorities, all of which heightened their ability to survive outside the palace eunuch system.

Capture

The frequency of eunuch flight suggests that palace security was not without its flaws; however, the number of eunuchs who were captured reveals that surviving and remaining hidden from the authorities outside the palace was challenging. Due to the nature of the source material, official notices of eunuch flight and documents concerning eunuch capture, it remains unclear how many eunuchs succeeded in permanently running away from the system. Sources in the imperial record either alerted people to a eunuch's flight from the palace so the authorities could be on the lookout, or recorded the confessions of eunuchs who had already been captured or turned themselves in.

Runaway eunuchs who managed to get outside the palace walls faced many obstacles, the first of which was the Inner City police. Having memorized the

---

32. The younger brother of the Xuantong emperor.
33. The two words in Chinese sound very similar but differ in tone. "Sugar" is pronounced *táng* (second tone); "soup: is pronounced *tāng* (first tone).
34. Pu Jie, "Huiyi chun qinwang de shenghuo," in *Wanqing gongting shenghuo jianwen*, ed. Zhang Wenhui (Beijing: Wenshi ziliao chubanshe, 1982), 241.
35. Pu Jie, "Huiyi chun qinwang de shenghuo," 241.

faces of the inhabitants of the ten-household groups assigned to them, Inner City patrolmen could easily have spotted anyone who did not belong to the group, such as "persons of unclear background" and "idlers."[36] Runaway eunuchs would have raised suspicions. Those who made it to the Outer City stood a greater chance of "disappear[ing] into the crowd and escap[ing] official notice" since this part of the city was "far less heavily policed."[37] However, even to reach this point, eunuchs would have had to pass through numerous gates and checkpoints, many of which had jails on site for holding suspicious people passing through.[38] Without a travel pass (*luyin* 路引) and an ID card (*zhizhao* 執照) issued by the Imperial Household Department, runaways would have found it exceedingly difficult to pass through the city unnoticed.[39] George Carter Stent, writing during the late Qing, mentions the presence of a special police corps, called the Palace Squad (*Neidaban'er* 內大班兒), whose duty it was to capture runaway eunuchs. Stent notes:

> The men composing this force are not eunuchs themselves, but know all the eunuchs of the palace; and it is rare that one of them succeeds in escaping, for no sooner is the flight of one reported than the members of the force—(who are adepts at disguises, and may be considered detectives) spread themselves all over the city, and speedily recapture the deserter.[40]

In sum, the tight security within the capital created many obstacles to eunuch escape and greatly contributed to the capture of most runaways.

Fear of the punishments waiting for them if captured led many runaways to turn themselves in. Understanding that, once captured, they would receive a punishment more severe than the beating they might have fled, some eunuchs created elaborate lies to avoid punishment. During the reign of the Kangxi emperor (1662–1722), Cui Zilu 崔子路, a eunuch in the *Dagaodian* (大高殿 Hall of High Heaven) music troop, was very familiar with the Qing punishment system. In 1714, Cui had dropped his flute while playing it and was sentenced to forty blows from the heavy bamboo rod and transferred to the *Zhangyisi* (掌儀司 Department of Ceremonial). Three months later, fearing that he would receive a beating for not studying well, he fled the palace but was caught. In order to avoid punishment for running away, Cui first lied in his confession, claiming,

> I used to be a eunuch in the service of the *Dagaodian*'s music company. On the first day of the third month of the 52nd year (April 14, 1714), I dropped my flute while playing it and received forty blows from the heavy bamboo and was issued

36. Alison Dray-Novey, "Spatial Order and Police in Imperial Beijing," *The Journal of Asian Studies* 52, no. 4 (Nov. 1993): 898–99.

37. Dray-Novey, "Spatial Order and Police in Imperial Beijing," 902.

38. Dray-Novey, "Spatial Order and Police in Imperial Beijing," 895.

39. Tang Yinian, *Qing gong taijian* (Shenyang: Liaoning daxue chubanshe, 1993), 109.

40. George Carter Stent, "Chinese Eunuchs," *Journal of the North China Branch of the Royal Asiatic Society* XI (1877): 175. I have yet to come across an archival document that refers to the Palace Squad (*Neidaban'er*). Here Stent may be referring to the *Fanyichu* 番役處. This was a division of the *Shenxingsi* 慎刑司 that was responsible for the capture of escaped eunuchs. See Kutcher, "Unspoken Collusions," 476.

a discharge certificate and sent back to my native place. I sold my certificate to my Department of Ceremonial co-worker, Cui Jinchao 崔金朝 for five *taels*. When I hired myself out for work, I was arrested. I am really not a runaway eunuch.[41]

In the end, Cui revealed the truth and was sentenced to wear the cangue for three months and to receive one hundred blows.

Punishment

The imperial court did not take eunuchs running away from the palace lightly. A runaway eunuch faced punishment varying in severity according to the length of time spent outside of the palace walls, where he fled, whether he was captured or turned himself in, and the number of times he had run away previously. For example, the *Qinding gongzhong xianxing zeli* (Imperially authorized laws and regulations of conduct within the palace),[42] hereafter referred to as the *QDGZXXZL*, records that first-time offenders who turned themselves in would receive sixty blows from the flattened bamboo (*ban* 板) and be sent back in to serve, with a reduction in food and salary for one year. First-time offenders who were caught and second-time offenders who turned themselves in would receive sixty blows from the *ban* and be sent to Wudian[43] 吳甸 to cut grass for one year. Second-time offenders who turned themselves in one of the times they had run away would receive eighty blows from the *ban* and be sent to Wudian to cut grass for one and a half years. Second-time offenders who were captured in both attempts would receive one hundred blows from the *ban* and be sent to Wudian to cut grass for two years. As the number of times the eunuch ran away increased, so did the number of blows from the bamboo and the length of time cutting grass.

These strict punishments did not prevent eunuchs from repeatedly running away. Clearly, the punishments were not an effective deterrent if it was necessary to have specific regulations for eunuchs who had run away three, four, or even five times. For example, the *QDGZXXZL* states that eunuchs who ran away three, four, or five times, no matter whether they turned themselves in or not, when caught were sentenced to one hundred blows from the *ban* and sent to Wudian to cut grass for three, four, and five years respectively. When the term of punishment was fulfilled, these repeat offenders were re-employed by the Qing but restricted to positions in

---

41. *Qingdai neige daku sanjian manwen dang'an xuanbian*, doc. 48, 康熙56年5月17日，126–27.

42. *Qinding gongzhong xianxing zeli* 欽定宮中現行則例 (QDGZXXZL) [Imperially authorized laws and regulations of conduct within the palace] (Reprint, Taipei: Wenhai chubanshe, 1979), 卷4，處分 (punishment of officials), 808–15.

43. Eunuchs were assigned to cut grass in Wudian 吳甸 to supply the Manchus with feed for their horses. During the Qing, Wudian was located in Nanyuan 南苑. According to Hu Zhongliang, in the sixteenth year of the reign of the Qianlong emperor, the location for cutting grass was moved from Weng Mountain 翁山 to Wudian. The emperor, who was fond of the scenery at Weng Mountain, renamed the location Wanshou Mountain in celebration of his mother's sixtieth birthday. For more information on this and the system of cutting grass at Weng Mountain, see Hu Zhongliang, "Tan tan Wengshan zha cao," *Gugong Bowuyuan Yuankan* 3 (1986), 92.

the outer court. Concern about security leaks and eunuch loyalty after they had been exiled and had the opportunity to be in contact with people outside the palace led to prohibitions against exiled eunuchs from serving in the inner court.[44]

Sentencing eunuchs to perform manual labor in chains such as cutting grass appears to have only increased the desire of some eunuchs to flee. Eunuchs arrested for running away from Wudian before completing their sentences and eunuchs who had fulfilled their five-year sentences of cutting grass only to run away again were sentenced to wear the cangue in perpetuity. Four-time offenders who ran away from Wudian would receive even more beatings and be sent to serve as slaves to regular soldiers in Dasheng Wula for three years. As will be seen, the system allowed for flexibility in sentencing runaway eunuchs and not all eunuchs served their entire sentence.

Running away to destinations such as Henan, Shandong, Shanxi and Heilongjiang, Jilin, and Fengtian (*Dongsansheng*) elicited even stricter punishments from the government. All eunuchs who ran away to these places, regardless of the number of times they ran away or whether or not they had been captured or had turned themselves in, were sentenced to wear the cangue for a year and sent to Heilongjiang to serve as slaves to officials.[45] In addition, if there was an amnesty, these eunuchs were not to be pardoned. As mentioned, such sentences were usually reserved for repeat offenders who had run away from exile. The harsher punishments for eunuchs who ran away to these destinations can be partially attributed to the prohibition against Chinese immigration to Manchuria, a policy that aimed to both maintain Manchu political control and lessen sinicization in the area.[46]

Eunuch natives of Zhili who fled back to their home province also faced closer scrutiny and harsher punishments. Eunuchs who had run back to Zhili were to be closely questioned. Eunuchs found to have lied in their confessions would have their punishments increased in severity by one degree. Eunuchs who ran away to departments or counties within Zhili that were more than 500 *li*[47] from their native places, regardless of whether they had been captured or turned themselves in, would be sentenced to wear the cangue for six months and be sent to Dasheng Wula and given to an official as a slave for three years.

Eunuchs exiled to the remote edges of the empire even ran away from these distant locales. In 1715, the Imperial Household Department noted that eunuch Li Fang 李芳, previously exiled to Weng Mountain for gambling, broke free from his iron chains and fled. Although the officials from the Imperial Household Department recommended sentencing Li to wear a large cangue weighing fifty

---

44. In reality, these regulations were not always enforced, especially during periods when eunuch supplies were not meeting demands.
45. *QDGZXXZL*, 卷4，處分，812.
46. Robert H. G. Lee, *The Manchurian Frontier in Ch'ing History* (Cambridge, MA: Harvard University Press, 1970), 182.
47. 1 *li* = .5 kilometer.

jin[48] (approximately thirty-three pounds) and incarceration in the city gate prison with no possibility of release, the emperor ordered that Li be excused from wearing the cangue and sent back to Weng Mountain.[49] As the number of repeat offenses increased or the eunuch ran away from his location of exile, so did the remoteness of his next exile destination. Eunuchs who fled from Dasheng Wula received sentences of exile to Heilongjiang.

According to Tang Yinian, during the reigns of Qianlong (1736–1795), Tongzhi (1862–1874), and Guangxu (1875–1908), eunuchs ran away in large numbers.[50] It remains unclear though, whether or not this statement is based upon the number of documents that have survived in the historical record from these periods or if in fact there were more eunuchs escaping during these periods.[51] As the Qianlong emperor is often depicted as relying on "coercive and punitive"[52] measures to manage his eunuch staff, one could assume that Qianlong's management style may have contributed to the higher number of eunuchs fleeing during his reign. In contrast, Kutcher, in his study of *Yuanmingyuan* eunuchs, argues that eunuchs stationed at this palace had fewer restrictions placed on their mobility, thus making it easier for them to run away.[53] In either case, as more and more eunuchs fled, their contact with society increased and thus the likelihood of the realities of eunuch life becoming common knowledge. Their illusions of the eunuch lifestyle shattered, many eunuch applicants may have reconsidered their decision to become a eunuch, which in turn may have contributed to a decrease in the eunuch supply. Faced with a demand for eunuchs that exceeded the supply, the Qing relaxed the age and native place restrictions and filled vacancies with eunuchs taken from the princely households.[54]

The failure of supply to meet demand during this period may also have necessitated leniency in the punishment of runaways. Despite the severity of the punishments for runaways as listed in the *QDGZXXZL*, not all eunuchs served their entire sentences. A record from the First Historical Archives in Beijing suggests that runaways might be sentenced to strict punishments, only to have their sentences reduced and be sent back into the palace to serve.[55] Spared from wearing the cangue in perpetuity, six-time runaways Li Shoutong 李壽通 and Zhang Fujun 張福均 were resentenced according to the legal precedent and discharged from service after wearing the cangue for only four years. Moreover, three-time runaways sent to Wudian to cut grass for three years, Wu Degui 吳得貴 and Jia Defu 賈得福, had their sentences reduced to one hundred blows, after which they were sent back to

---

48. 1 *jin* or Chinese "catty" = 1 1/3 lbs.

49. *Kangxi chao manwen zhupi zouzhe quanyi*, 1516, entry 3645.

50. Tang, *Qing gong taijian*, 109.

51. While some documents record the number of eunuchs sent to different areas to serve their punishments, most just record individual cases of runaway eunuchs.

52. Preston Torbert, *The Ch'ing Imperial Household Department: A Study of Its Organization and Principal Functions, 1662–1796* (Cambridge, MA: Harvard University Press, 1977), 50.

53. See Kutcher, "Unspoken Collusions," 451.

54. Tang, *Qing gong taijian*, 109.

55. First Historical Archives, Beijing, 宮中，雜件，敬事房 2462, n.d.

the palace to serve in the outer court. Records from the Xianfeng reign period even reveal that five-time runaways were sent back to serve at the palace, albeit restricted to service in the outer court, after only four years in exile in Heilongjiang.[56]

The possibility of obtaining their freedom from the system by paying off their bondage upon reaching their destination of exile and slavery also motivated some eunuchs to run away. In his work on the Manchurian frontier, Robert H. G. Lee notes that criminals exiled to Kirin (Jilin) could purchase their freedom from their masters.[57] An imperial decree from 1810 reveals:

> Eunuchs who were exiled for criminal causes also lived in freedom after paying their ransoms. Some of them bought business properties. When they were released, they deliberately recommitted crimes in order to be sent back to exile. Thus the intent of the national code for the strict punishment of criminals was being grossly violated through the practice of private redemption, which mitigated the criminals' fear of punishment and encouraged them to look upon the land of exile as paradise.[58]

The edict attempted to close this loophole in the exile system by instructing the military governor to prohibit the purchase of freedom by exiled criminals.

Eunuch Unfree Status

The abundance of cases of eunuch flight by repeat offenders in the historical record reveals the ineffectiveness of the Imperial Household Department's policies aimed at stemming the outward flow of eunuchs with harsh punishments. While the practice of reducing sentences for eunuch runaways may have been an immediate fix for the problem, it ultimately decreased the effectiveness of harsh punishments as a deterrent. The desire of eunuchs to escape the system continued unabated through the end of the Qing dynasty. After the fall of the dynasty in 1911, eunuchs ran away in great numbers.[59] The weakness of the imperial court and the newfound political rights of eunuchs as citizens of the Republic favored the ultimate success of eunuchs in their escape attempts.[60]

---

56. *Guoli Gugong Bowuyuan*, Taipei, 宮中檔奏摺，咸豐朝，406015891，故宮134838.
57. Lee, *The Manchurian Frontier in Ch'ing History*, 84. Lee notes that masters were often willing to allow slaves to buy their freedom due to the financial burden of owning slaves in urban areas.
58. *Jilin tongzhi* cited in Robert H. G. Lee, *The Manchurian Frontier in Ch'ing History*, 84.
59. Yu Huaqing, *Zhongguo huanguan zhidushi* (Shanghai: Renmin chubanshe, 1993), 508. Under the "Articles of Favourable Treatment," the emperor and his court were allowed to continue to live within the Forbidden City under certain restrictions. For more information, see Aisin-Gioro Pu Yi, *From Emperor to Citizen: The Autobiography of Aisin-Gioro Pu Yi*, trans. W. J. F. Jenner (Beijing, 1964; reprint, New York: Oxford University Press, 1987), 38. As discussed in Chapter 9, the emperor continued to rely on eunuchs to serve him and his court from 1911 until 1923, when he expelled eunuchs from the palace.
60. Article 6 of a document issued by the Republic on December 26, 1914, proclaims that "Criminal jurisdiction within the palace is abolished. Minor offenders among the eunuchs and other palace employees may be dealt with by commanding officers of the palace guards and punished in accordance with police regulations." Article 7 states that "All persons employed by the imperial household are citizens of the republic." Cited in Reginald F. Johnston, *Twilight in the Forbidden City* (London, 1934; reprint, Wilmington, DE: Scholarly Resources, 1973), 99.

The use of slavery as a punishment for runaway eunuchs also reveals the complexity of eunuch unfree status during the Qing. The majority of eunuchs during the Qing voluntarily underwent emasculation and then applied for service as an imperial court eunuch. Once eunuchs were admitted into the system, their terms of servitude were essentially for life, with discharge authorized only for illness, old age, or death. Eunuchs who chose to make an unauthorized exit from the system faced two options: suicide or running away.[61]

Eunuchs received salaries but lived out their lives governed by strict rules regarding deportment and mobility. Eunuchs assigned to the Forbidden City found themselves subject to more restricted rules than those assigned to other palaces or to princely establishments, due to the palace being the seat of imperial power. These rules, when coupled with an environment in which corporal punishment was used as a tool to ensure compliance, made daily life difficult for many eunuchs, especially low-level eunuchs, to endure.

Moreover, the term used to refer to eunuchs discharged from the palace eunuch system, *weimin taijian* (為民太監 commoner eunuch), clearly reveals that eunuchs were regarded as different from the rest of the population. The inability of eunuchs to leave the system of their own volition before being deemed unfit to perform their duties suggests that they were not free. However, the use of slavery as a form of punishment for runaway eunuchs further indicates that there were degrees of unfree status during the Qing. In other words, the punishment of banishment to the frontiers of the empire to serve as a slave was considered more restrictive than the life of a palace eunuch.

Motivations

Clearly aware that harsh punishments were not stemming the flow of eunuchs fleeing the palace, those conducting the investigations appear to have been very interested in the reasons why eunuchs fled. The imperial court feared that eunuch runaways could become involved with people on the outside who might wish to utilize or exploit the eunuch's knowledge of and access to the Forbidden City to gain entry into the palace or to obtain classified information. Alluding to this, the interrogators of five-time runaway Sun Yong'an asked him whether or not he had owed money and thus been coerced into running away.[62] This suspicion extended even to eunuchs in the service of princely establishments who applied to work in the palace. In the case of Gao Sheng 高升, a eunuch who ran away from his exile in Wula (for stealing clothing from his employer) only to return to the capital to work as an inner court eunuch, the Imperial Household Department desired to know who had encouraged Gao to obtain employment within the palace.[63] This fear of eunuchs

61. For a discussion of eunuch suicide, see Chapter 7.
62. First Historical Archives, Beijing, 內務府，掌儀司3779，熟火處太監孫勇案，嘉慶24年3月18日.
63. *Qingdai neige daku sanjian manwen dang'an xuanbian*, doc. 11, 雍正8年3月初7日, 26–28.

acting as counterintelligence agents proved well founded in 1813 during the Eight Trigrams Uprising, in which eunuchs facilitated the entry of rebels into the palace.[64]

While interrogations of captured runaways clearly reveal an interest in ascertaining whether or not the eunuch could pose a security risk, they also show that the Imperial Household Department was well aware of the more common causes behind flight. For example, during the twenty-third year of Jiaqing (1818), *Jingshifang* 敬事房[65] officials closely questioned eunuch Jihua 紀華 about why he fled: "was it that his *shouling taijian* had cursed at [him], or that he had gotten into a fight with eunuchs or others, or that he had habitually broken the rules against drinking alcohol and gambling, etc."[66] Kutcher argues that runaway eunuchs, when questioned about their reasons for running away, would choose "from a repertoire of excuses for their misdoings that conformed to the expectations that others had of them."[67] As Kutcher notes, the circumstances in which the confessions were made or recorded are unknown. This study finds that without this information and more importantly, any evidence to suggest otherwise, eunuch-professed motives, rather than being "formulaic," reveal that eunuchs were running away due to problems endemic to the eunuch system. The repetition of eunuch motivations for running away suggests that reasons such as fear of being beaten were indicative of problems eunuchs faced in their daily lives and those that were plaguing the eunuch system as a whole. Last, it is important to also recognize the purpose of recording these confessions in the first place. The imperial court's motives for ascertaining why eunuchs fled the system did not stem from a desire to improve the welfare of the eunuch population but rather the need to maintain the security of the emperor and his family.

This distrust of eunuchs appears evident in searches to make sure nothing had been stolen after a eunuch had fled. Memorials often cite whether or not official items or the eunuch's personal effects were missing.[68] These searches of the premises suggest that eunuchs fled because they committed theft. The historical record does reveal that eunuchs commonly fled after stealing items, to avoid suffering the consequences for their crimes. Eunuchs such as Ye Fu 葉福 fled after failing to cover up instances of petty theft. In 1770, Ye Fu, a eunuch in the service of the *Yuanmingyuan* kennel, turned himself in after attempting to flee. While Ye's *shouling taijian*, Wang Lin 王林, was away accompanying the hunt, Ye had used 2,000 *wen* 文 of the kennel's operating budget (*gongfei qian* 公費錢). It is unclear what Ye spent this money on. In an effort to replace the money, Ye stole Wang's silk outer coat and sold it, replacing six strings of cash. Still short of the money and fearing that Wang would want his coat upon his return, Ye fled and hid for two days. Despite Ye's confession

64. See Clara Wing-chung Lau, "Jiaqing jingji 'guiyou zhi bian' zhong taijian suo banyan de jiaose," *Dongfang wenhua* 2 (1984): 87–106.
65. The *Jingshifang* 敬事房 handled the screening, transfer, appointment and reward and punishment of the imperial palace eunuchs. See Yu, *Zhongguo huanguan zhidushi*, 451.
66. First Historical Archives, Beijing, 內務府敬事房 5245, 逃走太監, 內殿總管孫得祿, 嘉慶23年7月初6日.
67. Kutcher, "Unspoken Collusions," 462–63.
68. First Historical Archives, Beijing, 宮中, 雜件, 人事類太監1019.

about running away after misappropriating money and stealing from his superior in order to cover it up, the memorialist, a Vice Provincial Commander-in-chief (*futidu*) remained suspicious of the motives behind Ye's flight and feared there were other factors involved.[69]

Suspicions of eunuchs fleeing after committing theft were not unfounded. Eunuch Ma Yu 馬玉 stole silver vessels to pawn, was captured, and sent to Heilongjiang to serve as an armored soldier's slave. Ma's family was forced to pay for the items he had stolen.[70] *Shenninggong* (神寧宮 Palace of Earthly Tranquility) eunuch Ma Sheng 馬昇 fled after stealing several pearls. Ma later turned himself in and was exiled to Dasheng Wula to be a slave.[71] The possibility also exists that the items were stolen in the first place to do just that, to facilitate an escape from the palace by providing funds for traveling expenses and food. Some eunuchs during the Daoguang reign period were arrested after having run away from the palace when accused of selling opium.[72]

Tang Yinian attributes eunuch flight not only to beatings but also to a desire to see the outside world. Eunuchs who entered the palace at an early age essentially grew up inside the palace walls. Tang argues that, later on in life, these eunuchs desired to get out of the palace. Leave from the palace and time outside the palace only increased this desire.[73]

Eunuch runaways appear to have been more desperate than this. The historical record shows that more commonly eunuchs ran away to avoid being beaten or having to deal with harsh working conditions. Eunuchs who confessed that they could not bear the suffering anymore clearly reveal that they just wanted to get out of the system. Three-time runaway Yang Dehai 楊得海 ran away from his punishment of cutting grass at Wudian because his "daily grain ration was not enough and he was suffering."[74] In the 1716 case of Li Guoqin 李國秦, a runaway from Rehe, Li states: "Since my leg was hurting I requested a leave of absence from my *zongguan taijian*, Chen Qitai 陳齊泰. My *shouling taijian*, Wang Taiping 王泰平, urged me to return [to work] and rudely insulted and cursed at me. I got in an argument with him. Fearing being beaten by him . . . I ran away."[75] Other eunuchs such as Zhao Rong 趙榮, a fifteen *sui* eunuch learning a trade in the Prospect Hill's palace lower school (*Jingshan xiaoneixue* 景山小內學) was struck twenty-nine times with

69. *Zhongyang yanjiuyuan lishiyuyansuo xiancun Qingdai neige daku yuancang Ming-Qing dang'an* 中央研究院歷史語言研究所現存清代內閣大庫原藏明清檔案 [Ming-Qing archives in the collection of the Academia Sinica's Institute of History and Philology], ed. Zhang Weiren (Taipei: Academia Sinica, 1986–1995), A209-48, 2-1-2-2.

70. Du, *Zhongguo huanguan shi*, 123–24.

71. Du, *Zhongguo huanguan shi*, 123–24.

72. *Guoli Gugong Bowuyuan*, Taipei, 軍機處檔摺件 080428, 道光 27年12月23日.

73. Tang, *Qing gong taijian*, 111.

74. *Guoli Gugong Bowuyuan*, Taipei, 宮中檔奏摺, 咸豐朝, 406007139, 故宮125933, 咸豐5年11月20日. Yang Dehai was sentenced to eighty strikes from the *ban* and sent to Dasheng Wula for three years to serve as a military slave, after which time he was to be assigned to the outer court of the palace.

75. *Kangxi chao manwen zhupi zouzhe quanyi*, 1118, entry 2822.

the *ban* by *shouling* Shao Guoqin 邵國秦, after which he became depressed.[76] Shao, feeling melancholy after his punishment and desiring to avoid any future beatings, readily agreed to accompany two of his fellow eunuch co-workers who were planning an escape.[77] Eunuchs such as Gao Jingrui, a eunuch in the *Jingshifang*, even ran away due to losing his eunuch supervisor's dog.[78] Fear of being punished for returning late from running errands outside of the palace also contributed to the high incidence of eunuch flight.[79]

Labor Relations during the Qing

Cases of eunuchs running away from the palace provide important insight into labor relations between the Imperial Household Department and the eunuch workforce. Confessions from runaway eunuchs reveal that the eunuch hierarchy reinforced a management system based upon coercion and punishment. Eunuch runaways were commonly from among the largest population of palace eunuchs, those who were known simply as *taijian* who, at the bottom tier of the eunuch hierarchy, did not carry any rank. While the Imperial Household Department was officially in charge of the management of eunuchs, they relied heavily on the upper echelons of the eunuch hierarchy to supervise the majority of these unranked eunuchs.

Beatings of eunuchs at the bottom of the eunuch hierarchy by their eunuch supervisors (*shouling taijian*) reveal that beatings were a frequent management tool within the palace. Intended to be a deterrent to keep the eunuch workforce in line, it often proved too much for some eunuchs to bear and contributed to deteriorating labor relations within the palace. Although eunuch beatings by the imperial court masters was a common practice, cases of eunuch flight add to our understanding of corporal punishment within the palace. The prevalence of unranked eunuchs running away from the system suggests that the Qing's reliance on collective responsibility created a culture in which eunuch supervisors abused their subordinates. In sum, eunuch-on-eunuch beatings and fear of collective punishment were a practice used by the palace in its attempt to control its eunuch population by intimidation and force.

Descriptions of life within the palace by palace women and even the last emperor, Pu Yi, cast the realities of life within the palace in a negative light. In *A Palace Woman Talks about her Recollections of the Past* (*Gongnü tan wanglu*), He Rong'er, a palace woman during the late Qing, recalls, "In reality, there was no happiness within the palace . . . People were just like wooden people, going along according to the rules, nobody being allow to make a mistake or differ."[80] In his

---

76. 宮中檔嘉慶朝奏摺，No. 20, Part 2, 嘉慶13年7月24日，431–33.
77. 宮中檔嘉慶朝奏摺，No. 20, Part 2, 嘉慶13年7月24日，431–33.
78. First Historical Archives, Beijing, 宮中，雜件，敬事房2462，n.d.
79. First Historical Archives, Beijing, 宮中，雜件，敬事房2462，n.d.
80. Jin Yi and Shen Yiling, *Gongnü tan wanglu* (Beijing: Forbidden City Press, 1992), 18.

autobiography, *From Emperor to Citizen*, Pu Yi provides insight into the lives of eunuchs, revealing that eunuchs would make offerings to the palace gods (snakes, foxes, weasels, and hedgehogs), the protectors of eunuchs, in hopes "that the palace gods would protect them from the beatings and other forms of ill-treatment from which they often suffered."[81]

What do repeat offenders and laws addressing eunuchs running away up to six times say about Qing labor relations and management of palace eunuchs? Clearly, the palace's management style (characterized by beatings and corporal punishment) was not resolving the problem of eunuchs running away from the palace. The imperial court maintained a policy that dereliction of duty would not be tolerated. Harsh regulations and punishments were intended to show that the emperor's power was absolute and that any attempt to try to place one's independent will above the needs of the emperor and his family would be met with swift punitive action. Such shows of force and dominance were not always effective.

Ultimately, runaway eunuchs created a drain on the system of skilled servants for the palace. During reign periods such as Daoguang, in which supply was not meeting demand, harsh punishments were ineffective as deterrents and had to be relaxed in order to ensure that the imperial court had the necessary number of eunuchs. Security demands, however, dictated that repeat offenders could no longer serve within the inner court of the palace. Even these restrictions, though, could be relaxed if the demand for eunuchs outweighed the available supply.

Conclusion

The palace eunuch workforce served the imperial court in an oppressive work environment designed to ensure complete submission to the imperial will. Relying on coercion and punitive measures to manage its eunuch staff, the Imperial Household aimed to keep the palace eunuch population under control. Despite their efforts, the Imperial Household's management techniques and use of harsh punishments as deterrents for unwanted behavior had the unintended result of becoming too oppressive for some eunuchs to bear. Young Han Chinese boys and men voluntarily submitted themselves to undergo emasculation to apply for service as palace eunuchs. Once they were inside, some eunuchs who had initially wanted to enter the system soon desperately wanted to get out. Subject to frequent beatings, often restricted in their mobility, and deprived of the freedom to terminate their term of service of their own volition, running away presented eunuchs with a degree of agency rarely afforded to them in their daily lives.

During the Qing dynasty, eunuchs ran away repeatedly, some in excess of six times. The ability of eunuchs to escape from the palace and their duties suggest that palace security was severely flawed. Running away appears to have been the easy

---

81. Aisin-Gioro Pu Yi, *From Emperor to Citizen*, 67.

part; what proved most difficult for runaway eunuchs was surviving outside the system. Eunuchs who managed to get beyond the palace walls soon faced a host of obstacles that had the potential to impede their ability to sustain their escape: tight security within the capital, obtaining traveling expenses and food, and even the threat of receiving a harsher punishment if eventually captured as opposed to choosing to turn oneself in.

Despite the inherent difficulties in permanently running away from the system, eunuch flight continued unabated. Confessions from captured eunuchs reveal that, for many eunuchs, serving in the palace proved too restrictive and too oppressive to endure until old age or sickness enabled them to end their term of service. The repeated flight of eunuchs suggests that, for some eunuchs, punishment such as a year of manual labor cutting grass in Wudian was preferable to serving as eunuchs inside the palace. Eunuch confessions provide insights into the tense labor relations between eunuchs and their supervisors/superiors and overt acts of eunuch resistance to the system designed to keep them submissive. While flight from the palace empowered eunuchs and allowed them the opportunity to attempt to determine their own fate, this freedom often proved short-lived and led to much more oppression in the form of punishment. Concerns about the safety of the empire ensured that unauthorized exits from the system would be met with capture, followed by beatings, wearing the cangue, forced labor and, in more severe cases, slavery and exile.

Cases of eunuch runaways also add to our understanding of unfree status during the Qing and reveal that, in the case of eunuchs, it was complicated. On the one hand, palace eunuchs collected salaries. Service in the palace even offered a small number of eunuchs opportunities for upward mobility. Eunuchs were not considered slaves but in many ways had restrictions on their freedom and mobility like slaves. Moreover, eunuchs could not terminate their employment of their own volition. Eunuchs had few options for leaving the system; approved exits from the system such as sick leave, retirement, and death were determined by others. To the Qing, eunuchs occupied a type of unfree status outside slavery, as that classification was reserved as a punishment for repeat runaway offenders. Many eunuchs discovered only after entering the palace that life as a eunuch was much more restricted than they had originally imagined. In an act of agency, some eunuchs attempted to determine their own exit from the system by running away from the palace. For eunuch runaways, this taste of freedom was only fleeting.

7

Eunuch Suicide

Punishment, Not Compassion

During the thirteenth year of reign of Jiaqing (1808), Li Guangyu 李光玉, a eunuch in the *Yonghegong* (雍和宮 Palace of Eternal Harmony) hanged himself in the *Yuhuayuan* (御花園 Imperial Garden). In response, the Imperial Household Department dumped Li's body in the wilderness and exiled his relatives to Yili to serve as slaves to soldiers.[1] The deprivation of a proper burial for Li and the exile of six of his family members leaves no doubt that Li's suicide was considered a criminal act. Far from a solitary act, a eunuch's suicide posed a risk to the imperial court, his family members, and his fellow eunuchs.

Cases of eunuch suicide not only record the death of a eunuch, but they also reveal much about the eunuch's life and his status. An examination of how the Qing dealt with eunuch suicides provides insight into palace–eunuch labor relations, the complexities of unfree status, and further evidence of eunuchs pushing the boundaries of acceptable behavior as they attempted to express a degree of agency and self-determination in their lives.[2] The suicide of a eunuch warranted the direct involvement of the Imperial Household Department and its Judicial Department (*Shenxingsi* 慎刑司). Qing regulations sent a clear message that actions such as suicide that put the wants and needs of a servant before those of the emperor and his family and disrupted the harmony of the palace would be dealt with harshly. Moreover, they reveal that eunuchs did not have the right to leave their positions whenever they chose, especially when it involved the possibility of leaving the palace for good through suicide.

---

1. *Gongzhong dang Jiaqingchao zouzhe (GZDJQCZZ)*, no. 20, pt. 2, vol. 30 (Taipei: National Palace Museum, 1993–1995), 704.
2. As of February 2016, the First Historical Archives, Beijing, lists sixty-six cases of eunuch suicide in its database. The majority of digitized cases are from the reigns of Qianlong (nineteen cases), Daoguang (sixteen cases), and Jiaqing (eighteen cases). The Tongzhi, Yongzheng, Xianfeng, and Guangxu reigns each had one case on file. It remains unclear how many cases of eunuch suicide the archive holds, as only those digitized are currently accessible to scholars.

Suicide during the Qing

While the Qing regarded eunuch suicide as a criminal act, cases of suicide among the general populace were not considered illegal unless the act directly threatened the security of the government or resulted from the actions or coercion of another. During the early Qing, the government recognized and even commemorated cases of suicide by widows. Commemorative arches or plaques[3] stood as monuments to such acts of filial piety that brought recognition from the government and honor to these women and their families.[4] However, the government later realized that official recognition of such acts could contribute to widows ending their lives. As a result, in 1688, the government reevaluated its approval of such suicides and thereafter labeled widows who killed themselves solely because their husband had died (rather than to avoid forced remarriage) as "'treating life lightly.'"[5] Suicides by widows, despite being the focus of several scholarly studies, in reality only made up a small percentage of the suicides committed in China.

Suicide among the general populace was not uncommon during the Qing dynasty. Instances of females drowning themselves in wells to avoid unwanted arranged marriages or to make a statement against unjust treatment by their families are a familiar theme in Chinese literature. Huang Liu-hung, Qing dynasty magistrate and author of a manual for magistrates, noted that suicide was particularly prevalent in areas with populations living in extreme poverty. According to Huang, "Suicides by hanging were daily occurrences and self-destruction by cutting one's throat or drowning in the river were common events" in Tancheng (Shandong Province), where he served from 1670 to 1672.[6] It remains unclear, however, if Tancheng is representative of all of China or is an example of a particular locale over a two-year period. Further study on the topic of suicide during the Qing dynasty is necessary before one can assess the overall prevalence of suicide in China at the time. Nevertheless, these sources suggest that ending one's own life was not uncommon.

Among the general population, acts of suicide only warranted criminal prosecution when an injustice had occurred which caused the deceased to take his or her own life. According to Andrew Hsieh and Jonathan Spence in their work on suicide and the family in China, "for long periods of China's pre-modern history the act of suicide was not regarded as deviant . . . what was deviant was not the

3. J.-J. Matignon, *Superstition, Crime et Misère en Chine: Souvenirs de Biologie Sociale* (1899; reprint, Paris: Masson et Cie, 1900), 118.
4. Margery Wolf, "Women and Suicide in China," in *Women in Chinese Society*, ed. Margery Wolf and Roxane Witke (Stanford: Stanford University Press, 1975), 111.
5. Mark Elvin, "Female Virtue and State in China," *Past and Present* 104 (August 1984): 127–28.
6. Huang Liu-hung, *A Complete Book Concerning Happiness and Benevolence: A Manual for Local Magistrates in Seventeenth-Century China* (Tucson: University of Arizona Press, 1984), 356.

suicide act, but the pressuring of a person into suicide."[7] Rather than treating the person who committed suicide as a criminal, the Qing authorities often regarded the deceased as a victim of a criminal act committed by others. "The Chinese legal codes did not conceive of suicide as an act carried out in isolation. On the contrary, in suicide cases as in homicide cases, they looked for an instigator, and the major category under which acts of suicide can be found in the Ming and Ch'ing [Qing] Codes is that of 'Pressuring a person to commit suicide' (*Wei-pi jen chih-ssu* [*weibi ren zhisi*] 威逼人致死)."[8] Thus, when a person committed suicide, the main question asked was often not "Why?" but "Who?" "Who drove [him or] her to this? Who is responsible?"[9]

Questions about the motives behind the suicide act were usually answered in criminal proceedings focusing on those who had "pressured" the victim into committing suicide. In the twenty-five sub-statutes listed under "Pressuring a Person to Commit Suicide" detailed in the *Xing'an huilan* (Conspectus of penal cases), Hsieh and Spence found the following causes for suicide among the populace:

> Most of these sub-statutes concerned cases of adultery or sexual assault where shame or discovery was followed by suicide. The number of sub-statutes was partly due to the different ways in which suicide followed the occurrence: in some cases it was the party directly involved who committed the suicide out of guilt or shame, but more often the statute was invoked because the shock resulting from the discovery of the act led a third party within the family (whether husband, mother-in-law or parents) to commit suicide. Most of the remaining cases sprang from robberies—usually because the person was so desperate at his loss that he chose to end his life—or from money-lending, when either failure to pay or the sudden demand for payment might cause either party to kill themselves. There are also examples of threats, abuse, false accusation, blackmail or defamation of character, and forcing a woman into an unwanted marriage.[10]

Only acts of suicide in which the victim appeared to have been coerced or pressured into taking his or her own life elicited criminal prosecution against the suicide victim or even his family. Suicides engineered to settle grudges were labeled "acts of depravity" [that] "cannot be condoned."[11] Official responses to suicides among the general populace varied from condemnation to compassion, depending upon the circumstances of the suicide and the reasoning behind the act.[12]

---

7. Andrew C. K. Hsieh and Jonathan D. Spence, "Suicide and the Family in Pre-Modern Chinese Society," in *Normal and Abnormal Behavior in Chinese Culture*, ed. Arthur Kleinman and Tsung-Yi Lin (London: D. Reidel Publishing Company, 1981), 45.

8. Hsieh and Spence, "Suicide and the Family in Pre-Modern Chinese Society," 35. In 1772, this category became known as *bipo*, the change in wording reflecting a more "neutral tone" of "to press someone to do something," since "*weibi*" carried the connotation of a superior pressuring a person to commit suicide. See Hsieh and Spence, "Suicide and the Family in Pre-Modern Chinese Society," 36.

9. Wolf, "Women and Suicide in China," 112.

10. Hsieh and Spence, "Suicide and the Family in Pre-Modern Chinese Society," 36.

11. Huang, *A Complete Book Concerning Happiness and Benevolence*, 356.

12. Huang, *A Complete Book Concerning Happiness and Benevolence*, 355–56.

When a suicide among the general population was reported, the magistrate would go to the site and examine the corpse immediately, to ensure that the death was the result of a suicide and not murder.[13] Once this was verified, the magistrate would investigate to determine if the suicide had been committed due to provocation by another; in other words, attempt to determine who caused the suicide. In such cases, the person who provoked the act would be punished with blows from the heavy rod and fined, all in an effort "to pacify the spirit of the deceased."[14] If the magistrate's investigation determined no provocation was involved, the corpse would simply be returned to the family and the case would be closed. In sum, cases of suicide among the general population attracted little attention from the authorities during the Qing, unless they directly threatened the security of the government or resulted from the actions or coercion of another member of society.

Regulations

Qing regulations concerning eunuch suicide as stated in the punishment section of the *Qinding gongzhong xianxing zeli* (欽定宮中現行則例 Imperially authorized laws and regulations of conduct within the palace)[15] reveal that such acts involved far more than an individual ending his own life. Threatening the harmony, safety, and comfort of the imperial court, the focus on the act of suicide moved away from the deceased to the implications for the imperial court and its protection. In addition, these regulations emphasize the eunuch's servile status and the negation of his right to dispose of his body as he saw fit, without penalty. Viewed as a criminal act that terminated the eunuch's employment without authorization, disrupted the harmony of the Forbidden City and lives of the imperial family, eunuch suicide elicited a harsh response from the authorities.

Included in the laws of conduct within the palace are four regulations that specifically address punishments for eunuchs who attempted and/or committed suicide. In each of these regulations, eunuchs and women are grouped and singled out for punishment.[16] At first glance, one might assume that similarities in status, specifically servile status, dictated the joining of these two groups. On closer inspection, though, the use of the broader term for women (*nüzi* 女子) as opposed to palace maidservants (*gongnü* 宮女) suggests that the two may have been linked in

---

13. Huang, *A Complete Book Concerning Happiness and Benevolence*, 356.
14. Huang, *A Complete Book Concerning Happiness and Benevolence*, 356.
15. *Qinding gongzhong xianxing zeli* 欽定宮中現行則例 (QDGZXXZL) [Imperially authorized laws and regulations of conduct within the palace] (Reprint, Taipei: Wenhai chubanshe, 1979), 卷4，處分 (punishment of officials), 786–87. See Appendix 2.
16. Although eunuchs and women are grouped in the statutes, the focus of this chapter is on eunuch suicides. See Appendix 2 for a listing of the statutes. The study of suicide during the Qing has focused primarily on suicide among widows. At present, there are not enough studies to draw comparisons between eunuch suicides with those by palace women, palace maidservants, and non-emasculated males.

the statues due to their shared classification as subordinated groups.[17] This is further supported by the fact that no mention is made of punishment for suicides committed within the palace by non-emasculated males (e.g., bondservants).

The statutes differentiate between attempted suicide and those that ended the eunuch's life. Eunuchs "saved from" killing themselves soon died, but often at the hands of another. As will be seen, suicides attempted within the palace could warrant sentences ranging from strangulation to immediate beheading. At first glance this seems ironic since this punishment aided the eunuch in achieving his goal. However, it also deprived the eunuch of the freedom to decide how and when he would end his life. Eunuchs who committed suicide did not escape punishment even though they were already dead. The deceased eunuch was deprived of a proper burial and his family was exiled. The regulation states: "As for eunuchs and women who commit suicide within the palace, their corpses shall be discarded in the wilderness and their relatives sent to Yili to be given to soldiers to serve as slaves." Responding to all cases of eunuch suicide (attempted or completed acts) with either the death penalty or exile, the Imperial Household sent a message to the eunuch population that suicide would not be tolerated and was a criminal act warranting harsh punishment for the eunuch or, in his absence, his family.

Location and Mode of Suicide

Qing regulations concerning eunuch suicide varied in severity according to the method and location in which the suicide was either attempted or committed. Here, the Imperial Household differentiated between those committed within the palace (*zai gongnei* 在宮內) and those committed in the gardens (*zai yuanting* 在園庭). Suicides attempted or committed in the gardens (outside) carried a much lighter punishment. These eunuchs were spared from having their corpses cast out into the wilderness, but their relatives were still subject to exile to Urumqi to serve as slaves to soldiers. In cases of suicide attempted in a garden, the eunuch received a sentence of exile to Yili to serve as a slave to soldiers rather than death by strangulation. Such punishments minimized the loss of eunuch labor by ensuring his continued to service to the Qing (but in another capacity).

The punishment of slavery once again illuminates the complexities of eunuch status during the Qing. Rather than seen as a binary, of either free or unfree, status appeared along a spectrum or continuum. Cases of eunuch suicide further support the argument that eunuch status occupied a position closer to that of unfree but did not equate to slavery. The sentencing of a eunuch for an attempted suicide in the garden makes clear that, while eunuch status was low and eunuch lives were in many ways restricted, slavery occupied a position on the lower end of the servitude–slavery continuum. Eunuch suicide statutes also emphasize the point that

---

17. One can assume that *nüzi* 女子 referred to women living and working in the palace.

eunuchs were particularly restricted in their ability to terminate their employment at a time of their own choosing, especially when it involved ending their lives.

Sentences of deprivation of a proper burial for the deceased and immediate beheading for those still living clearly reveal the severity of punishments for acts of suicide committed within the palace. Why differentiate between the two locations and punish eunuchs who committed acts within the palace more severely? Committing an act of suicide within the palace carried a harsher punishment due to its proximity to the emperor. Eunuchs were not simply being punished for attempting to decide when and where to dispose of their bodies but also for possessing weapons within the palace, disrupting the Forbidden City, and potentially polluting the imperial residence.

Statutes not specifically dealing with eunuch suicide, such as those concerning fighting within the palace, reveal the Qing's lack of tolerance for disturbances and acts of violence within the palace.[18] Individuals charged with getting into an angry dispute within the palace received a beating of fifty blows from the heavy bamboo. If the fights occurred within a palace hall (*diannei* 殿內), the severity of the punishment would increase by one degree. In the Qing Code's section on fighting, the inclusion of the regulations concerning eunuch suicides committed with a knife reveals that eunuchs were not simply being punished for committing suicide but also for possessing weapons within the palace and disrupting the harmony of the imperial court. Furthermore, the differentiation between acts carried out within the palace (*zai gongnei*) and in the garden (*zai yuanting*) suggests that those acts committed within a building inhabited or utilized by the imperial court carried harsher punishments because of the increased threat of the deceased's spirit polluting the site and making the building uninhabitable. In sum, the severity of the punishment depended upon the location of the act, inside or outside, proximity to the emperor also being an important factor to consider.

The sub-statute dealing with suicides attempted by eunuchs within the palace clearly distinguishes between those committed with a knife (*jin dao* 金刀) and those involving other modes of killing. In cases of attempted suicide within the palace that did not involve a weapon (suicide by hanging, *ziyi* 自縊, *zijing* 自經, or unspecified means *zijin* 自盡),[19] eunuchs received the relatively lighter punishment of death by strangulation. While all attempted suicides by eunuchs within the palace received the death penalty, those who attempted suicide with a knife were sentenced to the harsher punishment of immediate decapitation. According to Derk Bodde and Clarence Morris in their work *Law in Imperial China*, strangulation might have been a slower and more painful death than decapitation, but due to the precepts of filial piety in which one's body is a gift from one's parents and as such should not

---

18. *Qinding Da Qing lüli* 欽定大清律例 [The Great Qing Code], Qing *Tongzhi* 9 清同治9年 (1870)，卷 27，行律，鬪毆上，宮內忿爭，1.

19. These unspecified means could include overdosing on opium, since some Qing eunuchs were known to have smoked opium. See *QDGZXXZL*, 卷 4, 處分, 818–22.

be harmed, decapitation and mutilation of the body would have been an unfilial outcome. Strangulation also maintained the body's "somatic integrity,"[20] leaving it intact so that the spirit could return.[21] Taking this into account, the use of the knife within the palace warranted the relatively harsher punishment of immediate beheading due to the presence of a weapon in proximity to the emperor. The use of the knife in the suicide act would also have led to blood being spilled and the potential for greater pollution of the palace.

The greater severity of the punishment of eunuch suicides committed in the palace may also be attributed to a fear of the eunuch's ghost inhabiting the palace and disrupting the harmony of the imperial court. Among the general populace, there were fears that men who committed suicide by hanging themselves from rafters or drowning themselves would become "wandering ghosts, hovering under the roofs or drifting within the waves."[22] Within the palace, buildings in which a suicide had occurred could be seen as housing evil spirits and if not properly decontaminated or exorcised could become regarded as uninhabitable or unusable. Tang Yinian's account of the case of Wang Bing 王炳, a eunuch who hanged himself from a rafter in a vacant building in the *Yuanmingyuan* in 1765,[23] reveals the elaborate decontamination process necessitated by Wang's suicide. First, people were sent to remove Wang's body and carry it out of the palace. Then the coroner (*wu* 忤) from the *Shenxingsi* (慎刑司 Imperial Household Department) was sent to examine the corpse.[24] At the same time, workers were sent to pull down the now inauspicious building's tiles and the wall next to the rafter. Inside, the floor was removed down three feet (*chi* 尺), replaced with new soil, and allowed to dry for three days. Thereafter, the wall and tiles were replaced. This process culminated with a lama 喇嘛 being called in to read sutras and sweep the floor with wine.

Such actions designed to decontaminate the site were warranted by the Qing if they wanted to continue to use the building in which the suicide had occurred. As noted in J. J. M. De Groot's *The Religious System of China*, after committing suicide, the victim's spirit (*po* 魄 or *gui* 鬼) would return to the earth on the spot where the act was committed. "'The p'oh [*po*] of a man is something lying under a hanged

---

20. Melissa Macauley, *Social Power and Legal Culture*, cited in Timothy Brook, Jerome Bourgon, and Gregory Blue, *Death by a Thousand Cuts* (Cambridge, MA: Harvard University Press, 2008), 11.

21. Derk Bodde and Clarence Morris, *Law in Imperial China: Exemplified by 190 Ch'ing Dynasty Cases* (Cambridge, MA: Harvard University Press, 1967), 92.

22. Huang, *A Complete Book Concerning Happiness and Benevolence*, 357.

23. One day in 1765, while the Hongli emperor and children were staying temporarily at the *Yuanmingyuan*, Wang Bing left the confines of the palace to settle an account at an oil and salt shop and never returned. Two days later, Wang was found dead, hanging from a beam in a vacant building within the *Yuanmingyuan*. See Tang Yinian, *Qing gong taijian* (Shenyang: Liaoning daxue chubanshe, 1993), 119.

24. It is interesting to note that in this case the eunuch's body was removed from the scene prior to the coroner inspecting it. In cases of suicide among the populace that occurred outside the palace, this was not the case. The magistrate, upon hearing of a suicide, would go to the scene of the suicide and "examine the corpse immediately." See Huang, *A Complete Book Concerning Happiness and Benevolence*, 356. Another case, discussed later in this chapter, also suggests that the body was not moved until after the coroner had been sent to inspect it. As will be seen, in other cases of eunuch suicide, coroners were sent in to examine the body.

person and resembling carbonized wheat-bran; if dug away immediately, it may be destroyed, but if this precaution is delayed, it sinks deep into the ground, and unless eradicated, a repetition of the incident is sure to occur.'"[25] Failing to exorcise the spirit from the site of the suicide could also result in another suicide, since ghosts of suicides did not rest until they had caused another to kill him or herself in a similar manner.[26]

Since the palace gods were "the protectors of the eunuchs,"[27] a eunuch suicide committed within the palace might have also involved upsetting the palace gods. According to the last Qing emperor, Aisin-Gioro Pu Yi, these gods "were not included in the offerings made by the royal family" and were worshipped by eunuchs in the hope that they "would protect them from the beating and other forms of ill-treatment from which they often suffered."[28] As the protectors of eunuchs, these palace gods might have become angry and thus vengeful at the thought of a eunuch being in such utter despair that he killed himself.

Thus, in acts of suicide committed within the palace, the loss of life of the eunuch clearly became overshadowed by the act's potential harm to the imperial court. The Imperial Household Department's response focused on exorcising the eunuch's spirit and punishing his corpse and his family. In dealing with a eunuch suicide, the priority was ensuring the harmony and safety of the imperial court and preventing such inauspicious acts from occurring in the future.

The location of the suicide and mode of killing were not the only factors in determining the severity of the punishment. The status of eunuchs also appears to have influenced the Qing's handling of such suicide cases. The disparity between the treatment of a eunuch committing suicide in the palace and a member of the general population doing the same is revealed in the handling of a case in which a eunuch's nephew committed suicide within the palace. In July of 1810, De Lin 得林, the nephew of Yu Jinzhong 于進忠, a eunuch in the *Waishanfang* (外膳房 Outer Imperial Kitchen), threw himself into a well within the Forbidden City and killed himself.[29] Rather than focusing on the act of the suicide itself, the Qing dealt with the matter as a breach in security, trying to determine how this person gained entry

25. *Pen-ts'ao kang muh* [*Bencao gangmu*], ch. 52, cited in J. J. M. De Groot, *The Religious System of China*, vol. 5, book 2 (Reprint, Taipei: Ch'eng Wen Publishing Co., 1976), 714.

26. *Pen-ts'ao kang muh* [*Bencao gangmu*], ch. 52, cited in J. J. M. De Groot, 714. H. Y. Lowe states that causing another to die in the same fashion would release the spirit and allow it to go before judges in the next world before being reincarnated. See H. Y. Lowe, *The Adventures of Wu: The Life Cycle of a Peking Man* (Princeton: Princeton University Press, 1983), 236.

27. Aisin-Gioro Pu Yi, *From Emperor to Citizen: The Autobiography of Aisin Gioro Pu Yi*, trans. W. J. F. Jenner (Beijing, 1964; reprint New York: Oxford University Press, 1987), 67. According to Pu Yi, "The ordinary eunuchs were very devout in their offerings to the 'palace gods': snakes, foxes, weasels and hedgehogs . . . On the first and fifteenth of every month, at New Year and at other festivals they would make offerings to them, usually of eggs, dried bean curd, spirits, and cake; at the New Year and other festivals, they would also offer whole pigs and sheep as well as large quantities of fruit."

28. Aisin-Gioro Pu Yi, *From Emperor to Citizen*, 67–68.

29. *Guochao gongshi xubian*, ed. Qing Gui et al. (Reprint, Beijing: Beijing guji chubanshe, 1994), 卷 6, 59–60, 嘉慶15年6月3日.

into the Forbidden City, proceeded to live there for two months undetected, and then committed suicide on the premises. Since this was considered an individual act, no mention is made of punishing the deceased's family for his suicide. In this case, even questions about why he might have committed suicide and the usual focus on who might have caused his actions were overshadowed by an investigation into how he was able to enter such a highly restricted area as the Forbidden City. As the deceased was not a eunuch himself and did not kill himself within a palace building, the act did not warrant the same treatment as a eunuch suicide. The record does not note anyone being punished, but one can assume that the deceased's family members avoided punishment for the suicide. Undoubtedly, the eunuch relative who facilitated his entry and stay in the palace would have been dealt with severely. Moreover, this case highlighted major flaws in a system designed to only allow emasculated males to live as servile staff within the palace.

Dumping the Body

Eunuchs who committed suicide did not avoid punishment even though they were deceased. The statutes on eunuch suicide stated that the bodies of eunuchs who had committed suicide within the palace would be dumped in the wilderness.[30] Eunuchs who had committed suicide in the gardens were spared from this treatment, once again revealing the relatively less offensive nature of their crime due to the location where it was committed.

In addition to leaving the corpse exposed to the elements, the deprivation of a proper burial left the eunuch without a grave and the regular rites. These suicides appear to have been singled out in not receiving a burial. Suicides among the populace in general appear to have at least been buried so as to protect the corpse from the ravages of animals and the weather.[31] Deceased felons even received a burial, albeit an anonymous one. Criminals sentenced to death by a thousand cuts, the most extreme of the Chinese punishments, were buried in a cemetery outside one of the city gates.[32] According to Michael Dutton, "With the body of the felon, the anonymity of disposal marked the ultimate social sanction against the body of the family and kin. It would symbolize the lack of social standing of the dead, the lack of a name and, ultimately, the indication of familial failure in relation to its criminal member."[33] Both anonymous burial and corpse dumping prevented the family from venerating the body. By depriving the deceased eunuch of a proper burial, the

---

30. The term used is *huangye* (荒野 wilderness). As lands around the capital were banner, farmland, or hunting reserves, it is likely that the wilderness in question was some distance from Beijing. If the corpse of a suicide was not welcome in the palace, one can assume it was also not welcome in other areas associated with the imperial court or banners.

31. Huang, *A Complete Book Concerning Happiness and Benevolence*, 357.

32. Brook et al., *Death by a Thousand Cuts*, 2.

33. Michael Dutton, *Policing and Punishment in China: From Patriarchy to 'the People'* (Cambridge: Cambridge University Press, 1992), 101.

Imperial Household Department expressed its resolve to ensure that acts of eunuch suicide would not go unpunished and made clear that a eunuch who committed suicide was considered lower than a criminal.

Magistrate Huang Liu-Hung's commentary on suicides reveals the lack of compassion that suicide in general elicited from the authorities. Huang wrote, "The human body is not only a bequest of one's parents but also a result of countless cycles of reincarnation. That anyone can be degraded enough to destroy it with his own hands and regard it no more important than that of a pig or a dog is something I detest most vigorously. Why should I value the body bequeathed to someone by his parents if he does not value it himself?"[34] In cases of eunuch suicide, where the act had the potential to disrupt the harmony of the imperial court, such acts only engendered feelings of contempt.

Collective Responsibility

As the statutes make clear, the response to eunuch suicide did not end with the punishment of the deceased; the eunuch's relatives were also held collectively responsible. As a result of the eunuch's actions, his relatives would receive sentences of exile to the frontiers of the empire to serve as the slaves of soldiers. While exile was a penal practice listed in the Ming Code with innovations such as gradations in penalties, "The Qing supplemented and topped these grades with the penalty of Great Deportation which entailed enslavement in a Tartar [Manchu] garrison."[35] Relatives of eunuchs who had committed suicide within the palace were exiled to Yili to serve as slaves for soldiers; relatives of eunuchs who committed suicide in the gardens were exiled to Urumqi to serve as slaves for soldiers.

In the case of the above-mentioned Li Guangyu, the Yonghegong[36] eunuch who had hanged himself in the Imperial Garden in 1808, Li's relatives suffered as a result of his actions. The Imperial Household Department dumped Li's body in the wilderness and exiled his relatives to Yili to serve as slaves.[37] Here, the punishment of Li's relatives (qinshu 親屬) reflects the patrilineal nature of Chinese society; Li's mother, younger brother, his younger brother's wife, and Li's two nephews and his niece were all sent to Yili to serve as slaves. Had Li's father not been deceased, he would have been included as well.[38]

---

34. Huang, *A Complete Book Concerning Happiness and Benevolence*, 357.
35. Brook et al., *Death by a Thousand Cuts*, 38.
36. By the Jiaqing era, this former residence of Prince Yinzhen (later the Yongzheng emperor) was used as a Tibetan Buddhist temple (as it is now). Li was assigned to the *Yonghegong* but committed suicide in the Forbidden City.
37. *GZDJQCZZ*, 704.
38. *GZDJQCZZ*, 705. Note that there is no mention of the mother's side of the family being punished. Since Chinese custom viewed the bride as becoming a part of the groom's family at marriage, his mother can be viewed as part of the father's side of the family.

While families of eunuchs who had committed suicide within the palace and in the gardens both received punishments involving exile, the location of the exile is important to note. According to Joanna Waley-Cohen in her work *Exile in Mid-Qing China*, "the general rule was that the more serious offenders were sent to Ili [Yili] and the less serious sent to Urumqi."[39] Moreover, located more than 400 miles farther away from the capital than Urumqi, Yili would have required an additional one or two months of travel by cart for the eunuch's family members even to reach their place of exile[40] and would have placed the eunuch's family even farther away from their Hebei, Shandong, or Zhili origins.

It is interesting to note that, although the above-mentioned eunuch, Li, committed suicide in a garden, his relatives were punished as if he had killed himself within the palace: they were sent to Yili rather than to Urumqi. While the site of the suicide, the Imperial Garden,[41] is located within the Forbidden City (technically on the palace grounds), the act was not committed inside. The divergence from the usual punishment in the suicide of Li may be explained by the flexible nature of the allocation of exile destinations. According to "a memorial submitted in 1766 by Shuhede, acting governor-general of Shanxi and Gansu: '. . . Ili is vast and they need people for reclamation work, so probably we should send more convicts there than to Urumqi.'"[42] Thus, labor needs on the frontier often took precedence over exile destinations determined by the severity of the crime.

Nevertheless, eunuchs' families were not punished unless their eunuch relative had committed suicide. If the eunuch only attempted suicide, he alone was either sentenced to death or to exile, the location depending upon where the act was attempted. Why punish a deceased eunuch's relatives? Such actions ensured that someone was punished for the eunuch's actions. If the eunuch was deceased, collective responsibility enabled the government to deliver a sentence of exile servitude as well as allowed it to recoup lost labor and benefit from the services of the eunuch's relatives. Cases of banishment to Yili and Urumqi also allowed the Qing to achieve its dual purpose of punishment and colonization of Xinjiang.[43] Last, punishment of the eunuch's relatives may have also stemmed from the idea of punishing the

---

39. Joanna Waley-Cohen, *Exile in Mid-Qing China: Banishment to Xinjiang, 1758–1820* (New Haven: Yale University Press, 1991), 70.

40. Waley-Cohen, *Exile in Mid-Qing China*, 131. According to Google Maps, Ili is located 3,838 kilometers (2384.82 miles) from Beijing; Urumqi is located 3,165 kilometers (1966.64 miles) away. Both are located in present-day Xinjiang province, China.

41. Located in the Western Section of the Forbidden City, close to seven minor residential palaces inhabited by female members of the imperial court. See L. C. Arlington and William Lewisohn, *In Search of Old Peking* (Shanghai: North China Daily News, 1935), 42–43, map 7.

42. Waley-Cohen, *Exile in Mid-Qing China*, 68.

43. "The Xinjiang policy on convicts' families reaffirms that colonization was as important a goal of the system of banishment to Xinjiang as was punishment. Previously, the primary purpose of exile had been to isolate the offender not only from his native community but also from his family. In Xinjiang this goal was partially defeated by the procedure recommended by Agui, who was prompted by an overriding interest in importing able-bodied Han Chinese, criminal or otherwise, to populate and cultivate Xinjiang." See Waley-Cohen, *Exile in Mid-Qing China*, 72–73.

eunuch's guarantor. Holding the guarantor responsible would also send a message to eunuchs and their families that a eunuch terminating his employment with the palace without authorization would not be tolerated.

Although only the deceased's family members were noted as being held collectively responsible for the suicide, in reality they were not the only group punished for his actions. In addition to the deceased's family, eunuchs serving alongside him and his eunuch supervisors would be held responsible for the suicide. Rather than being blamed for coercing the eunuch to commit suicide, these eunuchs, regardless of whether they claimed they had no knowledge of why the eunuch took his life or offered a possible motive, found themselves being held accountable. For example, in the case of Zhou Baoshi 周寶石, a eunuch whose emasculation wound had not healed well, his fellow eunuchs all were punished for his suicide. These punishments ranged from being fined six months' pay (for his *shouling taijian*), to thirty blows from the *ban*, or the loss of three months' pay for *zongguan taijian* implicated in the case.[44] In 1799, Zheng Furui 鄭福瑞 died in a well. Zheng had gone to get water and not returned. Ye Mingliang 葉明亮, a fellow eunuch, found the poles Zheng had used to carry the water next to the well and, upon looking into the well, saw a body. According to Ye, Zheng had not quarreled with anyone, but he had been sick recently. As a result of Zheng's death, six eunuchs received punishments of deductions in pay and food for one to two years.[45] Unable to punish the deceased, the Qing utilized collective responsibility as a deterrent and a management tool.

The Value of Official Suicide Reports

In addition to legal statutes, the Qing historical record includes official reports of eunuch suicide. These accounts serve as invaluable resources in the reconstruction of eunuch history, providing momentary yet vivid glimpses into eunuchs' lives. Within these reports one often finds a shift midway through the report from the Classical Chinese of the official to the vernacular of the eunuch witnesses. Here, the reader can essentially "hear" the eunuchs' own words, to picture the events leading up to the event, and the emotions involved in the discovery of the body. For example, following the death of eunuch Li Chao 李朝 in 1758, officials interviewed Li's fellow eunuchs who recounted the events leading up to and after the discovery of Li's body.[46] According to Tian Deming 田德明, who served with Li, he hadn't seen Li on the morning of the twenty-first but ran into him at noon and asked where he was headed. Li told him, "I'm headed to the *tatan* to eat lunch." Later, when Tian went to change his clothes, he found Li lying on the ground and called out to him saying, "What's going on?" but Li didn't answer. Looking more closely, he noticed the pool of blood under Li's head and sought help.

---

44. First Historical Archives, Beijing, 總管內務府, 005-0628-076, 09040321, 道光4年3月21日 (April 25, 1799).
45. First Historical Archives, Beijing, 總管內務府, 05-0475-067-068, 080405013, 嘉慶4年5月13日.
46. First Historical Archives, Beijing, 總管內務府, 05-0168-010, 072310023, 乾隆23年10月23日.

This report and others like it reveal an interesting fact about eunuch life experiences that directly contradicts one of the main misperceptions about the eunuch system. One of the pillars of the eunuch system was that it created a workforce of loyal servants who were uninfluenced by family ties. As stated, emasculation was designed to render the eunuch into a loyal servant who had severed his ties with his family and society (*chu jia* 出家, quitting home; see Introduction). Archival records documenting eunuch suicide clearly show that eunuchs kept in contact with their families either by traveling to see them or having their families visit them in the capital. In Li's case, his visit to his family may have contributed to his suicide. According to Tian Deming, prior to Li's suicide, he had come to him crying, asking to borrow money because during a visit with his family his parents had taken his fur gown (*pipao* 皮包), his outer jacket (*gua* 褂), and his padded gown (*mianpiao* 棉袍).[47]

In the case of Gao Yuwang 高玉枉, the report notes that, when questioned, Gao's family told officials that the twenty-nine *sui* 歲 eunuch had visited his family twice in the last month. In 1759, Gao's body was discovered with his throat slit after he had run away from the palace.[48] After Gao's disappearance, the authorities arrived at his family home looking for him and inquiring why he had run away. His family appeared to have no information regarding his motives for running away but in the end were of use to the authorities. Once Gao's body was found, the *Shenxingsi* called upon Gao's mother and brother to identify his body. Recognizing a scar on Gao's knee that he had received years earlier from a dog bite, the family was able to identify his body.[49] While one might expect eunuch contact with their families in the later years of the dynasty (when a series of young emperors ruled through regents), suicide cases such as this one reveal that such contact was occurring even during the Qianlong period (1736–1795). Clearly, the realities of eunuch life were not in line with one of the system's main reasons for being, to have servants who had no familial connections.

Motives

Despite the Qing's lack of compassion for the deceased, records do reveal that the *Shenxingsi* did its due diligence to send a coroner to examine the eunuch's body. It was the coroner who determined the cause of death and whether or not it was indeed a suicide and not a murder. In the case of Li Chao, the coroner's description

47. Tian claimed that he loaned Li the money to buy new clothes. Li's parents were ultimately exiled to Daxing wula. First Historical Archives, Beijing, 總管內務府, 慎刑司, 05-0168-010, 07231002, 乾隆23年10月23日.

48. First Historical Archives, Beijing, 總管內務府, 慎刑司, 05-1076-002, 082412002, 乾隆24年12月初2日.

49. In another case, the cousin of deceased eunuch, Liu Xin, identified the body by recognizing the markings (*huaban* 花斑 piebald) on the deceased's legs. See First Historical Archives, Beijing, 總管內務府, 慎刑司, 05-0337-076, 074306R25, 乾隆43年閏6月25日.

of the corpse notes the condition of each major part of the body and ultimately determines the cause of death as suicide due to a slit throat.

Qing reports on eunuch suicide shed little light on the motives of the deceased. Instead, the documents focus primarily on decontamination and exorcism and the use of punishment to deter future suicide attempts. Strikingly absent are those questions asked after a suicide had been committed among the general population, such as "Who drove this person to commit suicide?"[50] Undoubtedly, the Qing did not ask such questions in eunuch suicides simply because the guilty party might well have been members of the Imperial Household and the eunuch management system. Officials documenting cases of eunuch suicide did not always include questions aimed at ascertaining the motive. In those records in which the "why" was investigated, officials routinely asked if the eunuch had gambling debts or a drinking problem or had argued with his fellow eunuchs. The standard response from eunuchs was that "he had no reason to commit suicide." As will be seen, despite this response, later in the interview the fellow eunuch might share information that suggested that the eunuch was experiencing problems that might have contributed to his decision to take his own life.

In cases of suicide, records containing a eunuch's confession regarding what drove him to take his life are extremely rare.[51] The eunuch now deceased, we can only surmise what motivated his actions. In such cases, interviews conducted with the deceased's fellow eunuchs prove invaluable for helping one understand the challenges eunuchs faced in their daily lives. In the cases presented below, one is reminded that eunuchs were individuals and, as such, their motivations for committing suicide varied. One common motivating factor appears to be the harsh realities (physical, mental, and financial) of serving as a palace eunuch.

Within the confines of the Forbidden City, eunuchs found themselves living in an environment in which beatings of the palace staff were common. Collective responsibility for infractions and crimes committed by the eunuch staff ensured the perpetuation of violence within the palace. Supervisory eunuchs who did not keep their eunuchs in line faced punishment for their subordinate's actions. As a result, harsh punishments were used as a management technique to promote compliance. With mistakes and offenses being met with harsh punishments and the threat of receiving a beating for one's mistakes a daily reality, some eunuchs found such a working environment too much to bear.

While some eunuchs dealt with the threat of punishment by running away from the palace, others turned to suicide as an escape. For eunuchs such as Ma Feng 馬鳳, assigned to the Imperial Kitchen, the threat of receiving a beating (often for a minor infraction) proved to be a powerful motivating factor. According to Ma's confession, fearful that he would receive a beating from his superior for wearing

---

50. Wolf, "Women and Suicide in China," 112.
51. The majority of eunuchs were illiterate and as a result would not have left a note or a letter providing insight into why they committed suicide.

disheveled clothes, he slit his own throat. Ma survived the attempt on his own life and was sentenced to cut grass in perpetuity at Weng Mountain (Weng Shan 甕 山).[52] Without more information on Ma, it is unclear if this impending beating was one of many or a singular punishment. Regardless, the threat of punishment was enough to make this eunuch decide he no longer wanted to live.

Financial problems also contributed to eunuch suicides. In the 1770 suicide of Wang Bing 王炳,[53] a fifty-seven *sui* eunuch serving a Qing princess, five of Wang's fellow eunuchs did not think that he had a reason to commit suicide. They had noticed that he had a habit of drinking, though, and would return home from visiting his family visibly agitated. On the day of his death, Wang had requested time off to settle his debts but never returned. After a search, he was found hanging from the scaffolding. The report later suggests that Wang's fellow eunuchs should be interrogated about whether or not Wang had gambled and gotten drunk and quarreled with his fellow eunuchs. This inquiry suggests that the *Shenxingsi* was interested in determining whether or not eunuchs continued to drink and gamble despite prohibitions against such practice being listed in the statutes (see Chapter 5).

Medical problems may have also motivated eunuchs to commit suicide. In the case of above-mentioned Zhou Baoshi 周寶石, one of his fellow eunuchs, Ma Yubao 馬玉保, recalled that when Zhou, a new recruit, was first assigned to work in the Wutang (五堂 Fifth Hall) at the *Yuanmingyuan*, he looked sick and walked very slowly. When Zhou's supervisor inquired about this, Zhou responded that he was in poor health and had not recovered well after his emasculation. Zhou was later found hanging from the door of their living quarters (*tatan*). When pressed for more information, Ma stressed that no one had quarreled with Zhou and that his supervisor had not beaten him. According to the coroner's findings, Zhou's emasculation wound had not healed well.[54] One might surmise, then, that the new eunuch had killed himself as a result of complications related to his emasculation. Another possible motivating factor may have been depression brought on by emasculation

---

52. Du Wanyan, *Zhongguo huanguan shi* (Taipei: Wenjin chubanshe, 1996), 123. It is interesting to note that Ma was not exiled to Yili to serve as a slave for a soldier. Since the location of Ma's suicide attempt is not noted, it is possible that he attempted to kill himself in a location that was not considered as deserving of a harsh sentence as attempting suicide within the palace or in the gardens. The location of Ma's exile, Weng Mountain (Ziyang County, in nearby Shanxi province), further supports this conclusion. For the location of Weng Mountain, see Zhang Qiyun, ed., *Zhongwen da cidian*, vol. 22 (Taipei: Zhongguo wenhua yanjiusuo, 1967), 9420.

53. First Historical Archives, Beijing, 總管內務府,慎刑司,05-0281-035,073510002,全宗5,281卷,35 號,乾隆35年10月初2日. Why wasn't Wang exiled? This case occurred prior to the Qing establishing their rule in the Xinjiang region, and exile to the region was not an option for punishment. No mention is made of Wang's family being punished. Instead, Wang's eunuch brothers (*baoxiong* 胞兄) were each sentenced to wear the cangue for two months, receive forty blows from the *ban* 板, after which they were returned to their native place and placed under the supervision of the local authorities. In essence, they were effectively removed from the eunuch system.

54. Zhou's family was punished according to the statute of eunuchs who had committed suicide in the garden. His body was dumped in the wilderness and his family was sent to Urumqi to become slaves for the military. His supervisor (*shouling taijian*) had his pay docked for six months. Eunuchs serving alongside Zhou received thirty blows from the *ban* 板. First Historical Archives, Beijing, 總管內務府,005-0628-076,09040321,道 光4年3月21日.

due either to the psychological trauma accompanying the procedure or the sudden drop in testosterone following the removal of the testes.[55]

In addition to despair, suicide provided eunuchs with a way to express discontent or to criticize the system. Like the suicides of young Chinese widows that "made a strong statement about the status of women,"[56] eunuch suicides could also offer commentary about the status of Qing dynasty eunuchs. Faced with a lack of alternatives, eunuchs could view suicide, as some women did, as "an act of aggression." Commenting on female suicide, Emily Martin writes, "In fact, because the soul is not in its proper place in the underworld, and can harass the living, making them sick, troubled, and unsuccessful, suicide can be used as an act of aggression against one's kin."[57] In the case of eunuch suicide, rather than being aimed at their families, the suicide would be directed at their employers, the Qing government. Moreover, Margery Wolf writes, "suicide is not only an individual act, a gesture of personal despair, but also an act that implicates others. For a young person, it is the ultimate rebellion in a society that requires respectful submission to the will of one's seniors, and for a woman it is the most damning accusation she can make of her mother-in-law, her husband, or her son."[58] Hsieh and Spence term this type of suicide "purposeful suicide" and suggest that it could be an effective way of "pressuring the survivors . . . to pursue a better line of conduct . . . or it could contain an element of vengeance as the restless spirit of the deceased returned to haunt the living."[59] As servants, eunuchs could not have realistically put much hope in changing the system through their suicide. However, as evidenced by Qing efforts to exorcise ghosts after the eunuch Wang Bing's suicide, eunuchs could attempt to disrupt the harmony of the palace and bring bad luck to its inhabitants. Eunuchs could certainly use suicide as an "act of rebellion"[60] against the system.

Eunuch belief in transmigration may have also motivated some eunuchs to commit suicide. According to Yuan-huei Lin's study of suicide in traditional China, Buddhist belief in reincarnation "inspired" those in unbearable circumstances to end their lives in the hope of being reincarnated into a better life. Such a belief in reincarnation could have enabled eunuchs to look upon suicide not as a final exit from this world but merely a gateway into the next life.[61]

---

55. Medical studies today remain inconclusive on whether or not the loss of testosterone is linked to depression. See Revital Amiaz and Stuart Seidman, "Testosterone and Depression in Men," *Current Opinion in Endocrinology, Diabetes and Obesity* 15, no. 3 (Jan. 1, 2008): 278–83.

56. Wolf, "Women and Suicide in China," 111.

57. Emily Martin, "Gender and Ideological Differences in Representations of Life and Death," in *Death Ritual in Late Imperial and Modern China*, ed. James L. Watson and Evelyn S. Rawski (Berkeley: University of California Press, 1988), 177.

58. Wolf, "Women and Suicide in China," 112.

59. Hsieh and Spence, "Suicide and the Family in Pre-Modern Chinese Society," 45–46.

60. Tang, *Qing gong taijian*, 118.

61. Yuan-huei Lin, "The Weight of Mt. T'ai: Patterns of Suicide in Traditional Chinese History and Culture" (PhD diss., University of Wisconsin-Madison, 1990), 74–76. For a discussion of eunuchs and Buddhism, see Chapter 4.

Modes of Killing

The eunuch's choice of method in killing himself may also be indicative of his motivation in committing the act. An examination of the modes of self-destruction among the general populace shows a preference for methods that did not involve cutting oneself or spilling blood. For example, according to Hsieh and Spence in their work on suicide and the family in China, "suicide was presented as a swift and clean act. Though there are cases of suicide by sword or dagger and of self-immolation by religious fanatics, the most common methods were those that were literally bloodless; death was found either through poison, by drowning, by self-strangulation or (in the nineteenth century) by swallowing raw opium."[62] This is further evidenced by J.-J Matignon, who lists the different methods of suicide in China by order of frequency: "poisoning, hanging, drowning, [death by] sharp instruments, starvation, and self-immolation."[63]

In comparison, an examination of the methods used in Qing official documents to refer to acts of suicide committed by eunuchs involved harming oneself with a knife, suicide by hanging (*ziyi* 自縊, *zijing* 自經), or suicide by unspecified means (*zijin* 自盡).[64] The *QDGZXXZL* (欽定宮中現行則例) and the *Da Qing luli huiji bianlan* (大清律例彙輯便覽) specifically mention the use of knives (*jin dao* 金刀) in eunuch suicides. While this emphasis on the use of knives may reveal more about the Qing's concern about the safety of the imperial court in suicides in which a knife was involved than the frequency with which eunuchs killed themselves with knives, the use of the knife remains important. The fact that eunuchs would choose to kill themselves with a knife at all reveals a divergence from the preferred modes of killing oneself among the general populace.

Chinese ideas of filial piety may have contributed to the aversion among the general population to killing oneself with a knife. According to the *Xiao Jing* (孝經 The Classic of Filial Piety), "Our bodies—to every hair and bit of skin—are received by us from our parents, and we must not presume to injure or wound them:—this is the beginning of filial piety."[65] However, violating the code of filial piety by slitting their wrists or slashing their throat in order to kill themselves may not have been a moral dilemma for eunuchs. Having already violated this precept by becoming emasculated, eunuchs may have considered the possibility of being considered unfilial a moot point. As discussed in Chapter 2, a eunuch's life was essentially defined by the knife. With the cut of the knife, Chinese boys and men initiated their

62. Hsieh and Spence, 46.

63. Matignon, *Superstition, Crime et Misère en Chine* (1900), 40.

64. As stated previously, these unspecified means could include overdosing on opium, since some Qing eunuchs were known to have smoked opium. See *QDGZXXZL*, 卷 4, 處分, 818–22.

65. James Legge, *The Sacred Books of China*, part. I, *The Shu King, The Religious Portion of the Shih King, the Hsiao King. Sacred Books of the East*, vol. 3, ed. F. Max Muller (Clarendon Press, 1879; reprint, Delhi: Motilal Bunarsidass, 1978), 466.

transformation into palace eunuchs. It is conceivable that some eunuchs may have looked to the knife to terminate their existence as such.

The choice of the knife may have also increased the pollution of the site by causing blood to be spilled. Whether or not blood contaminated the scene any more than did the inauspicious nature of the act of killing oneself remains unclear. However, if the eunuch was motivated by a desire for vengeance and hoped to make a statement with his death, the choice of killing himself with a knife or a sharp instrument clearly would have made the scene more difficult to clean up and more unpleasant for those who came across the body.

Conclusion

Eunuchs who attempted or committed suicide were treated as criminals. This labeling of eunuch suicide as deviant behavior did not stem from any desire by the Qing to encourage a sense of value for human life among the eunuch population. Rather, Qing regulations and punishments concerning eunuch suicide made it very clear that servants did not have the right to put their wants and needs before those of the imperial court, especially when those needs might disrupt the harmony of the palace. More than glimpses into the end of a eunuch life, eunuch suicide reveals much about the status and treatment of eunuchs by the imperial court.

Linked in the suicide statutes, eunuchs and female inhabitants of the palace were singled out for punishment. While the motivations for the linkage are not stated, one can assume that this was motivated by their shared status as subordinated groups. Suicides committed by members of society did not warrant the government's attention unless someone had clearly instigated the act. In contrast, eunuch suicides triggered the involvement, investigation, and response of the Imperial Household Department every time. Rather than focus on the death of the individual eunuch, the Qing concentrated on the protection of the imperial court and deterring future such unwanted acts.

Although the death of a eunuch amounted to nothing more than decreasing the eunuch population by one, its potential harmful effects on others were significant. The location of the eunuch's suicide, within the palace or in the garden (within a building or outside), dictated the severity of the punishment as well as the level of the decontamination efforts. A suicide committed within the confines of the palace carried the greatest potential to disrupt the harmony of the imperial court and to impede service to the emperor and his family due to the loss of labor. Eunuch suicide also carried disastrous implications for the eunuch's family and coworkers. Collective responsibility ensured that a eunuch's family and fellow eunuchs would also suffer due to his decision to end his life. Even the deceased was punished with the deprivation of a proper burial by being dumped in the wilderness. Such an act ensured that there would be no grave to visit. Such harsh punishments served as a means by which the palace could educate the eunuch population on the fate that would await eunuchs and their families if they attempted to commit suicide and perhaps deter future acts.

Favoring the use of exile and slavery for eunuchs who survived their suicide attempt, or for eunuch family members in cases when the eunuch died, the Qing achieved the dual purpose of ensuring that, despite the loss of service for the palace, the empire continued to benefit in terms of labor and service on the frontier. In addition, the threat of the punishment of slavery further reveals that, despite their servitude while serving as palace eunuchs and their placement as closer to slavery on the free–unfree continuum, they were not considered slaves. Slavery was clearly another category.

Investigations into eunuch suicides reveal that the government did its due diligence to discover if the eunuch had been murdered. Reports also indicate that the palace was also occasionally interested in what had motivated the eunuch to end his life. More frequently, reports focused on informing superiors of the punishments and decontamination efforts following a suicide. In the few cases that delved into eunuch motivations, authorities appear to have been more interested in determining if eunuchs were breaking rules against gambling or drinking within the palace. Nevertheless, these reports provide valuable insights into the challenges (financial, work, and psychological) that eunuchs faced in their everyday lives. These records also add weight to the argument that some eunuchs continued to have contact with their families despite the severance of family ties being one of the reasons for the existence of the eunuch system.

Acts of attempted eunuch suicide receiving the death penalty show that clearly the individual eunuch's life was of little importance to his masters. Unlike members of society in general, the eunuch was not free to dispose of his body as he pleased or to leave his employment at a time of his choosing. The Qing response to eunuch suicide suggests that, although many eunuchs had entered the eunuch system voluntarily, they had essentially sold themselves into service for life.

8

Authorized Exits from the System

Sick Leave, Retirement, Discharge, and Death

Employment as an imperial court eunuch during the Qing dynasty often ensured a lifetime of service for the eunuch. However, as cases of eunuch runaways and suicide have demonstrated, many eunuchs desired to end their employment with the palace before reaching old age. Such unauthorized exits from the system carried harsh punishments for the eunuch and/or his family. These were not the only routes leading out of the palace available to eunuchs, though. An authorized exit could be obtained from the system; however, a eunuch might have to wait a lifetime for the chance.

The Imperial Household Department authorized only three types of exit from the eunuch system: sick leave, retirement due to old age or illness, and natural death. In very rare cases, eunuchs were released from the system due to disciplinary reasons. While sick leave provided many eunuchs with a temporary break from their duties, discharge from the system ended the eunuch's relationship with the palace. Upon discharge, eunuchs became known as *weimin taijian* (為民太監 commoner eunuchs), implying a return of the eunuch to commoner status. However, eunuch reintegration into society proved to be more of an ideal than a reality. Having spent the majority of their lives working behind palace walls, eunuchs faced a multitude of uncertainties once they left the system. Financial problems, discrimination, and even disassociation from family members complicated eunuch reintegration, causing some eunuchs to attempt to reenter the system, while others faced social ostracism in retirement and death.

As this chapter will show, the study of eunuch sick leave and discharge from the system contributes to our growing knowledge of how late imperial Chinese states such as the Qing managed the human resources required to govern its empire.[1] These cases provide a micro-level study of the Qing's management of one segment of its workforce operating within the seat of imperial power. Beyond labor relations, archival records add to our understanding of eunuch illnesses: what maladies they suffered from, how they were diagnosed, and the authority (or lack of authority) attached to a diagnosis. When reviewing these cases, one notices a stark contrast

---

1. For a study of the Qing's management of illness among its officials, see He Bian, "Too Sick to Serve: The Politics of Illness in the Qing Civil Bureaucracy," *Late Imperial China* 33, no. 2 (Dec. 2012): 40–75.

between the system's strict regulations and use of corporal punishment and the liberalness of Qing palace sick-leave policies. As will be seen, the palace's often lax sick leave policies ultimately created opportunities for abuse of the system, which increased the palace's distrust of its eunuch workforce.

Sick Leave

Eunuchs were essential to the daily functioning of the imperial court, handling duties ranging from guarding the gates and tending the fires, to taking care of the needs of the imperial family living within the palace, to escorting officials in to see the emperor, and transmitting memorials. When eunuchs were sick and unable to perform their duties, this could negatively impact the service provided to the emperor, his family, and the functioning of the government. Since eunuch service within the palace was essentially for life, sick leave was one of the few times in a eunuch's life when he was given extended time off from his duties to be taken outside the palace.

Terms of sick leave varied depending upon the severity of the eunuch's illness. Sick leave could be short term, allowing the eunuch time to recuperate for a couple of days before returning to work, or months long, when eunuchs could no longer perform their duties. When a eunuch became ill, he could request sick leave, which, if granted, would allow him to take time off to recuperate either inside or outside the palace. Eunuchs who were suffering from serious illnesses or who had been sick for over a month could request sick leave to return to their native place to recuperate. As will be seen, the ability of eunuchs to survive outside the palace during periods of extended sick leave proved problematic, as they struggled to survive at a time when their salaries were reduced and they were expected to arrange and fund travel to their native place to recuperate. Eunuchs who were sick for over a month were subject to a reduction in salary, according to their rank and the length of time they were away from their work. After recovering, eunuchs were required to return to service in the palace.

Throughout the Qing, the palace granted sick leave to eunuchs suffering from a wide variety of illnesses. A sampling of sick leave records from the ninth year of the Tongzhi reign (1870–1871) reveals the numerous maladies that prompted eunuchs to request sick leave.[2] Xian Delu 咸得祿, a eunuch assigned to the *Yuhuayuan* (御花園 Imperial Garden), was granted sick leave to recover from a pulmonary abscess (*feiyong zhi zheng* 肺癰之症). *Longfumen* (龍福門 Gate of Abundant Happiness) *shouling taijian* (supervisory eunuch) Wang Jinbao 王金寶 was spitting up blood and needed time off. Meng Zhangxi 孟長喜, who worked in the *Niaoqiangsanchu* (鳥槍三處 Fowling Office) was constantly vomiting. Other eunuchs complained of

---

2. First Historical Archives, Beijing, 宮中，雜件1272，人事類太監，同治9年.

leg pain and swelling and numbness.[3] Some eunuchs, like *shouling taijian* Wang Xi 王喜, requested sick leave to recover from dysentery. Han Fuqing 韓福慶, from the *Yuchafang* (御茶房 Imperial Tea Room), reported that he was suffering from headaches, typhoid fever (*shanghan* 傷寒), and the inability to walk. Xu Jinlu 許進祿, from the *Dasaochu* (打掃處 Sweeping Department), was granted sick leave for lower back pain (*mo yao* 抹腰). Wang Shuangxi 王雙喜 was suffering from *tanqi*[4] 痰氣, and the Cooking Fire Department's *shouling taijian* Gao Jinxi's 高進喜 request noted that had warm heat disease (*wenre zhi zheng* 溫熱之症).

Too Many Sick or Elderly Eunuchs in the Capital

Qing policies on where eunuchs were allowed to take their sick leave fluctuated throughout the dynasty. Prior to the 1800s, the Qing required seriously ill eunuchs to return to their native places to recuperate. During the reigns of Kangxi, Yongzheng, and Qianlong (1662–1795), seriously ill eunuchs were required to return home until they were well. Eunuchs suffering from contagious diseases were required to take sick leave outside the palace. Due to the proximity of the eunuch work environment to the emperor, these regulations may be attributed to the fear of infectious diseases spreading throughout the palace and afflicting the imperial court. Aware of the potential threat caused by eunuchs and others infected with smallpox, the Kangxi emperor ordered the removal of sick eunuchs from the palace. In 1674, it was ruled that eunuchs and others attached to the palace who did not exhibit symptoms of smallpox were to remain at home for one month. Those who had family members showing smallpox pustules were ordered to remain at home for one hundred days.[5] In another case from the Kangxi period, one eunuch who became seriously ill while in prison was even told to return home to recuperate, with the understanding that he would return to prison after he had recovered.[6]

Such policies requiring seriously ill eunuchs to return to their native places to recuperate proved problematic for both the eunuch and the imperial court. While they removed sick eunuchs from the palace, they also removed eunuchs from the oversight of the Imperial Household Department. The requirement also placed physical, logistical, and financial burdens on the sick eunuch. If the eunuch was too sick to work, he most likely was also too sick to travel. While some eunuchs were from the capital area and its environs, e.g., the cities of Beijing and Tianjin, others would have had to travel farther to reach their native places in the provinces of Zhili

---

3. See First Historical Archives, Beijing, 宮中，雜件1030，人事類太監，同治9年 and 光緒24年.
4. A psychotic disorder marked by oversensitivity, inactivity, and auditory and visual hallucinations.
5. *Qing shengzu xunyu*, 康熙13年6月11日. Cited in Yu Huaqing, *Zhongguo huanguan zhidushi* (Shanghai: Renmin chubanshe, 1993), 491.
6. First Historical Archives, Beijing, *Kangxi chao manwen zhupi zouzhe quanyi* (Beijing: Zhongguo shehui kexue chubanshe, 1996), 1666, entry 4142.

and Shandong, and Shuntian Prefecture.[7] Sick eunuchs would also have to pay for travel to their native place.

During the reign of Kangxi, the emperor acknowledged that many eunuchs were too old or too sick to return to their native place when he ordered the Board of Rites to "adopt" (*shouyang* 收養) such inner court eunuchs. Every four were to be given a house, and each was to receive a monetary payment of .5 *liang* (兩 tael) and 1 *hu* 斛 of rice and when the eunuch died he was to be buried in Wucheng.[8] This policy appears reminiscent of assistance provided for eunuch retirees during the Ming dynasty. Retired and disabled Ming eunuchs would be sent to the *Wanyiju* (浣衣局 Nursing Home Bureau), where they were provided with rice, salt, and other necessities.[9] It is important to note that Kangxi only extended this welfare assistance to eunuchs who had been assigned to the inner court, namely those had who worked directly for the imperial family.

A comparison of eunuch sick leave policies with those of officials discussed in He Bian's study on the politics of illness in the Qing civil bureaucracy[10] provides insight into how the Qing managed its human resources as well as how differences in status affected the treatment of each group. According to He, prior to the reign of Yongzheng (1722–1735), only officials stationed in the capital were allowed to request temporary sick leave; provincial officials who became seriously ill were forced to retire. Seeing this as a waste of valuable human resources, the emperor extended the right of provincial officials to take sick leave and to be reappointed after recovery; in doing so, he saved the careers of many officials. As time progressed, though, the emperor began to suspect that this privilege was being abused in order to evade duties; he suspected that many of these officials who were returning home to take their sick leave had never been sick at all. As a result, in 1735, he suspended the right of officials to take sick leave in their native place and instead required them to recuperate in their posts. When the Qianlong emperor came to power in 1735, believing that sick officials should be allowed to recuperate without having to shoulder the added financial burden of paying for sick leave in the provincial capital while their salary was suspended, he reversed the Yongzheng emperor's ruling. Thereafter, sick officials were allowed to recuperate in their hometowns.

In cases of eunuch sick leave, returning to one's native place was not a privilege but a requirement. Removing sick eunuchs from the palace and the capital

---

7. Yu Huaqing, *Zhongguo huanguan zhidushi*, 479. For a list of the specific provinces in Zhili and counties in Shuntian from which eunuchs originated, see Tang Yinian, *Qing gong taijian* (Shenyang: Liaoning daxue chubanshe, 1993), 36. (See Chapter 2).

8. Yu Huaqing, *Zhongguo huanguan zhidushi*, 491. Yu does not cite the original source. According to Playfair, Wucheng is a *chen* (zhen, market town) near Hsiu-ning (Xiuning) District, Anhui. See G. M. H. Playfair, *The Cities and Towns of China: A Geographical Dictionary*, 2nd ed. (Shanghai: Kelly and Walsh Ltd., 1910), entries 7110 and 5099.

9. Shih-shan Henry Tsai, *The Eunuchs in the Ming Dynasty* (Albany: State University of New York Press, 1996), 49.

10. He Bian, "Too Sick to Serve: The Politics of Illness in the Qing Civil Bureaucracy," *Late Imperial China* 33, no. 2 (Dec. 2012): 40–75.

allowed the imperial household to not only distance itself from potentially contagious diseases but also to avoid the responsibility of caring for its dependent eunuch workforce. Relying on eunuchs to manage their own travel and health-care needs once outside the palace suggests that the palace was unconcerned with the plight of members of its eunuch workforce after they were no longer of use to the palace. The palace's treatment of sick eunuchs also reveals that, despite the lowly status of eunuchs and their dependence on the palace for their livelihood and place in society, the welfare of sick eunuchs was often of no concern unless they were congregating outside the palace, where they were clearly visible and putting a strain on capital resources. As will be seen, the Yongzheng emperor, when faced with such a situation, felt compelled to offer eunuchs assistance when they were too old or too sick to serve. Yongzheng, like other Qing emperors, could quickly change his mind, though, when confronted with evidence that officials and/or eunuchs were abusing this leniency by feigning illness and evading their duties.

Despite the financial and logistic hardships sick leave could impose on eunuchs, sick leave policies appear to have been quite liberal, especially considering the strict disciplinary measures in place to deal with eunuch infractions and a work environment in which corporal punishment was the norm. Cases from the reign of the Guangxu emperor (1875–1908) reveal the often generous terms of sick leave the palace granted to eunuchs. In 1897, *Jinghemen* (景和門 *Jinghe Gate*) *shouling taijian* Li Jinxi 李進喜 received up to six months of sick leave to be taken outside the palace, during which time he was to recuperate from leg pain.[11] In 1899, *shouling taijian* Gao Chengxiang 高成祥, suffering from *tan* (痰 phlegm) and having difficulty walking, requested sick leave; his request was granted, and he was given three months leave to recuperate outside the palace.[12]

Given that corporal punishment was a common form of discipline utilized by the Imperial Household Department to manage palace eunuchs, one might assume that the historical record would show evidence of eunuchs seeking treatment for their wounds after having been beaten. However, this is not the case; archival documents regarding sick eunuchs do not mention injuries but rather symptoms related to illnesses. This can be attributed to the fact that most documents concerning eunuch illnesses appear in records related to eunuch sick leaves requests, the rules governing sick leave, and cases involving alleged eunuch abuse of sick leave. Eunuch treatment of health problems caused by beatings may simply have been too mundane an occurrence and deemed unworthy of a note in the historical record.

These cases do, however, provide insight into what illnesses were associated with the lifestyle of eunuchs. Despite the low mortality rate associated with emasculation, eunuchs faced a host of urological problems post procedure.[13] Eunuchs often

---

11. First Historical Archives, Beijing, 宮中，雜件1030，人事類太監，光緒23年11月.

12. First Historical Archives, Beijing, 宮中，雜件1199，人事類太監媽媽女子，光緒25年12月28日.

13. See Melissa S. Dale, "Understanding Emasculation Western Medical Perspectives on Chinese Eunuchs," *Social History of Medicine* 23, no. 1 (April 2010): 38–55.

suffered from the inability to pass urine or empty their bladders due to blockages in their urethra or bladders. Some eunuchs suffered from chronic problems such as urinary incontinence, a nuisance and an embarrassment more than an illness that would prompt a sick leave request. Eunuchs, like other segments of Qing society, suffered from a host of medical problems including eye ailments, leg pain, cough, stroke and cancer. Eunuchs, like Qing officials, also suffered in particular from *tan* (phlegm).[14] Without a clear definition of what was considered a "serious illness," eunuchs applied for and were granted sick leave for all sorts of symptoms. As a result, such liberal policies created a situation in which some eunuchs abused the system in order to evade their duties.

Were Eunuchs Feigning Illness?

During the early and mid-Qing, liberal sick leave policies, particularly those involving leave to be taken outside the palace and those involving permanent discharge, led to many hasty decisions that were later proven unwarranted. The suspicions of Qing emperors over fraudulent sick leave requests were heightened by cases in which a discharged eunuch was found to have feigned illness to avoid work. In the case of officials, Qing emperors were well aware that claims of illness could provide "a convenient pretext for evading one's duty."[15] For example, in 1780, Su Chang 蘇 常, a eunuch serving in the *Yuanmingyuan*, was retired due to an eye ailment, *tan*, and other medical problems. Later, Su's claims of being too disabled to serve were found to be false. Su was sentenced to wear the cangue, receive a beating, and be exiled to Yili, where he was to be given to the Oirat Mongols as a slave. Li Yu, the eunuch superior responsible for approving Su's discharge, committed suicide before being officially charged with not thoroughly investigating Su's claims of illness.[16] Such reports contributed to the Qing's decision to closely examine the veracity of eunuch sick leave requests before granting retirement due to illness.[17] Cases of fraudulent sick leave among eunuchs, when viewed alongside studies of official sick leave practices, suggest that this was a labor management problem that cut across status and position within the Qing bureaucracy and palace.

Eunuchs permanently discharged due to illness continued to arouse the suspicions of the government. Although no longer employed by the palace, these eunuchs continued to be under the supervision of the Imperial Household Department and by extension the local officials in the eunuch's native place. The passes[18] of these retirees explained that, if the eunuch recovered from his illness, the pass was to be

---

14. According to He Bian, the two most frequent maladies of Qing officials were heart palpitations and phlegm. See He Bian, "Too Sick to Serve," 60.
15. He, "Too Sick to Serve," 40.
16. *Guochao gongshi xubian*, ed. Qing Gui et al., 卷 72 (Reprint, Beijing: Beijing guji chubanshe, 1994), 669.
17. See He, "Too Sick to Serve," 40–75.
18. Identification showing that these eunuchs were authorized to be on sick leave.

handed in for cancellation.[19] Thus, retirement from the Qing eunuch system did not always mean freedom from the Imperial Household Department or an absolute end to one's obligation to serve the palace. Eunuchs discharged due to illness were subject to periodic investigations to determine if they had recovered or were still too sick to serve. If a eunuch was found to have recovered without reporting for service, his discharge would be revoked and he would be sentenced to cut grass at Wudian 吳甸 for three years, after which time he would be returned to service[20]

Eunuchs permanently dismissed due to illness often later recovered and struggled to support themselves outside the system. Some of these discharged eunuchs, desperate for a source of income, even returned to the capital region and obtained employment as a eunuch in prince's households under an assumed name. For those eunuchs who succeeded in returning to their native places, financial problems often impeded their ability to reintegrate into society. Since many eunuchs came from destitute families, it is not surprising that, after returning to their native places, eunuchs found themselves unable to feed and clothe themselves. One such eunuch, Ma Jinzhong 馬進忠, was arrested in 1763 for running back to the capital and working for a prince under an alias. When questioned by the authorities, Ma confessed:

> I am a native of Jinghai, Zhili. I am thirty-three *sui*. Originally, I served in the *Jingmingyuan* 靜明園. Last year during the sixth month, since I had contracted ulcers and could not serve, my *zongguan taijian* [assistant chief eunuch] memorialized to have me deported back to my native place, Jinghai County. It was my uncle, Ma Yongzhang who prepared the guarantee to receive me back. Since my family did not have any food to eat, I ran back to the capital on the 20th day of the 12th month and applied to work at a prince of the first degree's establishment.[21]

In his deposition, Ma revealed that he obtained employment at the prince's establishment under an alias, claiming that he was Hao Fu 郝福 from the Duke of Song's household 嵩公家. The ease with which Ma succeeded in obtaining employment under this alias, and the Provincial Military's Commander's criticism of the prince for not closely questioning Ma about his origins, reveals the problems the government had in controlling the relocation of discharged eunuchs. Furthermore, Ma's case highlights a problem that the imperial court was well aware of, that eunuchs discharged due to illness, once outside the palace, were recovering and returning to the capital to work for princes. Cases like Ma's also raise the question of why a recovered eunuch would not apply to return to work in the palace. One need only

---

19. *Qinding gongzhong xianxing zeli* 欽定宮中現行則例 (*QDGZXXZL*) [Imperially authorized laws and regulations of conduct within the palace] (Reprint, Taipei: Wenhai chubanshe, 1979), 卷4，處分，803.

20. *QDGZXXZL*, 卷4，處分，803.

21. *Zhongyang yanjiuyuan lishiyuyan yanjiusuo xiancun Qingdai neige daku yuancang Ming-Qing dang'an* 中央研究院歷史語言研究所現存清代內閣大庫原藏明清檔案 [Ming-Qing archives in the collection of the Academia Sinica's Institute of History and Philology], ed. Zhang Weiren (Taipei: Academia Sinica, 1986–1995), A204-61, 3-1-3-2.

recall the Qing's reliance on corporal punishment to manage its eunuchs and the frequency with which many eunuchs ran away from the palace to realize that, for many, this was not an option.

Suspicions that some eunuchs feigned illness to obtain a permanent discharge from service led the Qing to scrutinize sick leave requests more closely and to impose greater restrictions on sick leave overall. During the reigns of Jiaqing (1796–1820) and Daoguang (1821–1850), the number of requests for leave increased while simultaneously the supply of eunuch applicants was not meeting the demand and large numbers of eunuchs were running away.[22] In 1809, the following imperial decree was issued:

> Until now, among palace and *Yuanmingyuan shouling taijian* and eunuchs (*taijian*), if there were those who were old or crippled and could not serve, the *zongguan taijian* in charge and others would memorialize the throne and accordingly authorize dismissal. In every case, send a person to investigate. As for those feared to have fabricated stories, we must be ready for their gradual advance (increase). Hereafter, all elderly and/or crippled or sick eunuchs who cannot serve, after the *zongguan taijian* in charge has memorialized the emperor, let the Ministers of the Imperial Household Department and others pursue the details and personally investigate [the matter]. If there are those who are too sick to get out of bed, have the Imperial Household Department send a secretary over to carefully examine if it is true. [Only] after memorializing the emperor, then authorize the dismissal. If there are fabrications and fraud, stringently investigate the eunuch. Moreover, punish *zongguan taijian* who jointly memorialize the throne [in these cases]. Let this be made into a directive. Now, there are ten *shouling taijian* memorializing requesting dismissals. Handle them according to the new rules.[23]

This specification that Imperial Household Department ministers personally investigate a eunuch's claims of being too disabled to serve highlights the emperor's suspicion of eunuch superiors corroborating their subordinates' false claims of illness.

Eunuchs requesting discharge due to old age or illness who had been recuperating outside the palace for a year first had to be personally examined by a grand minister of the Imperial Household Department and the appropriate eunuch supervisor. If the sick eunuch could not get out of bed, the grand minister would select a secretary to inspect the validity of the claim. If the sick eunuch was truly bedridden and over sixty-five *sui* or seriously ill, the eunuch's *weimin* status would be approved.[24] In fraudulent cases, the eunuch would be interrogated, and the *zongguan taijian*, *shouling taijian*, and others named in the original joint memorial approving the eunuch's discharge, would all share in the punishment.[25]

22. Yu Huaqing, *Zhongguo huanguan zhidushi*, 491.
23. *Qinding Da Qing huidian shili* 欽定大清會典事例 (QDDQHDSL) [Imperially commissioned collected regulations of the Qing dynasty], ed. Li Hongzhang 李鴻章 et al. (Shanghai: Shangwu yinshuguan, 1909), 卷1216, 內務府 (Imperial Household Department), *taijian shilei*, 2.
24. *QDGZXXZL*, 卷4，處分，801–2.
25. *QDGZXXZL*, 卷4，處分，801–3.

Sick leave requests were routinely granted early in the dynasty, but by the Xianfeng reign (1851–1861), sick eunuchs were subject to an investigation by their eunuch superiors (*zongguan* and *shouling taijian*) prior to sick leave being granted. If a eunuch suddenly contracted a serious illness, his eunuch supervisor was to examine him and, if the claim was true, write a report. Then, an official from the Imperial Household Department would be sent to perform a second examination. If the two reports did not agree, the original investigating *zongguan, shouling taijian*, etc. would be punished.[26] Such procedures reveal that those given the power to approve eunuch sick leave were not medical professionals or at the very least individuals with some knowledge of the nature of diseases and the amount of time needed to recuperate from such illnesses. In cases of official sick leave, He Bian notes that the Qing required officials to submit an affidavit from a physician. However, in cases of eunuch sick leave, there was no such requirement.

Qing palace records provide few clues as to the medical treatment of eunuchs. Archives from the *Taiyiyuan* (太醫院 Imperial Hospital) list eunuchs along with other servants as having access to medical care at the hospital. Shan Shikui, in his article on the *Taiyiyuan* during the Qing dynasty, notes that records from the eighth year of the Guangxu reign show that eunuchs from the *Changchungong* (長春宮 Palace of Eternal Spring, located within the inner court) were prescribed medicine from the hospital.[27]

Qing palace archives do reveal that inner court eunuchs had greater access to medical care. The proximity of eunuchs to the emperor and the imperial court improved the likelihood of sick eunuchs receiving quality medical care. According to Tang Yinian, inner court eunuchs often enjoyed the privilege of being treated by the imperial family's physicians. In his work *Qing gong taijian*, Tang notes that documents held in the palace archives indicate that, in more than a few cases, doctors were sent to care for sick eunuchs.[28] Tang points out that the motivation behind providing the best medical care for these eunuchs was not genuine concern for the eunuchs' well-being or due to any high political position the eunuch held, but a desire to return eunuchs to service as quickly as possible and thus not disrupt the system. Tang also suggests that rulers treated sick eunuchs in order to pacify other eunuchs still in their service.[29] Although Tang argues that eunuchs enjoyed this privileged medical care, care that was better than what most people received, evidence suggests that this was a privilege reserved for the imperial court's favorite eunuchs and that eunuch status dictated which eunuchs were treated.[30]

Records from the *Yuyaofang* (御藥房 Imperial Pharmacy) further support the argument that inner court eunuchs had access to medical care within the palace.

---

26. *QDGZXXZL*, 卷4，處分，799–801.
27. Shan Shikui, "Qingdai Taiyiyuan," *Gugong bowuyuan yuankan* 1985, no. 3: 51.
28. Tang, *Qing gong taijian*, 58.
29. Tang, *Qing gong taijian*, 58–60.
30. Tang, *Qing gong taijian*, 58–59. I have yet to come across any evidence that this privilege was extended to eunuchs who worked in the outer courts or those who were among the unranked.

Chen Keji's research on the Imperial Pharmacy includes lists of prescriptions prepared for cases involving young inner court eunuchs.[31] While these records provide
little information about these eunuchs other than their inner court designation and
their name, they do reveal the treatment received by the eunuchs. Prescriptions
are recorded for eunuchs suffering from symptoms ranging from cough to *tan*. In
several cases, the same physician treated the sick eunuch for two or more consecu-
tive days, offering continuity of care. Outer court eunuchs may have had to find
their own medical care. Rare glimpses of eunuch doctors appearing in Qing archival
records lead one to believe that these eunuchs may have sought treatment from
palace eunuchs who had some medical training. However, as cases documenting
instances of malpractice by eunuch doctors have shown, the palace would most
likely not have relied on a eunuch doctor's assessment of the severity or veracity of
another eunuch's illness.

Eunuchs found to be truly sick were temporarily relieved of their duties and
allowed to recuperate in their place of work or their own quarters but not outside
the palace. This specification reveals the Imperial Household Department's desire
to keep a closer eye on sick eunuchs. After recovering from his illness, the eunuch
would be sent back to the palace to serve in his original position. If the eunuch's
illness was deemed to be very serious, he would be granted sick leave to recuperate
outside the palace or at the *Xinglongsi* (興隆寺 Temple of Prosperity).[32]

In an effort to further discourage abuse of sick leave, the Imperial Household
Department reduced the pay of sick eunuchs. Reductions in pay and the timetables
involved in achieving *weimin taijian* status depended upon the rank of the eunuch
in question.[33]

Zongguan and *shouling taijian* who requested sick leave and who had not worked
for over a year but who had already been removed from office and had their salaries
taken away were required to return home for a year to recuperate. After recovering,
they were required to return to service in the palace. If after a year, they still had not
recovered, they were allowed to request retirement. Those *shouling taijian* who were
retiring due to illness and whose service had been long and devoted could request
to receive one *liang* 兩 *enshangyin* (恩賞銀 gracious reward money) every month
and five hundred *wen dazhi qian* (大制錢 large-sized cash). If these *zongguan* and
shouling taijian had continued to serve for several days after requesting sick leave,
then all deductions from their salary would be returned to them.[34]

Eunuchs who had been sick for a year or more were dismissed and no longer
received a salary. These eunuchs were designated as *weimin taijian* 為民太監, a
term also used to refer to retired eunuchs that indicated that the eunuch was being
discharged from the system and returned to commoner status. Each *weimin taijian*

31. Chen Keji, ed., *Qing gong yi'an yanjiu* 清宮醫案研究 (Beijing: Zhongyi guji chubanshe, 2006), 1335–46.
32. *QDGZXXZL*, 卷4，處分，800.
33. Adapted from Tang, *Qing gong taijian*, 58–59.
34. Tang, *Qing gong taijian*, 58–59.

Table 8.1: Salary Reductions and Discharge Due to Illness

Title	Rank	Monthly Rations	Amount of Sick Leave Taken (Months)				
			<1 month	>1 month	<6 months	>6 months	12 months
Eunuch (*taijian*)	None	2 *liang* silver			No deduction	–1 *liang*	Cease paying salary and memorialize for *weimin* status
		2.5, 3, and 4 *liang* silver	No deduction	–0.5, 1, and 2 *liang* respectively		–1 *liang*	Cease paying salary and memorialize for *weimin* status
shouling taijian		2.5 and 3 *liang* silver		–0.5 *liang* salary		–1, 1.25 *liang* respectively	Cease paying salary
	Grade 7 and 8	3 and 4 *liang* silver		–0.5, 1 *liang* respectively		–1.25, 1.5 *liang* respectively; those with official positions, remove from office	Cease paying salary
zongguan taijian		4 *liang* silver		–1 *liang* salary		–1.25 *liang* salary	Cease paying salary
	Grade 6 and 7, Grade 5, Grade 4	5, 7, and 8 *liang* silver		–1, 2 *liang* respectively		–1.5, 2.5 *liang* salary and remove from office	Cease paying salary

During the Qing, the average eunuch's monthly salary could range from two to eight *taels* [*liang*] per month and from one to eight *hu* of rice. The minority of eunuchs in the upper echelons of the eunuch hierarchy received comparatively much higher salaries. During the reigns of Guangxu and Xuantong, *dazongguan* [received] 100 *taels* of food money . . . , 40 *pin* of vegetables, and 2 *tang* per month, *shouling taijian* [received] 50 *taels* of food money, 4 *pin* of vegetables, and 1 *tang* per month; each department's *shouling taijian* [received] 10 *taels* of food money, 3 *pin* of vegetables, and one *tang* (see Pu Jia and Pu Jie, *Wanqing diwang shenghuo jianwen*, Vol. 1 [Taipei: Juzhenwu chubanshe, 1984], 210). The allowance each eunuch received depended upon the location of one's duties rather than rank; some locations did not pay the allowance to those in the upper echelons of the eunuch hierarchy (see Yu Huaqing, *Zhongguo huanguan zhidushi* [Shanghai: Renmin chubanshe, 1993], 483).

would be given documentation that would be used in case authorities ever questioned why he was outside the capital.[35] On this pass would be noted the eunuch's age, appearance, and native place.[36] After receiving a pass, these eunuchs would then be under the management of their local officials. How the eunuch would travel and pay for this required return to his native place was not specified.

Too Many Discharged Eunuchs in the Capital

The Yongzheng emperor (r. 1722–1735) struggled repeatedly with how to solve the problem of discharged eunuchs (both sick and elderly) remaining in the capital. Just two years into his reign (1724–1725) the emperor commented on the large number of discharged inner court eunuchs and those from the princely households in the capital and expressed his concern that "these people would cause trouble" and should not be allowed to remain.[37] Aware of the problems eunuchs faced upon discharge from the palace, in 1726 the emperor remarked that eunuchs who had served the court for twenty and thirty years, now that they were old and sick, were suddenly finding themselves ordered to leave the palace. "If dogs and horses are supported, why not eunuchs?"[38] This is perhaps a reference to Confucius's comments to Zi Yu about filial piety. Confucius said, "'Nowadays a filial son is just a man who keeps his parents in food. But even dogs or horses are given food. If there is no feeling of reverence, wherein lies the differences?' [II:7]"[39] Yongzheng decreed that, among retired eunuchs desiring to remain in the capital, those found to be without family property and unable to make a living would receive a stipend of one *liang* per month in assistance from the *Ziwuzhong* (自鳴鐘 Clock Department) or the *Jingshifang* (敬事房 Office of Eunuch Affairs) and each person was to be given one or two rooms to live in the extra buildings of the official housing of the Imperial Household Department. Two *shouling taijian* would be sent to receive the rent, manage these eunuchs, and to provide for them in their old age.[40]

However, by the following year, 1727, the emperor's compassion for the welfare of discharged eunuchs was becoming tempered by problems associated with the growing number of *weimin taijian* remaining in the capital. Eunuchs now found to be living in the capital without a guarantor (*baoliu* 保留) were to be sought out and

35. *Qinding Da Qing huidian shili* (*QDDQHDSL*), 卷1216，內務府，太監視事例，乾隆33年.
36. During the early Qing, eunuchs discharged from service at a princely household were not given such certificates, making it difficult for authorities to determine whether or not a eunuch had indeed been discharged. In 1768, the Qianlong emperor rectified this problem by requiring that all retired eunuchs be issued a pass. See *QDDQHDSL*, 卷1216，內務府，太監事例，4.
37. *Qing shilu* 清實錄 (Taipei: Guofang yanjiuyuan, 1961), 卷20，雍正2年5月，段 28745, 329-2.
38. Preston M. Torbert, *The Ch'ing Imperial Household Department: A Study of its Organization and Principal Functions, 1662–1796* (Cambridge, MA: Harvard University Press, 1977), 47.
39. See Theodore de Bary et al., *Sources of Chinese Tradition*, vol. 1 (New York: Columbia University Press, 1960), 27.
40. *Guochao gongshi*, ed. Yu Minzhong (Taipei: Taiwan xuesheng shuju, 1965), 卷3，6–7，雍正4年11月12日.

returned to their native place.[41] Undoubtedly, the great numbers of unemployed, sick, and elderly discharged palace and princely establishment eunuchs residing in the capital were placing a strain on the capital area. The stipulation that guarantors of discharged eunuchs be held collectively responsible for the crimes of their guarantees suggests that the court was concerned that these eunuchs might cause trouble and/or break the law. Also, discharged eunuchs remaining in the capital posed a potential security risk since some might have been privy to the inner workings of the imperial court and could divulge palace secrets. It is interesting to note that Yongzheng's change in policy towards discharged eunuchs came about the same time as he was suspecting that officials were feigning illness to avoid their duties.[42]

By the late 1800s, measures appear to have been put in place to deal with some of the seriously ill eunuchs who remained in the capital; sick eunuchs could recuperate at the *Xinglongsi*.[43] George Carter Stent, writing in the late 1800s, remarked that the *Gangbing miao*[44] (剛秉廟 Gangbing Temple) and a temple built for the God of War (*Guandi*), in which Gangbing was given a niche by the Yongle emperor, were used as wards.[45] While such measures provided assistance to some eunuchs during periods of dire need, they did not resolve the problems created by lax sick leave policies. As the records show, suspicions about fraudulent sick leave requests continued unabated throughout the Qing.

Discharge Due to Disciplinary Problems

In addition to retirement due to old age or illness, eunuchs could be discharged from service due to disciplinary problems. Incorrigible palace eunuchs met with corporal punishment in the form of beatings from their superiors and, if the offense was deemed serious enough, harsher punishments such as beatings combined with wearing the cangue, and exile meted out by the *Shenxingsi* (Judicial Department). Cases such as that of Li Liandong 李連棟, found guilty of arson and theft, appear to be the exception. During the Qianlong era, it was not uncommon for eunuchs guilty of such crimes to receive sentences of execution. However, one cannot help but notice how the emperor handled the punishment of Li's co-workers. Here, the emperor found Li's eunuch colleagues to be unruly, a trait the emperor linked to them having been emasculated in middle age, and ordered that they be discharged from service.[46]

In contrast to the harsh punishments facing unruly palace eunuchs, eunuchs in the service of a princely establishment were simply dismissed from service and

41. *Qinding huidian shili*, 卷1216，內務府，*taijian shilei*, 4.
42. See He, "Too Sick to Serve," 65.
43. QDGZXXZL，卷4，處分，800.
44. Eunuch who served under the Yongle emperor during the Ming dynasty.
45. George Carter Stent, "Chinese Eunuchs," *Journal of the North China Branch of the Royal Asiatic Society*, New Series, no. 11 (1877): 158.
46. Du Wanyan, *Zhongguo huangguan shi* (Taipei: Wenjin chubanshe, 1996), 30.

remanded to the supervision of the local officials in their native places. For example, An Dexiang 安德祥, a eunuch in the service of a *junwang* 郡王, was sent to the *Libu* (禮部 Board of Rites) for discharge for being drunk and disorderly. The Board of Rites then deported An Dexiang to his native place, where the local officials were to supervise him.[47]

Retirement

Besides sick leave, eunuchs could gain an authorized exit from the system due to old age. In order to become eligible for discharge due to old age, a eunuch had to be sixty-five *sui* (sixty-four years old) or older. However, retirement at sixty-five *sui* was not automatic; the eunuch also had to prove that he was no longer able to serve. Authorized discharge from the Qing eunuch system involved an often complicated process of requests for retirement regulated by frequently changing requirements and stipulations. Once discharged, eunuchs faced financial and social challenges as they transitioned from life within the palace to life among Qing society. As evidenced by the large number of discharged eunuchs either remaining in or running back to the capital environs, eunuch retirement to their native place proved problematic.

Far from the ideal of eunuchs being restored to commoner status and being absorbed into society in their place of origin, retirees faced a much more difficult reality. While retirement was not a problem for powerful eunuchs such as Li Lianying 李蓮英 and Xiao Dezhang 小德張, the majority of discharged eunuchs faced a number of uncertainties once they left the eunuch system. Where would they go? And how would they survive after leaving the palace? Late Qing palace eunuchs attributed these uncertainties to two sources: discrimination by society and the origins of eunuchs.[48]

Eunuchs faced an unreceptive environment upon discharge from the palace. Despite their previous connection with the Imperial Household, eunuchs were often regarded as outcasts due to their disfigurement. Sayings or names that ridiculed eunuchs reveal the low esteem many in society had for eunuchs. For example, eunuchs would be cursed as *laogong* (Old Roosters),[49] or when referring to a foul odor, people might say, "'He stinks like a eunuch' . . . [or refer to] them as 'stinking eunuchs.'"[50] Genital mutilation and its accompanying physical changes immediately impeded eunuchs' efforts to reintegrate into society. To society, eunuchs were lowly freaks and the subject of ridicule.[51] Aware of the discrimination against retired

---

47. *Zhongyang yanjiuyuan lishiyuyan yanjiusuo xiaocun Qingdai neige daku yuancang Ming-Qing dang'an*, A221-101.

48. Ma Deqing et al., "Qing gong taijian huiyi lu," in *Wanqing gongting shenghuo jianwen*, ed. Zhang Wenhui (Beijing: Wenshi ziliao chubanshe, 1982), 196.

49. Stent, "Chinese Eunuchs," 181.

50. Stent, "Chinese Eunuchs," 179. Reference to the urinary incontinence some eunuchs suffered after emasculation.

51. Ma Deqing et al., "Qing gong taijian huiyi lu," 196.

eunuchs, some relatives, fearful of losing face for their association with the disfigured relative, even joined in the castigation of eunuchs.[52]

The lowly origins of most Qing eunuchs also complicated their attempts to reintegrate into society. Poverty had motivated many families to emasculate their sons in the first place and, despite their expectations to the contrary, it often continued to afflict these families even after the eunuch's service had ended. Thus, the return of eunuchs who had been designated as no longer fit to serve only further oppressed these families. Some eunuchs, upon leaving the palace after years of service, discovered that poverty had so oppressed their families that they did not even have a family to return to.[53] Moreover, some eunuchs who had been kidnapped when young and sold to the *daozijiang* (刀子匠 knife expert) for emasculation might not even remember where they had come from and thus not know where to return to.

Eunuchs also faced problems earning a living for themselves after retirement. Eunuch employment problems stemmed from the nature of their specialized employment within the palace. With the majority of eunuchs performing menial tasks and exiting with little savings, eunuchs found it difficult to apply the skills they had once utilized to serve and maintain the imperial court and clan and its surroundings applicable to their new lives outside the palace. In most cases, retirement proved fraught with difficulties since, at the time of discharge, eunuchs were either too sick or too old to work for a living and untrained in skills appropriate for earning a living outside the palace.

Contrary to reports that the government provided retirement assistance for all eunuchs, the majority of eunuch retirees were left to fend for themselves once their employment with the palace was terminated. The financial difficulties eunuchs faced after retiring from service clarify Stent's comment: "When eunuchs are seventy years of age, or are rendered unfit for duty through sickness, etc., they are allowed to retire on a pension varying from two to six *taels* [*liang*] per month, and those who wish to do so, have the privilege of living in the temples rent free."[54] Perhaps some eunuchs enjoyed these benefits, but not all did. During 1726, the emperor had bestowed a pension of one *liang* per month on eunuchs remaining in the capital who, after investigation, were found to be without family property or the ability to support themselves. Moreover, a select few eunuchs such as Chang Yonggui 常永貴, a Supervising Attendant of the Directorate of Palace Domestic Service (*Gongdianjian dulingshi* 宮殿監督領侍) under the Jiaqing and Daoguang emperors, did receive a pension. In fact, when one adds up the pension and the additional gifts of money bestowed on Chang, he ended up making just as much as his original salary.[55] However, the government fully expected the majority of

---

52. Li Guang, "Qingji de taijian," in *Wanqing gongting shenghuo jianwen*, ed. Zhang Wenhui (Beijing : Wenshi ziliao chubanshe, 1982), 170.

53. Ma Deqing et al., "Qing gong taijian huiyi lu," 196.

54. Stent, "Chinese Eunuchs," 158.

55. Tang, *Qing gong taijian*, 62.

eunuchs in the lower echelons of the eunuch hierarchy to be self-supporting upon exiting the system.

While Chinese society relied on children to provide for their parents in their later years, few Qing eunuchs found themselves with a family to provide care for them in their old age. During the Qing, the eunuch application process favored eunuchs emasculated prior to the onset of puberty. As a result, these eunuchs often remained single and did not have heirs. A small minority of eunuchs who became emasculated in mid-life, entered the palace as married men with children. Others managed to adopt male heirs. The majority, however, were left with no one but themselves and other eunuchs to rely on after retirement.

Aware of the difficulties facing them upon retirement, some eunuchs took measures during the prime of their life to ensure that they would be cared for in their later years. Those able to save money while working as a eunuch would then be able to make preparations for their retirement. Late Qing eunuchs recount that hard-working eunuchs even received *enjiayin* (恩加銀 gracious reward money) specifically for this purpose.[56] Some retirees would spend their money on land; others chose to donate money to a temple where they became the disciples of a *shifu* (師父 master) or helped fund the repair of a temple.[57] After leaving the eunuch system, the eunuch could then move to the temple to live out the remainder of his years, "enjoying both peace and stability."[58] A small number of powerful and wealthy eunuchs, such as one of the Empress Dowager Cixi's eunuchs, Liu Duosheng 劉多生, even became abbots.[59]

During the Qing, eunuch retirement associations housed in these eunuch temples provided retirees with the companionship and peace of living among their own kind without discrimination, as well as the assurance of receiving room and board in their later years. Unlike Ming eunuch retirees, who were sent to the *Wanyiju* (Nursing Home Bureau) where they were essentially isolated from society in order to prevent the revelation of court secrets,[60] Qing eunuchs spent their later years in self-imposed segregation. Moreover, whereas during the Ming the Palace Servants Directorate provided eunuch retirees with rice, salt, and other daily necessities, the majority of the discharged Qing eunuch population had to join self-help organizations in order to provide a livelihood for themselves outside the system.

One such organization was Beiping's Eunuch Retirement Association (*Beiping de Taijian Yanglaoyihui* 北平的太監養老義會). At the end of the Qing, the association required a membership fee of 180 *kuai*[61] 塊 per eunuch. Three years after joining the association, eunuchs would be entitled to retire at the temple and receive free

---

56. Pu Jia and Pu Jie, *Wanqing diwang shenghuo jianwen*, vol. 1 (Taipei: Juzhenwu chubanshe, 1984), 190.
57. Li Guang, "Qingji de taijian," 170.
58. Ma Deqing et al., "Qing gong taijian huiyi lu," 198.
59. Ma Deqing et al., "Qing gong taijian huiyi lu," 196.
60. Tsai, *The Eunuchs in the Ming Dynasty*, 49.
61. The colloquial term for the Chinese monetary unit, *yuan* 圓.

Figure 8.1
Group of former palace eunuchs at Gang Tie Miao, ca. 1933–1946. Photograph by Hedda Morrison, Harvard-Yenching Library, Harvard University.

room and board.[62] Some eunuch retirement associations required an introduction before the eunuch would even be considered for membership.[63] Due to the waiting period required to join the retirement community, this option only suited eunuchs who had saved enough money throughout their service to cover such an expense. Such associations benefited those who were either wealthy or who had planned well for their future. Eunuchs unexpectedly taken seriously ill and summarily discharged most likely would have found it difficult to meet both the monetary and the waiting requirements attached with such associations. Whether exemptions were made for such cases remains to be seen. Eunuchs without the money to become the pupil of a *shifu* or to join a retirement association often became itinerant and eventually froze or starved to death.[64]

During the Ming and Qing dynasties, eunuchs retired to some twenty-six eunuch temples located in the environs of the capital.[65] Such temples where retired

62. Ma Deqing et al., "Qing gong taijian huiyi lu," 198.
63. Du, *Zhongguo huanguan shi*, 36.
64. Li Guang, "Qingji de taijian," 171.
65. For a list of these temples, see Appendix 3.

eunuchs congregated to live out their retirement were often self-supporting. Eunuch tenants tilled fields, raising grains, vegetables, and fruit trees for the market.[66] In addition, the eunuch residents could rely on their property for both housing and rent. In 1934, Vincent Starrett visited *Gang Tie Miao* (剛鐵廟 Gang Tie Temple)[67] located at that time about one hour outside the walls of Beijing near the village of Xiazhuang.[68] This appears to be the same temple that Stent cited as a site where sick eunuchs could go to recuperate from illness. In the 1930s, the temple was home to more than thirty eunuchs who supported themselves by growing grains and vegetables for the Beijing market and tobacco, which Starrett found to be of "no particular merit."[69]

As havens for eunuch retirees unable to provide a livelihood for themselves among society and unwilling to endure the discrimination their disfigurement engendered among the masses, these temples resulted in a self-imposed segregation of eunuchs from the rest of society. Located outside the capital city limits, these temples allowed eunuchs to distance themselves from the discrimination that their disfigurement brought but also to enjoy the benefits of being close enough to the capital to sell their produce in the Beijing market.

Death and Burial

Eunuchs continued to be discriminated against even after death. Years after eunuchs were emasculated, their physical disfigurement translated into discrimination by denial of admission to burial sites, disownment from their families, and a lack of the heirs necessary to perform ancestor veneration. As in retirement, lack of help and support from members of the eunuch's family and society following the death of a eunuch engendered reliance upon their fellow emasculates to try to alleviate the problem of receiving a proper burial and rites.

According to Chinese custom, when a person reached old age he would return to his native place to live out the remainder of his life and be buried there.[70] Eunuchs shared this desire to be buried in their native place among their kin. However, ancestral cemeteries often denied burial to eunuchs, due to their physical disfigure-

---

66. Li Guang, "Qingji de taijian," 171–72.
67. See L. C. Arlington and William Lewisohn, *In Search of Old Peking* (Shanghai: North China Daily News, 1935), 309–10.
68. According to Arlington and Lewisohn, this temple, also known as *Gang Tie Miao* was named after Gang Tie (Gang Bing). A general under Yongle during the Ming dynasty, Gang was left in charge of the palace while the emperor was away on a hunting trip. Concerned that his enemies might attempt to harm him by fabricating stories of his relations with the palace women, Gang castrated himself. As feared, when the emperor returned, a minister charged Gang with such improper relations. Gang defended himself by revealing to the emperor his now castrated genitalia, stored in his saddle. Impressed by Gang's loyalty, the emperor made him his chief eunuch and deified him as the patron saint of eunuchs. See Arlington and Lewisohn, *In Search of Old Peking*, 309–10.
69. Vincent Starrett, *Oriental Encounters* (Chicago: Normandie House, 1938), 15.
70. Jin Yi and Shen Yiling, *Gongnü tan wanglu* (Beijing: Forbidden City Press, 1992), 110.

ment. While eunuchs attempted to fool the King of Hades (*Yanwang* 閻王) into thinking they were complete males by being buried with their *bao* (寶 treasure),[71] apparently clan members were not always willing to risk upsetting the spirits.[72] Moreover, even to attempt this, prior to death, eunuchs not in possession of their *bao* would have to have saved enough money to buy them back from the *daozijiang* who had emasculated them so many years earlier.[73] The practice of eunuchs buying back their *bao* was known as "returning one's flesh and blood to the family" (*gurou huan jia* 骨肉還家).

However, aside from fearing retribution from the gods, eunuch families shunned their eunuch relatives and barred them from burial in the ancestral cemetery to avoid disgrace and ridicule. With the deceased eunuch's usefulness to the family exhausted in terms of power and money, many families chose to disassociate themselves from their eunuch relative rather than lose face. Once the eunuch relative had left the palace, particularly if he was without wealth or power, he ceased being of use to the family financially or for connections and was often disowned.

In response to the need for a proper burial for Qing dynasty eunuchs, the Qing followed the Ming precedent of establishing cemeteries specifically for eunuchs. For example, in 1734, construction began on the *Enjizhuang* (恩濟莊 Village of Imperial Favor) Eunuch Cemetery and was not completed until the third year of the Qianlong reign (1738).[74] Qing records reveal that the government made lands available on which deceased eunuchs could be buried. An Imperial Decree from 1799 states that deceased *Nanfu* (南府 Court Theatrical Bureau) and *Jingshan* (景山 Prospect Hill) *zongguan* and *shouling taijian* no longer had to be buried in the Foreign Studies Scholar and Student Cemetery (*Waixue jiaoxi xuesheng yingdi* 外學教習學生營地) but could thereafter be buried in *Enjizhuang*. At the end of the Qing, it is said that some 2,700 eunuchs were buried at *Enjizhuang*. However, only 300 headstones remained in the cemetery at the time of the 1958 Beijing City Historical Relics' general survey. According to Arlington and Lewisohn, the cemetery was desecrated by Marshal Feng Yuxiang's soldiers. These soldiers knocked over tombstones, destroyed marble carvings, and cut down most of the old cypress trees.[75] Upon those headstones still existent in the late 1950s were noted the title, name, birth and death dates, and the native place of the eunuch. More elaborate headstones included facts such as the employment history of the eunuch, specifically

---

71. Preserved genitalia.
72. Stent indicates that the King of Hades would transform eunuchs into "she-mules." See Stent, "Chinese Eunuchs," 173.
73. Jin and Shen, *Gongnü tan wanglu*, 110.
74. Liu Jingyi and Lu Qi, "Qingdai taijian Enjizhuang yingdi," *Gugong bowuyuan yuankan* 3 (1979): 51. Arlington and Lewisohn locate the cemetery's origins much earlier, during the reign of the Ming emperor Yongle. This discrepancy may arise from Arlington and Lewisohn's contention that *Enjizhuang* was originally known as *Jingenzhuang*. See Arlington and Lewisohn, *In Search of Old Peking*, 309. During the late 1970s, Liu Jingyi and Lu Qi located the cemetery outside Beijing's *Fuchengmen* (阜城門), approximately two *li* west of *Balizhuang* (Eight Li Village). For a list of these cemeteries, see Appendix 4.
75. Arlington and Lewisohn, *In Search of Old Peking*, 309.

the age he became emasculated and entered the palace, and the different positions he held during his lifetime.[76] An examination of the remaining headstones reveals a preponderance of eunuchs who had achieved the rank of *zongguan* or *shouling taijian*.[77] This evidence suggests a correspondence between eunuchs who reached the upper echelons of the eunuch hierarchy and the privilege of being buried in this cemetery. Liu and Lu suggest that eunuchs of lesser or no rank, those below *shouling taijian*, were also buried in the cemetery but rarely received headstones.[78] While some powerful eunuch's graves, such as that of Li Lianying, were marked with tablets consisting of more than 800 characters, most eunuchs' burial sites consisted of nothing more than a grave.[79]

Cases in the archives of eunuch death appear in two forms: (1) announcements that a vacancy needed to be filled due to a death, and (2) suspicions of fraud. In some, the cause of death is stated; in others simply the eunuch's name and the fact that he had died were listed. Archival documents pertaining to eunuch vacancies such as one from 1719, while mainly about substantiating the need to fill eunuch positions, do record the cause of eunuch deaths. The document states that, during the previous year, two eunuchs had died.[80] Wang Guoqin 王國秦 is listed as having died from *tanhuo bing* 痰火病[81] and Zhao San 趙三 from dsyphagia[82] (*yege* 噎嗝). No further information or details are given. These are merely administrative records noting a vacancy due to death and making it clear that the position would need to be filled by another eunuch.

Cases of eunuch death, like cases of eunuch sick leave, often led the government to suspect fraud. A distrust of eunuchs attempting to exit the eunuch system by feigning death is apparent in memorials reporting the deaths of eunuchs. In addition to noting the date the eunuch died, the names and ranks of those who personally went to verify that the eunuch was indeed deceased were listed.[83] This verification was also necessary because the families of eunuchs who died while still employed by the palace could be eligible to receive a monetary payment upon the eunuch's death. The amount of the payment to the family of the deceased eunuch would be based upon his rank.[84] In some cases such as the death of *Ningshougong* (寧壽宮 Palace of Peaceful Old Age) grade seven *shouling taijian* Dong Shiyu 董世玉, money was paid even though the eunuch had already retired.[85] In an undated memorial one finds that from the twenty-seventh year of Kangxi to the

---

76. See Liu and Lu, "Qingdai taijian Enjizhuang yingdi," 52–58.
77. For a listing of information obtained from these headstones, see Liu and Lu, "Qingdai taijian Enjizhuang yingdi," 52–54.
78. Liu and Lu, "Qingdai taijian Enjizhuang yingdi," 57.
79. Liu and Lu, "Qingdai taijian Enjizhuang yingdi," 57.
80. First Historical Archives, Beijing, *Kangxi chao manwen zhupi zouzhe quanyi*, entry 3177, 1287.
81. A disease much like asthma, manifesting itself in a high fever and chest pains.
82. Difficulty or discomfort in swallowing, as a symptom of a disease.
83. First Historical Archives, Beijing, 宮中，雜件1030，人事類太監，光緒24年閏3月27日.
84. Tang, *Qing gong taijian*, 66.
85. First Historical Archives, Beijing, 敬事房5236，康熙27年–乾隆30年.

thirtieth year of the Qianlong reign (1688–1765), deceased eunuchs who had been employed in the *Yuanmingyuan*, the *Qin'andian* (欽安殿 Hall of Imperial Peace), etc. each received ten *liang*, presumably to be put toward burial expenses.[86] In 1821, families of deceased eunuchs such as Jiang Jinyu 蔣進玉, who had served in the *Yuanmingyuan*, still only received ten *liang* at the time of his death.[87]

It is unclear whether or not the Qing continued the Ming practice of providing a burial for eunuchs who died of illness while employed by the palace. During the Ming, sick eunuchs who had died while being treated at the eunuch infirmary would be provided with a copper tablet, a coffin, and wood for the cremation.[88] Mitamura Taisuke adds that, during the Ming, there was a crematorium where court ladies and eunuchs without kin were cremated.[89]

While the Imperial Household Department donated the land for eunuch cemeteries on which many eunuchs serving in the upper echelons of the eunuch hierarchy were interred, it appears that eunuchs were required to assume the financial responsibility for their own burial costs.[90] During the Qianlong reign (1736–1795), eunuchs had joined together to form the Enjizhuang Lifelong Society, an association aimed at providing funds for eunuch burial at *Enjizhuang*. This organization consisted of two chapters, the first headed by eight eunuchs from the *Jingshifang* 敬事房, *Beixiangsuo* 北祥所, *Dasaochu* 打掃處, *Zhangyisi* 掌儀司, *Yingzaosi* 營造司, *Nanfu* 南府, the *Yuanmingyuan* 圓明園, and the *Changchunyuan* 暢春園; and the second composed of more than one hundred eunuchs from the *Yuchafang* (御茶房 Imperial Tea Room), the *Yushufang* (御書房 Imperial Library), and the *Gudongfang* (古董房 Antiques Bureau). According to the records of the Enjizhuang Lifelong Society, each month every member was required to pay fifty *wen* 文 in dues towards the five thousand *wen* burial fee required by the Enjizhuang Eunuch Cemetery.[91] Eunuchs holding positions such as *zongguan* and *shouling taijian* had the opportunity or, more importantly, possessed the funds necessary to be buried at cemeteries specifically set aside for eunuchs by the government, such as *Enjizhuang*. Tang Yinian's research into the *Enjizhuang* organization reveals that, while essentially a privately run organization, the group did not enjoy complete autonomy from the *Jingshifang*. Extracting money from the Enjizhuang Lifelong Society's coffers to cover *Enjizhuang* cemetery repairs and sacrifices, the *Jingshifang* continued to control the management of the association. As a result, Tang classifies the association as a "government supervised privately run organization" (*guandu minban* 官督民辦).[92] The existence of this association suggests that not all eunuch families

---

86. First Historical Archives, Beijing, 敬事房5236，康熙27年–乾隆30年.
87. First Historical Archives, Beijing, 宮中，雜件1030，人事類太監，道光1年8月.
88. Tsai, *The Eunuchs in the Ming Dynasty*, 49.
89. However, Mitamura does not cite the source of this information. See Mitamura Taisuke, *Chinese Eunuchs: The Structure of Intimate Politics*, trans. Charles A. Pomeroy (Rutland, VT: Charles E. Tuttle Co., 1970), 127.
90. Tang, *Qing gong taijian*, 63.
91. Tang, *Qing gong taijian*, 63.
92. Tang, *Qing gong taijian*, 64.

received a monetary payment upon the eunuch's death. In sum, the remaining eunuch population, particularly those below the rank of *shouling taijian* or without rank at all and without the money required to be buried there, faced a much more uncertain final resting place.

With the majority of the eunuch population lacking heirs, eunuchs also faced the prospect of having no family members to burn incense or make offerings on their behalf after death. In order to alleviate this problem, emperors such as Jiaqing allocated government funds to cover the cost of incense and other eunuch cemetery expenses. In 1799, the Imperial Household Department bestowed upon palace, *Yuanmingyuan, Qingyiyuan* (清漪園 Garden of Clear Ripples), and *Jingmingyuan* (靜明園 Jingming Garden) eunuchs and others the rent obtained from one *qing* 零 nine *mu* 畝[93] of land located outside *Xizhimen* (西直門 *Xizhi* Gate) to be used to purchase incense for the Enjizhuang Temple and for other cemetery expenses.[94] Once it was realized that the money obtained from the rent of this land would not cover the costs of the incense burned, it allocated an additional one *qing* eighty *mu* of adjoining land to be given to the eunuch population, including eunuchs from the *Nanfu* and Prospect Hill. According to Stent, during the late Qing, the government provided "a yearly sum to enable a certain number of eunuchs to go to the cemeteries in the spring and autumn to burn paper money, and offer sacrifices at the tombs of those who have been buried there."[95]

Eunuchs, well aware of the uncertainties facing them after retirement from service and the unwelcome reception they would meet in attempting to reintegrate into society in the later years of their life and after death in being buried among their families, relied upon their own initiative and their fellow eunuchs to provide a proper burial for themselves. Retirement associations, in addition to providing a eunuch with room and board, provided the benefit of a burial site and the assurance that other eunuchs would stand in for the eunuch's kin and offer paper money, incense, etc. in the form of ancestor veneration after he was gone.

In sum, considered outsiders in life as well as in death, eunuchs continued to face discrimination and segregation from the rest of society, even in burial. While the government attempted to alleviate these problems and assuage eunuchs' unease about how they might survive in their later years and where they would ultimately be buried by allocating lands and funds for cemeteries and incense, and even money to be put towards burial expenses, these efforts tended to favor those in the upper echelons of the eunuch hierarchy. Despite these measures, many eunuchs found themselves forced to rely on one another through burial societies and retirement associations in order to ensure a proper burial for themselves.

---

93. 1 *qing* = 100 *mu* or approximately 15.13 acres. 1 *mu* = 733.5 square yards.
94. *Guochao gongshi xubian*, 661–62.
95. Stent, "Chinese Eunuchs," 158.

Conclusion

The Qing authorized three exits from the palace eunuch system: sick leave, retirement due to old age or illness, and natural death. In each case, the palace viewed these exits as a loss of valuable labor and as a potential disruption of the harmonious operation of the palace. For eunuchs, all three exits posed challenges as they attempted to leave the palace and to reintegrate into society either temporarily or permanently.

How the Qing handled eunuch sick leave and discharge from the system is an important lens through which to view the Qing's management of its human resources, or in this case, eunuchs serving in its palaces. In contrast to the palace's usual strict rules and regulations for eunuch behavior and deportment, sick leave policies appear quite lenient throughout the Qing. Rather than an indication of a genuine interest in the well-being of its eunuch workforce, these policies suggest that the Qing did not want to deal with sick eunuchs who were incapable of performing their duties or those who might infect the palace's imperial inhabitants. These records also provide a better understanding of the illnesses associated with the lifestyle of eunuchs and reveal that, aside from urological problems associated with their emasculation, eunuchs suffered from many of the ailments (such as phlegm) that afflicted non-emasculated Chinese men during the Qing.

Liberal sick leave policies had the unintended effect of providing eunuchs with an opportunity to abuse the sick leave system. While the Qing instituted salary reductions and ultimately discharged eunuchs who were not performing their duties due to illness, it is unclear the extent to which this prevented eunuchs from using sick leave as an opportunity to take time off or to escape from the eunuch system. It is not until the late Qing that "serious illness" meant that a eunuch was too sick to get out of bed and measures were put in place to ensure the validity of eunuch sick leave requests.

The requirement that eunuchs sick for over a month return home to recuperate suggests that the Qing considered that these eunuchs, despite being employed essentially for life as palace servants, were not their responsibility. If eunuchs were unable to perform their duties and to serve, they were removed from the palace until which time they could perform their duties again. Moreover, the inability of eunuchs to return home to recuperate underscores the difficulties they faced in trying to survive outside the palace walls. Sick eunuchs faced a myriad of problems when trying to return home, ranging from logistical problems due to distance to social ostracism from families to financial problems as they struggled to support themselves outside the eunuch system. Early Qing emperors such as Kangxi and Yongzheng were confronted with the difficulties eunuchs faced in having to return home, as many lingered in the capital. Early acts of compassion were soon replaced by fears of instability and eunuch crime, as sick eunuchs were required to have guarantors or risk being removed from the capital area.

Not all sick eunuchs were left to their own devices, though. Inner court eunuchs, due to their proximity to the imperial family, often enjoyed privileged medical care due to their higher status within eunuch society.[96] These eunuchs received treatment from palace physicians who tended to their needs over the course of several days and noted their prescriptions in the Imperial Pharmacy's archives. The treatment of inner court eunuchs who were being held in jail reveals the value of these eunuchs to the emperor and his family. The status of inner court eunuchs gave them access to medical care unavailable to outer court eunuchs.

Ideally, the Qing envisioned that its responsibility for the livelihood of a palace eunuch would end as soon as the eunuch was no longer able to perform his duties. The government restored the eunuch's commoner status, classifying him as *weimin taijian*. Having taken this action, the government attempted to sever all ties and relinquish all responsibility for its former employees. Qing regulations stipulated that retired eunuchs were to return to their native places and support themselves. However, eunuch reintegration upon retirement ran into obstacles upon implementation.

What appears as a lack of compassion on the government's part stemmed from suspicions of eunuchs feigning illness in an abuse of the sick leave system in order to avoid fulfilling their duties and/or to obtain a permanent authorized exit from the system. However, the government's desire to cease being responsible for its former employees and the expectation that eunuchs could fend for themselves after retirement proved ill founded. Repeatedly confronted with large numbers of eunuchs remaining in the capital after discharge, as well as eunuch retirees fleeing back to the capital, assuming aliases, and obtaining employment in princely establishments, Qing emperors found that eunuchs encountered many difficulties as they tried to reintegrate into society. Coming from poor backgrounds and returning to society with very little capital and highly specialized skills often not applicable to obtaining a livelihood, discharged eunuchs found it difficult to support themselves outside the system. Discrimination due to their physical disfigurement further compounded these problems, as family members disowned their eunuch relatives.

Well aware of these problems, Qing emperors such as Kangxi, Yongzheng, and Jiaqing in particular endeavored to address the problems eunuchs encountered in attempting to care for themselves while sick, to support themselves in old age, and to find a cemetery in which their bodies could be buried. While allocations of room and board for invalids, land for cemeteries, and funds for incense aided eunuchs, these acts of imperial kindness were not enjoyed equally by all eunuchs. Those in the upper echelons of the eunuch hierarchy often relied on government pensions (in some cases equal to their previous salary) to fund their retirement and in death

---

96. According to Tang Yinian, during the Qing, inner court eunuchs numbered 400–500, in other words twenty to twenty-five percent of the Qing palace eunuch workforce. In direct contact with the imperial family, inner court eunuchs enjoyed a higher status and considerably more power than outer court eunuchs. See Tang, *Qing gong taijian*, 24.

received a burial plot in a eunuch cemetery marked with a headstone commemorating their years of service to the imperial court.

The Qing providing retirement assistance for only a small percentage of the retired eunuch population resulted in eunuchs having to rely on their own initiative to survive outside the palace. Undoubtedly aware of the fate that awaited them once they left the employment of the palace, Qing eunuchs scrimped and saved for their retirement. Independently forming retirement associations, eunuchs pooled their money and resources to buy land where they would buy a temple and provide for their basic needs in old age and ultimately in death. These associations provided eunuchs with both a livelihood as well as a community in which they could retire with some degree of solace from the society in which they now lived as social outcasts. Many eunuchs longed for the day they would be discharged from service. However, having often waited a lifetime for this authorized exit from the system, eunuchs found themselves faced with a host of uncertainties and challenges in an often unreceptive environment.

9

Surviving the Fall of the Qing

Chinese Eunuchs Post 1911

On July 16, 1923, the residents of the capital noted an unusual sight around the Forbidden City, some 1,400 eunuchs exiting the palace under the escort of the palace guard. As a misty rain fell on the capital, eunuchs congregated in groups in front of the palace walls, some sighing, some quietly sobbing, others yelling out in anger. Earlier that day, the former Xuantong emperor 宣統帝 (r. 1908–1911/12), without prior notice, had expelled all but a select few eunuchs from the palace.

This was not the first mass exodus of eunuchs from the palace. Twelve years earlier, in 1911, approximately 1,600 eunuchs had "fled" the palace during the 1911 Revolution and subsequent fall of the Qing dynasty (1644–1911). In 1912, as China entered the Republican era, new political actors would emerge and garner attention while the Manchus and participants in their former government would recede into the background. The Manchus and their court, and by association eunuchs, became symbols of a past that many in China wished to forget.

Although histories of the end of empire and the emperor's transition from "emperor to citizen" (from the Xuantong emperor to Aisin-Gioro Pu Yi 愛新覺羅溥儀, or simply Pu Yi 溥儀) have attracted the attention of numerous scholars, often overlooked are the other male inhabitants of the palace who were negatively impacted by the fall of the Qing, the palace eunuchs. For eunuchs, the end of empire signaled the beginning of the end for the eunuch system as a whole. With the Qing now stripped of its political power, eunuchs found themselves in a precarious position. Not only was the palace a source of livelihood, but, for many eunuchs, the Forbidden City was home. While a few wealthy eunuchs, those who had held positions in the upper echelons of the eunuch hierarchy, transitioned into lives of luxury outside the palace, the majority struggled to survive. This chapter will chronicle the last days of the Qing palace eunuch system from the fall of the Qing in 1911 through the mass expulsion of eunuchs in 1923, and Pu Yi's eviction from the palace in 1924, focusing on the average eunuch's survival strategies in the interim and on into the early 1930s. Compounding their categorization as social outcasts, the end of empire solidified negative representations of eunuchs and restricted eunuch employment opportunities to stereotypical roles as servants for women.

The Beginning of the End: 1911

The fall of the Qing in 1911 did not signal an immediate end to the eunuch system and its some 3,000 eunuchs. Rather, the end of eunuch system came in a series of waves punctuated by key events in 1911, 1923, and 1924 that deprived the system of much of its purpose, reduced the number of eunuchs in service, and prevented the system from adequately replenishing its ranks with new recruits. By 1924, as a result of the eviction of Pu Yi from the palace, the palace eunuch system would be finished.

In the waning years of the Qing, the signs of its weakening power would have been difficult to ignore for eunuchs working and living within the palace. By the late 1800s, the Qing had already endured two Opium Wars[1] and the Boxer Uprising. In 1901, as the imperial court fled to Xi'an and the allied powers[2] moved in to take over the capital and the palace, those eunuchs left behind may have felt that the end was near. Some eunuchs may have taken advantage of the challenges facing the Qing to ensure their own livelihood in case of a permanent collapse of Manchu power. A *New York Times* article from 1901 suggests that eunuchs were already looting the palace some ten years before the fall of the dynasty.[3] The court's days were numbered, but it would eventually return,[4] allowing the Manchus to hold onto power until 1911.

Late Qing Reforms

In the first decade of the twentieth century, the Qing would embark on a series of reforms in an effort to stave off its immediate collapse. While the Qing court focused on political reforms and a possible transition to a constitutional monarchy, reform societies and Western missionaries worked towards ending practices they considered to be social vices that prevented China from joining the ranks of modern nations. These groups rallied to end concubinage, foot-binding, and opium smoking, but the practice of emasculating young boys and men to become eunuchs was overlooked. Chinese reformers such as Sun Yirang pointed out that world

---

1. First Opium War (1839–1842) and Second Opium War (1856–1860).
2. This Alliance was made up of eight nations: Japan, Russia, Britain, France, the United States, Germany, Italy and Austria-Hungary.
3. This *New York Times* article appears to be an attempt to make clear that occupying forces were not looting the palace, by placing blame instead on palace eunuchs. Eunuchs were accused of passing palace treasures over the palace walls and selling them. The author claims that no treasures had passed through the gates guarded by American and Japanese troops. "Fear for Chinese Treasure: Gold from the Forbidden City May Have Been Stolen—Eunuchs are Selling Valuables," *New York Times*, June 23, 1901.
4. In January 1902.

powers had left eunuchs behind while weak countries had retained them, but his argument was ignored.[5] As a result, the emasculations continued.

The Articles of Favorable Treatment

In 1911, the Qing dynasty collapsed, and on February 12, 1912, the Empress Dowager Longyu 隆裕太后 signed "The Articles of Favorable Treatment," an "abdication settlement"[6] that effectively brought an end to the Qing dynasty and China's imperial system. In return for the emperor's abdication, the new government allowed the former emperor and his court to remain within the Forbidden City. Retaining his "status and title" but divested of any political power,[7] the six-year-old Xuantong emperor (hereafter referred to as Pu Yi) would continue to inhabit most of the palace, the Republican government taking over several buildings located in the outer court area.[8] At that time, the emperor of the Great Qing Empire became essentially the emperor of the Forbidden City (less than seventy-two acres).[9] Among these eight articles, two carried very important changes for eunuchs and the eunuch system. First, Article 3 stipulated that the emperor may reside temporarily in the Forbidden City and eventually move to the *Yiheyuan* (頤和園 Summer Palace). This allowance had no set deadline by which the emperor would need to leave the Forbidden City and allowed Pu Yi and his court to remain at the palace until November 5, 1924, when he was evicted by Marshal Feng Yuxiang 馮玉祥.[10] With Pu Yi still in residence at the palace, the eunuch system continued to have a reason for being. Second, Article 6 stated that Pu Yi could continue to use the staff that was in place at the time but could no longer accept new eunuch recruits. According to Pu Yi, "although the Articles of Favorable Treatment specified that no more eunuchs were to be engaged the Household Department continued to take them on secretly."[11]

The Flight of the Eunuchs

Despite surviving the fall of the dynasty, the eunuch system did lose considerable numbers in 1911. According to Pu Yi's autobiography, "Most of the eunuchs fled

---

5. In the early 1910s, Chinese such as Sun Yirang and others argued that the world powers had left eunuchs behind while weak countries like Turkey had retained them. See Kuwabara Jitsuzo, "Shina no kangan," *Toyoshi setsuen* (1927): 358.

6. Reginald Johnston, *Twilight in the Forbidden City* (1934; reprint, Vancouver: Soul Care, 2011), Kindle edition, 86.

7. Johnston, *Twilight in the Forbidden City* (2011), 86.

8. According to Johnston, three large halls were taken over by the Republic. See Johnston, *Twilight in the Forbidden City* (2011), 38.

9. Johnston writes that the former emperor "reigned as titular monarch over a kingdom that was bounded by the walls of the Forbidden City." See Johnston, *Twilight in the Forbidden City* (2011), 96.

10. For a complete list of the articles in English, see Johnston, *Twilight in the Forbidden City* (2011), 87.

11. Aisin-Gioro Pu Yi, *From Emperor to Citizen: The Autobiography of Aisin-Gioro Pu Yi*, trans. W. F. Jenner (Beijing, 1964; reprint, New York: Oxford University Press, 1987), 62.

after the 1911 Revolution."[12] Although "most" is a bit of an exaggeration, approximately 1,600 eunuchs, over half the palace eunuch population did "flee."[13] Little to almost nothing is known about the fate of these eunuchs. Ease of survival outside the system for these eunuchs depended upon how well they had prepared for their departure while still inside the palace walls.

Eunuchs in the upper echelons of the eunuch hierarchy, former eunuchs favorites of the Empress Dowager Cixi 慈禧太后 who had amassed considerable wealth and power under her ascendance, left the palace in waves in the last years of the dynasty (in 1908 after Cixi's death, in 1911 after the revolution, and in 1913 after the death of the Empress Dowager Longyu). Such eunuchs transitioned quite easily from palace life to Republican society, living very comfortably in their own residences, some surrounded by a wife, children, and servants. According to Xu Jingru, Zhang Lande 張藍德, an assistant chief eunuch stationed in the inner court (*Neijian Zongguan taijian* 內監總管太監), left the palace in 1913 after the death of Longyu and moved to Tianjin, where he lived off money he had amassed through embezzlement and bribes.[14] Zhang even recruited palace eunuchs to serve him in his household.[15] The majority of eunuchs, however, found themselves in a precarious position, as the palace abruptly lost its position as the seat of Chinese power.

Elderly eunuchs who left just after the revolution may have been in a better situation financially than younger eunuchs. During the Qing, many eunuchs prepared for their retirement by contributing to eunuch retirement associations (see Chapter 8). At the time of retirement, eunuchs, without families to return to or children to care for them in their old age,[16] would often live together in eunuch temples owned by these associations, where they farmed and lived simple lives among their own kind. Eunuchs would pay a membership fee and then, after a three-year waiting period, be entitled to retire at the temple and receive free room and board. Some eunuch temples waived this waiting period due to the extreme circumstances in which many eunuchs found themselves in 1911.[17]

12. Aisin-Gioro Pu Yi, *From Emperor to Citizen*, 62.

13. In 1908, the Qing employed an estimated 3,000 eunuchs. See Pu Jia, "Qing gong huiyi," in *Wanqing gongting shenghuo jianwen*, ed. Zhang Wenhui (Beijing: Wenshi ziliao chubanshe, 1982), 22. If one subtracts the number of eunuchs expelled in 1923 from this number (approximately 1,400) one can surmise that 1,600 eunuchs "fled the palace" after the 1911 revolution.

14. Xu Jingru 徐靜茹, *Zhongguo gudai taijian* 中國古代太監 (Beijing: Zhongguo shangye chubanshe, 2014), 123.

15. Yu Chunhe, a eunuch who at one time served in the palace of the Empress Xiaoding, wife of the Guangxu emperor (later called Empress Dowager Longyu after the emperor's death), was recruited by Zhang Lande to serve in his residence in Tianjin. See Dan Shi, *Mémoires d'un Eunuque dans la Cité Interdite* [Memoirs of a eunuch in the Forbidden City], trans. Nadine Perront (Marseille, 1991 ; reprint, Marseille Editions Philippe Picquier, 1995), 208.

16. Some eunuchs became emasculated as adults after having fathered children. More common was the practice of eunuchs adopting children. See Jennifer Jay, "Another Side of Chinese Eunuch History: Castration, Marriage, Adoption and Burial," *Canadian Journal of History* XXVIII (Dec. 1993): 459–78.

17. See Jia Yinghua, "Temple of Prosperity," in *The Last Eunuch of China: The Life of Sun Yaoting*, trans. Sun Haichen (Beijing: China Intercontinental Press, 2008), 160–82.

For some eunuchs, the fall of the Qing may have brought immediate relief to a life that they had tried repeatedly to escape (see Chapter 6). For these eunuchs, the end of empire would have created an opportunity for emancipation after repeated failed attempts to leave the system without authorization. Throughout the Qing and into the Xuantong reign period, eunuchs had repeatedly attempted to escape the eunuch system by running away from the palace. When writing about the response of eunuchs to the 1911 revolution, Pu Yi's use of "fled" to describe their actions, suggests that the former emperor was well aware of the harsh realities of eunuch life for the majority of the eunuch population.

Many eunuchs who left in 1911 may have simply attempted to return home. This was not without its challenges though. As the last surviving eunuch, Sun Yaoting 孫耀庭,[18] recalled, because the Qing preferred to hire young emasculates, many eunuchs had lived their entire lives inside the palace walls. Moreover, for eunuchs whose fathers had "volunteered" them for service and taken them to be emasculated or performed the procedure themselves, relations were often strained at best or nonexistent. Given that most eunuchs came from very poor backgrounds, an unemployed eunuchs' return home may have caused challenges for both the eunuch and his family (see Chapter 8).

Eunuchs no longer part of the palace eunuch system in 1911 fell under the jurisdiction of the capital police. In eunuch interviews, arrest records, and interrogations, one gets a glimpse of the challenges eunuchs faced after leaving the palace system. Arrest records from the 1910s reveal eunuchs struggling with opium addiction and engaging in criminal activities such as the operation of opium dens and theft. Eunuchs smoking opium and operating opium dens within the palace had plagued the late Qing dynasty (see Chapter 5). Police reports reveal that, after the fall of the Qing, eunuchs continued these practices outside the palace. In a police report dated January 1, 1916, Bian Baoxiang 邊寶祥 was arrested for possessing opium paraphernalia.[19] A search of Bian's room at the residence of Prince Li 禮王府 turned up long list of items used for smoking opium, including numerous balls of crude opium and drug paraphernalia.

Beijing police reports reveal that, aside from criminal activities, eunuchs took advantage of their newfound rights as citizens of the Republic to file lawsuits. In a report from February 2, 1913, eunuch Liu Yourong 劉有榮, aided by his eunuch master (*shifu taijian* 師傅太監), dropped a lawsuit against the man who had been accused of running into Liu with his horse.[20] Liu had sustained injuries to his knee and abdomen during the incident but was not injured severely and had returned home to recuperate. It is unclear why the suit was dropped.

Bian Baoxiang's above-mentioned police report also includes another important clue about how eunuchs survived after 1911: they continued to work in princes'

---

18. The last eunuch, Sun Yaoting, died at the age of 93 at his home in a temple in Beijing, in December 1996.
19. Beijing Municipal Archives, J181-018-07451.
20. Beijing Municipal Archives, J181-018-00293.

households. Bian is identified as a eunuch working in a prince's household some two years after the fall of the Qing. In another police report from 1917, a eunuch who helped a nineteen-year-old maidservant escape an arranged marriage is described as serving with the woman in a prince's household.[21] As the Articles of Favorable Treatment do not mention the employment of eunuchs by princes, the practice appears to have continued post 1911.

The Eunuch System Post 1911

As stated, the Articles allowed the former emperor to continue to employ eunuchs within the palace. After the flight of some 1,600 eunuchs, this left the palace with approximately 1,400 eunuchs still employed by the system. Focused primarily on the emperor and the Manchus, the Articles do not address important issues for the other inhabitants of the palace such as citizenship, citizens' rights, legal rights, and under whose jurisdiction these eunuchs now fell. Without this clarification, eunuchs continued to be managed as they had been throughout the Qing, by the Imperial Household Department, with punishments being handled by the Judicial Department (*Shenxingsi* 慎刑司). In sum, within the Forbidden City, palace rules and regulations superseded those of the Republic.

Changing Power Dynamics within the Palace

Within the palace walls, at first glance it appeared that the Qing court continued to function in many ways as if nothing had changed. Eunuchs' days consisted of serving the emperor and his family and keeping up the grounds of the palace. Upon closer inspection, one finds that the Qing's devolution of power created a power vacuum within the palace that some eunuchs quickly filled. These eunuchs flaunted the formerly strict regulations of the palace and even openly operated opium dens and gambling houses within the palace, with high-level eunuchs acting as guarantors.[22]

Prior to 1911, Qing rulers had kept a watchful eye on eunuchs and endeavored to control their rise to power through illiteracy, menial jobs, strict regulations, and harsh punishments. As this study has shown, eunuchs, while not technically classified as slaves, occupied a place closer to unfree on the continuum between free and unfree status. Although eunuchs received pay and could request leave, they could not leave the system of their own free will until they were deemed too old or too sick to serve. During the Qing, eunuchs were constantly reminded that their wants and needs were irrelevant; the imperial will was paramount and complete. After 1908, with a young, weak emperor on the throne and the future looking bleak, some eunuchs took advantage of the situation to augment their personal power and

---

21. Beijing Municipal Archives, J181-019-27584.
22. Pu Jia, "Qing gong huiyi," 24.

wealth. Describing the atmosphere within the palace at that time, the last emperor noted, "Despite its superficial calm, the Forbidden City was in complete disorder."[23]

The palace administration in disarray, Pu Yi would attempt to assert his power by beating eunuchs for minor infractions and subjecting them to inhumane treatment. He writes:

> In the journal of my actions and utterances kept by my tutor Liang Ting-fen there is an entry for February 21, 1913:
>
>> His Majesty frequently beats the eunuchs; he has had seventeen flogged recently for minor offences. His subject Chen Pao-shen and others remonstrated but His Majesty did not accept their advice.
>
> That goes to show how by the age of eleven flogging a eunuch was a part of my daily routine. My cruelty and love of wielding my power were already too firmly set for persuasion to have any effect on me.
>
> Whenever I was in a bad temper or feeling depressed the eunuchs would be in for trouble; and their luck was also out if I was in high spirits and wanted some sort of amusement. In my childhood I had many strange tastes, and apart from playing with camels, keeping ants, rearing worms, and watching fights between dogs and bulls I took the greatest delight in playing unkind tricks on people. Long before I learnt how to make the Administrative Bureau beat people many a eunuch came to grief through my practical jokes. Once when I was about seven or eight I had a brainwave: I wanted to see whether those servile eunuchs were really obedient to the 'divine Son of Heaven.' I picked on one of them and pointed at a piece of dirt on the floor. 'Eat that for me,' I ordered, and he really knelt down and ate it. Another time an aged eunuch almost died as a result of my soaking him with a fire pump.[24]

In 1914, in an effort to address issues that had arisen in the two years since the abdication, the Republican government issued another document consisting of seven articles. Among these, Articles 6 and 7 addressed the rights of eunuchs and labor relations within the palace. Article 6 stated,

> Regulations should be drawn up specifying the function of the newly appointed *hu chun* (palace guards), whose special duty it is to exercise police functions in the palace . . . Criminal jurisdiction within the palace is abolished. Minor offenders among the eunuchs and other palace employees may be dealt with by the commanding officers of the palace guards and punished in accordance with police regulations; but criminal offenders must be sent to the ordinary courts for trial and punishment.[25]

Article 7 addressed the important issue of citizenship, stating, "All persons employed by the imperial household are citizens of the republic and should conform to Chinese custom in the matter of dress. They may remove their queues if they wish

---

23. Aisin-Gioro Pu Yi, *From Emperor to Citizen*, 70.
24. Aisin-Gioro Pu Yi, *From Emperor to Citizen*, 70.
25. Johnston, *Twilight in the Forbidden City* (2011), 89.

to do so."[26] The clarification of these jurisdictional and citizenship issues would be important for eunuchs who remained in the service of the court.

Despite the prohibition against recruiting eunuchs to fill vacancies in the Forbidden City, the Imperial Household Department continued to do so by allowing recruits to assume the identities of deceased or runaway eunuchs. China's last eunuch Sun Yaoting recounts how, not long after he recovered from his self-emasculation,[27] his family discovered that the emperor had abdicated and the Qing would no longer be accepting eunuchs. Sun's recollections reveal the stress and the disappointment this announcement had on him and his family. Already emasculated and in need of work, Sun would eventually serve at a prince's household and later enter the palace by assuming the name of another. By 1923, Sun had risen from a lowly eunuch to become a "eunuch-of-the-presence," serving the Empress Wanrong婉容 (Pu Yi's wife).

On July 16, 1923, the eunuch system would be dealt the most serious challenge to date. On that date, the Imperial Household Department would summon all eunuchs to the *Qianqingmen* (乾清門 Gate of Heavenly Purity) to inform them of Pu Yi's decision to expel them from the Forbidden City.[28] While the typical narrative stresses that Pu Yi expelled the eunuchs after discovering that they had attempted to cover up their theft of palace treasures by setting fire to the palace, this explanation is only part of the story. In reality, the abolition of the eunuch system stemmed from the influence of Pu Yi's foreign tutor, Pu Yi's desire to become more independent, and the financial problems plaguing the Imperial Household.

In 1919, some seventeen years after the fall of the dynasty, Sir Reginald Johnston, a Scottish mandarin in the British colonial service, would be recruited by the President of the Republic[29] to serve as the deposed emperor's English-speaking imperial tutor.[30] Johnston's record of his time as Pu Yi's tutor is replete with references that clearly reveal his dislike for eunuchs and his goal of abolishing the eunuch system. Over time, Pu Yi increasingly shared Johnston's contempt of eunuchs, especially for their involvement in blocking his "secret escape" from the palace. In an attempted flight to freedom and independence, Pu Yi had arranged to move to Tianjin with Pu Jie 溥傑 (his younger brother) as a first step toward realizing his goal of studying abroad in England.[31] After careful planning, Pu Yi attempted this

---

26. Johnston, *Twilight in the Forbidden City* (2011), 89–90.

27. Self-emasculation refers to emasculation performed by non-professionals (see Chapter 2). In this case, Sun's father emasculated his son. See Jia Yinghua, *Zuihou yi ge taijian*, Ch. 1, Part 3, 20–32.

28. Some scholars locate the end of the eunuch system in November 1924, when Pu Yi was forced to leave the Forbidden City. At this time, approximately 470 eunuchs remained in the palace. Given that the majority of eunuchs had left in July 1923 and those who remained only served the Empress Dowagers, this did not equate numerically to a eunuch system.

29. Shiona Airlie argues that Li Jiangmai (confidant of President Xu Shichang) told Johnston that President Xu and other government officials hoped China would become a constitutional monarchy and planned to educate the emperor in case that became an eventuality. See Shiona Airlie, *Scottish Mandarin: The Life and Times of Sir Reginald Johnston* (Hong Kong: Hong Kong University Press, 2012), 146.

30. Airlie, *Scottish Mandarin*, 142.

31. Aisin-Gioro Pu Yi, *From Emperor to Citizen*, 128.

escape on February 25, 1923, only to be blocked by eunuchs on orders from his father not to let the former emperor leave the palace.[32] Last, the financial problems plaguing the Imperial Household Department also contributed to his decision to expel the eunuchs. Despite receiving an annual stipend of 4,000,000 *taels*, the court's expenditures repeatedly exceeded its budget. The numerous eunuchs on the palace payroll certainly contributed to the palace's deficit.

In the early 1920s, the precarious political and financial position of the "little court" and the relative powerlessness of the former emperor contributed to an environment conducive to corruption and theft. Taking advantage of the power vacuum at the court, some eunuchs actively engaged in theft. Pu Yi's cousin Pu Jia 溥佳 witnessed the arrest of one eunuch who had attempted to exit the palace with a chair. When questioned, he claimed he was taking it out for repair, but on closer examination it was discovered that underneath the seat were hidden objects of gold.[33] Unsure of the future of the imperial court as it entered the Republican era, eunuchs and members of the Imperial Household Department, removed treasures from the palace. Even Pu Yi himself engaged in such activities, justifying his actions as safeguarding his belongings.[34]

The distrust[35] and disorder that plagued the palace culminated in the events of late June–mid-July 1923. In June 1923, with the palace suffering from an increasing number of thefts, the High Consorts ordered the questioning of eunuchs in charge of each location in which a theft had occurred and approved the use of torture if necessary.[36] When the interrogations did not produce any new information, Pu Yi decided to take inventory of palace treasures stored in the *Jianfugong* (建福宮 Palace of Established Happiness). According to Pu Yi, this decision led some eunuchs to set fire to the building on June 26, 1923, in order to cover up the theft of antiquities stored within its walls. The blaze destroyed the building and many of the surrounding structures and all potential evidence of theft. A few days later, another fire broke out in the *Yangxindian* (養心殿 Hall of Mental Cultivation). The discovery of a kerosene-soaked cloth only increased Pu Yi's suspicions of eunuchs having committed arson.

Pu Yi viewed the fire as revenge for his ordering the beating of eunuchs believed to be responsible for the theft of ten golden bowls just three days prior.[37] According to the 1914 agreement, eunuchs accused of serious crimes were to be sent to the police; however, in this case, only after the palace's failure to get a confession were eunuchs sent to be interrogated by the police. An account in the *Beijing Huabao*

---

32. Aisin-Gioro Pu Yi, *From Emperor to Citizen*, 130.

33. See Pu Jia, "Qing gong huiyi," 19.

34. Aisin-Gioro Pu Yi, *From Emperor to Citizen*, 132.

35. Ling Haicheng and Yu Binhua, *Zuihou yi ge taijian*, trans. Li Jie and Sun Mingde (Changchun: Jilin wenshi chubanshe, 1991), 158.

36. Aisin-Gioro Pu Yi, *From Emperor to Citizen*, 133.

37. "Qing huangshi quzhu taijian" 清皇室驅逐太監 [Qing Imperial House expels eunuchs], *zazu* 雜俎, *Xinghua* 興華 1923, 18.

records that sixteen eunuchs were brought to the Police Judicial Department, where they were rigorously questioned and interrogated about the cause of the fire, but the truth had yet to be discovered.

In the days that followed, Pu Yi became increasingly concerned that the eunuchs would retaliate for the flogging of their fellow eunuchs. This concern led to several sleepless nights, after which Pu Yi asked Wanrong to keep watch over him throughout the night to make sure he was not killed in his sleep. In the days that followed, while eavesdropping on eunuchs' conversations, Pu Yi heard them talking about him and commenting that his temper was getting "worse and worse." At the time, Pu Yi became convinced that the eunuchs were planning to murder him.[38]

On July 15, 1923, just a day before the expulsion order, it was discovered that numerous treasures had been stolen from the palace.[39] Greatly angered by this news and realizing that things could not continue as they were, the former emperor vowed to take action and "to deal with the problem once and for all by expelling all the eunuchs from the palace."[40] Not swayed by the objections of his father nor of the women of the court, Pu Yi ordered Shao Ying 紹英, head of the Imperial Household Department, to inform eunuchs that they would be expelled. To avoid the possibility of eunuchs stealing any additional items from the palace, they were to be given no warning. On the morning of July 16, 1923, as a light misty rain fell on the palace, Shao Ying ordered all eunuchs to gather at the *Qianqingmen*, where he would later ascend the steps and read the former emperor's decree expelling all but 175 eunuchs who would stay on to serve the High Consorts and Pu Yi's wives.[41] Those eunuchs whose names were not on the list, an estimated 1,137, were to immediately gather their personal belongings and exit the palace.[42]

As eunuchs faced their new fate, the light rain that had been falling turned into a heavy downpour, quickly transforming the palace into a "sea of water."[43] Eunuchs were seized, put in rows of ten, and escorted out of the palace by police.[44] Before exiting the palace, eunuchs were required to submit to a body search. One eunuch responded to this indignity by cursing the former emperor, "We've served the emperor for so many years and now upon leaving he treats us like criminals. Go

---

38. Aisin-Gioro Pu Yi, *From Emperor to Citizen*, 135.
39. "Pu Yi da zhu yansi" 溥儀大逐閹寺, *Mingguo ribao*, July 27, 1923.
40. Aisin-Gioro Pu Yi, *From Emperor to Citizen*, 136.
41. Aisin-Gioro Pu Yi, *From Emperor to Citizen*, 62. In addition to these eunuchs, the imperial women retained close to one hundred maidservants. Ling and Yu, *Zuihou yi ge taijian*, 160. According to Pu Yi's autobiography, "From that time on the palace staff was made up of members of the greatly depleted palace guard or else genuinely male servants known as 'attendants.'" See Aisin-Gioro Pu Yi, *From Emperor to Citizen*, 62.
42. The number of expelled eunuchs varies depending on which source one looks at. *Shenbao* recorded that 1,734 eunuchs were expelled. See "Qing gong quzhu taijian zhi yuanyin" 清宮驅逐太監知原因 [The reasons for the Qing palace expelling eunuchs], *Shenbao*, July 23, 1923. Other accounts list the number as 2,000. I've chosen to use Pu Yi's estimate of eunuchs from 1922. See Aisin-Gioro Pu Yi, *From Emperor to Citizen*, 62.
43. Jia Yinghua, *Modai taijian miwen: Sun Yaoting zhuan* (Beijing: Zhishi chubanshe, 1933), 177.
44. "Qingshi quzhu yanguan xuzhi" 清室驅逐閹官續誌 [More records on the Qing house expelling eunuchs], *Shenbao* 申報, July 21, 1923.

to hell, you bastard!"[45] As the guards searched through the eunuchs' belongings, a mountain of suitcases and personal effects formed by the gate.

Now unemployed as well as homeless, eunuchs congregated outside the palace with the few belongings they were able to gather together before leaving the palace. Outside the palace, the eunuchs stood in groups around the southern pond next to the *Shenwumen* 神武門,[46] hanging their heads in sorrow and sighing or cursing.[47] Distraught and uncertain about their future, some eunuchs even committed suicide by jumping into the Tongzi River (Tongzhi He 筒子河).[48]

That night, eunuchs groped in dark to retrieve their belongings.[49] Eunuchs without a place to go could still be found at the back gate (*houmen* 後門) past 10:00 p.m.[50] Their immediate concerns now revolved around finding food and a place to stay. The palace encouraged eunuchs to go and live with their relatives or to rely on friends. Those without a place to go to were allowed to temporarily stay at the *Yanchilou* 雁翅樓.[51] There, eunuchs could temporarily find a meal of rice porridge and receive their "dispersal money."[52]

This "dispersal money" was intended to assist eunuchs in leaving the area to return to their native places. Many eunuchs, having spent most of their lives in the service of the court, did not have families or native places to return to. According to the *Shenbao*, as of the night of the expulsion, the decision had not been made about whether eunuchs would be allowed to re-enter the palace to retrieve the remainder of their belongings.[53] The following day, the decision made, the eunuchs entered the palace one by one flanked by two palace guards. Pu Yi's institution of the new eunuch identification card, in which photo IDs had replaced the former leather *yaopai* 腰牌, ensured the expelled eunuchs would not be allowed to re-enter a second time.[54] Although this process was intended to be completed within one day, the use of the police escorts necessitated that the retrieval be carried out over several days. According to Johnston,

> For three or four days, the Peking populace enjoyed the unwonted spectacle of palace-eunuchs sitting in disconsolate groups on the parade-ground between the northern wall of the Forbidden City and Prospect Hill, awaiting their turn to return

45. Jia, *Modai taijian miwen*, 178.
46. At that time, the imperial court's main entrance to the Forbidden City.
47. "*Qingshi quzhu yanguan xuzhi*," *Shenbao*, July 21, 1923.
48. Jia, *Modai taijian miwen*, 178. The Tongzi River is the local name for the moat that surrounds the Forbidden City.
49. Pu Jia, "Qing gong huiyi," 27.
50. "*Qingshi quzhu yanguan xuzhi*," *Shenbao*, July 21, 1923.
51. Jia, *Modai taijian miwen* 176. This building, built in 1420, was located outside the palace's rear gate (Di'anmen 地安門 or 後門). During the Qing, it had served as a sentry post.
52. Jia, *Modai taijian miwen*, 177.
53. "*Qingshi quzhu yanguan xuzhi*," *Shenbao*, July 21, 1923.
54. Jia, *Modai taijian miwen*, 179.

to the palace in twos and threes to collect their personal property and to receive the grants of money which each one received according to his age and seniority.[55]

Another source notes, "They [eunuchs] left the Forbidden City the next morning, presenting a curious sight as they scattered about the city."[56] Expelled eunuchs were not hard to miss; they could be spotted carrying their worldly possessions (ranging from suitcases to cooking utensils to animals) on their back.[57] According to the *Shenbao*, the majority of these eunuchs eventually scattered to live in the temples surrounding Jingshan Park (Jingshan Gongyuan 景山公園).[58]

Public Response

Both Pu Yi and Johnston note that the decision to expel the eunuchs engendered praise from the general public. Johnston even comments that the Peking Foreign Press described the expulsion as the act of a "progressive" ruler, citing,

> This action on the part of the ex-emperor Hsuan-T'ung [Xuantong] is welcomed by the vernacular press and the people in general. Hsuan-T'ung is now hailed as one of the very few progressive Manchu princes of the present day, and probably there would have been no Chinese republic had he been born thirty or forty years earlier.[59]

The tone and wording of Western language reports made clear that there was little sympathy for the expelled eunuchs. One article in *The North China Herald* read, "Peking, July 18—The environs of the ex-Emperor's Palace presented an unusual and animated sight yesterday, when carriages and carts and scores of coolies were engaged in conveying eunuchs and their tawdry belongings from the palace."[60] Most accounts reported the events; those that did offer commentary either noted that the former emperor had made the decision on his own (without consulting the Republican government) or focused on the peculiarity of the Chinese eunuch system, one newspaper noting that "no other country in the world has this peculiar system. This expulsion has at last gotten rid of a blemish with a history of several 1000 years."[61]

---

55. Johnston, *Twilight in the Forbidden City* (2011), 339.
56. Curent events 清宮遣散太監 [Qing palace dismisses eunuchs]，中英文對照，英語週刊，1923，第408期5 頁。[Note "current" is misspelled in the original.]
57. *Shengjing shibao*, July 19, 1923.
58. "Qing gong quzhu taijian zhi yuanyin," *Shenbao* 申報，July 23, 1923.
59. *Foreign Press* of Peking, July 18, 1923, as cited in Johnston, *Twilight in the Forbidden City* (1934; reprint, Wilmington: Scholarly Resources, 1973), 340.
60. "July 15, 1923—Abolition of the Eunuch System," *The North China Herald and Supreme Court and Consular Gazette*, July 28, 1923, ProQuest Historical Newspapers: Chinese Newspapers Collection, 264.
61. "*Qing gong quzhu taijian*" 清宮驅逐太監 [Qing palace expels Eunuchs], *Shishihua* 時事話，1923.

One group that did not remain silent on how they felt about the expulsion was the eunuch community. Expelled eunuchs responded with criticism and even threats directed at those held responsible. Reginald Johnston recounts,

> Some of the press comments contained reference to myself and my supposed influence over the emperor, but the tone of such comments was not unfriendly. The same cannot be said of some of the remarks contained in numerous anonymous letters which I received during the months that followed the expulsion of the eunuchs. Every form of flattery and threat was employed to induce me to persuade the emperor to reverse his decision. Some of my correspondents were considerate enough to warn me that if I failed to bring about the reinstatement of the eunuchs they would see to it that I paid the forfeit of my own life.[62]

Other eunuchs focused their anger over the expulsion directly on the emperor and sought revenge by informing Marshal Feng Yuxiang of the ex-emperor's removal of antiques and artifacts from the palace, which resulted in the marshal's demand that these items be returned.[63]

In the days and months following the expulsion order, initial praise for the emperor's decision turned to concern and unease. Residents of the capital now found themselves presented with a large group of unemployed, homeless persons squatting at the *Yanchilou* and roaming the city as vagrants. These homeless eunuchs added stress to a city already dealing with a population which recorded twelve percent of its population as "poor" or "very poor" in 1917; 73.3 percent were living at or below the poverty line in 1926.[64] A photo dated September 1, 1923 (approximately seven weeks after the expulsion) of group of expelled eunuchs fighting with the police reveals how desperate the situation had become for some eunuchs.

Six months after the expulsion, more than 300 expelled eunuchs continued to live at the *Yanchilou*. Pu Jia recalls the condition of these eunuchs: "Whenever I passed by this place on my way to the palace, [I] always saw quite a few eunuchs in tattered clothes under the porticos cooking over open fires. [They] really looked like refugees fleeing from a famine. Their appearance was really heartbreaking."[65] Time after time the military police (*juncha*) moved in to expel the eunuchs, fearing that they would cause a fire. By the spring of 1924, all remaining eunuchs had dispersed.[66]

Public Proposals for the Remaking Eunuchs

In July 1923, the same month Pu Yi issued the expulsion order, newspapers such as *Dagongbao* and *Shengjing shibao* began printing proposals for how best to deal with

62. Johnston, *Twilight in the Forbidden City* (1973), 340.
63. Jia, *Modai taijian miwen*, 74.
64. Janet Y. Chen, *Guilty of Indigence: The Urban Poor in China, 1900–1953* (Princeton: Princeton University Press, 2012), 50. *eBook Collection* (EBSCOhost)
65. Pu Jia, "Qing gong huiyi," 27.
66. Pu Jia, "Qing gong huiyi," 27.

Figure 9.1
Eunuchs scuffling with police, September 1, 1923. Photo by Topical Press Agency, Getty Images.

the unemployed and homeless eunuchs that remained in the capital area. These articles attempted to present eunuchs as still useful despite the termination of their sole reason for being. The writers suggested eunuchs could be refashioned to meet Republican society's needs just as "one might get some more wear out of an old pair of pants by turning them into shorts."[67] In particular, the writers recommended that dispossessed eunuchs who remained in the capital find employment in the following six areas:

(1) service in girls' schools[68]
(2) working as errand boys/servants
(3) services in places which aid *liangren* (良人 good people)
(4) service in theaters or selling seats ("since recently female patrons have become more numerous")
(5) working as errand boys/servants at female bathhouses

---

67. *Shengjing shibao*, July 31, 1923.
68. Qing eunuchs had experience in the education of young women. In 1901, eunuch Xin Xiuming served in the household of a prince (*junwang*), where he tutored the prince's granddaughter. See Xin Xiuming, *Lao taijian de huiyi* (1992), 176.

(6) serving as errand boys/servants for big families with wives and many concubines (recommended for elderly eunuchs).[69]

In each case, eunuchs were advised to find work as servants catering to the
needs of women. Even beyond the confines of the palace walls in the society of the
new republic, the eunuch's lack of genitalia continued to both limit and define his
employment opportunities.

One writer concludes his article by suggesting that the placement of eunuchs in
such positions would give them a place to settle down and, in the process, avoid all
sorts of dangers.[70] While the writer leaves the object of the dangers to the reader's
imagination, the advantages of finding employment would be twofold. Not only
would it rid the capital of a group of unemployed vagrants but also protect the
eunuchs themselves from the dangers of life as beggars. Despite the writer's anxiety
over eunuchs becoming beggars, police reports have yet to be found that reveal
any mention of eunuchs being sent to Republican-era workhouses or of eunuchs
begging.

Eunuchs also became a subject of discussion among students and intellectuals
taking part in the discourse on modernity in China during the New Culture/May
Fourth Movements (1916—through 1920s). One of the earliest of these discussions,
titled, "A Use for Eunuchs" (*taijian liyong* 太監利用) appeared in *Minguo Ribao*'s 民
國日報, "Random Thoughts" section (*zagan* 雜感) in 1924.[71] The author, Xiao Ming
小明, focuses his attention on the use of chaperones in Chinese girls' schools that
follow the American model. Situating the discussion in the context of the debates
over Chinese culture, Xiao Ming cites calls for action such as *zhengli guocui* (整理
國粹 put in order the quintessence of Chinese culture) and *baocun guocui* (保存
國粹 preserve the quintessence of Chinese culture) and suggests rather than just
adopting another Western practice, one should find one with Chinese characteristics. The author's solution: these schools should employ eunuchs who had been
cast out by the former emperor, individuals who "did not have place to eat" (*meiyou
chifan de difang* 沒有喫飯的地方). He goes on to explain that using eunuchs as
chaperones would be converting waste into useful material (*feiwu liyong* 廢物利
用).[72] This article suggests that, some nine months after their expulsion, eunuchs
continued to struggle to survive. Xiao Ming's reasoning is clearly influenced by the
period of great political and social change in which he lives. While his call to employ
eunuchs is motivated by a desire to promote China's national essence, he is also

---

69. *Dagongbao*, July 25, 1923, 190.
70. *Dagongbao*, July 25, 1923, 190.
71. Xiao Ming 雜感, "Zagan: Taijian de liyong" 太監的利用，*Minguo ribao funü zhoubao* 民國日報婦女週報,
    April 9, 1924, 7. Rather than translating the English term "chaperone" into Chinese as *jianshi* (監視 attendant),
    the author prefers the term *yiniang* (姨娘 female maidservant). Xiao Ming argues that female maidservants
    should not be chaperoning female students as they, like other females, are damaged goods (*sunpin* 損品).
    He also finds fault with older maidservants, viewing them as hindered by poor eyesight and even subject to
    seizures.
72. Xiao Ming, "Zagan: Taijian de liyong," *Minguo ribao funü zhoubao*, April 9, 1924, 7.

highly influenced by the stereotypical thinking that eunuchs are only employable as servants for women.

Nine years after dispersal from the palace, in 1932, eunuchs would become a topic of discussion in the news again as reporters commented on the announcement from one Mr. Wu from Shanghai to hire twenty eunuchs to work in a women's bathhouse. Titled "A Way Out for Eunuchs," the story, picked up by several news outlets throughout China such as *Shenbao* and *Xinwang Zhoukan* told of a Mr. Wu from Shanghai who had had come to Peking to hire twenty eunuchs to return to Shanghai with him, first to become subjects of medical research and then work in a women's bathhouse. If the eunuchs performed well, he planned to return and hire more. An abbreviated version of the story appeared in *The Independent Weekly*'s "The Independent Tattler" column as follows:

> According to a Peiping [Beijing] dispatch, one Mr. Wu from Shanghai is recruiting twenty eunuchs from there. The man, who has put up at the China Hotel, told pressmen that these castrated male persons would be employed as attendants in a ladies' bathing house to be opened soon in Shanghai. He added also that a leading Shanghai hospital was interested in the physiological peculiarities of these persons and would engage a few of them for the purpose of research. More eunuchs would be engaged in the near future if they could render efficient services to lady bathers in Shanghai, according to Mr. Wu. It is understood that great numbers of eunuchs were thrown out of employment following the collapse of the Ching [Qing] House and have remained without any means of living to this day.[73]

The story attracted more attention in a longer article published a month later in *Xiwang Zhoukan* 希望週刊, titled "A Way out for Eunuchs" (*taijian de chulu* 太監的出路).[74] The author's first perception is that men who have had their "testicles cut off and lost their manhood (*taijian*)" are being made into research subjects and studied like "mad dogs and cats." In the author's opinion, "this shows contempt for a eunuch's human dignity [renge 人格]." The author comments that the unemployed must be able to find work in society. Putting aside the research study, a topic he considers to be a matter of science, he proceeds to focus on what he argues is a social problem that should be discussed. Likening eunuchs to students like him, he notes that eunuchs had become citizens of the Republic and under the law should enjoy the rights afforded to citizens. As such, eunuchs must have a "way out" (*chulu* 出路). The author asks himself why, if there are so many vocations in society, eunuchs must be engaged as research subjects or attendants in a female bathhouse. The author acknowledges that a eunuch's uniqueness is quite small and that, even though novels do mention eunuchs having experience in bathing women, eunuchs are not really suited for such work. Believing that sexual desire survives emasculation, the author also considers eunuchs working in a women's bathhouse to be inappropriate and

---

73. "Eunuchs to be attendants in Ladies' Bathing House" 社會諧談：太監充女浴室招待, *The Independent Weekly* 英華獨立週報, 1931, 卷1, 7.
74. "*Taijian de chulu*" 太監的出路，*Xiwang Zhoukan* 希望週刊, Shanghai, July 3, 1932, 36.

warns that to ignore this fact would be to turn a bathhouse into a brothel.[75] While attempting to move the nation forward, the author urges his reader to ponder this small but important problem.

The perpetuation of the stereotype of eunuchs as only being suitable for work as servants or attendants for women is fascinating since, while employed inside the palace, this was just one of many jobs assigned to eunuchs. As Pu Yi noted, "The duties of the eunuchs were very extensive."[76] Eunuch responsibilities ranged from transmitting imperial edicts, to leading officials to audiences, to recording the activities of the emperor, to checking the clocks for accuracy, to serving as lamas, to sweeping the palace grounds, to taking care of the palace animals. Perhaps unaware of the myriad responsibilities performed by eunuchs behind the palace walls during the imperial period, Republican-era authors based their suggestions on information they had learned about eunuchs from sources such as Qing dynasty novels.

The Realities of Eunuch Survival Post 1911

While immediate concerns such as unemployment and homelessness faced expelled eunuchs, they also had to face social ostracism. During the Qing, eunuchs relied on their association with the imperial court in order to gain some semblance of respect from society. However, once their employment ended (usually through retirement), eunuchs encountered a society that considered them to be freaks and social outcasts. Emasculation created more than physical scars; it also created social ones.

As has been discussed in earlier chapters, the act of emasculation ran counter to the Confucian tenet that one should not harm the body given to him by his parents. Moreover, it prevented eunuchs from honoring ancestors by perpetuating the family lineage through heirs. In addition, emasculation marked the body physically, making eunuchs look and sound different.[77]

Reintegration into Society

Eunuchs who left the system from 1911 to 1924 encountered many of the same difficulties that eunuch retirees faced during the Qing. However, one might argue that, while eunuch retirees often saved and planned for their retirement over the course of their lives within the palace, expelled eunuchs found themselves with little or no time to make arrangements for their future outside the palace. During the Republican era, one former Qing eunuch commented on the ultimate fate of the Chinese eunuch: "How could I foresee the Revolution? That was indeed a misfortune.

---

75. "Taijian de chulu," *Xiwang Zhoukan*, 37.
76. Aisin-Gioro Pu Yi, *From Emperor to Citizen*, 62.
77. For a discussion of the physical effects of emasculation upon the body, see Melissa S. Dale, "Understanding Emasculation: Western Medical Perspectives on Chinese Eunuchs," *Social History of Medicine* 23, no. 1 (April 2010): 38–55.

I have sacrificed my virility and my hope of begetting children for a dream which, passing fleetingly, stopped short and can never return."[78] Nevertheless, both retirees and expelled eunuchs found themselves removed from one environment in which they were the majority and placed in another one in which they were a social minority labeled as freaks and social misfits. As a result, eunuchs often attracted unwanted attention. Tang Yinian notes that privacy became a problem for eunuchs, as some members of the public attempted to satisfy their curiosity and catch a glimpse of the eunuch's emasculated body while he used the restroom.

Now viewed as relics of the past, many eunuchs struggled for survival among society. Some returned to their native places as the palace had intended. However, return to one's native place often became complicated by unresolved family issues, especially relationship problems between eunuchs and their fathers, stemming from the eunuch's forced emasculation by his family as a child. Poverty also impeded eunuchs' attempts to reintegrate into society, as poverty oftentimes was the strongest motivating factor for a young boy/man becoming emasculated.

Like the retired eunuchs who preceded them, expelled eunuchs chose to distance themselves from mainstream society. These eunuchs preferred to live out the remainder of their lives in seclusion in temples surrounded by their own kind. As discussed in Chapter 8, in the 1930s, Vincent Starrett visited one such temple, the *Gang Tie Mu*, located about an hour outside Beijing. In this "refuge for old eunuchs" consisting of more than seventeen acres, the inhabitants raised grains and vegetables for sale on the Beijing market, and tobacco for local consumption.[79]

Retirement associations offered eunuchs not only a refuge from society but also a safety net to ensure that they had housing and food in the years ahead. The last eunuch, Sun Yaoting, was fortunate to have received a gift of cash from the empress he had served,[80] which enabled him to pay the required deposit for the association. The fact that he found it necessary to move to such a retirement community at the age of twenty-two serves as just one example of the difficulties that expelled eunuchs encountered post expulsion.

Other eunuchs survived by actively exploiting their former proximity to the imperial court and their exoticism, in order to earn a livelihood in the tourist industry. During the early years of the Republic, eunuchs captured the curiosity of tourists and were even among the sights to see in Beijing. As described by Starrett, "young things from Arkansas" would exclaim, "Show me a eunuch!"[81] Casting themselves as palace insiders who had been privy to the secret life of the emperor, some eunuchs found employment as tour guides. In addition to showing their customers the sights of Beijing, eunuch guides could share secrets and first-hand accounts of

---

78. John Blofeld, *City of Lingering Splendour: A Frank Account of Old Peking's Exotic Pleasures* (London: Hutchinson, 1961; reprint, Boston: Shambhala, 1989), 59.

79. Vincent Starrett, *Oriental Encounters: Two Essays in Bad Taste* (Chicago: Normandie House, 1938), 15.

80. Ling and Yu, *Zuihou yi ge taijian*, 161. Sun received twenty *liangyin* 兩銀 from Empress Wanrong, who told him to use the money to return home and buy a few *mu* 畝 of land (1 *mu* = 0.16 acres).

81. Starrett, *Oriental Encounters*, 25.

imperial palace life, specifically of the ex-emperor and his court. In the mid-1930s, John Blofeld, while living in Beijing, encountered one such eunuch guide in Beihai Park. In response to Blofeld's questions regarding how he supported himself, the eunuch responded,

> 'I manage well. I am a guide—not one of those so-called guides who live by invent-ing history for foreigners and by making commissions on things they purchase. I have not yet fallen to that. Discriminating Chinese gentlemen arriving from the provinces prefer to obtain their guides through the Palace Eunuchs' Mutual Prosperity Association. Often they have heard my name from their friends and are kind enough to ask specially for my services. I charge highly, for I am able to tell them many things they could scarcely learn from other sources. You must have heard of the Grand Eunuch Li Lien-Ying [Li Lianying]? Of course! Well, I was one of his men and among those placed in charge of the Lord of Ten Thousand Years during all the time he lived in confinement after that occasion when he tried to circumvent the Old Buddha [the Dowager Empress].'[82]

Figure 9.2
Eunuch of the Imperial Court, Peking [Beijing],
December 1948. Photo by Henri Cartier-
Bresson, Magnum Photos.

82. Blofeld, *City of Lingering Splendour*, 59.

Former associations with the palace also enabled some eunuchs to earn a live-lihood in the curio business.[83] As noted, during the last years of the little court, inhabitants of the palace, including eunuchs, stole large numbers of antiques from the palace. During this same period, a number of antique shops featuring palace artifacts opened in the capital. According to Pu Yi, in the early 1920s, eunuchs oper-ated antique shops on Di'anmen Street (Di'anmen Jie 地安門街) that sold former palace treasures.[84]

Other eunuchs retained their imperial connections in positions attached to the old imperial order. In her 1934 work on the summer palaces, Carole Brown Malone lists two eunuchs, Ho [He] and Tung [Dong], as sources. These eunuchs served as caretakers at the *Yiheyuan*, the grounds of which continued to be the property of the last emperor after the establishment of the Republic.[85] By 1934, these eunuchs would have been employees of the Beijing Municipal Government that had oper-ated the former palace as a public space since expelling Pu Yi from the Forbidden City in 1924.

The Last Eunuchs Leave the Palace

On November 5, 1924, the Republican government informed Pu Yi of their revi-sion of the Articles of Favorable Treatment. Under the new agreement, the former emperor was denied the right to continue living in the palace and to use his title. Within the revised articles, one in particular addressed the remaining palace eunuchs. The Qing house would no longer have the right to employ eunuchs.[86] As a result, some 470 eunuchs and 100 palace maidservants were evicted from the palace along with the ex-emperor and his family[87] (see Figure 9.3). One cannot but note how the number of eunuchs had risen since Pu Yi's expulsion order in 1923. Clearly, some 300 eunuchs had been allowed to return to service. Each eunuch was given ten silver dollars (*yang* ten yuan) as severance pay.[88] Of these 470, only ten eunuchs and maidservants accompanied the ex-emperor to Prince Chun's household.

After Pu Yi's eviction from the palace in 1924, eunuchs continued to serve the ex-emperor and his entourage, with their duties limited to the role of personal servant. Brief mention of these eunuchs appears in histories recounting the movements and actions of Pu Yi and his "little court" first to Tianjin and then to Changchun. For example, one account notes that three eunuchs named Liu Zhenying, Liu Qingyan, and Wang Fuxiang served Wanrong during this period. Li Chang'an, a eunuch

---

83. Starrett, *Oriental Encounters*, 25.
84. Aisin-Gioro, Pu Yi, *From Emperor to Citizen*, 133.
85. Carole Brown Malone, *History of the Peking Summer Palaces Under the Ch'ing Dynasty* (Urbana: University of Illinois, 1934), 209, 231.
86. Yu Huaqing, *Zhongguo huanguan zhidushi* (Shanghai: Renmin chubanshe, 1993), 511.
87. Yu, *Zhongguo huanguan zhidushi*, 511.
88. "*Chu gong zhi jingguo*," 出宮之經過 [Experiences leaving the palace], *Shengjing shibao* 盛京時報, November 11, 1924.

Figure 9.3
Eunuchs waiting in front of the palace after being evicted by the Republican government, ca.
1924. Photo by Walter Gircke, published by *Berliner Illustrirte Zeitung*, Getty Images.

from the Guangxu period, served Pu Yi's second and third sisters and later also
served Tan Yuling.[89]

Once installed as the emperor of Manzhouguo[90] 滿洲國 in 1932, Pu Yi recalled
eunuchs to service. As described by Yu Huaqing, Pu Yi did not establish a new
eunuch system; rather, he hired several former Qing eunuchs to serve in the "new
capital."[91] After 1936, Pu Yi contacted the Qing house temporarily residing in
Tianjin to recruit former Qing palace eunuchs for service in Changchun. In a report
sent to Pu Yi on March 8 of that same year, Pu Yi was informed that two eunuchs
had arrived in Tianjin from Beijing and were awaiting permission to proceed to the
new capital.[92] In a letter dated August 25, 1938, Pu Yi was informed that six eunuchs
were in Tianjin waiting for assistance in obtaining their visas to enter Manzhouguo
to serve the emperor.

---

89. "*Chu gong zhi jingguo*," *Shengjing shibao*, November 11, 1924.
90. Manzhouguo (1932–1945) was a puppet state created by Imperial Japan in Manchuria and eastern Inner
    Mongolia, with the cooperation of former Qing Dynasty officials such as Pu Yi. Manzhouguo is often spelled
    as "Manchukuo" in English.
91. Yu, *Zhongguo huanguan zhidushi*, 511.
92. Wang Qingxiang, *Weidi gongnei mu* (Jilin: Jilin wenshi chubanshe, 1986), 108.

Now citizens of Republican China, not all eunuchs who were asked to return to service accepted the emperor's summons. In mid-February, 1938, after suddenly remembering Chen Xian'gui, a former *Yangxindian* eunuch, Pu Yi dispatched the following edict: "Summon the former *Yangxindian* eunuch, Chen Xian'gui, to come to the capital [Changchun]. From Beijing, have him first go to Tianjin. After obtaining the visa with him there, then proceed to the capital."[93] Apparently Chen changed his mind since, as of March 8, he had not appeared in Tianjin. In that same year, Yang Duoquan 楊多泉 declined the emperor's request under the pretext that, due to illness, he was unable to travel to Manzhouguo to serve.[94]

Pu Yi's retention of a small number of eunuchs during his years in Tianjin and his later attempts to recall eunuchs to serve him once established as the ruler of Manzhouguo suggests that he did not truly share Republican society's perception of eunuchs as "anachronisms." Once in power again, Pu Yi resumed his use of frequent beatings, cursing, and/or punishments to manage the eunuchs in his employment.[95] Since Pu Yi relied on his former Qing palace eunuchs to serve him in Manzhouguo, eunuchs who must have been familiar with his proclivity for corporal punishment, one cannot help but wonder why they would have accepted the emperor's invitation to return to such a difficult work environment. Accounts from this period repeatedly describe the eunuchs in the service of the court as "old."[96] Such a description suggests that elderly eunuchs, those with fewer employment options in their old age, might have been more likely to accept the emperor's invitation and subject themselves to serving the imperial court once again. Ultimately, desperation and the desire to have something to eat motivated former Qing eunuchs to return to servile status in the new capital. In fact, an edict from 1936 reveals that eunuchs were paid only a food allowance of ten yuan per month, a sum sufficient for a diet of nothing more than coarse rice porridge.[97] As described by Wang Qingxiang, eunuchs such as Liu Delu 劉得錄 and Chao Wuming 超五名 had no other recourse but to return to work for Pu Yi if they wanted to eat.[98] Some eunuchs, unable to endure the poor working conditions and abuses of their master, eventually ran away. By 1945, only ten eunuchs remained in Manchuria to serve the emperor. After the third and final dethronement of Pu Yi at the end of World War II,[99] former Qing palace eunuchs forever ended their terms of employment as imperial court eunuchs.

Thirty-four years after the fall of the Qing dynasty and the Republic's intention to allow the eunuch system to die a natural death by the prohibition of new eunuch hires, these remaining ten eunuchs finally brought to a close the more than 3,000-year-old history of palace eunuchs serving the imperial court. The

93. Wang Qingxiang, *Weidi gongnei mu*, 107–8.
94. Wang Qingxiang, *Weidi gongnei mu*, 109.
95. Zhou Junshi, *Weiman gongting zayi* (Chengdu: Sizhou renmin chubanshe, 1981), 99–100.
96. Zhou Junshi, *Weiman gongting zayi* (Chengdu: Sizhou renmin chubanshe, 1981), 95.
97. Wang Qingxiang, *Weidi gongnei mu*, 108–9.
98. Wang Qingxiang, *Weidi gongnei mu*, 108.
99. 1911, 1917 after the brief restoration of the Qing, and 1945 after the fall of Manzhouguo.

perpetuation of this system for decades beyond the fall of the Qing in an increasingly modernizing society reveals the tenacity of eunuchdom's place in imperial Chinese culture. Despite the attractiveness of Westernization and modernization, the Qing imperial court simply could not exist without its eunuch servants.

Conclusion

In 1911, the collapse of the Qing dynasty and the establishment of the Republic signaled the beginning of the end for China's palace eunuch system. Their reason for being, to serve the emperor and his imperial court, increasingly irrelevant, eunuchs found themselves in a precarious position. Their former association with the emperor and the seat of imperial power now irrelevant if not damaging to their reputations, eunuchs struggled to find a place in the new society. Thrust into a society that viewed them as social outcasts and remnants of a fallen empire, eunuchs found themselves with few opportunities for employment: either they would continue to capitalize on their association with the palace or find themselves restricted to stereotypical roles as servants for women.

The eunuch system would suffer a series of blows first in 1911, then in 1923, and then in 1924. With each key event, large numbers of eunuchs abruptly found themselves outside the palace in search of food, work, and housing. Eunuchs who remained within the palace became first-hand witnesses to the devolution of Qing power. For many eunuchs and members of the Qing household, the former decorum of the palace became replaced by total disregard for the imperial will and a survival strategy based on looting and self-indulgence. Unable to sustain itself, the eunuch system imploded in a series of events that started in 1919 with an imperial tutor keen on abolishing the eunuch system, an adolescent ex-emperor testing his power and yearning for independence in the winter of 1923, an orgy of looting and arson in late June, and then the expulsion of some 1,400 eunuchs on July 16, 1923.

In 1911, over half the remaining 3,000 eunuchs, realizing that the Qing was finished, fled the system. Little is known about these eunuchs and their fate. For the majority of eunuchs, leaving the system meant a loss of livelihood and housing. Leaving the palace also meant returning to a society that was less than welcoming. Preferring to avoid public scrutiny, many eunuchs joined together to live out their remaining years in eunuch temples, where they pooled their resources and farmed the land.

In 1923, the Qing house expelled all but those eunuchs they could not survive without. Evicted eunuchs were provided with funds to facilitate their exit from the capital, but no further thought appears to have been given to how they would survive. Neither the Qing house nor the Republican government offered any concerted effort to help eunuchs reintegrate into society or to retrain them to survive outside the eunuch system. With many eunuchs having spent almost their entire lives in the service of the imperial court, few had homes or options waiting for them. The expulsion relieved Pu Yi of both his eunuch and financial problems and appeared to set him on a path to independence and perhaps even a possible restoration. The Qing house's problem had now become the Republican government's problem. Some six months later, homeless eunuchs strained a city with the majority of its population already at the poverty line.

Increasingly anxious about how to deal with the eunuch problem, newspaper reporters and writers in China called on Republican society to find "a way out" for eunuchs. As a result, eunuchs became the subject of popular discourse as society endeavored to find eunuchs' future career paths. These writers had little or no former interaction with eunuchs and were perhaps unclear on the myriad responsibilities they formerly handled within the palace. As a result, these suggestions confined eunuchs to stereotypical roles of servants for women, albeit now applied to the context of Republican society. Eunuchs became cast as "useless things" that needed to be repurposed (in a very narrow sense). Not a part of this discussion, and perhaps not even aware of it (due to their illiteracy), eunuchs found their own way.

No longer subjects of the palace, eunuchs became citizens of the Republic, and as such were no longer subject to the harsh rules and regulations and frequent beatings of the eunuch system. Citizenship also emancipated eunuchs from the unfree status in which the eunuch system had kept them. Freedom from the palace meant freedom to choose a path forward, when to come and go, and where to go. While many eunuchs simply removed themselves from society and lived out their days in eunuch temples, entrepreneurial eunuchs capitalized on their former association with the ex-emperor to sell antiques or to serve as tour guides for those eager to have a piece of or some secret knowledge of the Qing imperial court. Although the Qing was now gone, the identity of eunuchs remained forever attached to the former empire.

Conclusion

The Chinese historical record has traditionally cast eunuchs as conniving, corrupt, and selfish individuals who interfered in politics and illegally amassed personal wealth. Eunuchs were seen as a necessary evil, essential for the administration of the palace yet troublesome if not managed properly. Dynasties that did not heed the warning to separate eunuchs and politics were considered doomed to collapse. While dynasties rose and fell, the eunuch system persisted for some three millennia.

The typical eunuch narrative in Chinese history revolves around power and women.[1] For the imperial court, power required symbolic manifestations of power such as a large palace complex and an imperial harem. Eunuchs contributed to the imperial aura by representing a large servile class waiting upon the emperor and assisting with the maintenance of his harem. Eunuchs also served a practical purpose, contributing to the administration of the palace and ensuring the purity of the imperial lineage. The story of palace labor relations with eunuchs also focuses on power, a power that emasculation was intended to deny them. Emasculation was designed to render eunuchs into the ideal servants: loyal, subservient, and free of familial obligations and ties. In reality, eunuchs consistently challenged the systematic measures put in place to ensure their subservience. In sum, the history of eunuchs has been defined by a tension between the role eunuchs were meant to play and the life they intended to live.

Histories of the imperial period in China are replete with stories of eunuchs testing the limits of their subservient status while other eunuchs blatantly stepped outside its boundaries to influence politics and amass wealth. When considering the number of eunuchs serving the imperial courts over the centuries, the reality is that only a select few ever achieved such heights. Nevertheless, the stories of this small number of infamous eunuchs have fascinated scholars and contributed to a one-dimensional, stereotypical representation of eunuchs in the historical record. When scholars broaden their focus to examine the lives of the majority of eunuchs, many of whom did not even hold rank, one finds that eunuchs are a much more complicated social group than has previously been presented.

---

1. Li Kan, "Tan Qingdai de taijian," *Gujin wenshi yuekan* 古今文史月刊 (March 1942): 29.

Carefully combing through Qing palace archival records reveals another side to eunuch history. These findings present a much more comprehensive understanding of eunuch society and show that Qing palace eunuchs were a complicated social group whose emasculation and subsequent employment located them at the center of the empire yet also subjected them to servile status and marginalization by society. Seeking agency in their restricted lives, palace eunuchs tested the boundaries of subservience to the emperor and the imperial eunuch system and recreated the social bonds and networks that emasculation was intended to deny them. This study has inserted the study of Qing eunuchs into current conversations about labor regimes and unfree labor during the Qing, gender and sexualities, the anxiety produced by unmarried men, and Qing palace life, in an effort to provide a more nuanced understanding of the life experiences and actions of the palace eunuch population.

With the cut of a knife, eunuchs found their lives changed forever. Emasculation was a transformative process both physically and socially. Genital mutilation would define the lives of eunuchs: gaining them entry into the palace, dictating their status and employment opportunities, creating uncertainty about their gender, and causing them to become social outcasts. Unlike earlier dynasties in which many eunuchs received sentences of emasculation as a result of their unfree status as criminals, prisoners of war, or tributes, the majority of Qing palace eunuchs voluntarily underwent genital mutilation as a prerequisite for service. While the Qing attempted to distance itself from this ugly side of the eunuch system by making emasculation an application prerequisite, the government's licensure of *daozijiang* and Qing emperors' preferences for eunuchs who had been emasculated before the onset of puberty contributed to a palace eunuch population peopled with young boys forced to be emasculated by their fathers; others were victims of human trafficking often involving *daozijiang* and other eunuchs. In reality, although termed "voluntary," coercion accounted for the majority of emasculations performed on young boys. The decision to become an emasculate was rarely an individual choice. Poverty among families and the potential for financial gain among human traffickers were powerful motivating factors behind emasculation.

An examination of the life experiences of the palace eunuch population reveals the complexities of unfree status during the Qing. Eunuch status does not fit neatly into the binary of free or unfree. As this study has shown, eunuchs occupied a position on the continuum closer to unfree but not one equivalent to slavery. Human trafficking by *daozijiang* resulted in some eunuchs having ties of servitude to their "creators." This was just the first of many forms of subjugation and servitude for eunuchs. Once inside the Forbidden City, eunuchs lived and worked in an environment in which their lives became restricted and eclipsed by the needs and desires of their imperial masters. The eunuch master–apprentice system also created another layer to the bondage of eunuchs. Eunuch apprentices could find themselves serving the emperor during the day and their eunuch supervisor at night. In reality, Qing palace eunuchs served under multiple masters.

When a new recruit entered the palace, the harsh reality of having become an imperial palace eunuch confronted him. Recruits found themselves delivered into the surreal world of the palace and the inner sanctum of the imperial court. Among society, limited contact with palace eunuchs and the conspicuous consumption among the eunuch elite may have contributed to the misrepresentation of a eunuch's life as one of opulence and power. Such misrepresentations led many eunuch candidates to envision a life of wealth and power waiting for them if they sacrificed their genitalia. Once a part of the palace eunuch system, though, eunuchs found their identities, activities, and desires eclipsed by those of the emperor and his court.

Eunuch histories have been dominated by the select few eunuchs who attained positions of power and wealth within a system designed to keep them suppressed. Few eunuchs ever attained positions of authority. For the vast majority, dreams of riches and glory quickly faded as they performed their duties in the outer court, far removed from the inner sanctum of the emperor. Relying on a management style based upon strict rules and regulations, beatings and corporal punishment, and collective responsibility, the Qing created an atmosphere of mutual anxiety and distrust. The determination of early and mid-Qing rulers to prevent eunuch interference in politics and a repeat of the problems that contributed to the downfall of the Ming dynasty motivated them to enact a host of edicts designed to control all facets of eunuch life. Restricted leave time and attempts to limit association with family members and fraternization with society revealed the hegemony of the emperor and his court in every aspect of the eunuch's life and showed the true nature of his status.

The act of emasculation also physically altered the eunuch body. Genital mutilation and its accompanying physical changes resulted in a being who shared many physical characteristics more representative of the female sex. Outward physical manifestations of emasculation such as smooth skin, lack of facial hair, wide hips, gynecomastia, and a falsetto voice, combined with social expectations that eunuchs could not fulfill due to their infertility, created confusion about the nature of eunuch gender. Biannual examinations to check for the regeneration of emasculated organs, the transfer of "thoroughly pure" eunuchs out of the inner quarters once they reached maturity, and prohibitions against eunuchs entering into domestic relationships with palace maidservants all suggest that the Qing harbored suspicions and at times even anxiety about the effectiveness of emasculation in eradicating sexual desire. Among eunuchs there was no confusion about their gender identity. Eunuch attempts to recreate a semblance of family life through marriage and adoption support the argument that emasculation did not alter the eunuch's perception of his gender as male. While others may have been confused by a eunuch's gender, eunuchs were not.

As indicated by the colloquial term for emasculation, *chu jia* (出家 leaving home), the act involved more than the physical mutilation of the body. Emasculation was also intended to sever family ties and filial responsibilities. In theory, emasculation and its accompanying social stigmatization and "reproductive death" would segregate the eunuch from society, increase his dependency, and ensure his loyalty to the court. In reality, eunuchs often retained varying degrees of contact with their families. Through monthly visits located at one of the palace gates, or through money sent home to support their families, the exchange of letters and visits during leave from the palace, some eunuchs managed to retain their connections with their families. For some eunuchs, the betrayal of trust and the pain endured at the hands of a *daozijiang* or their fathers proved too divisive to overcome. What this study has shown is that eunuchs as a group responded to social ostracism and segregation from society by actively recreating the familial and social bonds that emasculation was intended to deny them. Within the palace eunuch system, eunuchs formed social bonds with their fellow eunuchs and servants. The Qing utilization of the master–apprentice system for the training of eunuch novices indirectly encouraged the creation of bonds and networks among eunuchs within departments and even within palaces. Prohibitions against eunuchs forming familial bonds with palace maidservants reveal the ability of eunuchs to form family ties and even amorous relationships within the palace.

Eunuch social groupings, networks, and bonds of loyalty facilitated their efforts to manipulate aspects of eunuch society within the palace. Systematized suppression of eunuch freedoms only induced some eunuchs to create a society in which they could attain wealth and power. In a world parallel to the life of decorum of the imperial house, some eunuchs engaged in prohibited forms of entertainment such as drinking, gambling, and smoking opium. Viewed as a dereliction of duty, acts that subverted the imperial will and placed the individual eunuch's wants and needs above those of their masters such as drinking, gambling and drug use, were met with harsh punishments. The imperial court was well aware of these eunuch infractions. Moreover, the need to have so many specific regulations on the books to address such behavior reveals the frustration and challenges eunuch labor caused their imperial masters. Less rebellious eunuchs relied on relationships formed with coworkers and simple pleasures such as sharing a meal at one of the palace restaurants or raising dogs, to provide a counterbalance to the often oppressive nature of palace servant life.

"Volunteering" to become palace eunuchs, emasculates had essentially signed themselves up for a lifetime of service. Eunuchs who sought an authorized exit from the system might have to wait their entire lives for this chance. The Imperial Household Department only authorized three types of exit: discharge due to old age or illness, disciplinary problems, and death. Eunuchs who desired to leave the system without authorization faced two options: flight or suicide.

The abundance of archival information detailing eunuch flight from the palace reflects poorly on the government's treatment of eunuchs and its effectiveness in managing them. While intended to prevent a resurgence of eunuch political power, restrictions on eunuch freedoms had the unintended result of becoming too oppressive for some eunuchs to bear. Flight from the palace offered eunuchs an escape from the restrictions and oppressive nature of palace life. However, these periods of reprieve were often brief, due to difficulties in evading the authorities and financing their time spent outside the palace. Faced with harsh punishments upon capture, eunuch runaways routinely sought leniency and turned themselves in. However, for some, capture and sentences of cutting grass or serving as a slave on the frontier were preferable to their present term of forced labor within the palace.

Whereas flight from the palace exposed the eunuch to the possibility of capture and punishment, suicide alone gave some desperate eunuchs access to a final exit from the system at a time of their own choosing. During the Qing, suicides among the public rarely involved the authorities unless they directly compromised the security of the empire or resulted from the actions or coercion of another. In contrast, eunuchs who attempted or committed suicide were considered criminals. Eunuch suicide elicited a harsh response from the government, ranging from capital punishment for those who had attempted to end their lives to deprivation of a proper burial for those who were deceased. Eunuch motives for suicide attracted little attention from their masters. Due to high rates of eunuch illiteracy, one can only hypothesize about their motives. Was it desperation, empowerment, and defiance, or simply a desire to choose when and where they would exit the system? Responding to suicides with punishments and exorcisms, the government's actions exemplified the preeminence of the harmony and safety of the palace and its imperial inhabitants. Here again, denied the right to voluntarily terminate his employment and the freedom to determine the fate of his own body, the eunuch was ultimately not the master of his own fate. Qing regulations and punishments concerning suicide clearly reveal the unfree status of eunuchs and the lengths some eunuchs would go to exert a degree of agency in their lives.

The Qing authorized three exits from the palace system: sick leave, retirement due to old age or illness, and natural death. On rare occasions, some eunuchs were dismissed for disciplinary reasons. The Qing's handling of eunuch sick leave and discharge from the system reveals another area in which eunuchs challenged the system. Lacking an understanding of what constituted a serious illness and relying on eunuchs to police themselves in these matters, the palace initially had very liberal sick leave policies. Rather than deal with eunuchs who were not performing up to the required level, and wanting to distance itself from potential causes of disruption or disease, the Qing granted eunuch requests for time off to recuperate from illness. Sick leave allowed the Qing to remove nonperforming eunuchs while avoiding the responsibility of having to care for these sick eunuchs. Upon retirement, the palace also initially hoped to end their responsibility to their former eunuch. Once retired from service, eunuchs would again have to rely on their own initiative to create the social bonds and networks denied to them by emasculation. Retired from the palace at the age of sixty-five, eunuchs found themselves thrust back into society. In theory, the government viewed retirement as a restoration of the eunuch's commoner status and the severance of all government ties and responsibility with its former employee. In practice, eunuch reintegration into society ran into numerous obstacles. Trained for service within such a specialized and restrictive environment, eunuchs found their skills inapplicable to life among society.

Eunuchs' financial problems were often further compounded by society's rejection of them and the tendency of eunuch families to disown them in order to save face. Early acts of compassion for the welfare of retired eunuchs by Qing emperors such as Kangxi, Yongzheng, and Jiaqing attempted to alleviate many of these and other problems eunuchs encountered in their old age. At different times, the government offered room and board for the sick, land for cemeteries, and funds for offerings for the dead. However, these measures only provided assistance for a small percentage of the retired eunuch population. Aware of the unwelcome reception that awaited them upon their long-awaited retirement, eunuchs planned and saved for their future outside the palace. Retirement associations located in temples provided eunuch retirees with the livelihood and community that life among society often denied them. With access to such associations determined by connections and the ability to pay the required membership fee, a host of uncertainties faced many eunuchs upon their exit from the system.

The expulsion of the majority of the eunuchs from the Forbidden City in 1923 pushed the last of China's eunuchs toward a similar fate. Given little or no warning of their impending termination, these eunuchs found themselves cast out into a society that viewed them not only as social outcasts but also as remnants of an imperial past that they wished to leave behind as they entered the Republican era. As citizens of the republic, unemployed and homeless eunuchs now became society's problem. A topic of discussion in the media, eunuchs became part of the popular discourse as society thought of ways for them to move forward. Society's suggestions, however, revealed that few could think of eunuchs as anything but defined by their lack of genitalia. For the majority of late Qing eunuchs, reintegration into society proved difficult. Like eunuch retirees, many expelled eunuchs sought solace from social ostracism and financial security in voluntary segregation in the form of retirement associations located in temples. Here again, one finds an interesting parallel between eunuchs and monastic life, as temples served as refuges for eunuchs and members of society without family ties. Only when faced with the imminent extinction of palace eunuchs did society actively pursue relationships with these relics of the three-thousand-year-old palace eunuch system.

Appendix 1
Reign Titles and Dates of the Qing Emperors

Reign Name	Reign Dates
Shunzhi 順治	1644–1661
Kangxi 康熙	1662–1722
Yongzheng 雍正	1723–1735
Qianlong 乾隆	1736–1795
Jiaqing 嘉慶	1796–1820
Daoguang 道光	1821–1850
Xianfeng 咸豐	1851–1861
Tongzhi 同治	1862–1874
Guangxu 光緒	1875–1908
Xuantong 宣統	1909–1912

Appendix 2
Eunuch Suicide Regulations

According to the punishment (*chufen* 處分) section of the *Qinding gongzhong xianxing zeli* 欽定宮中現行則例 (Imperially authorized laws and regulations of conduct within the palace), the Qing punished eunuch acts of suicide as follows:

All eunuchs and women who use a knife to harm themselves within the palace shall be beheaded immediately. [Those] who are saved from committing suicide shall be [sentenced to] strangulation after the assizes.
一凡太監女子在宮內用金刀傷者斬立決欲行自盡經人救活者絞監後

All eunuchs and women who are saved while attempting to commit suicide in the gardens shall be sent to Yili to serve as slaves for soldiers. According to the law, women are authorized to be redeemed.
一太監女子在園庭欲行自縊自盡經人救活者發伊利給兵丁為奴女子準其照律收贖

[As for] eunuchs and women who commit suicide within the palace, their corpses shall be discarded in the wilderness and their relatives sent to Yili to be given to soldiers to serve as slaves.
太監女子在宮內自縊自經身死者將尸骸拋棄荒野其親屬發往伊利給丙丁為奴

[As for] eunuchs and women who commit suicide in the gardens, their corpses will be spared from being cast out into the wilderness [but] their relatives shall be sent to Urumqi to be given to soldiers to serve as slaves.
太監女子在園庭自縊自經身死者尸骸免其拋棄其親屬發往烏魯木齊給兵丁為奴

Appendix 3
Eunuch Temples

Baojinshan	寶金山
Chaoyangyuan	朝陽院
Dabei an	大悲庵
Dinghui si	定慧司
Enjizhuang	恩濟莊
Fotang miao	佛堂廟
Fushou si	福壽司
Gaogong an	高公庵
Hong'en guan	鴻恩觀
Huguo si	護國寺
Jinshan Baocang si	金寶山藏寺
Lianhua si	蓮花寺
Lima Guandi miao	立馬關帝廟
Lingguan miao	靈官廟
Puzhao si	普照寺
Sanguan miao	三官廟
Suyun guan	素雲觀
Wang'gui miao	王瑰廟
Wuhua si	五花寺
Xianxing guan	咸興觀
Xiuyun si	岫雲寺
Xiuyun guan	秀雲觀
Xuanzhen guan	玄貞觀
Yuantong guan	元通觀
Yuhua an	裕華庵
Zhenwu miao	真武廟

Appendix 4
Eunuch Cemeteries

In addition to Enjizhuang, Liu Jingyi and Lu Qi cite the following Qing dynasty eunuch cemeteries. See Liu Jingyi and Lu Qi, "Qingdai taijian Enjizhuang yindi," *Gugong bowuyuan yuankan* 3 (1979): 52. For additional locations, see Li Guang, "Qing ji de taijian," in *Wanqing gongting shenghuo jianwen*, ed. Zhang Wenhui (Beijing: Wenshi ziliao chubanshe, 1982), 172.

Dofu zha	豆腐閘	Located outside Xizhimen
Huaishu juguiguang si	槐樹居貴光寺	Located 20 *li* NW of Xizhimen
Juesheng si	覺生寺	Located NW of Xizhimen
Zaojun miao	皂君廟	Located 7 *li* NW of Xizhimen

Bibliography

Archival Sources

Academia Sinica 中央研究院, Taipei, 近史所 [Institute of Modern History]. *Neiwufu tang-renshilei* 內務府堂人事類 [Imperial Household Department ministers].

Beijing Municipal Archives 北京市檔案館.

First Historical Archives, Beijing 中國第一歷史檔案館. *Gongzhong* 宮中 [Palace], *zajian* 雜件 [Miscellaneous documents]. *Renshilei taijian* 人事類太監 [Eunuchs].

First Historical Archives, Beijing 中國第一歷史檔案館. *Gongzhong* 宮中 [Palace], *zajian* 雜件 [Miscellaneous documents]. *Renshilei taijian mama nüzi* 人事類太監媽媽女子 [Eunuchs, mamas, and women].

First Historical Archives, Beijing 中國第一歷史檔案館. *Gongzhong* 宮中 [Palace], *zajian* 雜件 [Miscellaneous documents]. *Jingshifang* 敬事房 [Office of Eunuch Affairs].

First Historical Archives, Beijing 中國第一歷史檔案館. *Neiwufu* 內務府 [Imperial Household Department]. *Kuaijisi* 會計司 [Office of Accounts].

First Historical Archives, Beijing 中國第一歷史檔案館. *Neiwufu* 內務府 [Imperial Household Department]. Shenxingsi 慎刑司 [Judicial Department].

First Historical Archives, Beijing 中國第一歷史檔案館. *Neiwufu* 內務府 [Imperial Household Department]. *Zhangyisi* 掌儀司 [Department of Ceremonial].

First Historical Archives, Beijing 中國第一歷史檔案館. *Zongguan Neiwufu* 總管內務府 [Imperial Household Department]. Daoguang 道光, *zalu dang* 雜錄檔 [Miscellaneous Archives].

First Historical Archives, Beijing 中國第一歷史檔案館. *Zongguan Neiwufu* 總管內務府 [Imperial Household Department]. Xianfeng 咸豐, *zalu dang* 雜錄檔 [Miscellaneous Archives].

First Historical Archives, Beijing 中國第一歷史檔案館. *Qinding zongrenfu zeli* 欽定宗人府則例 [Imperially commissioned regulations of the Imperial Clan Court].

Guoli Gugong Bowuyuan [National Palace Museum], Taipei 國立故宮博物院. *Gongci dang* 供詞檔 [Confessions].

Guoli Gugong Bowuyuan [National Palace Museum], Taipei 國立故宮博物院. *Gongzhong dang zouzhe* 宮中檔奏摺 [Secret Palace Memorials]. *Jiaqing chao* 嘉慶朝 [Jiaqing reign period].

Guoli Gugong Bowuyuan [National Palace Museum], Taipei 國立故宮博物院. *Gongzhong dang zouzhe* 宮中檔奏摺 403020746, Box 2743, Qianlong chao 乾隆朝.

Guoli Gugong Bowuyuan [National Palace Museum], Taipei 國立故宮博物院. *Gongzhong dang zouzhe* 宮中檔奏摺 [Secret Palace Memorials]. *Xianfeng chao* 咸豐朝 [Xianfeng reign period].

Guoli Gugong Bowuyuan [National Palace Museum], Taipei 國立故宮博物院. *Junjichu dang zhejian* 軍機處檔摺件 [Grand Council Archives].

Primary Sources

Aisin-Gioro Pu Yi 愛新覺羅溥儀. *From Emperor to Citizen: The Autobiography of Aisin-Gioro Pu Yi*. Translated by W. J. F. Jenner. Beijing, 1964. Reprint, New York: Oxford University Press, 1987.

Aisin-Gioro Pu Jie 愛新覺羅溥傑. *Pu Jie Zizhuan* 溥傑自傳 [The autobiography of Pu Jie]. Beijing: Zhongguo wenshi chubanshe, 1994.

Chen Keji, ed. *Qing gong yi'an yanjiu* 清宮醫案研究 [Research on Qing palace medical cases]. Beijing: Zhongyi guji chubanshe, 2006.

"*Chu gong zhi jingguo*" 出宮之經過 [Experiences leaving the palace]. *Shengjing shibao* 盛京時報. November 11, 1924.

Curent events 清宮遣散太監 [Qing palace dismisses eunuchs]. 中英文對照. 英語週刊 Chinese-English Translation. English Weekly], 1923，第408期5頁. [Note "current" is misspelled in the original.]

Dagongbao 大公報. April 1–July 25, 1923.

"Da Qing Lüli" 大清律例 [Code of the Great Qing] (1740), Legalizing Space in China, http://lsc.chineselegalculture.org/eC/DQLL_1740/5.6.13.387.3.

Da Qing lüli anyu 大清律例按語 [Code of the Great Qing with remarks and comments], 冊 33卷65.

Da Qing lüli huiji bianlan 大清律例彙集便覽 [A collection and convenient inspection of the great Qing code]. 1885.

de Bary, Theodore et al. *Sources of Chinese Tradition*, vol. 1. New York: Columbia University Press, 1960.

"Eunuchs to be attendants in Ladies' Bathing House" 社會諧談：太監充女浴室招待. *The Independent Weekly* 英華獨立週報, 1931, 卷1, 7.

"Fear for Chinese Treasure: Gold from the Forbidden City May Have Been Stolen—Eunuchs are Selling Valuables." *New York Times*, June 23, 1901.

First Historical Archives, Beijing. *Kangxi chao manwen zhupi zouzhe quanyi* 康熙潮滿文朱批奏摺全譯 [A complete translation of Manchu vermilion endorsements and palace memorials from the Kangxi court]. Beijing: Zhongguo shehui kexue chubanshe, 1996.

Gongzhongdang Jiaqingchao zouzhe 宮中檔嘉慶朝奏摺 (*GZDJQCZZ*) [Secret palace memorials of the Jiaqing period]. No. 20, pt. 2, vol. 30. Taipei: National Palace Museum, 1993–1995.

Gongzhongdang Qianlong chao zouzhe 宮中檔乾隆朝奏摺 [Secret palace memorials of the Qianlong period]. No. 28, 乾隆32年8–12月. Taipei: National Palace Museum, 1984.

Guochao gongshi 國朝宮史 [A history of the palace during the Qing period]. Edited by Yu Minzhong 于敏中. 5 vols. Taipei: Taiwan xuesheng shuju, 1965.

Guochao gongshi xubian 國朝宮史續編 [A supplemental history of the palace of the reigning dynasty]. Edited by Qing Gui 慶桂 et al. Reprint, Beijing: Beijing guji chubanshe, 1994.

Huang Liu-hung. *A Complete Book Concerning Happiness and Benevolence: A Manual for Local Magistrates in Seventeenth-Century China*. Tucson: University of Arizona Press, 1984.

"July 15, 1923—Abolition of the Eunuch System." *The North China Herald and Supreme Court and Consular Gazette*. ProQuest Historical Newspapers: Chinese Newspaper Collection. July 28, 1928.

Li Guang, "Qing ji de taijian" 清季的太監 [Late Qing eunuchs]. In *Wanqing gongting shenghuo jianwen* 晚清宮廷生活見聞 [Information on late Qing palace life], edited by Zhang Wenhui 張文惠, 157–72. Beijing: Wenshi ziliao chubanshe, 1982.

Ma Deqing 馬德清 et al., "Qing gong taijian huiyi lu" 清宮太監回憶錄 [Recollections of Qing palace eunuchs]. In *Wanqing gongting shenghuo jianwen* 晚清宮廷生活見聞 [Information on late Qing palace life], edited by Zhang Wenhui 張文惠, 173–97. Beijing: Wenshi ziliao chubanshe, 1982.

Matignon, J.-J. *Superstition, Crime et Misère en Chine: Souvenirs de Biologie Sociale*. Paris: Masson et Cie, 1899.

Matignon, J.-J. *Superstition, Crime et Misère en Chine: Souvenirs de Biologie Sociale*. 1899 ; Reprint, Paris: Masson et Cie, 1900.

Minguo ribao funü zhoubao 民國日報婦女週報, April 9, 1924 (民13年4月9日).

Morache, G. *Pékin et ses habitants: Étude d'hygiène*. Paris: J.-B. Baillière, 1869.

Pu Jia 溥佳, "Qing gong huiyi" 清宮會議 [Recollections from the Qing Palace]. In *Wanqing gongting shenghuo jianwen* 晚清宮廷生活見聞 [Information on late Qing palace life], edited by Zhang Wenhui 張文惠, 1–35. Beijing: Wenshi ziliao chubanshe, 1982.

Pu Jia 溥佳, and Pu Jie 溥傑. *Wanqing diwang shenghuo jianwen* 晚清帝王生活見聞 [Information on late Qing imperial life]. Vol. 1. Taipei: Juzhenwu chubanshe, 1984.

Pu Jie. "Huiyi chun qinwang de shenghuo." In *Wanqing gongting shenghuo jianwen* 晚清宮廷生活見聞 [Information on late Qing palace life], edited by Zhang Wenhui 張文惠, 206–72. Beijing: Wenshi ziliao chubanshe, 1982.

"Pu Yi da zhu yansi" 溥儀大逐閹寺. *Mingguo ribao*, July 27, 1923.

Qinding Da Qing huidian shili 欽定大清會典事例 (*QDDQHDSL*) [Imperially commissioned collected regulations of the Qing dynasty]. Edited by Li Hongzhang 李鴻章 et al. Shanghai: Shangwu yinshuguan, 1909.

Qinding Da Qing lüli 欽定大清律例 [The Great Qing Code]. Qing Tongzhi 9 清同治9年 (1870).

Qinding gongzhong xianxing zeli 欽定宮中現行則例 (*QDGZXXZL*). [Imperially authorized laws and regulations of conduct within the palace]. Reprint, Taipei: Wenhai chubanshe, 1979.

Qinding huidian shili 欽定會典事例 [Shanghai: Shangwu yinshuguan, 1909], 卷1216, 內務府. [Imperial Household Department], *taijian shilei* 太監事例 [eunuchs]: 2.

Qingdai neige daku sanjian manwen dang'an xuanbian 清代內閣大庫散件滿文檔案選編 [Selections from the archives of the Grand Secretariat of the Qing dynasty]. Tianjin: Tianjin guji chubanshe, 1991.

"*Qing gong quzhu taijian*," 清宮驅逐太監 [Qing palace expels eunuchs]. *Shishihua* 時事話, 1923.

"*Qing gong quzhu taijian zhi yuanyin*" 清宮驅逐太監知原因 [The reasons for the Qing palace expelling eunuchs]. *Shenbao* 申報, July 23, 1923.

Qingshi 清史 [History of the Qing dynasty]. Taipei: Guofang yanjiuyuan, 1961.

"*Qingshi quzhu yanguan xuzhi*" 清室驅逐閹官續誌 [More records on the Qing house expelling eunuchs]. *Shenbao* 申報, July 21, 1923.

"Qing huangshi quzhu taijian" 清皇室驅逐太監 [Qing imperial house expels eunuchs]. *Zazu* 雜俎. *Xinghua* 興華 1923, 18.

Qing shilu 清實錄 [History of the Qing dynasty]. Taipei: Guofang yanjiuyuan, 1961.

Qinding zongrenfu zeli 欽定宗人府則例 [Imperially commissioned regulations of the Imperial Clan Court].

Shenbao 申報. July 20–23, 1923.

Shengjing shibao 盛景時報. July 4, 1923–November 11, 1924.

Stent, George Carter. "Chinese Eunuchs." *Journal of the North China Branch of the Royal Asiatic Society*, New Series, No. 11 (1877): 143–84.

"*Taijian de chulu*" 太監的出路. *Xiwang Zhoukan* 希望週刊 . Shanghai, July 3, 1932: 36.

Xin Xiuming, 信修明. *Lao taijian de huiyi* 老太監的回憶 [An old eunuch's recollections]. Beijing: Beijing yanshan, 1987.

Xin, Xiuming 信修明. *Lao taijian de huiyi* 老太監的回憶 [An old eunuch's recollections]. Beijing: Beijing chubanshe, 1992.

Xin Xiuming 信修明. *Taijian tan wanglu* 太監談往祿 [A eunuch talks about his recollections]. Beijing: Gugong chubanshe, 2015.

Xiwang Zhoukan 希望週刊. Shanghai. July 3, 1932 (民20年7月3日).

Xu Ke 徐珂 *Qingbai leichao* 清稗類鈔 [Unofficial sources on the Qing arranged by categories]. 1917. Reprint, Taipei: Shangwu yinshuguan, 1966.

Zhang Wenhui 張文惠, ed. *Wanqing gongting shenghuo jianwen* 晚清宮廷生活見聞 [Information on late Qing palace life]. Beijing: Wenshi ziliao chubanshe, 1982.

Zhao Rongsheng 趙榮陞 and Wei Ziqing 魏子卿. "Jinggong he bai shifu" 清宮和拜師父 [Entering the palace and honoring your master]. In *Wanqing gongting yishi* 晚清宮廷軼事 [Anecdotes from the late Qing palace], edited by Ding Yanshi, 206–9. Taipei: Shijie wenwu chubanshe, 1984.

Zhongyang yanjiuyuan lishiyuyan yanjiusuo xiancun Qingdai neige daku yuancang Ming-Qing dang'an 中央研究院歷史語言研究所現存清代內閣大庫原藏明清檔案 [Ming-Qing archives in the collection of the Academia Sinica's Institute of History and Philology]. Edited by Zhang Weiren 張偉仁. Taipei: Academia Sinica Institute of History and Philology, 1986–1995.

Zhu Jiyan 朱季演. "Taijian tan wanglu: Ningshougong taijian Geng Jinxi tan" 太監談往錄：寧壽宮太監耿進喜談 [A eunuch talks about the past: A discussion with Ningshougong eunuch Geng Jinxi]. *Zijincheng* 紫禁城 1 (1980): 42–44.

Zhu Jiyan 朱季演. "Taijian tan wanglu: Ningshougong taijian Geng Jinxi tan" 太監談往錄：寧壽宮太監耿進喜談 [A eunuch talks about the past: A discussion with Ningshougong eunuch Geng Jinxi]. *Zijincheng* 紫禁城 2 (1980): 40–41.

Secondary Sources

Anderson, Mary. *Hidden Power: The Palace Eunuchs of Imperial China*. Buffalo: Prometheus Books, 1990.

Airlie, Shiona. *Scottish Mandarin: The Life and Times of Sir Reginald Johnston*. Hong Kong: Hong Kong University Press, 2012.

Amiaz, Revital, and Stuart Seidman, "Testosterone and Depression in Men," *Current Opinion in Endocrinology, Diabetes and Obesity* 15, no. 3 (Jan. 1, 2008): 278–83.

Arlington, L. C., and William Lewisohn. *In Search of Old Peking*. Peking, 1935; Reprint, New York: Paragon Book Reprint Corp, 1967.

Asian Art Museum of San Francisco, "Tomb Treasures" Exhibit. http://www.asianart.org/regular/tomb-pleasures.

Backhouse, E., and J. O. P. Bland. *Annals and Memoirs of the Court of Peking: From the 16th to the 20th Century*. London, 1909; Reprint, New York: AMS Press, 1970.

Blofeld, John. *City of Lingering Splendour: A Frank Account of Old Peking's Exotic Pleasures*. London: Hutchinson, 1961. Reprint, Boston: Shambhala, 1989.

Bodde, Derk, and Clarence Morris. *Law in Imperial China: Exemplified by 190 Ch'ing Dynasty Cases*. Cambridge, MA: Harvard University Press, 1967.

Brook, Timothy, Jerome Bourgon, and Gregory Blue. *Death by a Thousand Cuts*. Cambridge, MA: Harvard University Press, 2008.

Brownell, Susan, and Jeffrey N. Wasserstrom. "Introduction: Theorizing Femininities and Masculinities." In *Chinese Femininities and Chinese Masculinities: A Reader*, 1–31. Berkeley: University of California Press, 2002.

Cai Shih-ying 蔡世英. *Qingmo quan jian Li Lianying* 清末權監李蓮英 [Li Lianying, a powerful eunuch from the late Qing]. Shijiazhuang: Hebei renmin chubanshe, 1986.

Carl, Katherine Augusta. *With the Empress Dowager of China*. 1906. Reprint, New York: KPI Limited, 1986.

Chan, Albert. *Glory and Fall of the Ming Dynasty*. Norman: University of Oklahoma Press, 1982.

Chang Te-ch'ang. "The Economic Role of the Imperial Household in the Ch'ing Dynasty." *The Journal of Asian Studies* 31, no. 2 (Feb. 1972): 243–73.

Chen, Gilbert. "Castration and Connection: Kinship Organization among Ming Eunuchs." *Ming Studies* 2016, issue 74: 27–47, 29. http://dx.doi.org/10.1080/0147037X.2016.1179552.

Chen, Janet Y. *Guilty of Indigence: The Urban Poor in China, 1900–1953*. Princeton: Princeton University Press, 2012. eBook Collection (EBSCOhost).

Chen, Liana. "The Empress Dowager as Dramaturg: Reinventing Late-Qing Court Theatre." *Nan Nü: Men, Women and Gender in Early and Imperial China* 14, no. 1 (2012): 21–46.

Crawford, Robert B. "Eunuch Power in the Ming Dynasty." *T'oung Pao*. Second Series, vol. 49, livr. 3 (1961): 115–48.

Dale, Melissa S. "Running away from the Palace: Eunuch Flight during the Qing Dynasty." *Journal of the Royal Asiatic Society* 27, issue 1 (Jan. 2017): 143–64.

Dale, Melissa S. "Understanding Emasculation: Western Medical Perspectives on Chinese Eunuchs." *Social History of Medicine* 23, no. 1 (April 2010): 38–55.

Dan Shi. *Mémoires d'un Eunuque dans la Cité Interdite* [Memoirs of a eunuch in the Forbidden City]. Translated by Nadine Perront. Marseille, 1991; Reprint, Marseille: Editions Philippe Picquier.

De Groot, J. J. M. *The Religious System of China*. Vol. 5, Book 2. Reprint, Taipei: Ch'eng Wen Publishing Co., 1976.

Der Ling. *Two Years in the Forbidden City*. New York: Dodd, Mead, and Company, 1924.

Ding Yanshi 丁燕石, ed. *Wanqing gongting shi* 晚清宮廷軼事 [Late Qing palace anecdotes]. Taipei: Shijie wenwu chubanshe, 1984.

Dorn, Frank. *The Forbidden City: The Biography of a Palace.* New York: Charles Scribner's Sons, 1970.

Dray-Novey, Alison. "Spatial Order and Police in Imperial Beijing." *The Journal of Asian Studies* 52, no. 4 (Nov. 1993): 885–922.

Du Wanyan 杜婉言. *Zhongguo huanguan shi* 中國宦官史 [A history of the Chinese eunuch]. Taipei: Wenjin chubanshe, 1996.

Dutton, Michael. *Policing and Punishment in China: From Patriarchy to 'the People.'* Cambridge: Cambridge University Press, 1992.

Elliott, Mark C. *The Manchu Way: The Eight Banners and Ethnic Identity in Late Imperial China.* Stanford: Stanford University Press, 2001.

Elvin, Mark. "Female Virtue and the State in China." *Past and Present* 104 (August 1984): 111–52.

Fang Shiming 方詩銘, ed. *Zhongguo lishijinian biao* 中國歷史紀年表 [A commemorative table of Chinese history]. Shanghai: Shanghai cishu chubanshe, 1980.

Fu Shengke 浮生客. "Gudu zhi taijian shenghuo" 古都之太監生活 [Ancient capital eunuch life]. *Zhengfeng zazhi banyue kan* 正風雜誌半月刊 4, no. 1 (民26年2月16日): 73–75.

Fu Zhengyuan. *Autocratic Tradition and Chinese Politics.* New York: Cambridge University Press, 1993.

Fuchs, Walter. "Asitan." In *Eminent Chinese of the Ch'ing Period (1644–1912)*, edited by Arthur W. Hummel, 14. Government Printing Office, Washington, DC, 1943. Reprint, Taipei: SMC Publishing Inc., 1991.

Furth, Charlotte. "Androgynous Males and Deficient Females." *Late Imperial China* 9, no. 2 (Dec. 1988): 1–31.

Giles, Herbert A. *A Chinese English Dictionary.* Shanghai, 1912. Reprint, Taipei: Ch'eng Wen Publishing Company, 1972.

Gordon, Sir C. A. *An Epitome of the Reports of the Medical Officers to the Chinese Imperial Maritime Customs Service from 1871 to 1882.* London: Baillière, Tindall and Cox, 1884.

Gugong 故宮 [The Palace Museum]. Beijing: The Forbidden City Publishing House of the Palace Museum, 1990.

Hashikawa Tokio. "Kangan oboegaki" [Memorandum on eunuchs]. *Bungei Shunju* (Dec. 1959): 252–60.

Hay, John. "The Body Invisible in Chinese Art?" In *Body, Subject and Power in China*, edited by Angela Zito and Tani E. Barlow, 42–77. Chicago: The University of Chicago Press, 1994.

He Bian. "Too Sick to Serve: The Politics of Illness in the Qing Civil Bureaucracy." *Late Imperial China* 33, no. 2 (Dec. 2012): 40–75.

He Guanbiao 何冠彪. "Huanguan tongcheng 'taijian' kao" 宦官通稱「太監」考 [An examination of *huanguan*, a general term for *taijian*]. *Hanxue yanjiu* 漢學研究 8, no. 2 (1990): 201–20.

Headland, Isaac Taylor. *Court Life in China: The Capital, Its Officials and People.* New York: Fleming H. Revell Company, 1909.

Hershatter, Gail. *Dangerous Pleasures: Prostitution and Modernity in Twentieth-Century Shanghai.* Berkeley: University of California Press, 1997.

Hinsch, Bret. *Passions of the Cut Sleeve: The Male Homosexual Tradition in China.* Berkeley: University of California Press, 1990.

Hsieh, Andrew C. K., and Jonathan D. Spence. "Suicide and the Family in Pre-Modern Chinese Society." In *Normal and Abnormal Behavior in Chinese Culture*, edited by Arthur Kleinman and Tsung-Yi Lin, 29–47. London: D. Reidel Publishing Company, 1981.

Hu Zhongliang 胡忠良, "Tan tan Wengshan zha cao" 談談甕山鍘草 [Discussing cutting grass at Weng Mountain]. *Gugong Bowuyuan Yuankan* 3 (1986): 90–92.

Hucker, Charles. *A Dictionary of Official Titles in Imperial China*. Stanford: Stanford University Press, 1985.

Hummel, Arthur W., ed. *Eminent Chinese of the Ch'ing Period (1644–1912)*. Washington, DC: Government Printing Office, 1943. Reprint, New York: Paragon Book Gallery, Ltd., 1967.

Jay, Jennifer. "Another Side of Chinese Eunuch History: Castration, Marriage, Adoption, and Burial." *Canadian Journal of History/Annales canadiennes d'histoire* XXVIII (Dec. 1993): 459–78.

Jenkins, J. S. "The Voice of the Castrato." *The Lancet* 351 (June 20, 1998): 1877–80.

Jia Yinghua 賈英華. *Modai taijian miwen: Sun Yaoting zhuan* 末代太監秘聞：孫耀庭傳 [Secret news from a eunuch of the last dynasty: The biography of Sun Yaoting]. Beijing: Zhishi chubanshe, 1993.

Jia Yinghua. *The Last Eunuch of China: The Life of Sun Yaoting*. Translated by Sun Haichen. Beijing: China Intercontinental Press, 2013.

Jin Yi 金易, and Shen Yiling 沈義羚. *Gongnü tan wanglu* 宮女談往錄 [A palace woman talks about her recollections of the past]. Beijing: Forbidden City Press, 1992.

Johnston, Reginald F. *Twilight in the Forbidden City*. London, 1934. Reprint, Wilmington, DE: Scholarly Resources, 1973.

Johnston, Reginald. *Twilight in the Forbidden City*. London, 1934. Reprint, Vancouver: Soul Care, 2011. Kindle edition.

Junne, George. *Black Eunuchs of the Ottoman Empire: Networks of Power in the Court of the Sultan*. London: I.B. Tauris, 2016.

Kahn, Harold L. *Monarchy in the Emperor's Eyes*. Cambridge, MA: Harvard University Press, 1971.

Kessler, Lawrence. *K'ang-hsi and the Consolidation of Ch'ing Rule, 1661–1684*. Chicago: University of Chicago Press, 1976.

Kutcher, Norman A. "Unspoken Collusions: The Empowerment of Yuanming yuan Eunuchs in the Qianlong Period." *Harvard Journal of Asiatic Studies* 70, no. 2 (Dec. 2010): 449–95.

Kuwabara Jitsuzo. "Shina no kangan" [Chinese eunuchs]. *Toyoshi setsuen* (1927): 344–59.

Lan Jie 蘭潔. "Zai shi taijian Sun Yaoting tingyou gongji." 在世太監孫耀庭遊宮記 [Notes from the living eunuch Sun Yaoting's visit to the palace]. *Zijincheng* 紫禁城 4 (1993): 40–44.

Lau, Clara Wing-chung 劉詠聰. "Jiaqing jingji 'guiyou zhi bian' zhong taijian suo banyan de jiaose" 嘉慶京畿「癸酉之變」中太監所扮演的角色. *Dongfang wenhua* 東方文化 2 (1984): 87–106.

Lee, Robert H. G. *The Manchurian Frontier in Ch'ing History*. Cambridge, MA: Harvard University Press, 1970.

Legge, James. *The Sacred Books of China*. Part 1. *The Shu King, the Religious Portion of the Shih King, the Hsiao King. Sacred Books of the East*. Vol. 3, edited by F. Max Muller. Clarendon Press, 1879. Reprint, Delhi: Motilal Bunarsidass, 1978.

Li Ao 李敖, ed. *Modai huangdi yanjiu* 末代皇帝研究 [Research on the last dynasty's emperor]. Taipei: Li Ao chubanshe, 1988.

Li Kan 李堪. "Tan Qingdai de taijian" 談清代的太監 [A discussion of Qing dynasty eunuchs]. *Gujin wenshi yuekan* 古今文史月刊 (March 1942): 29–33.

Lin Yuan-huei. "The Weight of Mt. T'ai: Patterns of Suicide in Traditional Chinese History and Culture." PhD diss., University of Wisconsin-Madison, 1990.

Ling Haicheng 凌海成, and Yu Binhua 余斌華. *Zuihou yi ge taijian* 最後一個太監. Translated by Li Jie and Sun Mingde. Changchun: Jilin wenshi chubanshe, 1991.

Liu Jingyi 劉精義, and Lu Qi 魯琪. "Qingdai taijian Enjizhuang yingdi" 清代太監恩濟莊塋地 [Qing dynasty Enjizhuang eunuch tombs]. *Gugong bowuyuan yuankan* 故宮博物院院刊 [Palace Museum Journal] 3 (1979): 51–58.

Louie, Kam, and Louise Edwards. "Chinese Masculinity: Theorizing Wen and Wu." *East Asian History* no. 8 (1994): 135–44.

Lowe, H. Y. *The Adventures of Wu: The Life Cycle of a Peking Man*. Princeton: Princeton University Press, 1983.

McMahon, Keith. "The Polyandrous Empress: Imperial Women and their Male Favorites." In *Wanton Women in Late Imperial Chinese Literature*, edited by Mark Stevenson and Wu Cuncun, 29–53. Leiden: Brill, 2017.

Male Hypogonadism. http://www.mayoclinic.org/diseases-conditions/male-hypogonadism/basics/symptoms/con-20014235.

Malone, Carole Brown. *History of the Peking Summer Palaces under the Ch'ing Dynasty*. Urbana: University of Illinois, 1934.

Mann, Albert. "The Influence of Eunuchs in the Politics and Economy of the Ch'ing Court 1861–1907." MA thesis, University of Washington, 1957.

Mao Xianmin 毛憲民. "Wanqing gongting 'yanggou re'" 晚晴宮廷養狗熱 [The "raising dogs" craze of the late Qing]. *Zijincheng* 紫禁城 4 (1994): 46–48.

Meijer, M. J. "Homosexual Offences in Ch'ing China." *T'oung Pao* LXXI 71 (1985): 109–33.

Melicrow, Meyer M., and Stanford Pulrang. "Castrati Choir and Opera Singers." *Urology* 3, no. 5 (May 1974): 663–70.

Mitamura Taisuke. *Chinese Eunuchs: The Structure of Intimate Politics*. Translated by Charles A. Pomeroy. Rutland, VT: Charles E. Tuttle Co., 1970.

Morrisy, Raymond T., ed. *Lovell and Winter's Pediatric Orthopedics*. 3rd ed., vol. 1. Philadelphia: J.B. Lippincott Co., 1990.

Naquin, Susan. "True Confessions: Criminal Interrogations as Sources for Ch'ing History." *National Palace Museum Bulletin* XI, no. 1 (March–April 1976): 1–18.

Naquin, Susan. *Millenarian Rebellion in China: The Eight Trigrams Uprising of 1813*. New Haven: Yale University Press, 1976.

Playfair, G. M. H. *The Cities and Towns of China: A Geographical Dictionary*. 2nd ed. Shanghai: Kelly and Walsh Ltd., 1910.

Rawski, Evelyn S. *The Last Emperors: A Social History of Qing Imperial Institutions*. Berkeley: University of California Press, 1998.

Rideout, J. K. "The Rise of the Eunuchs during the T'ang Dynasty, Part One (618–705)." *Asia Major* 1.1 (1949): 53–65.

Shan Shikui 單士魁. "Qingdai Taiyiyuan" 清代太醫院 [The Qing Dynasty Imperial Medical Bureau]. *Gugong bowuyuan yuankan* 故宮博物院院刊 3 (1985).

Shi Keguan, ed. *Zhongguo huanguan mishi* [The secret history of the Chinese eunuch]. Xindian: Changchunshu shufang, 1985.

Shi Shuo 石碩, Duan Yuming 段玉明, Gao Weigang 高維剛, and Yao Yueye 妖樂野, eds. *Huanguan daguan* 宦官大觀 [A broad study of eunuchs]. Xi'an: Sanqin chubanshe, 1987.

Sommer, Matthew. *Sex, Law, and Society in Late Imperial China*. Stanford: Stanford University Press, 2000.

Spence, Jonathan. *Emperor of China: Self-portrait of K'ang-hsi, 1654–1722*. New York: Vintage Books, 1988.

Spence, Jonathan. *Ts'ao Yin and the K'ang-hsi Emperor*. New Haven: Yale University Press, 1988.

Starrett, Vincent. *Oriental Encounters: Two Essays in Bad Taste*. Chicago: Normandie House, 1938.

Tang Yinian 唐縊年. *Qing gong taijian* 清宮太監 [Qing dynasty palace eunuchs]. Shenyang: Liaoning daxue chubanshe, 1993.

Torbert, Preston. *The Ch'ing Imperial Household Department: A Study of Its Organization and Principal Functions, 1662–1796*. Cambridge, MA: Harvard University Press, 1977.

Tsai, Shih-shan Henry. *The Eunuchs in the Ming Dynasty*. Albany: State University of New York Press, 1996.

Wagenseil, F. "Beiträge zur Kenntnis der Kastrationsfolgen und des Eunchoidismus beim Mann" [Contributions to the knowledge of the consequences of castration and of eunchoidism in men] *Zeitschrift für Morphologie und Anthropologie* [Journal of Morphology and Anthropology], Band XXXII, Heft 3. d. 26, H. 2 (1933): 463–64.

Waley-Cohen, Joanna. *Exile in Mid-Qing China: Banishment to Xinjiang, 1758–1820*. New Haven: Yale University Press, 1991.

Wan Yi 萬依, Wang Shuqing 王樹卿, and Liu Lu 劉潞. *Qingdai gongtingshi* 清代宮廷史 [A history of the palace during the Qing dynasty]. Shenyang: Liaoning renmin chubanshe, 1990.

Wang Shuqing 王樹卿. "Jingshifang" 敬事房 [Office of Eunuch Affairs]. *Gugong buowuyuan yuankan* 故宮博物院院刊 [Palace Museum Journal] 2 (1979): 64, 61.

Wang Qingxiang 王慶祥. *Weidi gongnei mu* 偽帝宮內幕 [Inside story on the puppet emperor's palace]. Jilin: Jilin wenshi chubanshe, 1986.

Wang Yude 王玉德. *Shenmi de di san xing: Zhongguo huanguan daxiezhen* 神秘的第三性：中國宦官大寫真 [The secret third sex: a portrait of Chinese eunuchs]. Wuchang: Huazhong ligong daxue chubanshe, 1994.

Watson, James L., and Evelyn S. Rawski, eds. *Death Ritual in Late Imperial and Modern China*. Berkeley: University of California Press, 1988

Weisskopf, Michael. "Imperial Court Eunuch Now Ward of Chinese Communist State." *Houston Chronicle*. Nov. 19, 1987.

Wilson, Jean D., and Claus Roehrborn. "Long-Term Consequences of Castration in Men: Lessons from the Skoptzy and the Eunuchs of the Chinese and Ottoman Courts." *The Journal of Clinical Endocrinology & Metabolism* 84, no. 12 (1999): 4332.

Witek, John, SJ. "Reporting to Rome: Some Major Events in the Christian Community in Peking, 1686–1687." In *Echanges Culturels et Réligieux entre la Chine et l'Occident*, edited by Edward J. Malatesta, SJ, Yves Raguin, SJ, and Adrianus C. Dudink, 301–18. Taipei: Ricci Institute, 1995.

Wolf, Margery. "Women and Suicide in China." In *Women in Chinese Society*, edited by Margery Wolf and Roxane Witke, 111–42. Stanford: Stanford University Press, 1975.

Wu Chieh Ping, and Gu Fang-Liu. "The Prostate in Eunuchs." *EROTC Genitourinary Group Monograph 10—Urological Ontology: Reconstructive Surgery, Organ Conservation and Restoration of Function*. New York: Wiley-Liss, 1991.

Wu, Silas H. L. *Passage to Power: K'ang-hsi and His Heir Apparent, 1661–1722*. Cambridge, MA: Harvard University Press, 1979.

Xu Jingru 徐静茹. *Zhongguo gudai taijian* 中國古代太監 [Ancient Chinese eunuchs]. Beijing: Zhongguo shangye chubanshe, 2014.

Yang Zhengguang 楊爭光. *Zhongguo zuihou yi ge taijian* 中國最後一個太監 [China's last eunuch]. Beijing: Junzhong chubanshe, 1990.

Yu Huaqing 余華青. *Zhongguo huanguan zhidushi* 中國宦官制度史 [A history of the Chinese eunuch system]. Shanghai: Renmin chubanshe, 1993.

Zhang Qiyun 張其昀, ed. *Zhongwen da cidian* 中文大辭典 [The encyclopedic dictionary of the Chinese language]. Vol. 22. Taipei: Zhongguo wenhua yanjiusuo, 1967.

Zheng Hesheng 鄭鶴聲. *Jinshi zhongxi shiri duizhao biao* 近世中西日對照表 [Modern times East-West historical date concordance]. Taipei: Taiwan shangwu yinshu guan, 1972.

Zheng Tianting 鄭天挺. *Qingshi tanwei* 清史探微 [Studies in Qing history]. Zhongjing: Duli chubanshe, 1946.

Zhou Junshi 周君適. *Weiman gongting zayi* 偽滿宮廷雜億 [Miscellaneous recollections on the puppet Manchu palace]. Chengdu: Sizhou renmin chubanshe, 1981.

Index

actors, eunuch, 81–82, 86
adoption, 33, 94, 106, 196
adultery, 128
age requirements. *See* application process
Aisin-Gioro Pu Yi. *See* Pu Yi. *See also* Xuantong, emperor
aliases, 66, 111, 113, 151, 168, 177
An Dehai, 2, 26, 57, 94
An Dexiang, 158
ancestor veneration, 79, 95, 162, 166, 186
application process, eunuchs: age require-ments, 10, 29, 35–36, 41–47, 51, 57, 118; applicants, 28, 32, 35–36, 41, 43, 45; background checks, 30, 45; person-ality profiles, 45; rejected applicants, 46
apprentices, eunuch. *See* master-apprentice system
Articles of Favorable Treatment, 27, 172, 175, 189
Asitan, 73–74

banishment, 98, 120, 136. *See also* exile
banner, 20, 31, 44, 59, 70, 134
bannermen, 25, 44, 47, 70, 103
Bao Desheng, 111
bao, 39, 41, 163
bathhouses, 46, 183, 185–86
beatings, 6, 11, 72, 99, 107, 111, 114–15, 117, 122–25, 131, 133, 139–40, 149, 150, 157, 176, 178, 191, 193, 196. *See also* corporal punishment
beheading. *See* decapitation
Beijing, 37, 44, 48, 51, 64, 134n30, 136n40, 147, 162–63, 174, 185, 187–91

beile, 19, 113
Beixiangsuo, 165
Bi Wu, 31–34
Bian Baoxiang, 174–75
biannual physical examination, 57–58, 196
biological eunuchs, 42
blood, 38, 102, 132, 137, 142–43, 146, 163
Board of Rites. See *Libu*
Board of Works. See *Gongbu*
body, eunuch, 48–65. *See also* emasculation, physical effects; gender
bondage, 29, 33, 47, 94, 119, 195. *See also* slavery
bondservant, 3, 6, 20–23, 26, 66, 73, 89, 130
bribery, 58
Buddhism, 79, 141n61
burial: 162, 165–66, 169; eunuchs denied burial in cemeteries, 162–63; depriva-tion (of proper) 126, 130–31, 134, 143, 198; expenses, 165–66; societies, 166; with *bao*, 39, 41. *See also* cemeteries

cangue, 11, 83, 98–105, 116–18, 125, 140n53, 150, 157
capital punishment. *See* strangulation; decapitation
Carl, Katherine, 64, 81, 95, 97, 104
castrati, 51, 60–61, 81
castration: xi, 14, 15, 16, 39n61, 48n1, 51, 56, 61, 63; definition, 9
catechists, eunuch, 80. *See also* Christianity
catheters, 39, 63
celibacy, 60

cemetery: 45, 134, 163–64, 166, 168–69, 198; Foreign Studies Scholar and Student Cemetery, 163. See also *Enjizhuang*; Appendix 4

Chancery of Memorials. See *Zoushichu*

Chang Yonggui, 159

Changchun, 189–91

Changchunyuan, 165

Chao Wuming, 191

chaperone, 184

Chen Qitai, 122

Chenghua, emperor, 40

chief eunuch. See also *Gongdian jiandu lingshi taijian*

Christianity: 62, 80; Christian eunuchs, 80–81. *See also* catechists, eunuch

chu jia, 1, 60, 67, 138, 197

citizenship, 1, 119n60, 174–77, 185, 191, 193, 199

civil service examination, 4, 7, 54

Cixi, empress dowager, 4, 26, 57, 59, 62, 70, 74–75, 76 fig. 4.4, 82, 86, 93, 95, 97, 104, 160, 173

class, 4–5, 54, 97. *See also* slaves; slavery

Classic of Filial Piety. See *Xiao Jing*

clothing. *See* eunuch, attire

collective punishment, 35, 72, 99, 103, 113, 123, 130. *See also* collective responsibility

collective responsibility, 6, 15, 114, 123, 135–37, 139, 143–44, 157, 196. *See also* collective punishment

commandery prince, 36, 113

concubines, 4, 21, 68, 71, 77–78, 82, 85, 171, 184

Confucian: patriarchy, 16, 60; philosophy, 2, 49; social norms, 52; society, 28, 55–56; teachings, 2, 53, 56, 186; value system, 7, 53, 59, 61, 65

coroner, 132, 138, 140

corporal punishment, 6, 15, 98, 104, 120, 123–24, 146, 149, 152, 157, 191, 196. *See also* beatings

corpse dumping, 134. *See also* burial, deprivation of proper

corruption, 87, 178

crematorium, 165

cross-dressers, 58

Cui Jinchao, 116

Cui Zilu, 115

cutting grass, 102, 113, 116–18, 122, 125, 140, 151, 198

Dagaodian/Dagaoxuandian, 68, 115

Daoguang, emperor, 25, 26

Daoism, 79

daozijiang, xi, 28–35, 37–39, 41, 46–47, 49, 67, 86, 159, 163, 195, 197

Dasaochu, 147, 165

Dasheng Wula, 98, 100, 111, 117–18, 122

Daxing, 35

dazongguan. See *Gongdian jiandu lingshi taijian*

death: of a eunuch, 5, 11, 58, 86, 120, 125–26, 129, 137–40, 142–43, 145, 161–69, 191, 197–98; of a parent, 6; of a sibling, 92; penalty, 15, 33, 39, 98, 103, 105, 130–31, 134, 136, 144; reproductive, 2, 53, 95, 197. *See also* capital punishment; discharge

debt, 34, 98, 101, 106, 139, 140

decapitation, 40, 130–32. *See also* capital punishment

decontamination, 132, 139, 143–44

deviancy, 63

discharge, eunuch, 5, 11–12, 32, 85, 116, 118, 120, 145, 150–52, 154, 155 table 8.1, 156–61, 167–68, 197–98. *See* also retirement

disciplinary problems, 11, 106, 145–46, 157, 197–98. *See also* discharge, eunuch

discourse of power, 4

discrimination, 81, 145, 158, 160, 162, 166

dispersal money, 180

dogs, 96 fig. 5.1, 97, 106, 123, 135, 138, 156, 176, 185, 197

Dorgon, 21, 22

drinking, 11, 23–24, 38, 89–90, 98, 100–102, 106, 121, 139, 140, 144, 158, 197

drowning, 91; suicide by, 127, 132, 142. *See also* suicide

drugs, 90. *See also* opium

Du Ming, 101
duishi, 59, 96
duties, 78–82, 87

education, eunuch, 55, 67, 73–74, 87–88
Eight Trigrams Uprising, 25, 43, 55, 91–92, 121
emasculation: death rate, 39; definition, 9, 28; physical effects, 10, 48–51, 65, 196; procedure, 31–34, 37–39; psychological effects, 10, 48, 52; as punishment, 34–35. *See also* self-emasculation
employment prerequisites (eunuch), 10, 35–36, 41. *See also* application process, eunuch
enjiayin, 160
Enjizhuang: Cemetery, 45, 163; Lifelong Society, 163; Temple, 166
enshangyin, 154
ethnicity, 10, 36, 41, 43, 47
eunuch-of-the-presence, 23, 73, 84, 177
eunuch, attire: 27, 62–63, 70, 75, 77, 85, 109–11, 120; numbers of, 3; sources on, 28–47
eunuchs, inner court (*neigong taijian*), 18, 32, 77–78, 84, 86–87, 92, 97, 109, 120, 148, 153–54, 156, 168, 173
eunuchs, outer court (*waiwei taijian*), 54, 77–78, 82, 85, 87, 97, 153n30, 154, 168
eviction (Pu Yi from palace in 1924), 170
examination: pre-emasculation, 32; pre-employment physical, 41–42
execution, 15, 99, 157
exile, 6, 40, 59, 83, 98–101, 103, 105, 110–13, 117–20, 122, 125–26, 130, 135–36, 138n47, 140nn52–53, 144, 150, 157. *See also* banishment
exorcism, 139, 198
expulsion, eunuchs from palace, 8, 12, 117n13, 119n59, 170, 177–82, 184, 187, 189, 192–93, 199
extortion, 35–36

family, eunuch: life, 26, 43, 93–95, 173; ties, 89, 90, 138, 144, 197; relations with father, 39–40, 52, 90–92, 174, 177n27,

187, 195, 197. *See also* collective responsibility
Fanyichu, 112n23, 115n40
Feng Yuxiang, 163, 172, 182
Fengtian, 117
filial piety, 2, 28, 53, 90, 127, 131, 142, 156, 186. *See also* Confucian
filial responsibilities, 90
fire: 177–79; *Jianfugong*, 178; *Yangxindian*, 178
five mutilating punishments (*wuxing*), 15
flight (eunuch). *See* runaway, eunuchs
foot-binding, 48, 171
Forbidden City, 48, 170, 172, 175–77, 180–81, 189, 195, 199
forty-eight departments, 71
fushouling taijian, 75, 83

gambling, 11, 23–24, 90, 97–102, 104–6, 117, 121, 139, 140, 144, 175, 197
Gang Tie Miao, 161 fig. 8.1, 162
Gang Tie Mu, 187
Gangbing miao, 157
Gao Chengxiang, 149
Gao Jingrui, 123
Gao Jinxi, 147
Gao Sheng, 120
Gao Yuwang, 138
gender: 5, 6, 10, 49, 52–57, 60–61, 64–65, 94, 195–96; eunuch self-identity 16, 53, 56, 60, 65, 196; imperial court's perceptions of, 61; Western perceptions of 61–64
Geng Jinxi, 81, 86, 93
genital mutilation, 1–2, 9–10, 28, 40, 47–49, 64–65, 95, 107, 158, 195–96
ghost, 132–33, 141. See also *gui*; *po*
girls' schools, 183–84
Gongbu, 77
Gongdian jiandu lingshi taijian (chief eunuch), 75
Grand Council, 34, 107n1
Gu Wenxiang, 23
Guangxu, emperor, 173n15
guarantor, 43–44, 137, 156–57, 167, 175
gui (spirit), 132

gynecomastia, 50–51, 196

Han Chinese, 44, 47, 73, 74
Han Fuqing, 147
Han, dynasty, 1, 9, 17–18, 26, 61n68
hanging, 101, 127, 131–32, 140, 142. *See also* suicide, modes of
Hanshu, 74
harem, 1, 14, 17, 21, 78–79, 87, 194
He Rong'er, 84, 90, 123
Headland, Lady Marion Sinclair, 62
Headland, Sir Isaac Taylor, 62
Hebei, 45, 136
Heilongjiang, 26, 99–100, 103, 112–13, 117–19, 122
Hejian, 45
Henan, 117
hierarchy, 3, 11, 18, 26, 54–55, 66, 75, 77, 85, 87, 91, 107n1, 123, 138, 155 table 8.1, 160, 164–66, 168, 170, 173
homelessness, 180, 182–83, 186, 193, 199
homicide, 128
homosexuality, 94–95; male-male intercourse, 54
Hongtaiji, 19
hormone therapy, 61
hu chun (palace guards), 176
Hu Jinyu, 113
Huang Liu-hung, 127, 135
huanguan, 9
huanjian, 9
human trafficking, 10, 15, 28–29, 32, 33, 47, 195. *See also* kidnapping
hypogonadism, 50–51

identification (ID) card, eunuch, 115, 180
illiteracy, 8, 24, 74, 175, 193, 198
illnesses, eunuch, 11, 145–46, 149–50, 153, 167, 197, 198
Imperial Garden. See *Yuhuayuan*
Imperial Guards, 54
Imperial Hospital. See *Taiyiyuan*
Imperial Household Department, 6–7, 11, 21–23, 30–32, 35, 41, 57, 59, 67, 74, 75, 77–78, 82, 86, 92, 113, 115, 117, 119, 120–24, 126, 130, 132–33, 135, 143,

145, 147, 149–54, 156, 165–66, 175–79, 197
Imperial Pharmacy. See *Yuyaofang*
imperial prince, 36, 43, 54n33, 113
Imperial Tea Room. See *Yuchafang*
impotence, 42, 60–61
Inner City Police, 114
institutional history, eunuch system, 7, 9, 17
intimate politics, 4, 17, 26, 59

Jia Defu, 118
jian (sexual and political betrayal), 58
Jiang Jinyu, 165
Jiaqing, emperor, 25, 36, 43–44, 92, 166, 168, 199
Jihua, 121
Jilin, 83n94, 98n45, 111n19, 117, 119
Jin Tinglin, 100, 102n59
Jinghemen, 149
Jingmingyuan, 151, 166
Jingshan: 163; park, 181; *xiaonei xue* (palace lower school), 122
jingshen, 9
Jingshifang (Office of Eunuch Affairs), 23, 77–78, 121–23, 156, 165
Johnston, Sir Reginald, 8, 43, 177, 180–82
Judicial Department. See *Shenxingsi*
junwang, 36, 113, 158, 183n68

Kangxi, emperor, 4n13, 22n53, 23, 35, 56–57, 73–74, 80, 98, 101–2, 147, 167–68, 199
ketou, 69, 102
kidnapping, 29, 32–33, 47, 159. *See also* human trafficking
King of Hades, 163
Korean imperial court, 1
Korsakow, W., 38
Kuaijisi (Office of Accounts), 36n45, 41, 67

labor relations, 5–6, 11, 25, 61, 89, 107n1, 108, 123–26, 145, 150, 176, 194
lama: 79, 132, 186; eunuch, 80
leave: 92, 109; sick, 92, 145–57, 167, 198; comparison with sick leave for

provincial officials, 148; fraudulent, 150, 157, 168
Li Chang'an, 189
Li Chao, 137–38
Li Dongji, 109
Li Fang, 111, 117–18
Li Guangyu, 126, 135
Li Guoqin, 122
Li Liandong, 157
Li Lianying, 2, 3, 26, 59, 64, 93, 158, 164, 188
Li Shoutong, 118
Li Tianfu, 35
Li Yi, 109–10
Li Yu, 150
Li Zhu, 32
Li Zicheng, 20, 21
libido, 9, 42, 52, 56, 59–61, 65, 95, 185, 196
Libu (Board of Rites), 35–36, 40–41, 45, 77, 148, 158
literacy, 7, 73–74, 88. *See also* illiteracy
Liu Decai, 92
Liu Delu, 191
Liu Duosheng, 160
Liu Erqi, 101
Liu, "Fine Blade," 32
Liu Jinxin, 91
Liu Kuaizui, 102
Liu Qingyan, 189
Liu Yourong, 174
Liu Zhenying, 189
Liu Zhongtang, 58
living quarters, eunuch, 84, 109n6, 140. See also *tatan*
Longyu, empress dowager, 172–73
Longfumen, 146

Ma Deqing, 39, 52
Ma Feng, 139
Ma Jinzhong, 151
Ma Sheng, 122
Ma Yu, 122
Ma Yubao, 140
maidservant, 8, 16, 59, 61, 66, 75, 84, 87, 90, 93–94, 96–97, 129, 175, 179n41, 184n71, 189, 196–97

male-male intercourse. *See* homosexuality
Manzhouguo, 190–91
marquis, 23n62, 25, 42
marriage, eunuch, 56, 59, 60n59, 61, 93–95, 106, 196
masculinity, 5–6, 10, 49, 54–55
master-apprentice system, 11, 72, 87, 95–96, 105, 114, 195, 197
Matignon, J.-J., 38–39, 52, 77, 80, 142
May Fourth Movement, 184
medical care, eunuch, 153–54, 168
medical malpractice, 82, 154
Meng Zhangxi, 146
Miao Jinyu, 83
Ming, dynasty, 1–3, 9, 12, 17–20, 26, 31, 40, 42, 45–47, 54, 58, 89, 95, 128, 148, 160, 165
missionaries, 62, 80, 171. *See also* Christianity
monasticism, 46. *See also* monks
Mongolian, eunuchs, 45
monks, 46, 58–60, 67, 79, 109n7, 111–12. See also *chu jia*; monasticism
Morache, Georges, 37, 50–51
Mu Qi, 43

Nanfu (Court Theatrical Bureau). See *Shengpingshu*
native place: 12, 36, 42, 44–45, 70–71, 86, 96, 116–18, 140n53, 146–48, 150–51, 156–58, 162–63, 168, 180, 187; associations, 90, 95, 105
natural eunuchs. *See* biological eunuchs
Neidaban'er (Palace Squad), 115
neigong taijian. *See* eunuchs, inner court
Neishutang, 73
Neiwufu. *See* Imperial Household Department
New Culture Movement, 184
Niaoqiangsanchu, 146
Nurhaci, 19–20

occupations, eunuch, post expulsion, 188–89, 193
Office of Eunuch Affairs. See *Jingshifang*
Office of General Affairs. See *Zongwufu*

Oirat Mongols, 150
opium, 11, 103–6, 122, 131, 142, 171, 174–75, 197
Ottoman Empire, 1

Palace Eunuchs' Mutual Prosperity Association, 188
palace gods, 124, 133
pass: travel, 115; for retired eunuchs, 150, 156
physician: 79, 153–54, 168; eunuch, 82–83; Western, 31, 37–38, 48, 51–52, 62–63
po (spirit). See also gui; ghost
pollution. See blood
polygamy, 63
poverty, 2, 29–30, 31, 33, 35, 40, 46–47, 113, 127, 159, 182, 187, 193, 195
Prince Chun, 189
princely households, 9, 25, 36–37, 43–44, 46–47, 70, 114, 118, 151, 156–57, 174–75, 177
prostitution, 47, 61, 122
Pu Jia, 45, 104, 178, 182
Pu Jie, 45, 114, 177
Pu Yi, 8, 12, 27, 79, 123–24, 133, 170–72, 174, 176–82, 186, 189, 190–91, 193. See also Xuantong, emperor
punishment, 98, 123, 131. See also beatings; cangue; cutting grass; corporal punishment; exile, slavery; strangulation

Qianlong, emperor, 24–25, 34–36, 40, 45, 68, 73–74, 156n36
Qianqinggong zongguan. See Gongdian jiandu lingshi taijian
Qin, dynasty, 1, 17
Qingshu, 74
Qingyiyuan, 166
queue, 109, 111, 176

rank, eunuch. See social hierarchy
recruits, eunuch, 35–36, 41, 47, 66–71, 86. See also application process, eunuch
regeneration of genitalia, 58, 65, 196
Rehe, 40, 122
reincarnation, 135, 141

reintegration into society, eunuch, 5, 12, 46, 145, 158–59, 168, 186–89, 199
rent, allowance, 85
research subjects, eunuchs as, 185
restaurants, 86, 97, 106, 197
retirement associations, eunuch: 60n60, 160–61, 166, 169, 173, 187, 199; Beiping's Eunuch Retirement Association, 160
retirement: 5, 60, 85, 111, 145, 150–51, 154, 157–60, 162, 166–68, 186, 198–99; assistance, 169. See also discharge; retirement associations
revolution (1911), 5–6, 8, 12, 27, 119, 170, 171–75, 186, 191n99, 192
Ripa, Matteo, 62
Roman, empire, 1
runaway, eunuchs: 11–12, 31, 101, 107–25, 145, 175, 177, 197–98; escape routes, 108–11; notices 109–10

salary: 85, 113, 159, 168; reduction due to illness, 146, 154, 155 table 8.1, 167; reduction as punishment, 116
scholar-officials, 7, 18, 54–55
screening, eunuch. See application process
secondary sexual characteristics, 111. See also emasculation, physical effects
self-emasculation: 39–40, 177; definition, 177n27; prohibitions against, 40, 47
sexual desire. See libido
Shandong, 36, 44, 47, 95, 117, 127, 148
Shang, dynasty, 1, 14
Shanhai Pass, 21, 111
Shanxi, 102n57, 117, 136, 140n52
Shao Guoqin, 123
Shao Ying, 179
shed, daozijiang's, 32–33, 37
Sheng Liang, 101
Shengpingshu (Court Theatrical Bureau, Nanfu), 81–82, 163, 165
Shenwumen (Shenwu Gate), 90, 180
Shenxingsi (Judicial Department), 67, 112n23, 115n40, 126, 132, 138, 140, 157, 175

shouling taijian, 44, 72, 75, 77, 80, 85, 87, 100, 112, 121–23, 137, 140n54, 146–47, 149, 152–54, 155 table 8.1, 156, 163–66

Shuhede, 136

Shuntian, 35, 42, 44–45, 148

Shunzhi, emperor, 9, 20, 22–23, 30, 40, 74

sick leave. *See* leave, sick

slavery: 35, 77, 119–20, 125, 130, 144, 195; slave, 3n11, 6, 10, 15, 20, 26, 98–99, 101, 103, 112–113, 117, 119n57, 120, 122, 125–26, 130, 135, 140n52, 140n54, 144, 150, 175, 198, 202. *See also* unfree status

smallpox, 23, 147

social hierarchy, 11, 66, 77, 87; eunuch, 75, 77

social ostracism: 89, 145, 158, 167, 186, 197, 199; social outcasts, 16, 28, 66, 111, 169–70, 186, 192, 195, 199. *See also* stigma

spirit, 132. *See also po; gui*

status. *See* social hierarchy; unfree status

Stent, George Carter, 1n1, 30, 37, 39, 45, 57–58, 60, 63, 80–81, 94, 104, 115, 157, 159, 162, 166

stigma, 1, 2, 15–16, 53–55, 60n59, 94, 197. *See also* social ostracism

strangulation, 98–99, 103, 105, 130–32, 142, 202. *See also* capital punishment

Su Chang, 150

Su Wenzhi, 91n8

suicide: 11, 101, 126–44, 197–98; modes of, 127, 142; purposeful, 141; regulations, 129–30

sumptuary laws, 23, 36, 46

Sun Yaoting, 85, 104, 174, 177, 187

Sun Yirang, 171

Sun Yong'an, 112, 120

supply and demand, eunuch, 3, 10, 19, 25, 27–28, 32, 34, 36, 40, 42, 46–47, 93, 99, 118, 124, 152. *See also* application process, eunuch

taijian: 67–68, 75; definition 9

Taiwan, 34

Taiyiyuan (Imperial Hospital), 153

Tancheng, 127

Tang, dynasty, 1, 2, 9, 17–18, 26

tatan: 103, (shop) 109. *See also* living quarters (eunuch)

temple, 60, 78–79, 81, 111, 159–62, 169, 173, 174n18, 181, 187, 192–93, 199. See also *Enjizhuang, Gangbing Miao, Gang Tie Miao, Xinglongsi, Yonghegong;* Appendix 3

testosterone, 50–52, 110, 141

theft, 94, 98, 121–22, 157, 174, 177–78

third sex, 6, 53

Thirteen Yamen (Thirteen Bureaus), 22–23, 74

Tian Deming, 137–38

Tianjin, 44–45, 47, 61, 147, 173, 177, 189–91

Tibetan Buddhism, 79–80, 135

tongzhen (thoroughly pure), 57, 60

Tongzhi, emperor, 26, 118

Tongzi River (*Tongzi He*), 180

torture, 178

tour guides, 187, 193

training: art, 82; basic, 10, 67–70; medical, 83, religious, 87. *See also* master-apprentice system

transmigration, 141

twenty-four offices, 18

unemployment, eunuch, 185–86

unfree status, 6, 11, 28–29, 46–47, 108, 119–20, 125–26, 130, 144, 175, 193, 195, 198. *See also* slavery

urinary incontinence, 39, 158n50. *See also* urological problems

urological problems, 48, 63, 149–50, 167

Urumqi, 130, 135–36, 140n54, 202

violence, eunuch-upon-eunuch, 61, 101–2, 106, 131

Wagenseil, Ferdinand, 50

waiwei taijian. See eunuchs, outer court

Wang Bing, 132, 140–41

Wang Fu, 92

Wang Fuxiang, 189

Wang Guoqin, 164
Wang Jinchao, 83–84
Wang Lin, 121
Wang Shuangxi, 147
Wang Taiping, 122
Wang Xi, 147
Wang Xiangrui, 110
Wang Xilian, 103
Wang Zhide, 91n8
Wanping, 35
Wanrong, empress, 177, 179, 187n80, 189
Wanshandian, 73–74, 111
Wanyiju (Nursing Home Bureau), 148, 160
weapons, within the palace, 25, 55, 100, 131–32
Wei Zhu, 24
weimin taijian (commoner eunuch), 12, 120, 145, 152, 154, 155 table 8.1, 156, 168
wen-wu (literary-martial), 54
Weng Mountain, 102, 116n43, 117–18, 140
Western medicine, 39
widow: 94; suicide, 127, 129n16, 141
Wu Degui, 118
Wu, empress, 17
Wucheng, 148
Wudian, 116–18, 122, 125, 151
Wula, 83, 98n45, 120
Wuqing, 35, 42, 112
wuxing. See five mutilating punishments

Xian Delu, 146
Xiao Dezhang, 158
Xiao Jing (*The Classic of Filial Piety*), 142
Xiaodao Liu, 31–32
xiaojian, 9
Xin Xiuming, 8n18, 86, 97, 109, 183n68
Xinglongsi, 154, 157
Xinjiang, 59, 103, 136, 140n53
Xu Jinlu, 147
Xuantong, emperor, 12, 22n53, 27, 114n32, 170, 172, 174, 181. *See also* Pu Yi

yan, 9
Yanchilou, 180, 182
Yang Dehai, 122

Yang Duoquan, 191
yange, 9
Yangxindian: 70, 191; fire, 178
yaopai, 180
Ye Fu, 121
Ye Mingliang, 137
Yiheyuan, 172, 189
Yili, 126, 130, 135–36, 140n52, 150
yin-yang, 53, 65
yin, 23, 53–57, 65, 73. *See also* yin-yang
Yingzaosi, 165
Yonghegong, 79–80, 126, 135
Yongzheng, emperor, 24, 42, 44, 54–55, 148–49, 156–57, 167–68, 199
Yu Chunhe, 32–34, 61, 69, 72, 173n15
Yu Jinzhong, 133
Yu Jiqing, 43
Yuanmingyuan, 25, 34, 40, 68, 83, 91, 101–2, 109–10, 118, 121, 132, 140, 150, 152, 165–66
Yuchafang (Imperial Tea Room), 147
Yuhuayuan (Imperial Garden), 126, 146
Yushufang, 165
Yuyaofang (Imperial Pharmacy), 82–84, 153–54, 168

Zhang Delang, 61
Zhang Feng, 110
Zhang Fujun, 118
Zhang Lande, 173
Zhang Ming, 109
Zhang Qianhe, 76 fig. 4.3
Zhangfang Guanxue, 74
Zhangyisi (Department of Ceremonial), 41, 67, 115, 165
Zhao Ben, 42, 46
Zhao De, 110
Zhao Rong, 112, 122
Zhao San, 164
Zhao Shijie, 101
Zhao Yu, 112
Zheng Furui, 137
Zheng He, 19
Zhili, 44, 47, 117, 136, 147, 148n7, 151
Zhongzhengdian, 80
Zhou Baoshi, 137, 140

Zhou Jinchao, 24
Zhu Xiang, 111
Ziwuzhong, 156
zongguan taijian, 70, 72, 75, 76 fig. 4.3,
    77–78, 85, 87, 100, 137, 151–54, 155
    table 8.1, 163–65, 173
Zongwufu (Office of General Affairs), 92
Zoushichu (Chancery of Memorials), 24,
    73, 88